THE BELGIAN FRIENDSHIP BUILDING

Race, Place, and Justice

Louis P. Nelson, senior editor

Irene Cheng, Charles L. Davis II, and Mabel O. Wilson, consulting editors

THE BELGIAN FRIENDSHIP BUILDING

From the New York World's Fair to a Virginia HBCU

Kathleen James-Chakraborty,
Katherine M. Kuenzli, and Bryan Clark Green

University of Virginia Press
CHARLOTTESVILLE AND LONDON

The University of Virginia Press is situated on the traditional lands of the Monacan Nation, and the Commonwealth of Virginia was and is home to many other Indigenous people. We pay our respect to all of them, past and present. We also honor the enslaved African and African American people who built the University of Virginia, and we recognize their descendants. We commit to fostering voices from these communities through our publications and to deepening our collective understanding of their histories and contributions.

This project has received funding from the European Research Council (ERC) under the European Union's Horizon 2020 research and innovation programme (Grant agreement No 101019419).

Disclaimer:
Funded by the European Union. Views and opinions expressed are however those of the author(s) only and do not necessarily reflect those of the European Union or the European Research Council Executive Agency. Neither the European Union nor the granting authority can be held responsible for them.

University of Virginia Press

Printed in the United States of America on acid-free paper

First published 2025

9 8 7 6 5 4 3 2 1

LIBRARY OF CONGRESS CATALOGING-IN-PUBLICATION DATA

Names: James-Chakraborty, Kathleen, author. | Kuenzli, Katherine M. (Katherine Marie), author. | Green, Bryan Clark, author.
Title: The Belgian Friendship Building : from the New York's World Fair to a Virginia HBCU / Kathleen James-Chakraborty, Katherine M. Kuenzli, and Bryan Clark Green.
Description: Charlottesville : University of Virginia Press, 2025. | Series: Race, place, and justice | Includes bibliographical references and index.
Identifiers: LCCN 2024041116 (print) | LCCN 2024041117 (ebook) | ISBN 9780813952963 (hardcover) | ISBN 9780813952956 (ebook)
Subjects: LCSH: Belgian Pavilion (New York World's Fair, 1939–1940, New York, N.Y.) | Pavillon de la Belgique (Exposition internationale, 1937, Paris, France) | Modern movement (Architecture)—Belgium. | Velde, Henry van de, 1863–1957. | Belgian Friendship Building (Richmond, Va.) | Virginia Union University (Richmond, Va.)—Buildings. | Exhibition buildings—Conservation and restoration. | Richmond (Va.)—Buildings, structures, etc.
Classification: LCC NA6750.N5 B455 2025 (print) | LCC NA6750.N5 (ebook) | DDC 727/.9—dc23/eng/20250122
LC record available at https://lccn.loc.gov/2024041116
LC ebook record available at https://lccn.loc.gov/2024041117

Permission to reproduce artworks by Henry van de Velde granted by the estate of Henry van de Velde.

Cover art: Photograph of the Robert L. Vann Tower on the campus of Virginia Union University, Richmond, from *A Decade of Progress, Virginia Union Bulletin* (Vol. 51, No. 6, June 1951). (Courtesy of Virginia Union University Archives)
Cover design: David Fassett

CONTENTS

ILLUSTRATIONS

FOREWORD

The story about the Belgian Friendship Building on the campus of Virginia Union University in Richmond, Virginia, is a complex and improbable tale of international cooperation and African American higher education that is woven together by the authors of this book, Kathleen James-Chakraborty, Katherine M. Kuenzli, and Bryan Clark Green. The Belgian government built an avant-garde pavilion for the 1939 World's Fair in New York City. Nazi Germany occupied Belgium the following year. The Belgian government went into exile and decided to sell the pavilion to Virginia Union University, a historically Black, American Baptist institution in Richmond. The pavilion was disassembled in New York City and partially reinstalled on Virginia Union's campus. The United States government entered World War II and rented this large shell of a building as an induction center for the War Department. After the war, Virginia Union continued its fundraising campaign and completed the conversion of the building's interior into science laboratories, a library, an auditorium, and a separate gymnasium in 1949. The renamed Belgian Friendship Building and the adjoining Robert L. Vann Memorial Tower, named in honor of the influential Black newspaper editor of the *Pittsburgh Courier,* have remained in active use on the campus until the present day. Today, the building and bell tower are recognized as both Virginia landmarks and as historic structures on the National Register of Historic Places.

Like many people, I wasn't aware of the full history surrounding the Belgium Friendship Building, even though I had a strong family connection to Virginia Union University. My in-laws, the Rev. Drs. Henry and Ella Mitchell, taught on the faculty of the School of Theology during the 1980s. My father-in-law served as dean of the theology school from 1982 to 1988. Yet I was aware of Virginia Union's importance in Richmond, and especially the Black community of Jackson Ward that surrounded the Virginia Union campus.

I grew up in Durham, North Carolina, in a similar Black neighborhood to Jackson Ward that surrounded a publicly supported, Black college, named North Carolina College for Negroes (the name was later changed to North Carolina Central University in 1972). My mother was on the faculty and taught in the Nursing Department. My father had served as a trustee of the college during the late 1960s and 1970s.

These educational institutions played an important role in anchoring the Black communities in Richmond and Durham. In addition to their educational impact, these institutions provided meaningful employment for African Americans; they attracted well-educated professionals who taught on the faculty and administered the college, and they offered cultural and sports events that enriched the local Black community that was walled in by segregation and Jim Crow laws. I grew up with other children whose parents were also connected to the college. We were all supported and encouraged by this protected Black village of educators, administrators, business professionals, and community leaders to carry forward the torch of racial pride, representation, and leadership. During my childhood, my brothers and I delivered the *Pittsburgh Courier*, each week on our bicycles as we rode through our neighborhood and across the North Carolina College campus.

On Sunday afternoons, my family often attended the Sunday Vespers services held in the B. N. Duke Auditorium on the North Carolina College campus. Prominent civil rights leaders of the day spoke at these services. The list included Martin Luther King Jr. of the Southern Christian Leadership Conference, Roy Wilkins of the National Association for the Advancement of Colored People, James Farmer of the Congress for Racial Equality, and Whitney Young Jr. of the Urban League. We also heard from important Negro educators such as Mordecai Johnson, president of

Howard University, and Benjamin E. Mays, president of Morehouse College. These speakers challenged us not to falter in the fight against segregation and inequality.

The Belgian Friendship Building story is also an important marker in the history of Virginia Union University. The university's procurement of the pavilion symbolized the transition of ownership and control of the institution to a local board of trustees led by its first African American president, Dr. John M. Ellison, in 1941. The American Baptist Home Mission Society (ABHMS) had controlled the Virginia Union University since its founding in 1865 and had guided the institution through subsequent mergers and the move to its present location on North Lombardy Street in 1897. The ABHMS raised funds for the magnificent granite Romanesque style buildings designed by John Coxhead. By the 1930s, however, support from ABHMS for its Black colleges, which included Virginia Union University, had waned. The General Education Board (GEB), funded by John D. Rockefeller Sr., had become the largest supporter of Virginia Union, which achieved accreditation as a four-year "Negro college" in 1935. The GEB was also the major funder of the Belgian Building's conversion during the 1940s. Although negotiations began with the outgoing president of Virginia Union, Dr. William J. Clark, Dr. Ellison's leadership and stewardship of the fundraising effort, the physical relocation and erection of the building, and the outfitting of its interior for academic use occurred under Ellison's first decade as president. I would say Dr. Ellison is the unsung hero of the story of how the Belgian Building became such an important treasure on the Virginia Union campus. Ellison had to balance so many competing constituencies, some friendly and some adversarial, which the authors describe in detail. Ellison's plight was typical of other African American college presidents who served during this era.[1]

Another important insight into the Belgian Building's story that the authors describe was the significance of its architectural style. Designed in a modern European style by Belgian architects, the building clashed with the older Romanesque Revival Buildings on campus. The simple geometry of the building, its materials and facades, conveyed a different aspiration for the institution. The Belgian Building was given a prominent location near the front of the campus facing North Lombardy Street. The final configuration of the building and bell tower faced outward to the neighborhood, not inward like the Romanesque buildings clustered together. The Belgian Friendship Building and bell tower became visual landmarks not only in the Jackson Ward neighborhood but across the Richmond skyline.

The authors group the Belgian Friendship Building among other contemporary buildings designed by European architects in the United States during the 1940s and 1950s. This list included Ludwig Mies van der Rohe at the Illinois Institute of Technology campus in Chicago and Walter Gropius at Harvard University in Cambridge, Massachusetts. The Finnish father and son duo, Eliel and Eero Saarinen, also designed two important American buildings that represented the emerging modernist architecture, namely the First Christian Church in Columbus, Indiana (1942), and the Christ Church Lutheran in Minneapolis, Minnesota (1949). Both buildings have simple massing and geometries, restrained but dignified facades, and tall belfry towers. The Belgian Friendship Building at Virginia Union is rightfully compared to these early, modernist buildings designed by European architects.

The final conversion of the former Belgian Pavilion into a multipurpose, academic facility was completed in 1949. Thus, Virginia Union became one of the first Black colleges after World War II with a major modern-style building on its main campus. Howard University, Tuskegee Institute (now University), and Hampton Institute (now University), three of the largest and best endowed of the historically Black colleges and universities (HBCUs), didn't construct their first modernist buildings until the 1950s. Modernist buildings didn't appear on the campuses of the Atlanta University Center, another important HBCU enclave, until the early 1960s.

Finally, the transfer of Belgium's pavilion to a small, historically Black college countered the then prevailing world of segregation. Race relations in the country during the 1940s were at a low ebb. Richmond, like other southern cities, was deeply divided socially and economically. But World War II provided new opportunities for African Americans. This upswing culminated in 1948, when President Harry Truman's executive order desegregated the armed services in this country. This executive order became a harbinger of future racial progress that occurred during the next two decades. In addition, Richmond elected its first Black city councilman, civil rights lawyer Oliver W. Hill, in 1948. Hill would go on to become an important civil rights attorney who led numerous legal battles that tore down racial segregation in Virginia and in this country. Yet, Black colleges remained one of the few venues where different constituencies came together supporting "Negro" higher education. Whites and Blacks, southerners and northerners, all worked together to raise funds to create a new home for the Belgian Friendship Building and Vann Memorial Tower.

Let us applaud the book's authors for so ably drawing attention to this important story and for explaining how the Belgian Building became the ground upon which the student demonstrations of the 1960s' civil rights movement played across Richmond and other southern cities.

ARTHUR J. CLEMENT
Preservation Architect
Atlanta, GA

ACKNOWLEDGMENTS

This project began with Bryan Clark Green's engagement with Virginia Union when it received a Getty Conservation Grant to develop a historic preservation master plan for the campus in 2007. His work as director of historic preservation for Commonwealth Architects in Richmond, Virginia included a trawl of Union's extensive archives, ably managed by Selicia Gregory Allen, to whom members of the team express their heartfelt thanks, and of the relevant material in the holdings of the New York Public Library. In April 2018, Green presented a paper based on this research at the annual conference of the Society of Architectural Historians, held that year in St. Paul, Minnesota, which Johan Lagae attended.

Two years later, when Kathleen James-Chakraborty told Lagae that she would like to write a book about the building, he encouraged her to contact Green. The two collaborated that summer on a lecture for the Global Architectural History Teaching Collaborative; Eliana Abu-Hamdi offered key support at that point. The following spring James-Chakraborty received the European Research Council Advanced Grant for her project "Expanding Agency: Women, Race, and the Global Dissemination of Modern Architecture," which has provided much of the funding for this book; that grant in turn was based on seed funding from University

College Dublin's Humanities Institute, which she received in collaboration with Douglas Smith. In September she visited Green in Richmond, where they toured the building in the company of David Gordon, and where Allen graciously guided James-Chakraborty through the archives. James-Chakraborty spent the following academic year as an Ailsa Mellon Bruce Senior Fellow at the Center for Advanced Studies in the Visual Arts at the National Gallery of Art in Washington, where the extraordinary community of scholars assembled by director Steven Nelson, most especially Luke Fidler, proved fundamental to her thinking about the Belgian Friendship Building.

At this point Green got in touch with Mark Mones at the University of Virginia Press, whose encouragement has been invaluable in seeing this book through to timely completion, as have been his colleagues Jane M. Curran and J. Andrew Edwards. As the project developed further under his guidance, Katherine M. Kuenzli joined the team. She and James-Chakraborty visited Richmond and Green in May 2022. Kuenzli also secured the assistance of the Henry van de Velde Family Foundation to hire historian Ruben Mantels, who expertly undertook research in Belgian government and literary archives and served as an ambassador for the project, putting the team in contact with local experts and supplying valued bibliographic recommendations. We are also grateful to the foundation for their assistance with illustration permissions. In July Kuenzli conducted archival research in Brussels, where James-Chakraborty joined her on walking tours of the city's architecture, a meal with Lagae, and an excursion to Leuven, where Mantels arranged for Luc Verpoest, professor emeritus at KU Leuven, to take them to the KU Leuven university library and archive, to the Leuven city archives, and to Tweebronnen, a former technical school, now the city's public library, designed by van de Velde.

Green laid the foundations for the entire volume, and his expertise particularly informs its final chapter. Kuenzli and James-Chakraborty co-wrote the book, with Kuenzli as the primary author of chapters 1 through 3 and James-Chakraborty of the introduction, conclusion, and chapters 4 through 7. Both made substantive contributions to all chapters; James-Chakraborty took the lead in unifying the material into a seamless narrative. All three authors would like to express their deep appreciation to their peer reviewers and to Richard Longstreth for their careful and very helpful reading of the initial manuscript, which has improved greatly as a result of their comments. They also thank Charles L. Davis II, Louis Nelson, and Mabel Wilson for their insights, which helped guide the final revisions.

Besides their shared debt to Allen, James-Chakraborty would like to begin by thanking Glenda Gilmore, who offered her important early encouragement and advice. She cannot think of HBCUs without remembering Terra Deaton's devotion to Morgan University and the memory of Terra's brother Ralph, another proud Morgan alum, as well as the many HBCU graduates, especially Terra and Ralph's great-aunt, the late Fannie Wilson, who were her teachers. In the United States the artist Debra Ambush, Marisa Bourgoin of the Archives of American Art, Donald Corner of the University of Oregon, Brian Goldstein of Swarthmore College, Michelle Wilkinson of the Smithsonian Institution's National Museum of African American History and Culture, and Angela Zimmerman of George Washington University all shared inspiring perspectives in the early stages of the project. Inge Bertels, Dirk Laureys, and Johan Lagae gave invaluable guidance regarding the Belgian side of the story. The tour Arthur Clements provided James-Chakraborty of Atlanta University provided deeply appreciated context. The staffs of the American Baptist Historical Society at Mercer College in Atlanta, Rockefeller Archive Center in Sleepy Hollow, the Virginia State Library in Richmond, and the Vlaamse Architectuur Archieven in Antwerp all provided ideal conditions in which to conduct archival research, and Jenny and Pierre du Pont provided congenial conversation and quarters close to Sleepy Hollow.

Above all James-Chakraborty is grateful to the team of Expanding Agency and to the staff of the School of Art History and Cultural Policy and the James Joyce and Richview Libraries at University College Dublin. Kate Buckley assembled the illustrations, always a laborious job, and put the manuscript in good order. Jenny Devine handled the accounts and kept morale high. George Francis-Kelly, who is also researching the history of HBCU architecture, generously shared the fruits of his research. Alborz Dianat, Nokubekezela Mchunu, and Pooja Sastry contributed valuable perspectives. James-Chakraborty also benefited greatly from conversations with and encouragement from countless colleagues, friends, and relatives, especially Catesby Leigh, Sally Murray James, Robert Wojtowicz, and Sibel Zandi-Sayek.

James-Chakraborty presented preliminary versions of this research at the Bauhaus University in Weimar, the University of Edinburgh, the University of Toronto,

Trinity College Dublin, and the Humanities Institute at University College Dublin, for which she thanks her hosts Pappal Suneja, Alex Bremner, Joseph Clarke, Christopher Cowell, and Anne Fuchs, respectively, and the attentive audiences whose probing questions furthered her thinking.

Kuenzli gratefully acknowledges the late Léon Ploegaerts, professor emeritus at the University of Ottawa, who was the first scholar to publish on the Belgian Friendship Building and who offered generous advice and encouragement. Prof. Dr. Werner Adriaenssens, curator of twentieth-century collections at the Musées Royaux d'Art et d'Histoire in Brussels, shared his deep knowledge of the Belgian Pavilion at the 1925 Paris Exposition and helped locate works of applied art in his museum's collection that had been exhibited in the Belgian Pavilion in New York. In addition to contributing excellent archival research in Belgium to this project, which helped to make Flemish sources accessible, historian Ruben Mantels's informed perspectives on Belgian history and the Belgian Congo and his comments on preliminary drafts have been invaluable. Tom Packet, a PhD candidate in architecture at Vrije Universiteit Brussels, provided insight into architectural politics and debates in interwar Belgium and shared his research related to the conflict between Victor Horta and van de Velde. Researcher and writer Bert Govearts was equally generous and supportive regarding Jan-Albert Goris and Albert de Vleeschauwer and thoughtfully read and commented upon preliminary drafts. Benjamin Zurstrassen, curator of the Horta Museum and Camille Paget, the museum's research assistant, kindly made accessible archival sources from Horta's archive and shared their informed perspectives on them. At Wesleyan University Professor Joseph Siry's expertise regarding ceramic tiles and their use in architectural construction was invaluable, as were his comments on draft chapters. Michael Printy, librarian for Western European Humanities at Yale's Sterling Memorial Library, provided essential research support and read chapter drafts, while Rudolf Kuenzli, professor emeritus at the University of Iowa, was a continuous source of wise counsel and a careful reader of drafts. Project grants from Wesleyan University funded Kuenzli's travel to and research at Virginia Union University and the Rockefeller Archive Center.

Finally, we join together in thanking Arthur Clements for agreeing to write the inspiring foreword.

A NOTE ON TERMINOLOGY

This book describes Americans of African ancestry throughout as African American. Historical quotations employing terms of polite usage at the time, including "Negro" and "colored," have been retained.

THE BELGIAN FRIENDSHIP BUILDING

INTRODUCTION

An article published on June 21, 1941, in the *Pittsburgh Courier* described the Robert L. Vann Memorial Tower, for which the cornerstone had just been laid on the campus of Virginia Union University in Richmond, Virginia, as "the largest memorial ever built for a Negro in America" (fig. 1).[1] It may still hold that record. The *Courier,* a weekly newspaper that at the time had the largest circulation of any publication in the United States edited by and written for African Americans, took a particular interest because the tower was named for Robert L. Vann, an alumnus of Virginia Union, Richmond's only historically Black university, who served for thirty years as the paper's editor. Some eighty years later, the tower and the Belgian Friendship Building of which it is a part are no longer the statements of African American pride they once were and might again become. For instance, the 165-foot-high structure did not feature in the public debate over the fate of the city's individually much smaller Confederate memorials on nearby Monument Avenue (fig. 2). Erected between 1890 and 1929, these were finally removed in 2020 and 2021.[2]

The Vann Memorial Tower remains one of Richmond's most recognizable buildings, even if it is rarely referred to by name. It rises just to the east of Interstate 95 as the freeway slices through Jackson Ward, once one of the country's most vibrant

Figure 1. Robert L. Vann Memorial Tower, Virginia Union University, Richmond, Virginia, 1939–49. (ART Collection / Alamy)

African American neighborhoods and today the focus of public history and regeneration efforts, including the JXN project and the Jackson Ward Collective.[3] The tower's imposing height, surpassing that of any church spire in the city and at a remove from its downtown skyscrapers, establishes the location of Virginia Union University to the inhabitants of automobiles and trucks whizzing by on the highway that runs from Maine to Miami. Those walking or driving past on North Lombardy Street get a different view. They see the entire U-shaped Belgian Friendship Building

Figure 2. Robert E. Lee Monument, Antonin Mercié, Richmond, Virginia, 1890, shown with lighting installation by Dustin Klein, 2020. (Bryan Clark Green)

for which the tower serves as a linchpin. Students, faculty, and other staff have a yet more intimate experience, as do those who come to cheer on the Panthers basketball team in the gymnasium. For them, the building carries a mixed legacy: it symbolizes Virginia Union's considerable academic and sporting achievements on the one hand, and, on the other, it reminds them of the outdatedness of some of its facilities.

Restoring the Belgian Friendship Building and recovering its importance in the history of education, politics, and architecture in the United States, as well as its ties to both Africa and Europe, provides an opportunity to counter the racist circumstances out of which it emerged. An earlier version of the building, containing most of the material used in Richmond, originally showcased Belgium at the World's Fair held in New York's Flushing Meadows in 1939 and 1940. In addition to presenting Belgian culture and products, the pavilion advertised the purported benefits of Belgium's colonial control of the Congo, which had begun in 1908, following the end of Belgian King Leopold II's personal rule over the Congo Free State, initiated in 1885. The Congo Free State comprised one the ugliest chapters in imperial history, one that African Americans George Washington Williams and William Henry Shepherd played a key role in exposing.[4] Belgium's conduct of what it viewed as its "civilizing mission" in the colony was more often one of continued exploitation, as African Americans well knew. However, displays at the Belgian Pavilion in 1939 told a different narrative, in which the United States had been among the first enablers of Belgian colonization, beginning with Henry Morton Stanley's expedition to the Congo River in the 1870s.[5] One of the purposes of the Belgian Pavilion at the New York World's Fair was to "sell" its resource-rich colony to the American public as well as to enterprising investors. The building's purpose began to shift in May 1940 when Germany invaded Belgium and imposed a miliary occupation. Responsibility for it then fell to Belgium's government in exile, whose deputies "donated" the building to Virginia Union in December 1940 in order to spare themselves demolition costs and to generate favorable publicity for their cause.

When Robert Vann's capable widow, Jessie, who became the *Courier*'s publisher upon her husband's death, pledged to raise $50,000 to ensure the tower's reerection in Richmond as a memorial to her husband, she completed the pivot toward a new, more equitable direction for what now became the Belgian Friendship Building that would eventually bear rich fruit. In April 1941 the *St. Louis Argus,* an African American newspaper, described the building as "an unusual and significant project dedicated to International Friendship, Interracial Good-Will, and Negro Education" and boasted of the tower, "No such Memorial has so far been erected anywhere in the world to the memory of a colored person."[6] The national importance of the project to African Americans is clear from the constitution of the Tower Fund Committee, which comprised a who's who of the community. Members included Mary McLeod Bethune, the founder of what is now Bethune-Cookman University as well as of the National Council of Negro Women; Nannie H. Burroughs, the president of the National Association of Colored Women; Herbert T. Delany, New York city's first African American judge; C. A. Franklin, the founder and editor of the *Call* (Kansas City); W. J. Hale, the president of Tennessee State University; West A. Hamilton, the commander of the 366th Infantry; Jane E. Hunter, the founder of the Phillis Wheatley Association; Daisy Lampkin, the national secretary of the NAACP; Adam Clayton Powell Sr., the former pastor of Harlem's Abyssinian Baptist Church; John H. Sengstacke, the publisher and owner of the *Chicago Defender;* David Henry Sims, the African Methodist Episcopal bishop of New York; the Los Angeles architect Paul R. Williams; and P. B. Young, the founder of the *Journal and Guide* (Norfolk, Va).[7]

Thanks to Vann and to John Malcus Ellison, Union's first African American president who organized the star-studded Tower Fund Committee, a building intended in part to garner support for a notoriously oppressive colonial regime instead came to provide a historically Black university with vastly improved facilities. These included an expanded library, up-to-date science laboratories, and a gymnasium that doubled as an auditorium. Together these spaces better equipped Virginia Union to provide students with a liberal arts education that prepared them for leadership roles in their communities. Many white supporters of the reconstitution of the building in Richmond hoped to reorient Virginia Union away from its roots in training clergy and other African American professionals and toward a less threatening focus on vocational education. Thankfully they failed, as the university instead became an incubator for the civil rights movement.

When Vann made her pledge, and again in 1949 when the completed tower was dedicated in her presence, she would have been barred from staying in Richmond's best hotels or eating in its downtown restaurants. If she had taken the train from Pittsburgh, she would have had to transfer into a segregated car with lesser facilities for her journey's last leg. She also could not have tried on clothes or shoes at the city's finest stores or had her hair done in its downtown beauty salons. And she certainly would not have been able to buy or rent a house in its most upscale neighborhoods. These were among the many indignities that Richmond's African American residents endured on a daily basis, as were the city's vastly inferiorly equipped segregated schools and hospitals. The pushback against Jim Crow—the system of legal segregation that had circumscribed African American life throughout the southern United States since at least the 1890s, and that extended a larger pattern of discrimination reaching back to slavery—had begun, but progress toward its elimination remained uncertain.

These circumstances ensured that in 1941, little overt celebration of the challenge the Vann Tower posed to Monument Avenue—the ceremonial artery of a city that had from 1861 to 1865 been the capital of the Confederacy, a breakaway regime established to preserve slavery—was possible. Pointing out how the Vann Memorial towers over its Confederate predecessors might not have provoked actual violence, but it definitely would have threatened the white financial support upon which Virginia Union relied. It also would have fatally undermined the fundraising required to transfer the building from New York to Richmond. This campaign began as an effort by white Baptists to assist the Belgian government in exile. Little, however, better symbolized the use to which African Americans would put the Belgian Friendship Building than the tower's conversion into a monument to a man who had been one of the country's best known and most powerful African Americans.

Born in 1879, Vann obtained a law degree from the University of Pittsburgh following his studies in Richmond. Shortly after participating in the *Pittsburgh Courier*'s founding in 1910, he took over as its editor; under his leadership the weekly became one of the country's two most widely read African American newspapers, along with the *Chicago Defender*. Throughout his career, Vann was a highly regarded spokesman for his race. His decision in 1932 to break with the party of Lincoln, for which most enfranchised African Americans then voted, and instead to endorse Franklin Delano Roosevelt's candidacy for the presidency garnered him an appointment as a special assistant to the attorney general. Vann resigned, however, in 1935 to return to the *Courier*, where he rightly felt he would have more influence. The cause for which he was best known in his late career was lobbying for expanded rights for African Americans within the country's armed forces. Although full desegregation would occur only in 1948, when Harry Truman signed an executive order to that effect, the pressure Vann exerted ensured that the issue was alive even before the United States entered World War II.[8]

By the time it might have been possible to celebrate the tower as a rival to the Confederate statues and memorials on Monument Avenue, the discussion had moved on. Vann's achievements were eclipsed after 1945 by a new generation of African American leaders. The civil rights movement focused on access to public schools, public space, and the ballot box rather than on issues of commemoration. Not surprisingly, the Virginia Union alumni who were active in city and state politics, such as Henry Marsh, Richmond's first African American mayor, and Douglas Wilder, Virginia's first African American governor, concentrated on more obviously tangible deliverables than the spire of their alma mater. The construction of Interstate 95 in the 1950s meant that the tower was marooned on the other side of the freeway from their new offices in city hall and the governor's mansion. Moreover, memorial culture took new forms in the United States in the postwar years. Living memorials, which included everything from highways to sports stadiums, increasingly replaced bronze equestrian statues of generals on horseback.[9] The downside to this development, however, was that the commemorative purpose of even recent, modern memorials became less visible.[10] The current lack of widespread recognition—of Robert Vann's importance to the later civil rights movement, of the tower named for him as a memorial to his achievements, and of the importance of the Vann Tower to the history of architecture in the United States—number among the many ways in which the struggles for equality remain incomplete.

In 2016 Michelle Obama pointedly noted of the White House in a speech at the Democratic National Convention that "I wake up every morning in a house that was built by slaves."[11] There is finally a growing awareness of the many contributions that African Americans have made as architects, as clients, and as artisans to the built environment of the United States. A rapidly expanding scholarly literature details the impact of this participation in the construction of our most cherished monuments as well as of the backdrops to everyday lives.[12] It also exposes the racism that remains deeply embedded in architectural culture. Less concerted attention has been paid, however, to the architecture of post-Emancipation African American institutions and enterprises, although this, too, is beginning to change. The African American church is certainly the most important of these, but the campuses of historically Black colleges and universities (HBCUs) and other educational infrastructure are also beginning to receive the detailed investigation they merit, while a recent study of the buildings housing the African American press in Chicago further demonstrates how much is to be gained through looking at businesses.[13]

To be sure, it was not until the middle of the twentieth century that African Americans gained control of most of the decisions made regarding the appearance of buildings on HBCU campuses, although there are important exceptions, such as

Tuskegee Institute (now University). Already beginning in the 1890s, its founder, Booker T. Washington, commissioned many buildings from Robert Taylor, the first African American to obtain a university degree in architecture. Today the enormous pride that HBCU alumni take in their institutions typically focuses on an iconic historic structure at the center of campus, often built in a Colonial Revival style, or on the most up-to-date facilities, leapfrogging over the presence of mid-century modernism, which can now appear tired and dated. With the notable exception of public housing, African Americans' roles as designers, makers, and users of modern architecture have been less documented and appreciated than their contributions to modern art, literature, and music in the United States.[14]

Already when the pieces of what became the Belgian Friendship Building arrived on freight cars in Richmond in 1941, African American artists were envisioning alternatives to the prominent visual reminders of institutionalized racism and colonial subjugation that were loaded into these cars and reconstituted in Richmond. Included in the shipment were two monumental bas-reliefs celebrating Belgium's "civilizing mission" by Belgian sculptor Arthur Dupagne (fig. 3). The two friezes depicting heroic Congolese figures lend credence to the myth that the Congolese adopted Western innovations without sacrificing their "native spirit." In the first, muscular figures dance, make music, and pound manioc, while in the second they engage in formal education, modern medicine, and mining with the same vigor and vitality. These panels purporting to depict the Congo before and after colonization marked the outside corner of the New York pavilion's Colonial Section and were reattached to the Vann Memorial Tower when it was reassembled in Richmond.

In contrast to this colonial propaganda, there is an uncanny resemblance between the Vann Memorial Tower and the triumphantly modern skyscrapers that African American artist Aaron Douglas began to paint as early as 1930 in his murals at Cravath Hall at Fisk University. Following Alain Locke, the intellectual father of the Harlem Renaissance, Douglas, its leading visual artist, believed that Africa was the cradle of art as well as civilization, and that only through the study of precolonial African creative achievements could he create an appropriately modern art of his own time.[15] Douglas's easel painting *Building More Stately Mansions* (1944), also at Fisk, includes two of these tiered towers on the far left of a celebration of African and African American construction prowess over which the silhouette of an Egyptian pharaoh presides (fig. 4). With a title derived from Oliver Wendell Holmes's

Figure 3. *Belgian Congo,* Arthur Dupagne, 1939. (Katherine M. Kuenzli)

1858 poem "The Chambered Nautilus," it suggests the racial pride and ambition that led generations of African Americans to harness African traditions to new forms of expression that articulated modern forms of African American identity and self-awareness. Upon arriving in Richmond, the Belgian Building would become part and parcel of this emancipatory movement evoked by Holmes in these lines:

> Build thee more stately mansions, O my soul
> As the swift seasons roll!
> Leave thy low-vaulted past!
> Let each new temple, nobler than the last,
> Shut thee from heaven with a dome more vast,
> Till thou at length art free.[16]

Figure 4. *Building More Stately Mansions*, Aaron Douglas, 1944, oil on canvas, 55 5/8 x 43 5/8 in. (Fisk University Galleries, Nashville, Tennessee, 1991.2147; photograph by Jerry Atnip)

It was this freedom that the Belgian Friendship Building was eventually harnessed to help achieve. It became a place where Virginia Union students could hear African American leaders inspired by the independence of Ghana exhort them to work for justice at home in Virginia, and where they could read newspapers detailing the Congo's struggles to break free from Belgium. That they did so in the earliest example of European architectural modernism to appear on a university campus in the United States has been ignored by architectural historians. Richmond—a city that, like the rest of the South, excluding Florida and Texas, was seldom in the forefront of twentieth-century architectural experimentation—is an unlikely site for the work of a quartet of major Belgian architects on the campus of an HBCU. The literature on the building to date has been authored by specialists in Belgian architecture; it remains to be integrated into the history of the country in which it stands.[17]

The acquisition by Virginia Union of the Belgian Friendship Building predated Harvard University's erection of Walter Gropius's Graduate Center and coincided with Ludwig Mies van der Rohe's Master Plan for the Armour Institute of Technology (now Illinois Institute of Technology). Gropius and Mies had directed the Bauhaus, the most influential twentieth-century school of art, architecture, and design, founded in Germany in 1919. They were part of a wave of immigrants from Central Europe whose presence helped transform the postwar practice of architecture and design in the United States in ways not always anticipated by "The World of Tomorrow," as the New York fair of 1939–40 was subtitled.[18] The design of the Belgian Pavilion for the fair was overseen by Henry van de Velde, who had recommended Gropius as his successor as applied art school director when, as a Belgian, van de Velde was forced to resign his position at the Grand Ducal School of Applied Arts in Weimar, Germany, in 1915.[19] Following a period of exile, van de Velde rebuilt his career in Brussels, where he founded the Higher Institute of Decorative Arts (Institut Supérieur des Arts Décoratifs, today's National Higher School for the Visual Arts, or École Nationale Supérieure des Arts Visuels, ENSAV) also known as La Cambre, after the former monastery in which it is situated.[20] Two of its faculty members, Victor Bourgeois and Léon Stynen, designed the Belgian Pavilion in collaboration with van de Velde, while a fourth Belgian architect, Hugo van Kuyck, oversaw the building's reconstruction in Richmond, where he was initially assisted by Charles Russell, an architect who was a linchpin of Richmond's African American community with a distinguished history of literally and figuratively building its institutions.[21]

The approach to modernism taken by the Belgians encompassed the rejection of all historicist ornament, although their marriage of abstract volumes and tactile cladding ran counter to Mies's and Gropius's preference to expose a building's underlying skeletal frame. Moreover, the emphatically civic character of the original design, which was cleverly tailored to the irregular site it occupied on the fairgrounds, was no longer as obvious when it was reconfigured for a more open setting in Richmond by an architect who was not involved in the initial design. The Belgian Friendship Building remains, however, a masterpiece of mid-century modern architecture in the United States, comparable to the contemporary work of Eliel and Eero Saarinen in its careful attention to massing and materials.

For much of twentieth century, historians of architecture focused their attention on a building's design process and how it fit into the oeuvre of its architect. They might also account for how it had been constructed in terms of the available technologies, how its plan was shaped by its intended use, and how it aesthetically impacted the resulting spaces. This book includes such stories, but any accounting of why the Belgian Friendship Building is the most significant structure that survives from "The World of Tomorrow" takes us well beyond such a narrow focus. The Belgian Pavilion marks a key moment in the history of modern European architecture, in which modernity was represented in terms of new construction systems, abstract forms, and an impressive scale but clad in familiar materials and put to civic uses. However, the true importance of the Belgian Friendship Building is as something neither its architect nor his original patrons could ever have imagined. At its very best it served as an inspiration to challenge Jim Crow. And although desegregation was by no means the intent of many of those who supported its reconstitution in Richmond, their goals, too, were different from those of its architects and the Belgian government. The story of the Belgian Friendship Building is thus not simply a biography of the meanings that can become attached to a single architectural form and the way in which they can help transform society, but an accounting of how divergent goals can coexist within the same form.

The story told in the pages that follow weaves together people and resources from three continents: Africa, Europe, and North America. It uncovers how a modestly resourced historically Black university in Richmond came to have the first important example of European modern architecture erected on a campus in the United States, ahead of such elite institutions as the Massachusetts Institute of Technology and Harvard University, and how its students engaged in significant political activism already several years before the Free Speech Movement began at the University of California, Berkeley or the anti–Vietnam War movement got underway on other historically white campuses. This extraordinary story of the Belgian Friendship Building occurred despite Virginia Union being located in a city and a state whose white community had little interest at mid-century in moving beyond architectural styles closely associated with its colonial past and with the exploitation of enslaved labor that had generated much of the region's early wealth, and whose white political leadership beginning in 1956 organized a campaign of Massive Resistance to the school desegregation mandated by the United States Supreme Court. The story of the Belgian Friendship Building reveals how white northern philanthropists imposed their own agendas upon African Americans seeking economic and political empowerment, but also how the two groups collaborated to create a campus and a university of considerable architectural and academic distinction that propelled the civil rights movement forward in Virginia. This remarkable achievement could nevertheless not always overcome the discrimination that ripped the heart out of Jackson Ward and continues to hamper African American economic equality. Finally, the design and reconstruction of the Belgian Pavilion demonstrates that buildings shape as well as are shaped by the societies in which they are embedded, which in the case of the Belgian Building were multiple, thus underscoring the interconnectedness of what has long been a global world.

The following chapter introduces three of the building's architects—van de Velde, Bourgeois, and Stynen—and situates them in the context of interwar Belgian architecture. Reconstructing its origins also requires explicating the rivalry between van de Velde and Victor Horta, two of the pioneers of Art Nouveau, that dated back to the 1890s and lasted throughout their careers. Both men engaged early in their careers in commissions for Edmond van Eetvelde, who oversaw the administration of the Congo Free State. Horta presided over Belgium's contribution to the International Exposition of Modern Decorative and Industrial Arts held in Paris in 1925; when Belgium's showing there failed to impress, van de Velde was granted authority over its participation in international expositions in Paris in 1937 and in New York in 1939. Together van de Velde, Bourgeois, and Stynen arrived at a design that repeated the constructional system van de Velde had developed with engineer Paul Célis and architects Jean-Jules Eggericx and Raphaël Verwilghen for the Belgian Pavilion in Paris, but they changed the building's massing, organizing it loosely around a courtyard and adding the tower, which held a carillon.

Chapter 2 recounts the pavilion's place on the fairgrounds in the context of the dominant commercial attractions such as Futurama as well as other national pavilions. Prominently sited at the entrance to the Lagoon of Nations, the building received considerable favorable publicity on both sides of the Atlantic, including from Lewis Mumford, the foremost architecture critic in the United States of the time. The Belgian Pavilion was designed to showcase Belgium's friendship with the

United States and to advertise the quality of Belgian-made handcraft and industrial products as well as of raw materials, especially diamonds, from the Congo. Belgium invested at least a million dollars in New York displays, which expressed gratitude for the role that the United States had played in saving its people from starvation during Germany's occupation in World War I and in rebuilding the county afterward. Belgium also wanted to convey to an international audience that it was a leading location for modern art, architecture, and design, and that the country had many desirable goods available for export. Organizers of the Colonial Section wanted to communicate to a sometimes skeptical public in the United States the purported benefits of its rule over its chief colony.[22] Organized by the ministry of the colonies, this part of the pavilion included an impressive display of Congolese art, which was already appreciated on both sides of the Atlantic. This foregrounding of Congolese culture was particularly notable, as the achievements of African Americans were sidelined at the fair; the community launched protests in order to get even a meagre share of mostly unskilled jobs.

The story of what became of the Belgian Pavilion after Germany invaded Belgium in May 1940 is the subject of chapter 3. Jan-Albert Goris, the Belgian civil servant who was the Belgian deputy commissioner for the fair, conspired to repackage the pavilion for any university that would pay for the cost of disassembling the original structure. He falsely claimed that only the war had prevented the building from being returned to and reerected in Belgium. Goris was also probably anxious to find employment for the Belgian engineer and construction laborers who had remained on the fair site through the summer of 1940 and who were now stranded in the United States. Made aware that the General Education Board (GEB), a Rockefeller family philanthropy that funded higher education, had already agreed to co-fund a new library at Virginia Union, Goris worked to persuade its officials to support the transfer of the building there. As a major donor, the GEB exerted a great influence over VUU, as it did over a number of Baptist HBCUs, and the Rockefeller family had already contributed generously as well to Belgium.

Chapter 4 details the history of Virginia Union and of Jackson Ward, the African American neighborhood on whose edge it sits. Virginia Union had, not uniquely but certainly unusually for an HBCU, always expressed its ambition for excellence through its distinctive architecture. Its turn-of-the-century campus was graced with the "noble nine," a series of Richardsonian granite-faced buildings that comprised one of the most impressive architectural ensembles at any university in the southern United States and cut strongly against the grain of the local white enthusiasm for reviving the neoclassicism Thomas Jefferson had popularized a century earlier. Equally notably, while many HBCUs, following the example of Hampton and Tuskegee Institutes (now Universities), focused on vocational training, Virginia Union was committed from the beginning to the highest possible academic standards it could manage on such a thin budget and in the face of such overwhelming racial discrimination.[23] It was particularly and rightfully proud of how many of its former students had become presidents of other HBCUs. The university benefited greatly from its location in Jackson Ward, which some of its residents experienced as an oasis of African American achievement and where that success was funneled into support for organizations, such as the NAACP and the Urban League, that sought to improve conditions for all African Americans. The chapter also introduces the web of white associations, staffed almost exclusively by Baptists, responsible for the governance and funding of Virginia Union, and the men who would help determine the Belgian Pavilion's fate.

As shown in chapter 5, the cost of reconstituting what became the Belgian Friendship Building in Richmond rose to several times the initial estimates, making the building more expensive than a new library alone would have been. The poor management of Sidney Hening, the university's white treasurer and a major figure in securing the building for Virginia Union, contributed to the overrun. It was exacerbated by the rising cost of materials and labor, as well as by shortages of both occasioned by the impending war, which the United States finally entered in December 1941. Ellison eventually successfully raised absolutely unprecedented sums for the university, ensuring the building's completion in 1950. Although he gained his position in part because he was able to convince his white backers that he would be able to substantially increase African American support for Union, many aspects of the campaign highlighted the degree to which HBCUs remained controlled by white interests.

This chapter also describes the impact of the war upon many of the parties involved. That the Belgian "donors" wanted—in addition to offloading the costs of disassembling their pavilion—to garner African American as well as white support for their country's eventual liberation from the Germans is undeniable. Probably no one involved was aware of the key role that the Congo would play in the conflict, supplying much of the uranium for the Manhattan Project and the bombs dropped on Hiroshima and then Nagasaki.[24] African American participation in the war would heighten demands for equality, or, in the words of the *Pittsburgh Courier* campaign, for a "double victory," one abroad and one at home.[25] University officials were careful to describe their institution and its goals in terms that would not threaten whites, but even faculty termed moderate or conservative by subsequent historians reached the end of their patience and were ready to challenge segregation head-on. For example, Gordon Blaine Hancock, a sociologist with a national reputation in what was then termed race relations, helped convene the 1942 meeting of southern African American leaders that issued the Durham Manifesto, now understood as an important move toward their eventual rejection of Jim Crow.[26] While white Baptists ensured that Ellison rather than Hancock became president in an effort to promote African American leadership they believed should be focused on economic rather than political empowerment, demands for real change proved impossible to constrain.

The most famous sites associated with the civil rights movement are located in Georgia, Alabama, Mississippi, and Arkansas, and the subsequent Black Power movement was based in major northern and western cities, yet HBCUs also played an outsize role in galvanizing communities across the Upper South.[27] When the Richmond 34, a group of Virginia Union students, was arrested on February 22, 1960, for taking seats at the lunch counter of Thalheimer's department store, it was inspired not only by recent events in Greensboro, North Carolina; Norfolk, Virginia; and Nashville, Tennessee. Speeches that the Rev. Dr. Martin Luther King had delivered in Richmond, including four he had given in the Belgian Friendship Building to which he would return for a final time later that year, also motivated these influential and nonviolent sit-ins by Virginia Union students, which helped to desegregate the city of Richmond.

Chapter 6 addresses these developments, which it places in the context of African American reactions to the crisis that developed in the Congo when Belgium proved unwilling to relinquish complete control of its entire former colony. The chapter also reconstructs the Cold War context in which modern architecture was increasingly adopted in the postwar period on the campuses of HBCUs as well as of predominately white campuses in the North. New architectural forms, these examples demonstrate, were not always informed by progressive politics, a conclusion confirmed by the damage that the new highways would do to neighborhoods such as Jackson Ward.

The Belgian Friendship Building, and particularly the Vann Tower, are less imposing today than they were when their reconstruction in Richmond was finally completed in 1950. Designed to be a temporary structure, the building was reerected by a largely Belgian construction crew that failed to take the necessary steps to ensure that water did not seep through the terra cotta skin and corrode the underlying steel skeleton. Virginia Union's resources remained conscribed by the structural racism that undercut all HBCUs, even as they operated as important engines for African American educational and economic attainment. In consequence, maintenance has been a challenge. This has particularly affected the appearance of the tower, which has been reclad in inappropriate materials. Chapter 7 recounts the efforts since the 1960s to preserve the building, including the Bells for Peace campaign in the early 2000s, in the face of these circumstances.

The Belgian Friendship Building is a place where the history, including the travails, of three continents intersect. Its story is one of aspirations, albeit often divergent ones. Above all, there was the aspiration that better educational opportunities could improve the economic standing of African Americans. There was also the hope on the part of African Americans that impressive architecture in line with national and international trends could help forge an identity distinctive from that of Jim Crow Virginia. Our hope as authors is that this book can draw attention to the circumstances that caused the Belgian Building to be designed and then reconstituted in Richmond and to the way in which it bolstered African American achievement and pride there. Beyond this, we draw attention to Virginia Union University and the contribution it has made to United States society, in the hopes of enhancing the resources it brings to both its crucial educational mission and to the care of its impressive and distinctive architectural heritage.

1

BELGIAN MODERNISM

From Art Nouveau to the World of Tomorrow

On February 12, 1938, a speed boat darted away from the *Normandie* when the French luxury liner was still in quarantine in a New York harbor. The boat carried a representative of the Belgian government, who when he reached the shore promptly hailed a cab and rushed to the Empire State Building (fig. 5).[1] His destination was easy to spot. Finished fewer than seven years earlier, the Empire State Building was then the world's tallest structure. For anyone coming from the piers lining the Hudson, the skyscraper completely dominated lower Midtown Manhattan. Moreover, at more than five times the height of Belgium's highest office building, the sight of it must have clearly communicated to our nameless courier the economic and technological, if not necessarily the aesthetic, dominance the United States had recently achieved in relationship to Europe, especially in the wake of World War I. Less apparent was the degree to which New York, and the rest of the country, had not yet fully recovered from the Great Depression nearly a decade after the stock market crashed in Lower Manhattan. After all, in 1938 the Empire State Building was not yet fully occupied and would not turn a profit for more than a decade. Its power at that moment was more aspirational than actual as the most potent and striking symbol of an ambitious effort to raise employment by increasing international trade and domestic consumption.[2] That same effort motivated the 1939 New

Figure 5. Empire State Building, Shreve, Lamb, and Harmon, New York, 1930–31. (Dpa picture alliance / Alamy)

York World's Fair, subtitled "The World of Tomorrow," which opened in the city's Flushing Meadows in the outer borough of Queens in April 1939.

Probably with the help of a porter, the Belgian found the right elevator bank to take him to the fair's offices located on one of the higher floors of the Empire State Building. There he became the first representative of a foreign government to deliver the plans for its pavilion to Grover Whalen, the president of the New York World's Fair Corporation, who was charged with organizing the event that officially commemorated the 150th anniversary of George Washington's inauguration in New

York as the first president of the United States. Whalen immediately took the plans to a meeting of the fair's Board of Design, where the Belgian Pavilion became the first of its kind to be approved. Articles celebrating this triumph published in two of the city's leading dailies, the *New York Times* and *Herald Tribune,* observed with interest that the Belgians had beaten out the French, despite their arrival on the same ship.[3] The pavilions of these two countries would face each other at the fair, where they flanked the entrance to the International Zone.

Today a design like this could be dispatched in seconds from Brussels to New York via the internet, but in 1938, the *Normandie,* launched just three years earlier as the world's fastest passenger ship, took over four days to cross the Atlantic. Telegraph and radio messages could be relayed quickly, but neither was capable of conveying images, let alone elaborate architectural and site plans. At a time when even television remained in its infancy (RCA would introduce consumers to it at the 1939 fair), world's fairs provided visitors with unrivaled firsthand experience of new products and dazzling artisanship, typically packaged in impressive, if temporary, architecture and spectacular, even entertaining displays.[4] And lots of people came, with attendance nearly crossing the forty-five million mark over the fair's two seasons in 1939 and 1940, suggesting that most of the city's seven and a half million residents attended at least once, and that they were joined by millions from across the country as well as visitors from other parts of the world.[5]

Belgium's pride in securing such a prominent location, and its determination to make a splash, indicated the continued economic and political importance of such events, as well as the significance of their architecture. Ever since the Great Exhibition was staged in London's Hyde Park in 1851, world's fairs, although intended above all to announce advancements in manufacturing and spur international trade, had also showcased the latest design trends. Originally the focus had been on technology, with London setting the bar high already with the Crystal Palace, a vast greenhouse-like structure assembled out of standardized pieces of plate glass, cast iron, and timber in a matter of months rather than years. The wrought iron Eiffel Tower, built for a fair held in Paris in 1889 and the tallest structure in the world until 1930, dazzled spectators with its demonstration of the tensile capacity of industrially produced materials. By the time the nations of the world assembled again in the City of Light just eleven years later, however, national pavilions, including those of places such as Finland that were not yet independent states, were becoming a popular alternative to this focus on engineering. These more modestly scaled contributions instead provided an important way to advertise distinctive national identities. The challenge was to balance recognizable references to the past, an approach that dominated early national pavilions, with striking demonstrations of one's modernity, an increasingly popular choice by the 1930s.

In the plans presented to Whalen, Belgium attempted to do both (fig. 6). The *Herald* quoted fair officials as declaring, "With plate glass forming approximately half of the exterior, the building will be unique in its modernity without sacrifice of quality."[6] The *Times* provided more details, emphasizing a number of features that would dominate later press coverage. The choice of terra cotta cladding atop a schist base was described as a response to a red and blue color scheme for that part of the fair. Here Belgian haste may have been misplaced, as in the end most buildings at "The World of Tomorrow" were white, although the high quality of the materials employed by the Belgians made an excellent impression in surroundings that consisted mostly of more obviously temporary structures.[7] The pavilion's art gallery

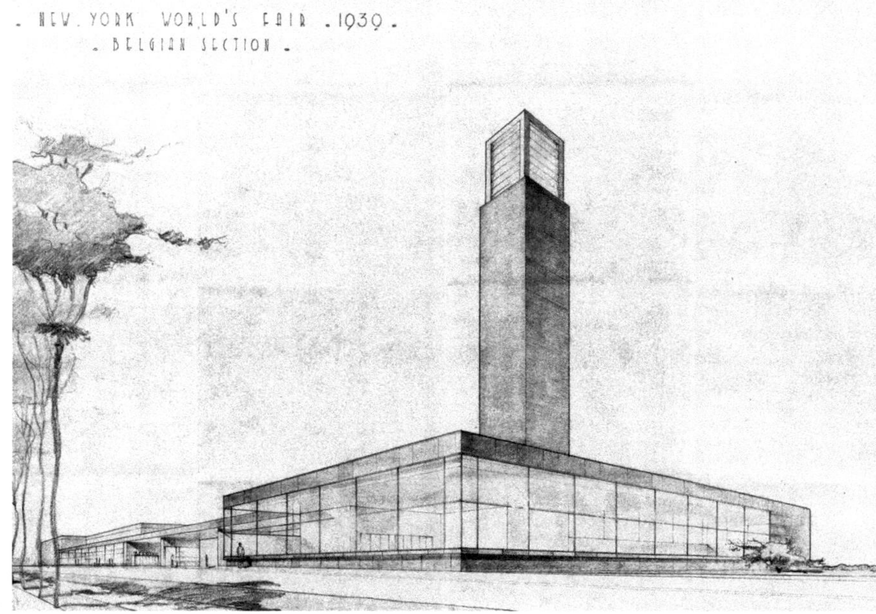

Figure 6. Preliminary perspective drawing of Belgian Pavilion, Henry van de Velde, Léon Stynen, and Victor Bourgeois, 1938. (Flanders Architecture Institute—collection of the Flemish Government, archive of Léon Stynen)

mentioned in the account failed to materialize, however, although "an exhibit from the Belgian Congo featuring mining and raw materials" did, with consequences that would, along with the choice of quasi-permanent materials, influence the building's subsequent history. The total cost of the structures and the exhibitions it housed was estimated at $1,000,000. This was quite substantial for a relatively small nation with a population only slightly larger than that of the host city, although the sum amounted to only a quarter of what the British soon announced they would spend advertising themselves and their empire.[8]

The 1939 Belgian Pavilion also marked a dramatic break with that country's last showing at a fair in the United States. In 1933, the Belgian village at the Century of Progress exhibition in Chicago had been a great success, but this entirely private venture had presented Belgium almost exclusively in terms of its historic architecture, much of which had been damaged or destroyed by German invaders during World War I.[9] In New York, there would be no such sentimental nostalgia. Instead Belgium presented itself as an industrial nation that was nonetheless determined to preserve cherished artisanal traditions, especially when they could be harnessed to modern forms of expression, not to mention the resources of a major colonial power.

Victor Horta versus Henry van de Velde: From Art Nouveau to the 1930s

The design presented to Whalen, which was subject to slight refinements over the following months, was the product of a decade-and-a-half-long debate in Belgium about what direction its architecture and design should take. This debate was epitomized by the rivalry between the country's two most vocal proponents of modern architecture and design, Victor Horta and Henry van de Velde. Both men had established their reputations in the 1890s, when Horta had pioneered Art Nouveau in a series of luxurious Brussels townhouses in which he fused structure and ornament to create a new alternative to historicist design. Beginning with the Hôtel Tassel of 1893–96, Horta employed an exposed iron skeleton to open the building's narrow and deep floorplan to the free circulation of light and air (fig. 7). In his private homes, Horta combined these structural innovations with the use of luxurious and colorful materials including ivory, onyx, marble, minerals, and precious woods. For his part, van de Velde worked on larger parcels of land on the outskirts of Brussels to fuse handcraft and industry, nature and technology, in designs indebted as much

Figure 7. Hotel Tassel, Victor Horta, Brussels, 1892–93. (Henry Townsend / Wikimedia Commons)

to the British Arts and Crafts movement as to European aesthetic innovations. The international dimensions of his career led him to pursue projects beyond Belgium, first in France and subsequently in Germany and the Netherlands before returning to Belgium in the mid-1920s. The Belgian Pavilion for New York represented a late chapter in the half-century-long competition between Horta and van de Velde, a rivalry that also encompassed the tensions between the country's French-speaking Walloon and Dutch-speaking Flemish communities. Both men wrote in French, but van de Velde identified as Fleming, whereas Horta had trained in part in Paris and embraced French architectural traditions. Both Horta and van de Velde would jockey to receive prestigious government commissions in the interwar years.

Art Nouveau, the movement that launched the careers of both men, was an umbrella term encompassing a broad range of approaches. Horta's creations displayed forms from the vegetal and animal kingdoms; by contrast, van de Velde's were nonrepresentational, mobilizing his scientific conception of line as a virtual force. Horta's compositions for mosaics and stained-glass windows suggest the fugitive movements of plant tendrils, smoke plumes, and insects. He combined these natural forms with a visual and structural emphasis on industrial materials. By contrast, van de Velde, who trained as a painter, was inspired by the expressive compositions of Vincent van Gogh and Georges Seurat. He fused these painters' dynamic and abstract approach to line and color with an appreciation for "honest" construction stemming from the British Arts and Crafts movement. The result was an influential articulation of sinuous and structural ornament.[10] The swelling curves that animate the contours and hardware of a wooden desk and matching chair van de Velde designed in 1899, for instance, are both dynamic and functional, as the shelves and drawers curve in to accommodate the arm span of the desk worker while affording ample workspace and storage. Such pieces anchored a modern interior, complete with wall coverings, carpets, and shelving, all designed by van de Velde (fig. 8). In his highly influential writings, van de Velde argued for the integration of fine art—that is, architecture, painting, and sculpture—with craft, and for abstract, structural ornament that did not imitate nature or history. He also praised modern engineering as the origin of a "new style."[11]

Like Louis Sullivan's architecture in the United States, which Charles L. Davis II has described as "reject[ing] the practice of European revivalism because he believed these historical styles were not capable of expressing the peculiarities of American life," and "replac[ing] these conventions with an ahistorical brand of botanical ornament that he created from scratch," Art Nouveau eradicated Neo-Renaissance, Neo-Gothic, and Neo-Baroque ornament.[12] The new, ahistorical architectural expression known as Art Nouveau quickly reverberated throughout Europe, where it was often associated with progressive social principles. The movement's leftist reputation was encouraged by the ties both Horta and van de Velde had to the Workers' Party of Belgium (Parti ouvrier Belge or POB), the client for Horta's most ambitious early work, the House of the People (Maison du Peuple) which opened in Brussels in 1899. Van de Velde was equally supported by the Workers' Party, which invited him to deliver important lectures on aesthetic and social matters, including on the British Arts and Crafts reformer William Morris, in which he acknowledged the

Figure 8. Desk, Henry van de Velde, 1899. (Museum of Applied Arts, Vienna; photo: © MAK/Georg Mayer)

reformer's unrequited efforts to yoke aesthetic and moral improvement to principles of social justice. "Imagine," van de Velde exclaimed, "here is a man, one single man, who was an accomplished poet, who was an accomplished artisan, practicing every craft—I say every craft of art—and who was, moreover, an ardent, sincere, and practicing socialist!"[13]

For van de Velde, Horta, and members of the Workers' Party of Belgium, however, principles of social justice applied primarily to their white brethren. Art Nouveau's ties to the oppressive, racist regime that the Belgian king Leopold II had established in the Congo Free State are notorious.[14] Leopold obtained the Free State in 1885 as his own possession by outmaneuvering the rival powers of England, France, Germany, and Portugal. Although he consistently cloaked his purely commercial interests in a rhetoric of humanitarianism and scientific progress, these noble claims became increasingly difficult to uphold amid evidence of serious abuses under a domanial system established to increase his profits from ivory and wild rubber.[15] As the Belgians were well aware as they prepared their New York exhibits, Americans—specifically African Americans—had been among the earliest and most vocal critics of the Free State. A decade before the publication of Joseph Conrad's unsettling novel *Heart of Darkness* in 1899 and fifteen years before the Irish-born British official

Roger Casement issued his Congo report in 1905, African American historian and journalist George Washington Williams alerted the world to colonial abuses there.[16] In "An Open Letter to His Serene Majesty Leopold II" and "Report on the Proposed Congo Railway," Williams exposed the brutal and inhumane treatment of the Congolese under Leopold's exploitative system.[17] For his part, African American Presbyterian missionary William Henry Sheppard documented the massacre and mutilation of local populations (including the appalling practice of cutting off the right hands of victims) in a report published in the *New York Times* in 1900. Sheppard, with the help of Casement, among others, created the Congo Reform Association in 1904. Its incontrovertible findings ultimately brought the Belgian state to dispossess Leopold of his colony in 1908. However, even though Belgium sought to curb the worst atrocities committed under Leopold II's reign, abuses persisted and were again exposed by Sheppard, who was taken to trial by the Kasai Company for libel in 1909.[18]

Edmond van Eetvelde, who administered the Congo for Leopold from his desk in Brussels, was one of the most enthusiastic supporters of the new style. In 1895, he commissioned Horta to design his private town house in Brussels, sparing no expense to provide his architect with lavish hard woods and precious minerals from the colony that comprise the house's sumptuous décor.[19] Two years later, again at Van Eetvelde's request, van de Velde—along with two other pioneers of Art Nouveau, Gustave Serrurier-Bovy and Paul Hankar—created displays for the Congolese Pavilion in Tervuren as part of the 1897 Brussels International Exposition.[20] At the Belgian Export Room in that Congolese Pavilion, for instance, van de Velde designed multidirectional display tables whose curved contours activated the surrounding space and enticed visitors. A stenciled frieze encircled the room with dynamic, abstract arabesques, representing a departure from the touristic landscapes and ethnographic scenes that accompanied earlier Congolese exhibits (fig. 9).[21] For the pavilion's Import Room, Sérrurier-Bovy created a series of large, circular archways that doubled as display cases and furniture; the arches' interior and exterior surfaces displayed Congolese minerals, while seats at their base provided resting spots for fairgoers. Such novel designs led to Art Nouveau occasionally being termed "Congo Style."[22]

The European-wide enthusiasm for Art Nouveau collapsed relatively quickly in the early years of the twentieth century, although it lingered longer in Belgium than in most other places. Both Horta and van de Velde were able to regroup, however.

Figure 9. Export Room in the Congolese Pavilion, a section of the Brussels International Exposition, Henry van de Velde, 1897. (HP.1971.28.1-1, collection RMCA Tervuren; photo Alexandre, 1897)

Van de Velde moved to Berlin in 1901, before accepting a position as adviser to manufacturers in the Grand Duchy of Saxe-Weimar in 1902. There, he founded an influential school, the Grand Ducal School of Applied Arts, which provided the foundations for the Bauhaus, which from 1919 to 1924 was housed in buildings van de Velde had designed. Denied reentry into Belgium during the war due to his status as a German civil servant, van de Velde took refuge in Switzerland in 1917 before finding employment in the Netherlands in 1921. Throughout these peregrinations, he remained committed to innovative abstract form.[23] Meanwhile, Horta, following a lecture and study tour in the United States during World War I, increasingly returned to the Beaux-Arts classicism in which he had been trained, even as he took on major new commissions.[24]

Of all Belgium's modern masters, Horta seemed the best positioned to take the reins of the modern movement after the First World War. Although Horta's wartime departure to the United States had caused him to lose his position as director of the Academy of Fine Arts in Brussels, he nevertheless received high-profile commissions upon returning in 1918, including for a growing number of public projects, such as the Brugmann Hospital (1919–23) and the Palace of Fine Arts (1929). However, rather than spearheading a second wave of modernism in Belgium, Horta in his postwar projects increasingly pursued a more traditional sense of monumentality by endowing his buildings with classical architectural elements, including columns, pilasters, and figural friezes in keeping with his French architectural education. This stylistic shift, combined with his pursuit of elaborate sculptural ornamentation, put him out of step with a younger generation of Belgian architects focused on the design and construction of affordable social housing.[25]

Horta's design for the Belgian Pavilion at the 1925 International Exhibition of Modern Decorative and Industrial Arts in Paris marked a decisive moment in his separation from modernism. Planning for the exhibition had been delayed, due to the urgent imperative to rebuild homes and infrastructure after the destruction wrought by the German invasion and occupation of Belgium during World War I. Nevertheless, a national pavilion was hastily erected in Paris, thanks to the efforts of Count Adrien van der Burch, who, as commissioner general, organized a national lottery to help fund Belgium's participation in the Paris Exposition. With no time to hold a national architectural competition for the Belgian Pavilion, members of the planning committee fast-tracked Horta's proposal, but only after Horta had maliciously discredited van de Velde's candidacy to serve as Belgium's commissioner general for the fair on the grounds that he was "German."[26]

In the final design, Horta replaced his signature Art Nouveau curves with rigid geometry drawn from Egyptian, Mayan, Greek, medieval, and modern architecture that perplexed fairgoers (fig. 10).[27] A central temple structure ornamented with a sculptural frieze by Pieter Braecke recalled the language of classical architecture. However, this became confused in the temple's stepped roof, whose profile recalled the pyramidal tiers of a Mayan temple or a Mesopotamian ziggurat. A low corridor resembling a nave introduced elements of a basilica plan into the pavilion but culminated, not in a choir, but in a rectangular tower that evoked Austrian architect Josef Hoffmann's Palais Stoclet, completed in Brussels in 1911. The building's archaism extended to the larger-than-life-size gilded sculptures by Marcel Wolfers

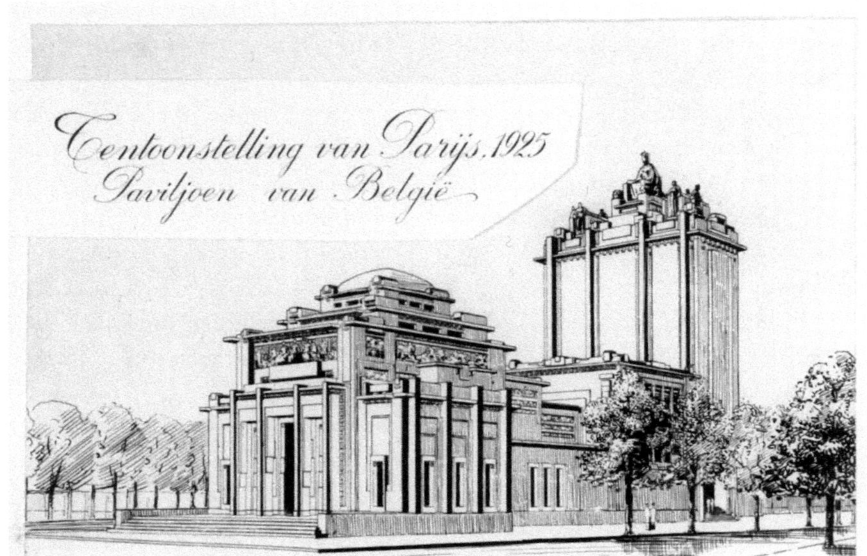

Figure 10. National lottery announcement to finance Victor Horta's Belgian Pavilion at the 1925 Paris Exposition Internationale des Arts Décoratifs et Industriels Modernes [International Exhibition of Modern Decorative and Industrial Arts]. His architectural design illustrates the advertisement. (State Archives of Belgium)

representing allegories of Belgium's four historical eras that marked the tower's four corners, with a central figure of Belgium enthroned rising to twice their height at the tower's center. Reviews of Horta's pavilion faulted the sculptures for encumbering its architecture, with the crowning personification of Belgium as a medieval queen flanked by two lions coming in for especially withering criticism. The outcry was so great that Horta agreed to remove the sculpture, but the pavilion continued to be viewed by modern architects as a travesty of his earlier and more progressive architecture. "This is Horta of the new manner: very few soft and gracious curves that were the quintessence of Horta's style," lamented critic L. Pierard.[28] Similarly disappointing were the pavilion's exhibits, which showcased luxury goods by an older generation of Belgian designers.[29] The 1925 Belgian Pavilion appeared tone-deaf to postwar Belgium's pressing social and economic concerns and marked Horta's distance from the pursuit of a more rational, efficient architecture.

The failure of the 1925 pavilion opened the door to van de Velde, as Belgian cultural officials began in earnest to look elsewhere for senior leadership in the applied arts and architecture. Already in 1922, Émile Vandervelde, leader of the POB, had proposed van de Velde as the best person to coordinate Belgium's participation in the 1925 Paris exposition, but this proposal was thwarted by Horta.[30] Nevertheless, Vandervelde had planted a seed that was nurtured by Pierre and Victor Bourgeois, leaders of Belgium's interwar artistic avant-garde, who took steps to restore van de Velde's reputation.[31] In 1923, they published a Belgian edition of van de Velde's most recent book of essays, *Formules d'une esthétique moderne* (1916–17) under the slightly altered title *Les Formules de la beauté architectonique moderne* (1923). A few months later, the Bourgeois brothers invited van de Velde to deliver a lecture in Brussels. These coordinated initiatives paved the way for the "lost son's" return, which was hastened by Belgium's lackluster showing in Paris.

After an extensive campaign to prove his Belgian loyalty, van de Velde was reinstated as a Belgian citizen in 1926 and returned to his homeland with a government mandate to found and direct a state-supported applied arts school.[32] He received his appointment from Camille Huysmans, a member of the POB and minister of arts and education, who envisioned the artist forming new generations of architects and designers and making Belgian applied and industrial arts more internationally competitive. Instead of reforming the Academy of Fine Art along lines proposed by Horta, van de Velde was hired to create a new school, the Higher Institute for Decorative Arts (Institut Supérieur des Arts Décoratifs, or ISAD) on the site of what had been La Cambre Abbey, a former Cistercian monastery in Brussels. It opened in 1927 and quickly gained an international reputation for a wide-ranging curriculum that synthesized fine and applied arts, traditional craft and industrial design, architecture and urbanism.[33] Much as was the case at the Bauhaus, its mission was to reconnect the arts with the daily life of most citizens, so as to overcome artists' social alienation and to disseminate good design among the broader population. Art was a necessity, not a luxury, van de Velde had long maintained. His vision gained urgency amid the world economic crisis triggered by the New York stock market crash of 1929. Seeking to equip artists with a practical trade alongside fine arts training, the school's curriculum encompassed courses in "pure form" alongside ones with a more applied focus in technical and ornamental drawing, architecture and urbanism, decorative and monumental sculpture, mural painting, textiles, metalwork, ceramics, graphic design and advertising, book binding, and theater set and costume design.[34] Artistic training would ensure students' participation in the modern movement, van de Velde reasoned, while the acquisition of a trade would increase their likelihood of employment. As was the case at historically Black colleges and universities in the United States, so too in Europe a healthy debate existed over the respective intellectual and economic benefits of liberal arts learning versus mastery of the trades. Rather than taking a side, van de Velde sought to merge fine and applied art education in order to elevate the trades.

Van de Velde received a warm welcome from the younger generation of modern Belgian architects and designers for his ability to advance their work and win government commissions. In constituting the faculty of La Cambre, van de Velde cast his net wide, hiring architects with varying approaches. He recruited faculty from the progressive and modern architectural association, the Belgian Society of Modernist Urbanists and Architects (Société Belge des Urbanistes et Architects Modernistes, or SBUAM), including urban planner Louis van der Swaelman, Antoine Pompe, Huib Hoste, and Victor Bourgeois. The latter two represented Belgium at the first International Congresses of Modern Architecture (Congrès internationaux d'architecture moderne, or CIAM) meeting at La Sarraz, Switzerland, in 1928 and espoused social housing built according to strict principles of economy and functionalism. By contrast, Pompe adopted a moderate position that defended the creative freedom of individual architects. Fearing that the principles adopted at La Sarraz would become school doctrine, Pompe in 1929 led a campaign in defense of regional styles and ornamentation against the demands of extreme standardization. Van de Velde supported both sides of the debate; as school director, he understood his role as that of encouraging and synthesizing the various strands of modernism within Belgium to attract an expanding circle of artists and clients, including the Belgian government.

Van de Velde's directorship of ISAD reflected an inclusive approach to the modern movement, as he sought to hold the school above narrow political and ideological divisions. Despite its political nonaffiliation, La Cambre appealed to members of the POB because of van de Velde's emphasis on the dignity of the trades.[35] In 1935, the POB minister of public works Hendrik de Man appointed van de Velde to serve in his newly created Office of Economic Recovery (Office de Redressement Économique, or OREC), which accorded unprecedented sums to modernizing and expanding public infrastructure throughout Belgium. The leading Belgian socialist intellectual of the 1930s who would later ruin his reputation by collaborating with the Nazis upon their invasion and occupation of Belgium in 1940, De Man heavily favored the social principles embraced by modern architects, designers, and urbanists associated with La Cambre.[36] However, van de Velde's work appealed equally to the Catholic minister Philip van Isacker, who appointed him artistic adviser to the Ministries of Transportation and Economic Affairs, beginning in the early 1930s.[37] As minister of economic affairs from 1934 to 1938, Van Isacker sought to address his country's trade imbalance in light manufacturing by expanding the international market share for Belgium's applied and industrial arts, whose sales had stagnated, if not declined. Rising unemployment could be addressed, Van Isacker reasoned, by employing artists to work with Belgian manufacturers to elevate the quality and distinctiveness of their products.[38]

Artistic advisory work in manufacturing had long been van de Velde's line of operation since his work for the Grand Duchy of Saxe-Weimar and leading role within the German Werkbund, an association founded in 1907 to elevate the quality and market share of German manufacturing.[39] Upon returning to Belgium, van de Velde received an unprecedented number of government contracts and appointments, rising to preside over what his detractors, partisans of Horta, would term an "aesthetic dictatorship."[40] His unrivaled power in the 1930s—arguably greater than that of any other modern architect or designer of his day or since—threatened existing professional associations and institutions in Belgium, earning him scores of enemies who sought to discredit him as a "foreigner." Some went so far as to dub him the "Stalin of architecture."[41]

Van de Velde's rise to power in Belgium is an extraordinary story that can be explained, in part, by the nation's attempt to reassert its international prominence after a humiliating defeat in World War I, followed by a series of lackluster performances that failed to restore its international reputation and struggling economy. The nation's real and symbolic wealth rested on recovering its former prowess in both heavy and light manufacturing. Yet Belgium's weakness was again exposed at the 1935 Brussels Exposition, with cultural officials viewing its artistic stagnation as portending larger problems. Exhibits exposed a rift between artists and Belgian industry, the very motor of its economic well-being. A model train station by Victor Bourgeois was the exception that proved the rule that Belgian fine artists showed little ability or interest in the applied arts and manufacturing.[42] A disheartened Commissioner General Van der Burch asked of Belgium's painters and sculptors: "Could they not attempt to collaborate with industry? Stained glass, tapestry, publicity art, and many more forms of industrial art demand their collaboration."[43]

Paris 1937: Van de Velde Ascendent

Van de Velde's contribution to Belgium's national pavilions for Paris in 1937 and New York in 1939 are best understood as attempts on the part of the government to recover from these missteps and to reassert Belgium's primacy as a leader of the modern movement. Van Isacker saw in these international exhibitions an opportunity to renew Belgium's arts of manufacturing by redirecting artistic displays away from the Academy of Fine Arts toward ISAD. To this end, he placed van de Velde in charge of designing the Belgian pavilions and selecting their exhibits. Works by core ISAD faculty members Victor Bourgeois, Oscar Jespers, and Elisabeth de Saedeleer were showcased in Paris and New York to present Belgium as once again a leader of the modern movement.

Van de Velde was well positioned to ensure that the Belgian Pavilion succeeded in Paris. Here, as it also would in New York, Belgium enjoyed a prominent site, thanks in this case to its location as France's immediate neighbor as well as its status as a victim of Germany's violation of its neutrality at the outbreak of World War I. Nestled between the northeast corner of the Eiffel Tower and the Seine River, the Belgian Pavilion appeared just to the left of the Pont d'Iéna to visitors standing on the steps of the fair's signature building, the Palais de Chaillot, and across the river from the tense standoff between the monumental German and Soviet pavilions (fig. 11). These three showcases, which have dominated later discussions of the fair and of 1930s monumental architecture in Europe more generally, represented a bombastic "return to order," in which monumental classicism was stripped of much of the detail that had given it a human scale.[44] Amid these hyperbolic expressions, the welcoming yet striking structure van de Velde designed in collaboration with Jean-Jules Eggericx and Raphäel Verwilghen, assisted by the engineer Paul Célis, achieved an elastic form that was much appreciated. Clad in terra cotta tiles hand-molded by Flemish artisans—the very same tiles that would be employed in the New York

Figure 11. Belgian Pavilion, Henry van de Velde, Jean-Jules Eggericx, and Raphaël Verwilghen, International Exposition of the Art and Technology of Modern Life, Paris, 1937. (© AML [Archives et Musée de la Littérature])

pavilion—the low-lying steel-framed structure, with three continuous bands of ribbon windows curving out toward the Seine River, provided a horizontality that counterbalanced the neighboring Eiffel Tower's soaring verticality and celebration of heavy industry, as well as the upward thrust of the coolly white Soviet and German pavilions.

The 1937 Belgian Pavilion was an answer to the challenge Fascist classicism and Soviet Socialist Realism posed to modern architecture and its perceived inability to represent civic and symbolic content.[45] Already in his contribution to the conference "Art and Reality, Art and the State" sponsored in 1934 by the League of Nations and held in Fascist Italy, van de Velde had struck a middle ground between asserting the independence of the artist and affirming his partnership with the state. Rejecting government policies toward the arts in both the Soviet Union (before and after the doctrine of Socialist Realism) and Nazi Germany, van de Velde put forward an idea of architecture and design as a dynamic synthesis of tradition and modernity that freely engages the broader community.[46] Van de Velde realized his vision of synthesis—between past and present and between the individual and the collectivity—in the Belgian Pavilions in Paris in 1937 and its successor in Queens, New York.

Not only the exterior but also the interior of the 1937 Belgian Pavilion was more imposing and grand than those of other examples of modern architecture on view at the fair, including the much smaller and less prominently located pavilion of the doomed Spanish Republic designed by Josep Lluis Sert, perhaps the fair's most avant-garde structure. Although in 1943 Sert would coauthor the position paper "Nine Points on Monumentality," in 1937 his Spanish Pavilion displayed a functionalism premised on straight lines, industrial materials, and an economical distribution of space. By contrast, van de Velde's interior was much more ceremonial. Visitors to the Belgian Pavilion entered via a soaring Hall of Honor featuring black marble walls adorned with monumental tapestries and a ceiling fashioned of gold and silk. A similar Hall of Honor, complete with imposing black marble walls and monumental Flemish tapestries, would be a signature feature of the New York pavilion, but in Paris the tapestries' theme was Flemish customs rather than Belgian-U.S. relations. Jan-Albert Goris, then secretary to Belgium's Technical Committee for the 1937 exhibition, hailed the display as "a triumph of Flemish art," a fact that must have galled the jealous Horta.[47] Off of the Hall of Honor, a black marble staircase led visitors into a suite of exhibition rooms organized from the top down, from luxury rooms to popular ensembles, all outfitted by professors and students at ISAD. The sense of quiet order, both aesthetic and social, pursued by van de Velde and his associates could not have been more different from the Spanish Republic Pavilion's strikingly modern gridded box sheltering Pablo Picasso's enormous painting *Guernica,* a celebrated exposé of the horror wrought by the recent Nazi German and Italian Fascist aerial bombardment of the town of that name in support of Franco's side in the ongoing Spanish Civil War. In 1937, Belgium successfully provided an alternative to all extremes, whether artistic or political.[48]

In a book whose French title can be translated as "Modern Belgian Architecture," published in the same year as the fair, Marcel Schmitz, an ally of van de Velde who organized a display of religious art in the 1937 Belgian Pavilion, wrote:

> Modern Belgian architecture is more sensual, seeks powerful harmonies, distinctive combinations of materials. Belgium easily combines them, alternating

> brick and colored mortar with marble and ceramic. By the same token, Belgians willfully endow their forms with a certain heaviness, the robust pleasure of a temperament that prizes comfort, well-being, and opulence. An architecture of earthiness, we would say: well-grounded, in the image of an active, realist, vigorous people ill-inclined to fantasy or elegance, but knowing how to find true pleasure in the interplay of formal relations.[49]

Schmitz's analysis certainly applies to van de Velde's designs from the 1930s. He was, with Frank Lloyd Wright, one of the few originally experimental designers of his generation not to eventually retreat into conventional classicism. Instead, in van de Velde's work from the 1930s, when he received a series of large and prestigious commissions that included the Book Tower that serves as Ghent's university library (1936–42) and the Technical School, also known as Tweebronnen, now occupied by Leuven's public library and city archive (1937–42), he synthesized modern principles of simplicity, functionality, and efficiency without resorting to the industrial aesthetic espoused by younger avant-garde architects such as Bourgeois and Sert. That artisans would work in concert with industry to lend timeworn trades new relevance for the modern era had been central to van de Velde's writings, pedagogy, and designs since the 1890s.[50]

The idea of fusing regional craft with transnational and lucrative industrial production led van de Velde to select regionally specific natural materials for the Belgian pavilions of 1937 and 1939—hand-molded tiles made of the red clay of Courtrai and black schist from the Ardennes—as cladding for a steel skeleton no longer visible once the building was completed.[51] With the assistance of Célis, he devised a system of attaching the removable clay and schist facing to the industrially produced steel frame. He selected the same local, hand-made red tiles he was using in Leuven but passed over the reinforced concrete skeleton and brick infill employed in this permanent structure in favor of steel beams and a system of bolts, which were easier to remove than rivets.[52] Van de Velde proudly noted of it, "It can be disassembled and all of its materials can *be easily recovered!* The government favors such a reconstruction and has encouraged me to pursue the work which I initiated."[53]

The novel construction system responded to Van Isacker's proposal for a dismountable pavilion that could be shipped back to Brussels at the conclusion of the exhibit, where it was to house a state-sponsored Institute for Applied Arts and

Manufacturing headed by van de Velde. Van Isacker had initially proposed this idea for the 1937 Paris pavilion.[54] When support did not materialize in time, he commissioned van de Velde to design a similar structure for the 1939 New York World's Fair, again with the intention to rebuild it as a governmental institute in Belgium.[55] Unfortunately, this plan also did not materialize. In February 1938, the Catholic Van Isacker resigned as minister of economic affairs after the election of a new, Liberal prime minister. Two weeks later, the new prime minister, Paul-Émile Janson, terminated the plan to rebuild the pavilion in Brussels. [56] Despite these difficulties and disappointments, van de Velde, who was discouraged but not vanquished, consistently prioritized matters of efficiency and mobility in his oversight of both pavilions. His statements, combined with the Commissariat General's highlighting of the building's novel design and planned permanence, sowed confusion as to whether the Belgian Pavilion was a temporary or permanent structure.[57] Goris would turn this confusion to his advantage in 1940 when he liquidated the pavilion.

From Paris to New York

From the beginning, the Belgian Pavilion in New York was the joint creation of two government ministries: the Ministry of Economic Affairs under the direction of Van Isacker, who took charge of the pavilion's exhibits related to Belgian applied and industrial arts and tourism, and the Ministry of the Colonies under the direction of Edmond Rubbens, followed by De Vleeschauwer, who administered the pavilion's Colonial Section. In Paris, the Congolese displays had been in a separate building.[58] Now they would be folded into one structure. Van Isacker appointed van de Velde to head the Applied and Industrial Art section's Artistic Committee and Lucien Graux to head its Technical Committee. The former was to oversee the artistic quality of exhibits, while the latter was to determine their overall orientation and emphasis. The combined goal of these two committees was to present high-quality, modern manufactured goods to increase the market share for Belgian exports. For his part, the head of the Colonial Section, Jules d'Ans, working with the newly formed Fund for Economic and Colonial Propaganda, sought to present the Belgian Congo to audiences in the United States as a model colony that brought material and moral improvements to the lives of the Congolese, whose natural resources enriched Belgium and the world's economy. Together, these two ministries presented a strong showing of Belgium's artistic and cultural prowess while portraying its largest colony, the Belgian Congo, as a site for international tourism and economic investment.

Van de Velde recruited Victor Bourgeois and Léon Stynen to help him design the pavilion. Célis reprised the role he had played in Paris. A generation younger than van de Velde, Bourgeois and Stynen both taught at La Cambre. They were among the leaders in the French and Flemish halves of Belgium, respectively, in advocating for an unornamented overly modern approach to form divorced from all traces of classicism. Bourgeois made his name in the 1920s as an architect of social housing in Brussels (fig. 12). The stepped volumes of his "modern city" cooperative housing estate, completed in 1925, communicated a practical and functional approach to design, in which a skillful composition, including glazed stair towers and cantilevered projections over the entrances, saved the otherwise spare design from sterility. Bourgeois was the Belgian architect of his generation whose work was most appreciated by the international avant-garde. He was, for instance, the only Belgian contributor to the Weissenhofsiedlung, a housing exhibition organized by Ludwig Mies van der Rohe and held in Stuttgart, Germany, in 1927.[59] Two years Bourgeois's junior, Stynen had fully mastered the style in which Bourgeois worked, but in the 1930s he experimented with a wide variety of textures that gave the facades of many of his buildings a greater warmth. The casino he built in Chaudfontaine in 1939, clad in the same terra cotta tiles as the Belgian Building, featured a jaunty entrance porch and oversize lettering that made an effective substitute for more conventional ornament (fig. 13).[60]

The team began with a plot plan dated October 27, 1937.[61] Stynen began work on the initial proposal the following month. His early drawings show a concave volume attached by a hyphen to a fan-shaped mass, anchored in one corner by a tower and with a stumpy cylinder huddled between them. His rather awkward series of volumes emphasized the irregular shape of the site without completely filling it (fig. 14).[62] Two aspects of these designs are notable. The first is the degree to which the rather gawky composition of separate volumes follows the precedent established by two Swiss architects, Le Corbusier and Hannes Meyer, in their submissions a decade earlier to the competition to design the League of Nations in Geneva. This mattered because the jury that had rejected both had been headed by Horta. The jury's decision to bypass Le Corbusier's and Meyer's proposals in favor of a much more conventional classically inspired design earned it the permanent enmity of the inter-

Figure 12. Cité moderne, Victor Bourgeois, Sint-Agatha-Berchem, Brussels, 1925. (EmDee / Wikimedia Commons)

national avant-garde to which both Le Corbusier and Meyer belonged.[63] The second notable feature of Stynen's initial design is the prominence of a tower, an element that had been notably absent from the Belgian Pavilion in Paris.

The tower was a feature that attracted the attention of the *New York Times* reporter who noted that the design the Belgians submitted fewer than three months later included a carillon tower, which he incorrectly stated would be 155 feet tall, rather than 165 feet (fig. 15). Carillons are ensembles of bells that can play complex musical arrangements. They date back to the sixteenth century in what is now Belgium and underwent a revival in the nineteenth century. Their popularity there and in the Netherlands spread to the United States in the early twentieth century. It was furthered by the greater familiarity that World War I gave residents of the United States with Belgian culture and especially the widespread sympathy for Belgium following Germany's violation of the small nation's neutrality.[64] Not surprisingly, the carillon had been a popular feature of the Belgian Village in the Chicago Exposition of 1933.

The presence of the carillon established the first link between the building and

Figure 13. Casino Chaudfontaine, Léon Stynen, Chaudfontaine, 1939. (Flanders Architecture Institute—collection of the Flemish Government, archive of Léon Stynen)

the Rockefeller family, then the wealthiest in the United States, if not the world. Rockefeller money would prove key in financing the building's reconstitution in Richmond. John D. Rockefeller Jr. paid for two celebrated carillons. Named for his mother Laura Spelman Rockefeller, the first was located on the campus the University of Chicago, an institution that his father's philanthropy had revived. The other resided in the steeple of New York's Riverside Church, which opened in Upper Manhattan in 1930. Although Riverside's bells were English, its tower, which rises to a height of nearly four hundred feet and contains classrooms and offices, was loosely modeled on Flemish as well as northern French Flamboyant Gothic examples (fig. 16).[65] Over the course of the New York fair, Riverside's carillonist, Kamiel Lefevere, who was himself Belgian, frequently played the Belgian Pavilion's instrument.[66] There was also a music-box-like drum that ensured its bells could be played automatically.

The presence of a carillon also attracted the attention of Robert Moses, the powerful commissioner of New York City's Department of Parks from 1934 to 1960. On March 7, 1938, he wrote Whalen, the president of the world's fair:

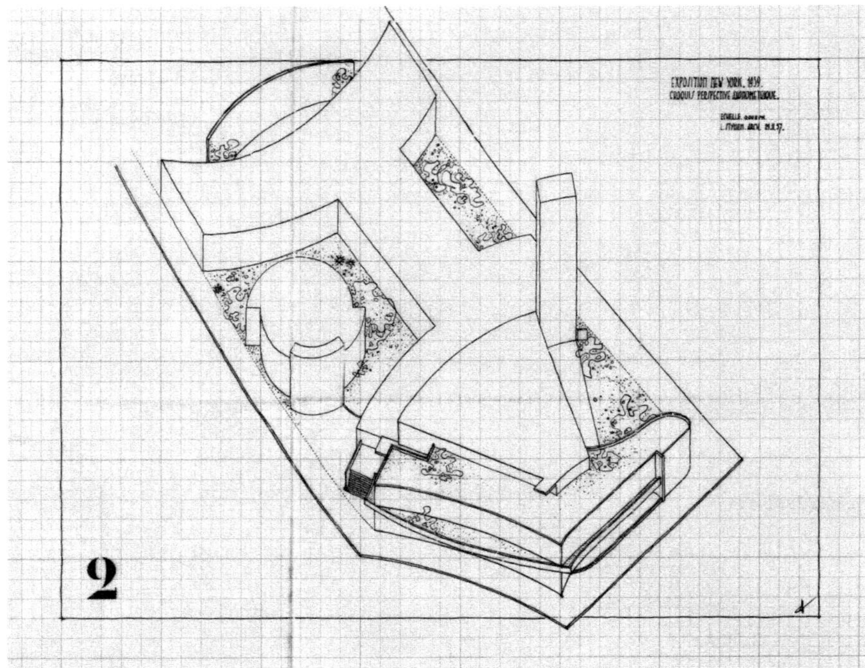

Figure 14. Preliminary design for Belgian Pavilion, "The World of Tomorrow," New York, 1937, drawing by Léon Stynen. (Flanders Architecture Institute—collection of the Flemish Government, archive of Léon Stynen)

> It occurred to me that if we could have a permanent SINGING TOWER like the Bok Memorial in Florida, this would be a tremendous asset to the park [in Flushing Meadows]. The temporary tower in the Belgium building with the carillon bells naturally suggested itself, and I communicated with Mr. Hoover in Belgium as to the possibility of persuading the Belgian government to make the tower section of the building permanent and leave the bells. This would be a sort of Statue of Liberty from Belgium and would be a recognition of what we did for that country during and after the war.[67]

Although the suggestion of making the "liberty" tower a permanent feature of Flushing Meadows Park was presented to van de Velde, who is identified in the correspondence as "the architect of the building," nothing came of it, because at

Figure 15. Carillon, Belgian Pavilion, New York World's Fair, 1939. (Manuscripts and Archives Division, The New York Public Library)

that stage van de Velde still hoped to bring the building back to Belgium. It demonstrates, however, that from the beginning former president Herbert Hoover took an interest in the carillon, which he indeed acquired after the fair for the tower named after him on the campus of his alma mater, Stanford University. It also indicates what powerful friends Belgium had. Although Hoover lost his 1932 reelection bid to Franklin D. Roosevelt in a landslide, he remained a hero in Belgium because of his role during and after World War I as the leader, in turn, of the Commission for Relief in Belgium, the United States Food Administration, and the American Relief Association. These roles had marked the beginning of his political career.[68]

The inclusion of the bell tower may have been the only aspect of Stynen's design to meet with the approval of van de Velde, who vetoed the rest of it.[69] What was probably read in New York as a clear nod to the late medieval spires, secular as well as

Figure 16. Riverside Church, Henry Pelton and Allen & Collens, New York, 1930. (Chris06 / Wikimedia Commons)

sacred, that punctuate the largely low-lying Belgian landscape may have begun, however, as a tribute to a series of more modern towers (fig. 17). It reprised, for instance, the tower Stynen had designed for an earlier building for a fair held in Antwerp in 1930 (fig. 18). By late December the team was at work on an entirely new design, one that retained little from Stynen's original scheme beyond the tower. Its details would slowly evolve across the course of 1938, with the final ones dated to October of that year, long after Whalen and his team had signed off on the basic design (fig. 19). Van de Velde probably suggested that the team reorganize the building's slightly irregular volumes around a rectangular courtyard, the approach he had himself adopted in the composition of the major commissions he had underway in Ghent and Leuven (fig. 20).[70] He also insisted on leaving room in front of the pavilion for those listening to carillon concerts to gather, as happened in Belgium in town squares in Mechelen and Bruges.[71] The team also gradually edited the scheme in order to generate the much tighter plan of the final design and to reduce the amount of glazing in order to produce a better defined sense of volume; this change also had the advantage of providing greater security for an exhibition that included valuable diamonds.[72]

These changes meant that, although the construction system was very similar to

Figure 17. Belfry, Ghent, Belgium, begun 1313. (Benoit Brummer / Wikimedia Commons)

the one used in Paris, the building's outward appearance was quite different. The way that the New York building responded to the irregular site dimensions, its organization around a courtyard, and the prominence of the tower all gave it a far more civic character, while the color and texture of its materials distinguished it from the obviously temporary nature of most fair buildings. While it proved quite different from anything else in Flushing Meadows, it was very much representative of the

Figure 18. Decorative Arts Pavilion, World's Fair, Léon Stynen, Antwerp, 1930. (Flanders Architecture Institute—collection of the Flemish Government, archive of Léon Stynen)

architectural mainstream in the Low Countries, where towered compositions featuring abstract, contrapuntal volumes, although more often clad in brick than tile, were a common expression of modern civic identity and community.

In the 1930s, Belgian architecture was often influenced by its counterpart the Netherlands, especially the work of Willem Dudok.[73] His city hall for Hilversum, completed in 1931, won him the Gold Medal of the Royal Institute of British Architects just four years later (fig. 21).[74] Dudok's emphasis on cubic massing clad in brick provided a compelling updating of the vernacular traditions of the Low Countries, which constituted a single political unit for much of the fifteenth and sixteenth centuries, as well as between 1816 and 1830. His attentiveness to the local was also infused, however, with his respect for Frank Lloyd Wright's Prairie Style houses. Van de Velde was very familiar with Dutch architecture and knew Dudok personally, as

Figure 19. Model of the Belgian Pavilion, 1939 New York World's Fair, Léon Stynen, 1937 (© AML [Archives et Musée de la Littérature])

he had lived in the Netherlands from 1921 until 1926; his Kröller-Müller Museum, which opened in the Dutch village of Otterlo in 1938, remains one of his most significant late works. In 1937 van de Velde and Dudok served together as jurors on the Mont des Arts competition for Brussels.[75]

The impact of Dudok's commitment to distinctively modern towers can be seen in the abundance of secular as well as sacred spires erected in Brussels in the 1930s. Two of the most prominent modern towers in Belgium anchored the Brussels headquarters for Belgian radio, completed in 1937, and the town hall for the Brussels district of Woluwe-Saint-Lambert, completed in 1938 (fig. 22). Both were the work of Joseph Diongre.[76] Towers were equally popular during the interwar period for strikingly new Belgian churches, including Diongre's own church of St. John the Baptist in Molenbeek, another Brussels neighborhood. Less tightly knit than the Belgian building and clad in brick or stone rather than tile, these buildings exemplify the modern mainstream in Belgian architecture of the late 1930s. Even taller and tauter was van de Velde's library tower for Ghent university (fig. 20). He delib-

Figure 20. Boekentoren (University Library), Henry van de Velde, Ghent, 1933–1942. (Geert Roels / Wikimedia Commons)

erately kept the structure slightly shorter than the belfries of its medieval cousins in Ghent, the spires of St. Bavo Cathedral and St. Nicholas's Church, while ensuring that his building contributed an obviously twentieth-century grace note to the city's skyline. Although the profile of the Boekentoren (Dutch for "book tower") was far from identical with its New York cousin, both featured unusually bold, clean-cut compositions.

Aligned with the architecture of Dudok and Diogre, van de Velde's Belgian Pavilion for New York was emphatically civic more than monumental. The choice of cladding materials nodded respectfully toward longstanding artisanal traditions

Figure 21. City Hall, Willem Dudok, Hilversum, 1931. (Roundtheworld / Wikimedia Commons)

and established a sense of scale related to that of the human hand, even as the steel frames that supported the building, as well as the presence of elevators, were resolutely up to date. Although constructed on a grand scale, the Belgian Pavilion in New York marked a break with the neoclassical national pavilions erected by the Soviets and the Germans that had dominated the view from the steps of the Palais de Chaillot at the Paris International Exposition in 1937. The Belgian Pavilion's steel or concrete bones may have been tucked out of site, but the embrace of the new it did display encompassed an awareness of the contrapuntal rhythms of the latest abstract painting to which was added a refusal to wallow in either the sentiment of the Arts and Crafts movement or the imperial ambitions that too often accompanied the latest iterations of classicism. Although the label "regional" is often applied to this approach, the fact that it resonated closely with developments in places as far afield as Hilversum and Finland suggests the limitations of such categorization, even as

Figure 22. District city hall, Joseph Diongre, Wolowe-Saint-Lambert, Brussels, 1938. (Benoit Brummer / Wikimedia Commons)

the form it took in Belgium and in the Netherlands was tied above all to the region's strong history of baked construction materials, whether brick or tile.[77]

The final design was the result of what Stynen himself described as an equal collaboration between himself, van de Velde, and Bourgeois.[78] Most of the drawings display the names of all three or are simply signed "the architects." Bourgeois designed the pavilion's cinema, where films on Belgian culture, history, and tourism, as well as those of its colony, were shown. He is, however, absent in the photographs of Stynen and van de Velde with Célis and Goris, seated around a table atop which sits a model of the final scheme (fig. 23). Stynen had sole responsibility for the restaurant, the bar, and the interior of the Congo exhibition. Van de Velde took credit above all for the construction system first used successfully in Paris and certainly played a role in refining all of the building's details.

The official guidebook described the building as "having been conceived by the Belgian architects M. Victor Bourgeois and M. Leo Stijnen [more often written Léon Stynen], under the direction of Professor Henry van de Velde."[79] The apportioning of credit for the building was marred, however, by the feud underway back in Brussels between supporters of Horta, who remained the éminence grise of French-speaking Belgian architectural culture, and the circle clustered around van de Velde

Figure 23. Photograph of Jan-Albert Goris, Henry van de Velde, Léon Stynen, and Paul Célis with a model of the Belgian Pavilion, 1938. (Flanders Architecture Institute—collection of the Flemish Government, archive of Léon Stynen)

at La Cambre. Without providing any evidence, Horta's backers maliciously alleged that van de Velde had had no hand in the design of either the Paris or the New York pavilions.[80] Stynen explicitly denied the charges, which he aptly attributed to jealousy and envy.[81]

The laying of the building's cornerstone on May 25, 1938, occasioned van de Velde's first trip to the United States; he returned the next year for the building's opening (fig. 24). For most European architects who traveled to the United States in the interwar years, the main attraction was its cities, especially New York.[82] With over ten million people in its metropolitan area, New York was the largest city the world had yet seen, its streets and subways teeming with people, cars, and trains that astounded and often frightened newcomers.

Van de Velde was, like many thoughtful Europeans, initially almost appalled and certainly overwhelmed, as he recalled in his memoir:

I did not approach Manhattan and its multitude of skyscrapers with the overwhelming enthusiasm experienced by the majority of first-time visitors glimpsing it from the ocean. As I stood watch at daybreak to await the expected shock, I was overcome with a curious and most involuntary vision. Hardly had I glimpsed the monsters standing erect, higgledy-piggledy, on the bank of the island on the Hudson when an image instantly superimposed itself on this impression, similar to an effect of double exposure intentionally obtained on cinematographic film. I distinctly saw the image of the Grand Trianon superimposed on the reality before me!

Who was the mischievous mountebank or pedant who, abruptly diverting the lens, turned it on an image that I apparently carried within me? And through what ripened and irresistible impulse? I was more than a little troubled. It took all the commotion of disembarkation, handshakes with the captain and his officers, distribution of tips to the stewards, and what have you;

Figure 24. Groundbreaking ceremony, May 25, 1938, with Henry van de Velde third from right. (Manuscripts and Archives Division, The New York Public Library)

> the formalities of customs and passport control, the loading of trunks and suitcases into the car, the arrival at the Dorset hotel, and finally the comfortable room and armchair into which I sank for me to come to my senses and find an explanation for the mirage, for the double exposure.
>
> The sense of order that came over me was caused by disorder. The same taste for order and equilibrium had caused me to quickly turn away from the inappropriate or excessive lines dating to the time of my first ornaments and furniture pieces—to wrest myself from this chaos. It never occurred to me to contrast Versailles to New York![83]

The sense of calm and order to which van de Velde alludes in his poetic recounting of his first approach to Manhattan speaks to the sense of balance, however contrapuntal, he pursued in his designs from the 1930s that present a uniquely modern expression of civic, collective identity. Nevertheless, despite his initial shock and confusion, which may have been caused as much by the spectacular skyscrapers as by the unbridled capitalistic economy that spawned them, van de Velde eventually warmed up to the spectacle New York City offered. He later recounted an experience, in his characteristically visually vivid and metaphoric language, that probably dated to his second visit:

> I also recall a memorable evening spent with Victor Bourgeois on the top floor of a skyscraper where we lingered late in conversation. We could not tear ourselves away from the magical spectacle of Manhattan at night, as seen from one of the numerous skyscrapers piled on top of each other. One only needed to thrust one's arms into the heap in order to gather the treasures of precious stones that sparkled with their thousands upon thousands of fires in this vault of the heavens fallen from the sky.[84]

The spectacle of night lighting plunged van de Velde into a state of reverie, in which electric lights metamorphose into cosmic entities. During his short stay in New York City, van de Velde also admired the glimmering shop windows on Fifth Avenue but did not linger, traveling instead to Virginia, where he hoped to build a house for Baroness Johanna "Hansi" Lambert, an art collector of Austrian origins whose husband and sons, members of a wealthy Belgian banking family, had ties to the Belgian Congo.[85]

If New York epitomized modernity, Virginia offered a different spectacle, one rooted in conventions of racial subordination that he probably understood in ways influenced by Belgian propaganda about the Congo. Van de Velde admired Virginia's landscape, where he described finding "a paradise populated entirely by Negros" deferential to the Baroness.[86]

This misreading is striking and telling, as is van de Velde's unusual interest in rural rather than urban conditions. Most European architects, Horta among them, were particularly fascinated by the prowess of the construction industry in the United States, which had produced taller buildings than those found anywhere else in the world. Van de Velde, however, was quite proud of Belgium's own building technologies. Except for the electric, plumbing, and ventilation systems, Belgium's entire pavilion was assembled in New York out of Belgian-made parts. Although by the time these were shipped, there were no longer plans to reerect the building back in Brussels after the fair, the choice to rely on Belgian parts and labor was probably made in part to dodge the labor disputes that delayed the erection and raised the construction costs of many of the other national pavilions. Belgium sent to New York not only the materials out of which the building was constructed but also most of the men responsible for erecting it. Goris later recalled having to pay a union man $2.75 an hour for several weeks to sit at the base of the tower while Belgian experts installed its bells. He also accused locals of forcing the Belgians to rely upon a generator, which was repeatedly sabotaged.[87] Interestingly, considering the central role the Congo would play in the building's relocation to Richmond, prefabrication had been a prominent feature of early Belgian construction in the Congo, as well as in other European colonies.[88]

Work on the building began already on April 6, 1938, seven weeks before the pavilion's cornerstone-laying ceremony. Construction photographs document the erection of the steel skeleton (fig. 25). *L'ossature métallique,* a Belgian trade journal, reported that it sat atop a foundation of wooden piers capped in concrete. This method of construction was chosen in part because of the marshy site (reinforced concrete, the obvious alternative, was heavier) as well as because it prevented delays. It had the further advantage, the article noted, that the building's materials could be salvaged following the obligatory demolition at the end of the fair. It was the pres-

Figure 25. Construction photo of Belgian Pavilion for the 1939 New York World's Fair. (© AML [Archives et Musée de la Littérature])

ence of the steel that made the building's extensive glazing possible, as it meant that the skin of the building was no longer supporting the roof. While steel skeletal framing was hardly new in the United States, where it had been used for the construction of office blocks in Chicago since the 1880s, this was the first—and may remain the only—example of a metrically sized frame constructed in the country, something that has complicated efforts to conserve the structure as it aged. A section drawing shows the arrangement of the trusses; the cinema is to the right (fig. 26). The Belgian firm of Debusschère and Tedesco was responsible for the building's erection, with carpentry being provided by Ateliers de Braine-le-Compt. Usines de Braine-Le-Compte S.A. supplied the nine hundred tons of steel. The Chamebel firm donated sixteen tons of metal and door framing; the specialist crafting of its details was executed by the Longtain rolling mills. S. A. Ardoisières L. Donner, a quarry in the village of Martelange, provided the schist, while the terra cotta tiles were manufac-

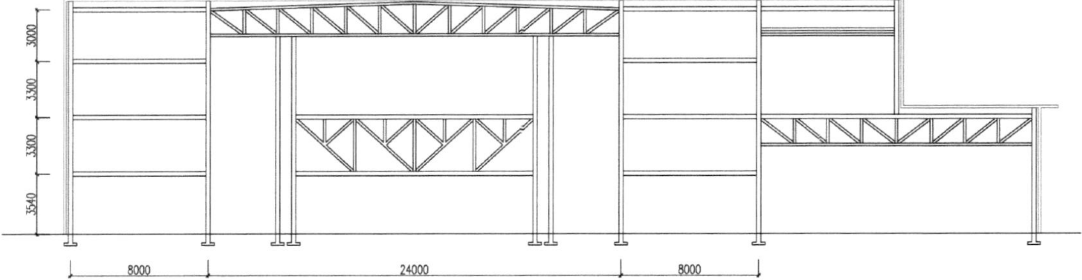

Figure 26. Belgian Pavilion, cross section of the truss. (Niall Howard)

tured by Comptoir Tuilier de Courtrai (Kortrijk in Dutch). Construction was swift, with the exterior shell completed by November 10, the day before the celebration of the twentieth anniversary of the armistice that had ended World War I.[89]

The pavilion opened on time, with only the completion of the Colonial Section delayed by several weeks. All three architects were present for the ceremonial opening. So were former president Hoover and New York's popular mayor Fiorella LaGuardia, along with Whalen, Joseph Davies (who had recently served as the United States ambassador to the Soviet Union), and Baron de Gruben of the Belgian embassy. For the architects, another highlight of the trip may have been dinner at a New York restaurant run by the famous boxer Jack Dempsey, who came to their table to greet them.[90]

The architects returned to a Europe on the brink of disaster. They left behind in New York many other Belgians involved in the construction and running of their country's contribution to the fair. Although war clouds were very clearly on the horizon, it would have been impossible for any of those involved to predict how the turn of events would affect the fate of their building, leaving it the most important remnant of what is now very much yesterday's "World of Tomorrow" to still be standing, albeit in a rather different form, well into the twenty-first century.

2

DISPLAYING MODERN BELGIUM

Design, Diplomacy, and Colonial Propaganda

The child narrator of E. L. Doctorow's semi-autobiographical novel *World's Fair,* published in 1985, described his visit to the grounds of "The World of Tomorrow":

> From the elevated station I could see the famous Trylon and Perisphere. They were enormous. They were white in the sun, white spire, white globe, they went together, they belonged together as some sort of partnership in my head. I didn't know what they stood for, it was all very vague in my mind, but to see them, after having seen pictures and posters and buttons for so long, made me incredibly happy. I felt like jumping up and down, I felt myself trembling with joy.[1]

Doctorow, who was born in the Bronx in 1931, may have remembered feeling such a sensation himself upon visiting New York's Flushing Meadows, where the fair opened in April 1939 and where it was on view for a second summer the following year. The world's fair captured hearts and minds retrospectively, if not always at the time. A cartoon published in a local newspaper in September 1938, a year before Germany invaded Poland, depicted the same white globe as a bomb about to explode in Europe (fig. 27). "The World of Tomorrow," as the fair was subtitled, was

Figure 27. The World's Fair Theme, *Yonkers Daily Times*, September 6, 1938. (Manuscripts and Archives Division, The New York Public Library)

remembered afterward for having provided an escape from the Great Depression at a time when the United States was still at peace, even as war threatened. It supplied a vision of peaceful economic progress and international good will, which, although dimmed by the arrival of the war, nonetheless doubled as a template for what prosperity might look like afterward.

It was not only New Yorkers who were captivated by the escapism the fair offered. The Belgian artist and architecture critic Pierre-Louis Flouquet labeled New York "the capital of all modern phantasmagorias." And he asked of "The World of Tomorrow," "We simple mortals, inhabitants of a temperate Europe, cultivated in the idea of moderation and prudent mores, what do we think of and anticipate from the explosive, somewhat savage luxury of a fair?"[2]

The vision of the future that visitors to the fairgrounds found was certainly neither moderate nor prudent. Whereas political regimes of various stripes had competed for attention at the Paris 1937 exposition, in New York in 1939 national pavilions were certainly not the center of attention. The key difference between the international expositions in Paris in 1937 and in New York in 1939 was the dominance in New York of homegrown corporations, an approach pioneered six years earlier at the Century of Progress fair held in Chicago. Internationalism at the New York World's Fair played distinctly second fiddle to capitalist advertising. Chrysler, Ford, General Motors, American Radiator, American Tobacco, Budd Manufacturing, the Carrier Corporation, Consolidated Edison, Du Pont, Eastman Kodak, Equitable Life, General Electric, Heinz, U. S. Steel, and Westinghouse were among the large corporations sponsoring their own pavilions. Moreover, industry no longer focused simply on showing off new machines; instead, the intent was above all on how the public could use their wares to transform daily life.[3] Nowhere was this truer than in the Transportation Zone, located between 111th Street and Grand Central Avenue. Goodrich and Firestone, two brands of tires, and the big three automakers—Chrysler, Ford, and General Motors—were clustered there and drew the biggest crowds.

By far the most successful attraction at the fair was Futurama (fig. 28). Mounted

Figure 28. Futurama, Norman Bel Geddes, New York World's Fair, 1939. (Norman Bell Geddes, *Magic Motorways*, published 1940 / Wikimedia Commons)

by General Motors, the popular exhibit was designed by Norman Bel Geddes and housed in its pavilion. The theatrically inclined set and industrial designer collaborated with the office of Albert Kahn, the Detroit-based architect and engineer who had long enjoyed the patronage of the car manufacturers. Visitors traveled on moving chairs for an eighteen-minute tour that allowed them to look down upon bold visions of towns and cities planned around the automobile. Mesmerized spectators left the mobile attraction wearing buttons proclaiming "I have seen the future."[4] Although certainly the most beguiling and arguably the most influential of all the fair's displays, Futurama was not the only vision of tomorrow on offer, however. The most admired national pavilions pleased more thoughtful critics by providing less obviously conspicuous advertising, even as they showcased products, histories, and cultures.

Belgium's Place at the Fair

What would the architecture of "The World of Tomorrow" look like? Those looking forward largely agreed that it would no longer derive so great a share of its trimmings from the history of European architecture stretching from the temples of ancient Greece to the domed cathedrals of the Baroque. It was time to break with the past and adopt forms in keeping with the spirit of the times, a spirit that included enormous technological changes in how buildings were constructed. The economic downturn of the 1930s was another spur toward change, as clients with all but the deepest pockets became reluctant to pay for the ornament that had earlier communicated cultural sophistication and decorum.

Commercial attractions such as Futurama mostly featured a streamlined aesthetic inspired in part by the appearance of the fastest diesel train locomotives and the most stylish automobiles of the day.[5] But many of the nations whose pavilions were clustered on the opposite side of the Trylon and Perisphere at the fair's eastern edge favored more subtle approaches (fig. 29). Their formulations of progress and international good will were more illusory than real; after all, Germany had refused to participate because it feared becoming the target of vocal protests.[6] Nonetheless, a number of the displays, including Belgium's and Sweden's, attracted the attention and garnered the praise of influential writers, while the esteem the cognoscenti accorded the Brazilian and Finnish pavilions was a crucial step in elevating their

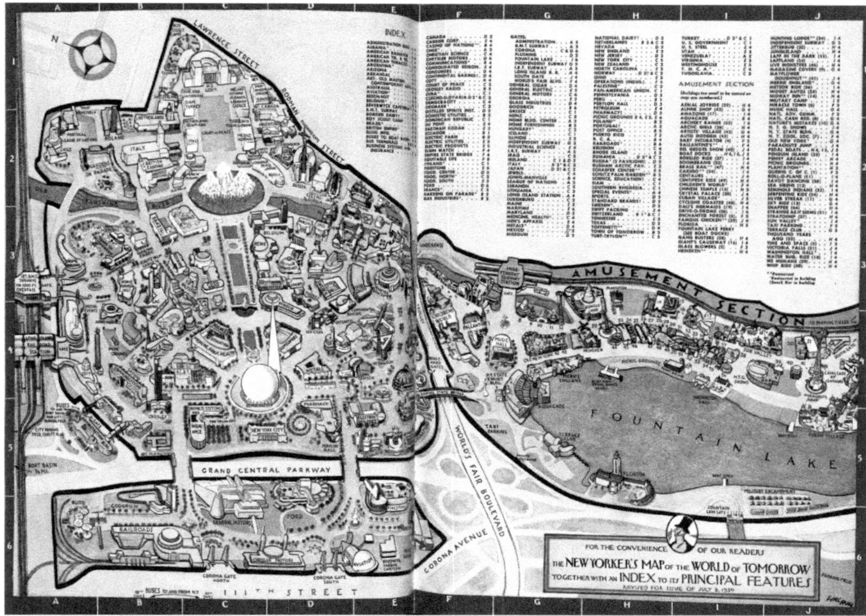

Figure 29. Plan of Fairgrounds, *New Yorker* (July 8, 1939). (The New Yorker)

architects to the superstar status they would later enjoy at home and abroad, especially in the United States.

The list of the nations participating at world's fairs expanded, without becoming nearly as comprehensive as one might expect today. European countries dominated the roll call of national pavilions, although a number of other nations from the Americas were represented in the government zone and the Hall of Nations. Morocco and Southern Rhodesia (now Zimbabwe) were the only Africans in attendance; Asian representation was also limited. Even Australia and New Zealand exhibited only as appendages of Great Britain. That most of Africa and Asia then comprised colonies ruled by Europeans or, in the case of the Philippines, the United States, was taken for granted by the fair's organizers, and most of their cultures and products were presented only in relatively isolated instances and through the eyes of the foreigners who governed them in order to extract their wealth. Challenging this situation would not be an aim of either side in the coming conflict, although it would prove increasingly difficult to maintain either segregation at home or colonialism abroad following the eventual Allied victory.

Although rising to only a fraction of the height of the Trylon, the Belgian Pavilion's bell tower made it difficult to miss. The building benefited from an outstanding location; along with the French Pavilion, it defined the entrance to the Lagoon of Nations (fig. 30). The fairgrounds were carefully arranged to give primacy to the two countries whose invasion by Germany twenty-five years earlier had helped catapult the United States to the world power status the fair was meant to showcase. The bells also contributed to the Belgian Pavilion's prominence. American patriotic and national hymns emanating from the Belgian and Dutch Pavilions' carillons punctuated the fair's opening ceremony and remained a much beloved feature of the fair. In addition to automated chimes sounding on the quarter of the hour, thrice-weekly

Figure 30. Belgian Pavilion with Lagoon of Nations in foreground, Henry van de Velde, Léon Stynen, and Victor Bourgeois, New York, 1939. (Manuscripts and Archives Division, The New York Public Library)

Figure 31. Postcard of Belgian Pavilion, 1939 New York World's Fair. (Boston Public Library, Print Department)

live concerts were performed on the Belgian carillon, accompanied by a light and water display at the Lagoon of Nations.[7]

Many aspects of the Belgian Pavilion, including its materials, attracted favorable comment (fig. 31). The reactions of visitors were undoubtedly shaped by the official guidebook, which described the building as representing "the true national unity of Belgium by using to full advantage the characteristic red tiles of Flanders, the gleaming black slate of the Ardennes and the famous plate glass of the Walloon provinces." "The upper outer walls," it continued, "are composed of purplish-red colored terra cotta slabs flecked with sand, slate-black schist being used for the majestic belfry which dominates the entire building as well as for the window casing and lower walls."[8]

The choice of the tiles and schist on the building's exterior, not to mention the black marble lining the Hall of Honor inside, demonstrated that obviously modern forms could evoke the past without repeating it. Blue-gray schist or slate was already commonly employed in Belgian construction; indeed, the French word for slate is *ardoise,* a reference to the Ardennes, the hills stretching across France, Belgium, Luxembourg, and Germany in which it is quarried. Schist was often placed at the base of Belgian buildings, where it reassuringly suggested a solid stone foundation that was, however, by the twentieth century seldom actually present. The terra cotta tiles provided a rich red-brown tone and coarse, handcrafted texture reminiscent of handmade brick.

Just as much as the diamonds, lace, and glassware on display within, the building materials doubled as advertising for the Belgian companies that supplied them. Van de Velde, who characterized the finished pavilion as both an official and a commercial structure, was frank about the good chance the materials had of conquering the American market.[9] While North America had alternative sources of building slate, Comptoir Tuile de Courtrai, who made the tiles, undoubtedly hoped to avail itself of the popularity of terra cotta in the United States, where the material had often provided an excellent and often inexpensive source of manufactured ornament since the late nineteenth century. The firm remained active in the area of exhibitions, providing a restaurant for the 1958 fair in Brussels that remains one of the most cherished relics of that event.[10] Because the building was erected entirely of Belgian materials, it did not feature, however, in the many advertisements for American construction products that filled the pages of trade journals published in the United States. The single exception was the Ru-ber-oid roof, one of twenty-three at the fair, its manufacturer proudly proclaimed.[11]

Not only the materials of the Belgian Pavilion synthesized tradition and modernity, craft and industry; so did its architectural language. The pavilion consisted of a central patio, flanked by three large volumes and two covered passages, over which a 165-foot bell tower housing a thirty-five-bell carillon presided (fig. 32). The monumentality of the bell tower and building, which occupied an area of 100,000 square feet, was softened by a series of asymmetrical curves and angles that lent the complex a more informal, additive appearance (fig. 33). Indeed, Jan-Albert Goris, deputy commissioner of the Belgian Pavilion who had helped oversee its design, underscored that the structure's central patio resembled a traditional Belgian town square flanked on all sides by an accretion of buildings and marked by a tall bell tower whose soaring verticality announced the square's civic importance; covered spaces between building volumes allowed for the passage of pedestrians.[12] And yet the structure was fully modern in its extensive glazing and unadorned surfaces that communicated principles of efficiency and rationality. Nothing could be more tradi-

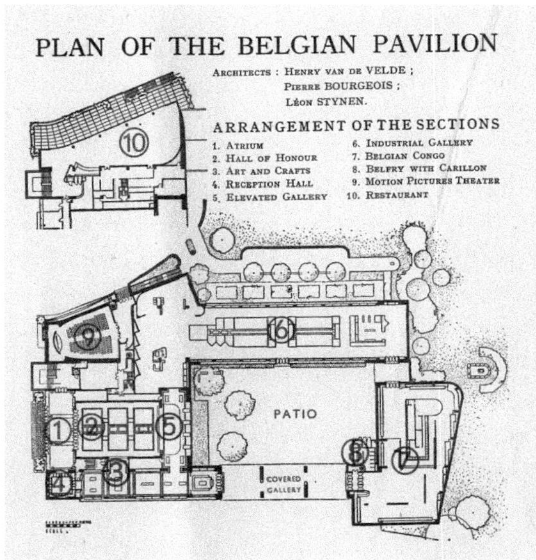

Figure 32. Plan of the Belgian Pavilion, *Belgian Pavilion Official Guide Book*, New York World's Fair, 1939. (Virginia Union University Archives and Special Collections)

tional than a bell tower, but here it acquired a new relevance, imbued with the sleek dynamism characteristic of an American skyscraper (fig. 34). Light reflected off the tower's smooth schist facing, whose dark materiality was broken by corner glazing that allowed natural light into the staircase; electric lighting at night afforded even more dramatic optical effects.

Even without American advertising, the building garnered generally good press on both sides of the Atlantic. A *New York Times* reporter covering the arrival of Albert de Vleeschauwer, the Belgian minister of colonies, described the pavilion as "one of the most imposing of the foreign buildings at the World's Fair, with a commanding place on the Lagoon of Nations."[13] The *Architectural Forum* less generously noted that the building was "handsome in appearance and well planned," but that "its monumental interiors house displays which are drab and inferior."[14] Two of the most important notices came in publications that were much more widely read and influential than any architecture journal, the *New Yorker* and *House Beautiful.* In his regular "Sky Line" column for the first of these, Lewis Mumford was generally dismissive of the fair, writing that "it has buildings as good as the drive-in markets of Los Angeles, and . . . monuments to salesmanship vying with the incredible milk bottles and ice-cream freezers that line the great highways of movieland." But he admired the Belgian contribution:

> The Belgian building, with its dark slate tower and its unglazed, slightly rough-textured red tiles, is one of the handsomest pieces of real architecture at the Fair. The great bay of windows that faces the water display, reflecting it at night as in a mirror, is a dramatic point of emphasis that vies with its own open-terraced restaurant on the Lagoon. Belgium produced some of the best of the early modern architectural leaders, particularly Van de Velde and Horta, and it has no reason, on this showing, to be ashamed of its present generation.[15]

Figure 33. Belgian Pavilion, New York, Henry van de Velde, Léon Stynen, and Victor Bourgeois, 1939. (RIBA Collections)

Figure 34. Bell Tower of the Belgian Pavilion, 1939 New York World's Fair. (© AML [Archives et Musée de la Littérature])

Mumford's opinion mattered. He was one of the country's foremost public intellectuals and its most widely read architectural critic. While he was particularly committed to regional-scale planning that would decant what he viewed as overcrowded unhealthy cities, he was also well aware of the latest architectural developments on both sides of the Atlantic. His own contribution to the fair was the script of the documentary film *The City* that provided a thoughtful alternative to Futurama's splashy spectacle. In his "Sky Line" columns, Mumford was equally dismissive of sentimental historicism and of industrial modernism. He excoriated what he viewed as crass commercialism, preferring understated, unornamented forms that served modern purposes with an efficiency scaled to humans, not machines.

Depending on its location at the edge or center of cities, new building, according to Mumford, should either be integrated into nature or into the spatial fabric of a community.[16]

House Beautiful's anonymous critic was equally enthusiastic about the Belgian Pavilion. He—or more likely she—enthused:

> Belgium: Many people will argue as to which is the most beautiful single building in the fair and many will select this pavilion . . . you will catch your breath at the handsomeness of it, its color and the outline. Inside your first thought will be there was never so much marble. And what a setting those great shiny blocks made for the airy Belgian laces, for the massive Belgian glass, for the modern rugs . . . You will like the silver which depends wholly upon its shape to be decorative, lacks every ornate touch . . . You will be enchanted with the linens and organdies and chiffons which have been worked and monogrammed for the table and the bed. This is French taste with a difference, as it is a fresh, rather than a derivative version of it.[17]

Established in 1896, *House Beautiful* was the first of what became known as shelter magazines, titles aimed at a largely female readership that focused upon domestic architecture, interior design, and gardening. In the 1920s and early 1930s, during the editorship of Ethel Power, it featured the latest European modernism as one of several possible approaches about which well-informed consumers in the United States should know.[18] Particularly representative of *House Beautiful*'s emphasis is the writer's insistence on reconciling high style with livability, distinction with practicality.

Especially since the Stockholm exhibition of 1930, the magazine had been enthusiastic about contemporary Swedish design, which in many ways provided a striking parallel to what Bourgeois, Stynen, and van de Velde achieved in New York in 1939 as they balanced industry and artisanship, modernity and tradition. Of the Swedish displays *House Beautiful* proclaimed, "In the wonderful glass and silver you reach a pitch of craftsmanship that surely cannot be surpassed. These manage to retain the inherent honesty of all Swedish objects but add to it that refinement of design which is art."[19] *House Beautiful* was not the only one to be impressed by the country's showing at the New York World's Fair. The critic for *Architectural Forum* termed Sweden's pavilion "unquestionably the most civilized piece of modern architecture in the entire Fair grounds" (fig. 35).[20] Writing in the rival publication *Pencil Points,* Talbot Hamlin profiled its architect Sven Markelius and termed the pavilion his "masterpiece." Like the Belgian contribution, it was organized around a courtyard and featured both a cinema and a restaurant, although its colorful awnings helped set a less formal tone.[21]

That van de Velde's approach was quite similar to that of Markelius, a leading architect a generation his junior, showed how well he had kept abreast of expectations for such events. Europeans, too, were impressed by the degree to which Belgium's contribution ranked in the forefront of the pavilions. Not surprisingly, positive notices appeared in the Belgian press.[22] Even the francophone satirical weekly *Pourquoi pas?,* which had earlier disputed van de Velde's authorship of both the 1937 and 1939 world's fair pavilions, found Belgium to be "magnificently represented in New York." This celebration was followed by the predictable jab that the pavilion

Figure 35. Swedish Pavilion, Sven Markelius, New York World's Fair, 1939. (Manuscripts and Archives Division, The New York Public Library)

was ultimately an example of "Flemish imperialism," for which it blamed both Goris and van de Velde.[23] Undercutting this critique, however, were positive comments appearing in the French press as well as in that of the Netherlands, where one critic admitted that their national pavilion paled in comparison.[24] Flemings, of course, were also positive, with the *Gazet van Mechelen* proudly quoting both Mumford and *House Beautiful!*[25]

The Belgian Pavilion was in no way futuristic. Rather than presenting "The World of Tomorrow," as the fair in Flushing Meadows aspired to do, it was an example of the best progressive European architecture of the day. As the person overseeing the architectural design as well as selecting the building's decorative schemes and exhibits, van de Velde coordinated the work of architects, urban planners, and artists to invent new forms of civic expression free of historicist bombast. Optimistic in its use of steel and glass, the Belgian Pavilion nonetheless displayed a respect for the silhouette of historic Belgian cities and the warmth of their brick-lined streetscapes, whose construction was more imposing than experimental. On the fairgrounds itself, and in such proximity to Manhattan, it was thus easy to overlook the degree to which the Belgian Pavilion presented a far more sophisticated example of twentieth-century European architecture than could yet be found in the United States, and this on a patently a civic scale.

This being said, this dynamic synthesis of handcraft and industry was not without parallels in the United States. The leading European-born exponents of this position stateside were the father and son duo of Eliel and Eero Saarinen. A decade younger than van de Velde, Eliel first made his name internationally with his picturesque design for the pavilion of his native Finland at the 1900 Universal Exposition in Paris. Modernism would be introduced to Finland in part by Sigurd Frosterus, van de Velde's former assistant in Weimar, through his pathbreaking competition entry in 1904 for the Helsinki railway station. This submission provided the catalyst for the elder Saarinen's revision of his winning entry, realized between 1909 and 1919.[26] The Saarinen family emigrated to the United States in 1923, settling just outside Detroit in Cranbrook, Michigan, where Eliel designed a pair of boarding schools and established an Academy of Art that had an outsize influence on postwar American design and craft; the academy's achievements, like those of La Cambre with which it shared a commitment to modern artisanship, have been too often overshadowed by the Bauhaus.[27] Eliel's late work was often designed in collaboration with his son Eero and sometimes also Robert Swanson, who in 1926 married Eliel's daughter Eva Lisa, also known as Pipsan.

Whether or not the Michigan-based architects were aware of van de Velde's pavilion, they certainly shared a predilection for slightly contrapuntal compositions of interlinked, low-slung volumes punctuated by a soaring vertical. The parallels between the Belgian Pavilion, as configured in New York and published already in 1938, and the winning entry that Eliel, Eero, and Swanson submitted for a design for a Smithsonian Museum in the spring of 1939 may be more than coincidental (fig. 36).[28] Furthermore, the Saarinens' Kleinhans Music Hall in Buffalo, completed in 1940, also shared several of the same features, including an arcade and a tiered extrusion. In the Belgian Pavilion, the stepped tiers supported the exterior stairs to the restaurant; in Buffalo they were the exterior expression of an interior staircase. In almost all of their work together, the Saarinens clad their well-defined volumes in brick, providing qualities similar to those of the Belgian building's terra cotta tiled surfaces. Eero Saarinen would go on to embrace a greater plasticity and tactility than his father in works that were often suffused with his admiration for the German

Figure 36. Competition entry for a Smithsonian Museum, Eliel Saarinen, Eero Saarinen, and Robert Swanson, project for Washington, D.C., 1939. (Smithsonian American Art Museum / Art Resource/Scala, Florence)

architect Erich Mendelsohn, again in ways that were colored by Mendelsohn's own respect for van de Velde.[29] In 1940, commissions such as these placed Eliel Saarinen near the apex of the architectural culture of his adopted homeland, a status Eero would enjoy in the 1950s. Neither, however, was present at the New York Fair.

The International Style, the Museum of Modern Art, and the Rockefellers

Two other national displays at the fair struck off in what have been understood ever since as highly productive new directions. Alvar Aalto, who was responsible for the Finnish installation, tucked exhibit space, including a model of a Finnish village, behind a sinuous and tilted plywood wall onto which he affixed photographs of the national lumber industry that featured as well in its construction (fig. 37). *Architectural Forum* labeled it "the fair's most exciting demonstration of what can be done with a bare rectangular room."[30] An L-shaped box in plan, Brazil's national pavilion

Figure 37. Finnish Exhibition, Alvar Aalto, New York World's Fair, 1939. (Finnish Heritage Agency)

Figure 38. Brazilian Pavilion, Lucio Costa and Oscar Niemeyer, New York World's Fair, 1939. (Manuscripts and Archives Division, The New York Public Library)

designed by Lúcio Costa and Oscar Niemeyer conveyed an openness entirely at odds with the strong sense of enclosure that characterized the Belgian Pavilion (fig. 38). Parts of both blocks were raised off the ground on thin concrete columns called *pilotis,* while perforated grill work and a sweeping ramp leading to the upper story communicated the dissolution of a conventional sense of volume. Michael Scott's shamrock-shaped Irish Pavilion, and the Venezuelan entry by the Chicago-based partnership of Skidmore and Owings, were further examples of national pavilions that helped launch practices that would play prominent postwar roles in Ireland and the United States, respectively.[31]

All four of these national pavilions were examples of the International Style that New York's Museum of Modern Art (MoMA) had been promoting since its 1932 exhibition "Modern Architecture: International Exhibition," to which Mumford and Catherine Bauer had contributed a section on housing.[32] Fairgoers interested in modern architecture probably added the museum to their itinerary, which moved into purpose-built quarters in Midtown Manhattan the same month that the gates opened in Queens (fig. 39). Designed by Philip Goodwin and Edward Durrell Stone, the MoMA building featured expansive glazing that, like two facades of the Belgian Pavilion, had much in common with the city's shopfronts that van de Velde so admired. Both the Museum of Modern Art's new headquarters and the Belgian Pavilion broke with a revival of classical architecture in the 1930s, which Mumford had dismissed in a 1936 column as the "laborious limestone counterfeits of civic grandeur in which most art institutions across the country [are] housed."[33]

The Museum of Modern Art had been established a decade earlier by three women, of whom Abby Aldrich Rockefeller, as wife of John D. Rockefeller Jr.,

Figure 39. Museum of Modern Art, Philip Goodwin and Edward Durrell Stone, New York, 1939. (The Museum of Modern Art, New York / Scala, Florence)

had the deepest pockets. In the interwar years, the architectural patronage of the Rockefeller couple offered an excellent example of the way in which informed people in the United States could simultaneously espouse what might appear as highly divergent positions. Rockefeller largesse contributed to the creation of the Cloisters, a branch of the city's Metropolitan Museum perched on the heights of northern Manhattan and housed in a pastiche that included authentic fragments of medieval European architecture, and built Riverside Church, a fusion of Gothic Revival styling and modern construction technology.[34] Rockefeller philanthropy also had a transformative impact in Virginia, where Colonial Williamsburg's sanitized version of the eighteenth century provided a template for single-family suburban houses that nodded respectfully toward preindustrial simplicity, while featuring such modern amenities as central heating and hot and cold running water. Just to the south of MoMA, Rockefeller Center set a jauntier, more modern note and established a precedent for postwar urban redevelopments, few if any of which matched its popular flair (fig. 40). Its RCA building, an 850-foot-tall slab, was capped by the Rainbow Room, a glamourous nightclub, while the cinema in Radio City Music Hall, the city's largest, catered to a broader public.[35] In comparison the new museum was much more austere.

In the 1930s, in addition to championing avant-garde architecture from Europe, the Museum of Modern Art prepared fairgoers for other aspects of what they would see in Flushing Meadows. It held an exhibition in 1934 entitled "Machine Art." In its catalog, curator Philip Johnson acknowledged that the British Arts and Crafts movement "was not acknowledged as a modern movement until it was transplanted to the Continent, where it thrived in Vienna and Brussels under the leadership of such men as Josef Hoffmann and Henry van de Velde."[36] In 1935 the MoMA exhibition "African Negro Art" included 150 works from the Belgian Congo.[37] Their relevance to contemporary art was confirmed two years later when the museum acquired Pablo Picasso's *Demoiselles d'Avignon* (1907), a key work in the assimilation of African influences into modern European art.[38] This landmark painting was joined in November 1939 by Picasso's mural *Guernica,* which remained on loan to the museum (although it often traveled) until its return to Spain in 1981. In 1938 MoMA devoted an entire exhibition to Aalto, paving the way for his success at the fair.

If the patronage of the elder Rockefellers often appeared quite conservative compared to much of what was on view at the Museum of Modern Art or at "The World

Figure 40. RCA Building, Rockefeller Center, Associated Architects, New York, 1933. (David Shankbone / Wikimedia Commons)

of Tomorrow" just six miles to its east, the fair helped push their son Nelson as well as the museum's staff in new directions. Perhaps its most enduring impact upon subsequent architectural culture was its introduction of contemporary developments in Brazil. The museum's 1943 exhibition "Brazil Builds" solidified the careers of Costa and Niemeyer in both Brazil and the United States and established their architecture and urban planning as templates for projects that Nelson Rockefeller helped sponsor when he served as governor of New York State between 1959 and 1973.[39]

By the late 1940s, MoMA's Department of Architecture was instrumental in determining that architectural culture in the United States would privilege not only Aalto and Brazilian modernism but also Walter Gropius and Ludwig Mies van der

Rohe, European architects whose work it showcased in 1932 and in subsequent exhibitions. These included an exhibit on the Bauhaus in 1938 that Gropius, its founding director, helped organize, and a 1947 show devoted entirely to Mies, the school's third and final director. By 1939, both men were already in the United States, with Gropius at Harvard and Mies at the Armour Institute of Technology (soon to be renamed the Illinois Institute of Technology), but the presence at the fair of the German modernism van de Velde had done so much to encourage was slight. Gropius and three of his former students, Herbert Bayer, Marcel Breuer, and Xanti Schawinsky, designed the installation that the state of Pennsylvania housed within a replica of Independence Hall (fig. 41). It would be nearly another decade before Gropius and Mies would become influential figures in their adopted homeland.

Figure 41. Pennsylvania Exhibition, Walter Gropius and Marcel Breuer with Herbert Bayer and Xanti Schawinsky, New York World's Fair, 1939. (Breuer Archive, Special Collections Research Center, Syracuse University Libraries)

Displays of Modern Design at the Belgian Pavilion

Van de Velde's artistic directorship extended from the building down to its exhibits, where a similar synthesis of tradition and modernity held sway (fig. 42). Part of the Artistic Committee's task was to commission designs from modern artists to be carried out by Belgium's finest artisans, manufacturers, and industrialists, in the hopes of regaining global markets that had eluded them, beginning in the twentieth century when manufacturers in Germany and the United States rose to the fore.[40] Seeking to correct the mistakes of 1925, when late planning had left little time to commission new work for the pavilion's exhibits, the Belgian minister of economic affairs, Philip van Isacker, started early to secure funding for Belgium's Artistic and Technical Committees, resulting in works of quality and innovation that drew international recognition. The pavilion's entrance spaces featured works of ceremonial and thematic importance that presented modern Belgium as a resourceful and

Figure 42. Hall of Honor, Belgian Pavilion, 1939 New York World's Fair, Photograph by Robert E. Coates (Flanders Architecture Institute—collection of the Flemish Government, archive of Léon Stynen)

Figure 43. Rendering of Floris Jespers's tapestries hanging in the Hall of Honor, Belgian Pavilion, E. P. Chrystie, New York World's Fair, 1939, watercolor. (E. P. Chrystie, 41.44.2, Museum of New York)

dynamic country, with close ties to America since the 1600s. Upon entering the Hall of Honor, visitors gazed upon five monumental tapestries, each measuring 490 by 582 centimeters: *The Founding of New York by Walloons and Flemings, Missionary Work in the United States, Traditional Belgium, Modern Belgium,* and *The Relationship between Belgium and America during and after the First World War.* All of them were designed by the Flemish painter Floris Jespers and were woven by traditional tapestry manufacturers Braquenié, De Wit, and Chaudoir. The imposing effect produced by these bright tapestries is captured in a watercolor by E. P. Chrystie that shows their brilliant colors reflecting off the Hall of Honor's polished black marble walls (1939, fig. 43).

By commissioning designs from a modern painter, van de Velde sought to revive a Belgian tapestry tradition, which had fallen on hard times since the French Revolution. New manufactures had opened in the nineteenth century, but attempts to rekindle the art had been stymied by a lack of new designs; copies were produced that were a pale imitation of the older, esteemed weavings.[41] In his choices, van de

Velde continued the work he had begun as director of La Cambre. In 1937, critic René Lyr observed of its impact, "A renascence has manifested [in tapestry] as well in hand weaving. . . . By establishing a workshop and a class, the Higher Institute of Decorative Arts has largely contributed to this resurrection."[42] Although Jespers did not teach at La Cambre, he would have been familiar with and sympathetic to its aims through his close collaborations with his brother, Oscar, who taught monumental sculpture at the school from 1927 to 1952. Along with the Flemish Dada painter Paul Joostens and poet Paul van Ostjaijen, the Jespers brothers had founded one of the first groups in Belgium that engaged with the modernist languages of Fauvism, Expressionism, Cubism, and Futurism. Floris Jespers went on to collaborate with Jean Metzinger and Albert Gleizes on the important theoretical text *On Cubism* (*Du Cubisme,* 1913) before exhibiting with a Dutch group "De Branding" alongside Kurt Schwitters. In 1925, the brothers became members of The Art of Today (Kunst van Heden).[43] The tapestries Floris Jespers designed for the Belgian Pavilion are representative of his work from the 1930s, when he fused an avant-garde, Cubist language of collage, evidenced in such works as *Susanna and the Elders* (1927, fig. 44), with more traditional figural and narrative elements.

The sophistication of Floris Jespers's work can be seen by looking more closely at one of his tapestries exhibited in New York, *The Relationship between Belgium and America during and after the First World War* (fig. 45). At the center of the composition, red flames symbolize the burning of the university library in Leuven, Belgium's oldest university, which the German military torched in August 1914. Yet the new library and collection funded by Americans, including the Rockefellers, between 1921 and 1928 defies these flames of destruction. Designed by Whitney Warren, the architect of New York's Grand Central Station, the neo-Flemish-Renaissance building is presented by Herbert Hoover. Food sacks stamped with "CRB" indicate Hoover's Commission for Relief in Belgium. Standing next to the Statue of Liberty draped in the American flag, Hoover represents America's role as peacemaker in Europe. His outstretched hand is repeated, on a larger scale, by the colossal blue hand at the top of the composition cradling two doves of peace symbolizing the United States and Belgium. The open hand bridges the geographical divide between the Manhattan skyline and war-torn Belgium. In the bottom left and right corners, help arrives from Great Britain and France, common allies, who seek to contain the

Figure 44. *Susanna and the Elders,* Floris Jespers, 1927. Oil on canvas, 105 x 70.4 cm, Koninklijk Museum voor Schone Kunsten, Antwerp. (© Estate of Floris Jespers / SABAM Brussels, IVARO Dublin, 2023; hoto: Hugo Maertens, Collection KMSKA—Flemish Community)

violence. In the bottom center, superimposed fragments of a gas mask, cannon, and classical column crush a soldier's body, a dismemberment expressed through a Cubist language of broken lines and overlapping planes. Countering this fragmentation, an overall color scheme of red, white, and blue unifies the composition. An inscription woven into the tapestry's lower border reads: "The United States saved Belgium from starvation during the war. When peace came, they helped to rebuild the country and its scientific institutions."[44] The tapestry further paid homage to the United

Figure 45. *The Relationship between Belgium and America during and after the First World War,* Floris Jespers, 1939. Tapestry, 16 ½ x 18 ½ ft., Hoover Institution, Stanford University, Palo Alto, California. (© Estate of Floris Jespers / SABAM Brussels, IVARO Dublin, 2023; Stanford University, Hoover Institution, exhibition view 'Ravaged' © M Leuven 2014, photo: Dirk Pauwels)

States by engaging recent artistic and cultural developments. The abstract, pulsating geometry of skyscrapers in the tapestry recalls Georgia O'Keeffe's mural painting *Manhattan* (1932, fig. 46), a seven-by-four-foot panel she created for an exhibition at the Museum of Modern Art.[45] Both Jespers and O'Keeffe associated the faceted, overlapping planes of Cubism with New York architecture, which became the basis for dynamic and expressive formal tensions.

These exhibited tapestries fused modern design and traditional craft, as did another ceremonial artwork by two sculptors, Oscar Jespers and Henri Puvrez.

Figure 46. *Manhattan,* Georgia O'Keeffe, 1932. Oil on canvas, 84 3/8 x 48 ¼ in., Smithsonian American Art Museum. (Smithsonian American Art Museum / Art Resource / Scala, Florence)

Entitled *Belgium at Work,* this monumental ceramic bas-relief was mounted to the pavilion's patio wall at the base of the bell tower, where it appeared next to a statue of the recently deceased and immensely popular Belgian king Albert I positioned close to the ground at arm's length (fig. 47). Jespers and Puvrez's bas-relief adopts an even more populist ethos. Like his brother, Oscar Jespers trained at the Royal Academy of

Figure 47. *Belgium at Work*, Oscar Jespers and Henri Puvrez, 1939. Ceramic bas-relief, Belgian Pavilion, 1939 New York World's Fair. (© AML [Archives et Musée de la Littérature])

Fine Arts in Antwerp before contributing to international avant-garde movements. His first sculptures, dating to the 1920s, consisted of nudes and heads, whose form is simplified into a series of overlapping volumes and planes inspired by Cubist painting and sub-Saharan African sculpture (fig. 48). The commission for the New York pavilion gave Jespers the opportunity to work on a monumental scale, and he introduced Realist and narrative elements into his composition to appeal to a broader audience. Following its theme, "Belgium at Work," his ceramic frieze depicts monumental workers in low relief, where they constitute an architectural frieze measuring fifteen by three meters (fig. 49). From left to right appear full-length, heroic Belgian workers with square jaws and defined musculature, among them fishermen, peasants, coal miners, and glass blowers.[46] Full-scale laborers are punctuated by half-scale figures engaging in leisure pursuits of dance and music. The positive image of labor and up-to-date social content would have been familiar to U.S. audiences attuned to Works Progress Administration (WPA) public art projects funded by Franklin

Figure 48. *Sitting Nude,* Oscar Jespers, 1925. Polished hardstone, 34 x 75 x 28 cm, Mu.Zee, Ostend, Belgium. (© Estate of Oscar Jespers / SABAM Brussels, IVARO Dublin, 2023; Collection Mu.ZEE, Ostend. Photo Cedric Verhelst, 2021)

Figure 49. *Belgium at Work,* 1939, Detail, Oscar Jespers and Henri Puvrez. Ceramic bas-relief, Belgian Pavilion, 1939 New York World's Fair. (© AML [Archives et Musée de la Littérature])

Delano Roosevelt's New Deal. Modeled in clay with a deliberately rough surface, the bas-relief conveys the physicality of the medium, presenting sculpture as an art of manual labor. Placed at the ground level for all to see, this sculpture could not have been more different than the regal allegorical figure of Belgium perched atop Horta's 1925 pavilion! Taking the pulse of the times, van de Velde ensured that Belgium would be represented, not by medieval royalty, but by modern workers.

Beyond these ceremonial and thematic artworks, the Belgian Pavilion featured commercial products and equipment intended for sale in U.S. markets; throughout the planning period, Belgian government officials highlighted the applied arts as a specific area of national distinction that had fallen into decline. Just as in Germany, so too in Belgium van de Velde was called upon to breathe new life into these failing economic sectors that were also connected to regional and national identity and pride. Success in 1939 was to be both economic and symbolic. Located just off the Hall of Honor, the Arts and Crafts Gallery featured handmade lace by members of the Belgian Lace Syndicate, along with artistic bookbinding, deluxe editions, cast and stamped medals, fine tableware, crockery, and ornamental ceramics by acclaimed firms such as Keramis Boch Frères (figs. 32, 50). Products from La Cambre were well represented, giving fuel to van de Velde's enemies who alleged that he favored his friends to the detriment of established art schools and professional organizations.[47] To take only one example: four smaller tapestries woven by Elisabeth de Saedeleer, a weaving instructor at La Cambre, after designs by painter Edgard Tytgat, were displayed above vitrines in the Arts and Crafts Gallery. Intended for private consumption, these tapestries featured poetic subjects, such as *The Suppleness of Women Is Like the Tides* (fig. 51). Their combination of traditional artisanry with modern, Symbolist-inspired poetry instantiates how traditional applied arts were endowed with a uniquely modern subjectivity.

Accompanying these unique pieces of artisanry, the Industrial Gallery featured larger-scale manufacturers, including makers of musical instruments (with the saxophone, invented by Belgian musician Adolphe Saxe prominently featured); graphic arts and publicity; photography and film; heating, ventilation, and refrigeration; metallurgy and chemical industries; furniture and interior decor, including work by the reputed furniture firm De Coene Frères; electric lighting by the Belgian subsidiary of Philips S.A.; aeronautics, tourism, and travel; mines and quarries; building material and equipment; construction technologies and processes; and ceram-

Figure 50. Exhibits in the Arts and Crafts Gallery, Belgian Pavilion, 1939 New York World's Fair, Photograph by Robert E. Coates (Flanders Architecture Institute—collection of the Flemish Government, archive of Léon Stynen)

ics and glass industries, including the renowned Cristallerie Val St. Lambert (fig. 52). Unlike the unique objects displayed in the Arts and Crafts Gallery, items in the Industrial Gallery were exhibited to express principles of seriality, wherein quality was matched by efficiency and mass production.[48]

These firms and products had been handpicked by the Artistic and Technical Committees to present merchandise and services of the highest quality that exemplified modern design principles, including a focus on the material properties of the medium and lack of applied ornament. Objects in historical styles were excluded from the outset. The goal was to represent distinctive, modern products to increase the volume of Belgian exports to the United States, which, thanks to Van Isacker's efforts, had steadily risen from 594 million francs in 1934 to over 2 billion francs in 1937.[49] By all estimation, the exhibition was a critical success, with the Arts and

Figure 51. Tapestry, *The Suppleness of Women Is Like the Tides*, designed by Edgard Tytgat and woven by Elisabeth de Saedeleer. Tapestry exhibited at the Belgian Pavilion, 1939 New York World's Fair. (University Archives KU Leuven, Raphael Verwilghen Foto 1/6)

Crafts section receiving the highest praise from international juries and viewers. A critic from the Netherlands observed of the Arts and Crafts Gallery, "It was all original without being bizarre, testifying to exquisite craftsmanship, great imagination, and dedication."[50] Along with the pavilion's architecture, these displays attested to Belgium's prowess as a modern, industrial, and cultured nation.

The cinema and the restaurant designed respectively by Victor Bourgeois and Léon Stynen also contributed to the pavilion's success. The V-shaped cinema and the lobby through which it was accessed helped account for the flair on one end of the building's longest facade (fig. 32). The Motion Picture Theater seated up to three hundred people, who watched a series of short documentaries on the country's artistic heritage—including the Ghent altarpiece, painted by Hubert and Jan van Eyck and completed by 1432, plus the outstanding collection of paintings in Saint John's Hospital Museum in Bruges by their successor Hans Memling—as well as promotional films on the Congo (fig. 53).[51] Photomontages presenting stills from these

Figure 52. Glasses manufactured by Cristallerie Val St. Lambert, exhibited at the Belgian Pavilion, 1939 New York World's Fair. (University Archives KU Leuven, Raphael Verwilghen Foto 1/6)

Figure 53. Cinema lobby, Belgian Pavilion, Victor Bourgeois, New York, 1939. (CIVA Collections, Brussels)

Figure 54. Restaurant, Belgian Pavilion, Léon Stynen, New York, 1939. (CIVA Collections, Brussels)

films decorated the walls of the cinema's lobby. Stynen's restaurant, which could seat five hundred diners, was located above the cinema, with half of the cinema's roof serving as a roof terrace overlooking the Lagoon of Nations that could be accessed by an exterior stair (fig. 54).

The Colonial Section and Colonial Propaganda

Although many interwar European fairs, including one held in Glasgow in 1938, had been dedicated to exhibiting empire, those in the United States typically shied away from such overt displays of colonialism.[52] Nonetheless, in addition to showcasing Belgian industry and artisanship, the pavilion included a Colonial Section, designed by Stynen, through which the organizing committee sought to appeal alike to white U.S. investors and to African Americans. Organized by the Ministry of the Colonies, the Colonial Section was no less tied to Belgium's cultural, social, and economic prestige. In keeping with the fair's theme, "The World of Tomorrow," the Colonial Commission shifted its emphasis from displaying Indigenous arts and culture to documenting processes of modernization. In previous fairs, such as the Paris 1937 Exposition, Belgium's colonial pavilion had been architecturally and spatially distinct from its national pavilion, with colonial displays prioritizing traditional Congolese arts and cultural expressions.[53] By contrast, in 1939 the Congolese displays were housed in a wing of the Belgian Pavilion located adjacent to the bell tower. Like the entire building, this section was also equipped with state-of-the-art air-conditioning, but it had additional security to protect the displays of diamonds, resulting in its being the only section of the pavilion without fenestration.[54] The open expanses of glazing that marked the pavilion's Applied and Industrial Art Sections gave way in the Colonial Section to an uninterrupted expanse of terra cotta facing, whose irregular surface and curved corner lent the wing a sculptural presence (fig. 55).

The fair's themes of moral and material progress dovetailed with colonial propaganda, as the Colonial Section foregrounded the "improvements" that Belgium had introduced to its colony. Nowhere was this narrative of progress more evident than in a two-part monumental bas-relief of the Belgian Congo marking the entrance. The architectural sculpture was the work of Arthur Dupagne, who had lived in the Congo from 1927 to 1935, where he worked by day as an engineer for the International Society of Forestry and Mining and studied sculpture in the evenings. Dupagne continued to draw on Congolese themes for much of the rest of his career, including in reliefs for the 1937 Belgian Pavilion in Paris and a heroic statue of Henry Morton Stanley in Leopoldville (present-day Kinshasa).[55] His sculptural reliefs for the New York pavilion measure sixteen by ten feet and are unusual in his oeuvre for their degree of Art Deco stylization. The first panel depicts the Congolese engaging in traditional pursuits: pounding manioc root, motherhood, making music, dancing, market going, warfare, and hunting (fig. 56). The second frieze represents developments introduced by the Belgians: formal schooling, the conquering of sleeping sickness through Western medicine, the rubber harvest, shipping, and mining (fig. 57).[56] Europeans are absent from the scenes, which are populated exclusively with heroic Congolese figures; stylized, two-dimensional motifs based in African textiles

Figure 55. Colonial Section and Bell Tower, Belgian Pavilion, Henry van de Velde, Léon Stynen, and Victor Bourgeois, New York, 1939. (© AML [Archives et Musée de la Littérature])

frame the figural scenes in which Dupagne simplified the language of classical relief sculpture and infused it with modern rhythms.[57] The message of his panels is clear: under the civilizing efforts of the Belgian colonial government, "primitive" energies would be harnessed to serve science and industry. The frieze monumentalized the Congolese while communicating the benefits of Belgium's "civilizing mission." It operated through a series of contrasts that the Colonial Commission consistently mobilized in its propaganda to demonstrate how the Belgian government had improved the quality of life for the Congolese while preserving their "native spirit."

This logic is articulated in an article from *L'illustration congolaise,* an illustrated

Figure 56. *Belgian Congo,* Arthur Dupagne, 1939. First panel of a two-part bas-relief mounted on the exterior corner of the Colonial Section of the Belgian Pavilion, 1939 New York World's Fair. This panel depicts the Congolese prior to colonization. (© AML [Archives et Musée de la Littérature])

monthly published by the Ministry of the Colonies beginning in 1924 to instill in the general public interest in and support for the Belgian Congo.[58] Entitled "Contrasts," the 1939 article presents the Congo as a land where the spirit of ancient traditions coexists with modernization. "In no way have we abolished what I would gladly call the 'savage's genius,'" claimed the editors. "Whereas the voyager goes into raptures before the long iron train tunnels, the hanging bridge, a masterpiece of primitive aerial transport formed simply out of vines and stakes, constitutes a point of contrast."[59] These arguments are illustrated by photographs juxtaposing a modern truss railway bridge spanning the Congo River with a footbridge made of local vines (fig. 58). Lest readers and viewers deem the Congo's "primitive" and modern technologies equal, the editors declared, "The nightmare is over. The white man erects in its place the framework for all possible dreams" by cleaning up the country and opening it to international tourism, investment, and travel.[60] Dupagne's bas-relief conveyed a similar message, in which "primal" impulses were trained to form com-

Figure 57. *Belgian Congo*, Arthur Dupagne, 1939. Second panel of a two-part bas-relief mounted on the exterior corner of the Colonial Section of the Belgian Pavilion, 1939 New York World's Fair. This panel depicts the Congolese enjoying the purported fruits of colonization. (Katherine M. Kuenzli)

pelling rhythms that unify the two parts of the frieze, all the while foregrounding the material and moral benefits of colonization.

Just as exhibits in the Belgian section underscored the benefits of Belgian-American cooperation, so too those in the Colonial Section highlighted Americans' contributions to developing the colony. Upon entering, viewers were greeted by a plaster cast of Thomas Vinçotte's monumental equestrian statue of Leopold II, Belgium's second king, whose ambition and greed led him to acquire the Congo as his private fiefdom. Figured with his patriarchal beard and full-length coat, Leopold II appeared as a visionary and explorer, even though he never set foot in Africa (fig. 59). Lest fairgoers assume that Leopold had worked in isolation, his sculpture stood adjacent to a mural painting entitled *The Discovery of the Congo by Stanley* (fig. 60) by Pierre de Vaucleroy, a Cubist painter who had also contributed a decorative panel to the Congolese Pavilion at the 1935 Brussels International Exposition.[61] In 1878, Leopold II had hired the British explorer as his agent to locate the sources of the Nile and Congo Rivers; the resulting five-year mission enabled the Congo

Le pont de chemin de fer sur l'Inkisi et...
(Cliché Ministère des Colonies.)

De brug van de spoorbaan over de Inkisi en...
(Plaat van 't Ministerie van Koloniën.)

l'invitation au grand voyage, et les portes de notre colonie s'ouvrent toutes larges pour accueillir ce nouveau « MONDE COLONIAL ». C'est celui que l'on convie à se débarrasser pour quelques mois seulement d'une civilisation gênante afin de mieux s'éprendre devant tant de beautés naturelles, de richesses accumulées. C'est celui qu'attendent les curieuses populations pacifiques qui clament leur reconnaissante affection et c'est celui sur lequel on compte pour affirmer, une fois de plus, que d'autres Belges ont réalisé, là-bas, en quelques années, une œuvre de TITANS!

Nul pays ne présente d'aspects plus divers et plus séduisants!

Tous les contrastes simultanés ou successifs nés de l'opposition des ombres, de la lumière, des couleurs, font valoir les choses les unes par les autres en renforçant leurs caractères; d'ailleurs, rien n'excite plus fortement l'attention, le rapprochement des causes, des objets, des êtres que d'en provoquer la comparaison.

Ainsi, le Katanga avec sa forêt naissante de cheminées d'usines, ses hauts fourneaux d'où le cuivre sort par tonnes, contraste singulièrement avec la terre voisine dont le lac, les vallées, les plateaux et les cônes volcaniques hachées de crevasses ne sont décrits qu'avec surprise et admiration.

Le Kivu? dans son incomparable beauté, ne demande aucune impression de détails, son ensemble seul tyrannise l'attention.

... le plus antique des ponts, celui en lianes.
... de meest ouderwetsche brug uit lianen.

Figure 58. Illustrations in the article "Contrastes," *L'illustration congolaise* 212 (May 1939), 7328. (KBR)

Figure 59. Colonial Section, Belgian Pavilion, 1939 New York World's Fair. At left is a plaster cast of Thomas Vinçotte's monumental equestrian statue of Leopold II. In the center is Pierre de Vaucleroy's mural *The Discovery of the Congo by Stanley.* Léon Stynen designed the interior. (© AML [Archives et Musée de la Littérature])

Free State's occupation of the Congo basin in 1885. The mural represented Stanley as a larger-than-life figure at the center, flanked by smaller scenes of Congolese who energetically and obediently follow his orders. To create an American context for Stanley's labors, Vaucleroy included a scene of Stanley's earlier mission to the Congo in 1871 sponsored by the journalist James Gordon Bennett Jr., editor of the *New York Herald.* Stanley's famous encounter with the missing Scottish missionary, Dr. David Livingstone, appeared in the mural's upper left corner, with a U.S. flag prominently featured. Stanley's published account of his voyage made his international reputation and brought him to the attention of Leopold II.

To further establish the American dimensions of Stanley's person and career, the mural was accompanied by a brochure entitled *Stanley Goes Back to America* (fig. 61). A masterpiece of Belgian propaganda, the brochure presented Stanley as an "American" journalist.[62] Its author, Gaston Denys Périer, a high-placed official in Belgium's Ministry of Colonies, recounted how Stanley was born in Wales in 1841 as John Rowlands. He ran away from an English workhouse to settle in the United States, where he took the name of his guardian, Henry Stanley. After joining the Confederate Army, being taken prisoner, and fighting for the Union Army, Stanley launched a career as an adventurer and journalist. Périer enumerated the American newspapers to which he contributed: the *Missouri Democrat, The Times, The Tribune,* the *Chicago Republican,* and the *Cincinnati Commercial,* not to mention the *New York Herald.* The commercial success of Stanley's Congolese travelogue led him to briefly adopt U.S. citizenship to copyright his publications.

Figure 60. Study for *Seven Episodes of H. M. Stanley's Travels*, Pierre de Vaucleroy, 1939. Gouache on paper, 43 x 63cm. (IVARO HO.0.1.910, collection RMCA Tervuren All rights reserved)

Stanley and Bennett were two of three exemplary "Americans" whom Périer credited as enabling Belgian colonization, along with General Henry S. Sanford. As special envoy and minister plenipotentiary of the United States in Belgium, Sanford helped Leopold create the International Africa Association and gave Stanley the commission on behalf of Leopold II to launch a Belgian expedition to the Congo. When Leopold converted the International African Association into the Congo Free State with himself as supreme leader, Sanford lobbied the U.S. government to be the first to acknowledge Leopold's territorial acquisitions. More generally, Périer credited the United States with inspiring what he presented as Leopold's humanitarian actions: "Were it not the United States," he asked, "which had freed several millions of negroes and created the Republic of Liberia, where the negroes have a self-government?"[63] Such efforts allegedly spurred Leopold to abolish the slave trade conducted by Arab merchants in the Congo. Périer downplayed the "abuses and errors" committed in the Congo Free State as "inherent to the occupation of faraway countries," in the Congo as well as in other European colonies. These abuses, Périer

Figure 61. Cover of Gaston Denys Périer, *Stanley Goes Back to America* (Belgium, 1939). Brochure distributed at the Belgian Pavilion, Colonial Section, at the New York World's Fair. (KBR)

alleged, were far outweighed by the economic and moral improvements that the king introduced to his colony.[64]

Other displays emphasized the technological progress and humanitarian improvements introduced since 1908, when Belgium acquired the Congo Free State from Leopold II. A series of photomontages, statistics panels, and tourist and mining maps created by the graphic designer Jos Léonard documented how the railway lines and port and river infrastructure begun by Leopold II had been updated and extended (fig. 62). Belgium's national airline Sabena, founded in 1923, offered a

Figure 62. Colonial Section, Belgian Pavilion, New York World's Fair. A tourism photomontage of Congolese flora, fauna, and people by Jos Leonard (center). At right, displays of transportation by water and air in the Congo. Léon Stynen designed the interior. (© AML [Archives et Musée de la Littérature])

growing number of flights to and within the Congo; hospitals and primary schools were established to better the bodies and minds of local populations; and national parks were created to protect local flora and fauna. These investments soared in the 1920s, when a renewed flow of private Belgian capital placed Belgium ahead of its European rivals in terms of per capita expenditure. By 1938, the Belgian Congo was receiving $48 of foreign monies per inhabitant, as compared to $8 in British India, $36 in the Dutch Indies, $25 in French Africa, $32 in British Africa, and $18 in Portuguese Africa.[65] These investments stood behind the Colonial Commission's claim that Belgium had effectively developed a vast and resource-rich territory while assisting local populations.

Mining, above all of diamonds, occupied pride of place among the displays in the Colonial Section. While exploitation under Leopold II had focused on ivory and rubber, mining became the focus of development beginning in the 1920s, when the Belgian Congo became one of the leading global producers of copper, cobalt, industrial diamonds, uranium, gold, and tin. Displays included samples of

Figure 63. Colonial Section, Belgian Pavilion, 1939 New York World's Fair. View includes an old diamond cutting machine. Léon Stynen designed the interior. (© AML [Archives et Musée de la Littérature])

a broad range of mining products, with diamonds receiving the most attention, due in part to their high display value. An old diamond cutting machine (fig. 63) threw into relief the precision and efficiency of modern equipment demonstrated by a fleet of technicians (fig. 64). The finished products were displayed in sleek, alarm-protected glass vitrines showcasing the wares of Antwerp's leading diamond merchants. This priceless jewelry was temporarily removed from the vitrines and modeled by glamourous women parading on stage at the "Diamond Ball" in New York City hosted by the Belgian commissioner general a few weeks after the Fair's opening (fig. 65).

Displays in the Colonial Section ignored the human cost of mining development, specifically the toll it took on the Congolese population. Between 1921 and 1948, minerals represented between 52 and 72 percent of the total value of Congolese exports, and this increased production put a strain on Congolese labor.[66] Masses of workers were forcefully recruited and transported to underpopulated mining regions, where they fell victim to workplace accidents and malnutrition. To counter depopulation trends among the Congolese, private companies, such as the Mining Union of Upper-Katanga, introduced mechanization and increased protections for their African workers, beginning in the 1920s. To support the operations of private companies, the Belgian state invested in basic education and health care. However, these efforts were stalled by the economic crisis of the 1930s, so that the harsh living conditions of the African population only began to improve in the second half of

Figure 64. Colonial Section, Belgian Pavilion, 1939 New York World's Fair. Demonstration of modern diamond cutting technologies. Léon Stynen designed the interior. (© AML [Archives et Musée de la Littérature])

the 1940s. These shortcomings were nowhere evidenced in the Colonial Section's displays touting Belgian investments in Congolese health care, education, and the environment.

Predictably, displays in the Colonial Section also sidestepped the Belgian Congo's antidemocratic government. In 1908, Leopold's supreme rule had been replaced by a joint government consisting of the Belgian parliament, which managed the Congolese budget, and a minister of the colonies, whom the parliament empowered to make unilateral decrees—a special power that would become decisive upon Germany's invasion of Belgium. Democracy in the Congo was nonexistent: the Colonial Charter adopted by the Belgian parliament stipulated that those civil rights guaranteed by the Belgian constitution—including freedom of association, freedom of the press, and the right to vote—did not apply to Congolese residents, whether Black or white.[67] However, the number of white Belgians living in the colony represented just 0.2 percent of the total Congolese population in 1938; whites numbered 20,795 and Blacks 10,304,084.[68] Although Belgium explicitly rejected a South African–style apartheid system, the Belgian Congo had a definite color line, so that economic and governing power remained the exclusive domain of an elite white minority. Education for Blacks would not, with very few exceptions, expand beyond the primary level until the 1950s.[69]

These shortcomings were well-known to U.S. audiences, and so the Colonial Commission faced significant headwinds in its attempt to convince the public in

LE BAL DES BIJOUX DANS LE PAVILLON BELGE

Ci-dessus: Le défilé des mannequins parés des plus pures merveilles de la joaillerie.

Hierboven: Het defile van de modejuffers met een schat van juweelen getooid.

Ci-dessous, de droite à gauche: M. J. Holmes, adjoint au président de la World's Fair; Mme J. Gevaert; M. de Vleeschauwer, ministre des Colonies; M. J.-H. Goris, commissaire général adjoint.

Hieronder, van rechts naar links: de heer J. Holmes, adjunct van den voorzitter der « World's Fair »; Mevr. JJ. Gevaert; de heer de Vleeschauwer, minister van Koloniën; de heer J.-H. Goris, adjunct commissaris generaal.

– 7442 –

Figure 65. "The Jewelry Ball at the Belgian Pavilion," *L'illustration congolaise* 212 (May 1939), 7442. (KBR)

the United States of the benefits of colonization. From the beginning, questions had arisen as to whether a small country could—and should—govern an enormous territory more than seventy-five times its size. From the 1870s onward, Leopold II had consistently cloaked his purely commercial interests in a rhetoric of humanitarianism and scientific progress. These noble claims became increasingly difficult to uphold amid evidence of serious abuses under the domanial system he established to increase profits from ivory and wild rubber.

The sophisticated propaganda campaign launched by the Belgian Colonial Commission in New York tried to mask the fact that Americans, and especially African Americans, had been among the earliest and most vocal critics of the Congo. The whitewashing of Leopold II had ensured that his reputation rose in Belgium after his death in 1909, even as his exploits continued to cast a shadow over the country's international reputation.[70] Rather than disputing specific charges, the Colonial Commission sought in 1939 to discredit disgruntled Americans, including African Americans, as ill-informed and incapable of understanding Africa. In a monthly write-up of recent events pertaining to Belgium's colony, the editors of *L'illustration congolaise* reported on De Vleeschauwer's trip to the New York World's Fair. By way of commentary, the editors relayed the challenges facing the Belgians in countering American and especially African American "ignorance." In a move that completely undercut the message of Belgian-American friendship purveyed by the pavilion, the editors condescendingly invoked the trope of American provincialism and simplemindedness. Published only in French, these comments were intended solely for a Belgian audience and lacked the diplomatic veneer that normally was applied to official discourse. They declared, "It's just that, if North Americans have a very poor understanding of Europe, which tires them because it is all too complicated, they have extremely imprecise notions of Africa."[71] The editors singled out midwesterners before taking aim at southerners, "the majority of whom are black." These comments especially undercut the work of Protestant African American missionaries, who traveled to Africa and worked directly with local populations; their success in interacting with the Congolese, along with their effectiveness in documenting abuses, had caught the attention of the Belgian state, which responded by restricting the number of Congolese visas accorded to African Americans.[72] These racist measures were part of a larger attempt on the part of the Belgian state to protect their

Catholic missions and to bolster white supremacy. American Protestant churches adhered to Belgium's restrictions, as they sought to ensure a role in the Congo for their own precarious operations.

L'illustration congolaise's editors targeted the Pan-African movement as well, by charging African Americans with racial essentialism that conflated Africans with African Americans: "Their idea of the black primitive is of a kind of black American with less clothing, whereas the latter has principally American reflexes, modified by a black brain."[73] The efforts of Marcus Garvey were alluded to in the editor's invocation of the misguided actions of "seasoned militants," who were incapable of understanding the "indigenous mentality" and the "reality of Congolese Blacks," which allegedly remained entirely foreign to them. "American blacks," claimed the editors, "have become, in a psychological sense, strangers to Africa." The editors then engaged in their own form of racial essentialism by characterizing southern African Americans as essentially incapable of understanding Africa. As proof, the editors referred to discussions of colonialism with leaders of the Pan-African movement in the United States, whose "scarce" knowledge was "based on the propaganda of yesterday." Such misconceptions, they continued, explain the absurdity of political ideas related to the Congo in the United States, not just among Black but also white populations.[74] These comments pointed to an enormous gulf separating the Belgian fair commissioners from their American audiences.

To bypass these areas of controversy and identify areas of mutual interest, the Colonial Commission included a vitrine of African art (fig. 66) in the Colonial Section and published a brochure addressed to American audiences. Despite its decision to emphasize the colony's modernization over its traditional arts and cultures, the Ministry of Colonies recognized the value that these objects held for Americans, and especially African Americans associated with the Harlem Renaissance.[75] The appeal to African Americans was a half-hearted attempt; although the center of this vibrant modern art movement was located only ten miles away from the fairgrounds, its accomplishments were poorly represented in "The World of Tomorrow." In the end, the arts of the Congolese were better represented than those of African Americans at the fair, where the Colonial Section featured some sixty "native art" objects drawn from private collections and the Royal Museum of Central Africa at Tervuren. Following display practices at the Royal Museum, located just outside of Brussels, pieces appeared without any identifying information, but a few can be identi-

Figure 66. Colonial Section, Belgian Pavilion, 1939 New York World's Fair. Vitrine of "Native Arts" from Belgian collections. Léon Stynen designed the interior. (© AML [Archives et Musée de la Littérature])

fied from period photographs. These include a *ndop,* or royal, figurative sculpture of a Bushongo king from the Kuba kingdom (fig. 67) and a Female Mboko Bowl Bearer (fig. 68) used by royal diviners in the Luba kingdom, alongside numerous carved wooden statues, vessels, ornamental textiles, and implements.[76]

A brochure entitled *Native Arts & Craftsmanship in Belgian Congo* accompanied this display and addressed common points of reference among Belgian and American art enthusiasts. In his capacity as founder and president of the Commission for the Protection of Indigenous Arts, the brochure's coauthor Gaston Denys Périer was the principal motor behind the promotion of colonial art in Belgium in the interwar years. Art, he believed, could instill a love for the colony and a yearning for its expansiveness and exoticism, qualities he calculated would have equal appeal to Americans. Périer's handsomely illustrated brochure underscored the importance and sophistication of visual imagery to cultures that did not develop a form of

Figure 67. *Ndop* sculpture of a Bushongo king from the Kasai region. Wood, 56 x 24 x 24 cm. RMCA Tervuren. (EO.0.0.27655, collection RMCA Tervuren; photo R. Asselberghs, CC-BY 4.0)

writing. He referred to the objects in terms of "art" rather than ethnography, noting admiringly that "if [African art] is still included in the category of 'primitive arts,' it holds first place there."[77] Moreover, he articulated how the "pure plastics," or formal logic, of African sculpture "equals and sometimes surpasses that of classic productions of the West."[78] Indigenous weaving, basketry, pottery, and wood carving came in for praise for their "abstract and inventive qualities," which, freed from "servile model copying," lend the works a "lyric sense."[79]

As a highly educated Belgian civil servant, Périer went to significant lengths to ground his account of Congolese art in authoritative texts familiar to U.S. audiences.

Figure 68. Female Mboko Bowl Bearer from the Katanga province. Wood, 46.5 x 22 x 26.4 cm. RMCA Tervuren. (EO.0.0.14358, collection RMCA Tervuren; photo J.-M. Vandyck, CC-BY 4.0 [PRO_01])

For example, his appreciation of Congolese sculpture featured a lengthy quotation from English art historian and critic Roger Fry's influential account of African sculpture. Fry was the foremost anglophone writer on modern art before Clement Greenberg. Although other influential accounts of African art existed, such as those by German art historian Carl Einstein and French gallerist Paul Guillaume, Périer quoted Fry because he was an accepted authority in New York. Before making his name by mounting the exhibit "Édouard Manet and the Post-Impressionists" (1910–11) at the Grafton Gallery in London, Fry had served as curator of modern European painting at the Metropolitan Museum of Art. His articulate writings on modern art, Renaissance painting, and African sculpture, beginning in 1910, shaped the twentieth-century discourse on art in the United States.[80] Périer cited at length Fry's account of "Negro sculpture" as among the world's most powerful visual expressions:

> We have the habit of thinking that the power to create expressive plastic form is one of the greatest of human achievements, and the names of great sculptors are handed down from generation to generation, so that it seems unfair to be forced to admit that certain nameless savages have possessed this power not only in a higher degree than we at this moment, but than we as a nation have ever possessed it.[81]

Fry's reference to "nameless savages" notwithstanding, Périer was among the more progressive interpreters of Congolese art in Belgium. His account of African art improved on that of the Royal Museum of Central Africa of the 1920s, which had emphasized the helplessness of the Congolese prior to European contact. Périer's arguments would help shape Museum policies after World War II, when its director Frans M. Olbrechts—following studies with Franz Boas at Columbia University in New York—came to emphasize the role of the individual artist within African culture in his scholarship and museological displays.[82]

Périer's account was closer to that of leading African Americans, including Alain Locke, doyen of the Harlem Renaissance and professor of philosophy at Howard University. In his influential essay "The Legacy of the Ancestral Arts," which appeared in his pathbreaking anthology *The New Negro* (1925), Locke presented Africa as "one of the great fountain sources of the arts of decoration and design."[83] Locke quoted the same essay by Fry on African sculpture in which the critic admitted "that some of these things are great sculpture—greater [. . .] than anything we produced in the Middle Ages." Locke further endorsed Fry's claims that

> they have indeed complete plastic freedom, that is to say, these African artists really can see form in three dimensions. Now this is rare in sculpture. . . . So—far from the clinging to two dimensions, as we tend to do, the African artist actually underlines, as it were, the three-dimensionalness of his forms. It is in some such way that he manages to give to his forms their disconcerting vitality,

> the suggestion that they make of being not mere echoes of actual figures, but of possessing an inner life of their own.[84]

African art offered a key example of what Fry termed "significant form," a concept he had developed in his appreciation of "Post-Impressionism" beginning in 1910. However, unlike Fry, who appreciated the importance of African sculpture for modern European art, Locke perceived how the study of African sculpture could empower African Americans to reconnect with their "ancestral traditions" as a means of formulating their own modern, urban, and American voice and means of expression.

Beyond Congolese art's formal sophistication, Périer identified its symbolic import. For example, the sculpture of a Bushongo king exhibited in the Colonial Section belonged to a genre representing the ideal characteristics of a specific ruler. Certain features of the sculpture were generalized, such as the flat, rectangular headdress, the seated, cross-legged position, the left hand holding a weapon, the neck ring, shoulder hoops, and smooth polished surface rubbed with palm oil. Within these conventions, individual rulers were identified by a small emblem, or *ibol,* at the base of the sculpture. The portrait of Mikope Mbula, from the collection of Belgium's Royal Museum of Central Africa, for instance, depicts a freed slave in front of the base, whereas the king Bope Pelenge, depicted in the sculpture at the British Museum, sits beside an anvil, which testifies to his activity as an iron worker.[85] These effigies were kept in the king's quarters with other sculptures believed to be endowed with royal authority. When the ruler was absent from the capital, the *ndop* was rubbed with oil and served as his surrogate, and the statues were believed to preserve the spirit of a king after his death. Such historical and cultural details were available to viewers in the brochure accompanying the display at the colonial pavilion, through which Belgian officials sought to bridge the considerable cultural gulf between Belgium and the United States.

Yet even as they agreed on the aesthetic criteria and symbolic import of Congolese sculpture, Périer and Locke disagreed about their political ramifications. Beginning in the early twentieth century, African American artists and intellectuals developed an independent appreciation of African Art that allied it to an explicitly anti-colonial and anti-imperial agenda, as evidenced in William Sheppard's collection. Over the course of his missionary work in the Congo, the ardent critic of King Leopold II and the Belgian Congo administration amassed *the* leading early collection of Kuba art, whose importance superseded even those of Hungarian collector Emil Torday and German collector Leo Frobenius. Sheppard's collection consisted of Kuba textiles, spears, knives, and other ceremonial objects he collected or received through his close contacts with native populations and the royal court at Mushenge. There he recognized the significance of *ndop* statues but refrained from collecting them, as opposed to Torday, who acquired several important statues for the British Museum. In his selection and presentation of objects, Sheppard resisted the colonial codification of African art. Not only British colonizers, but also Leopold II acquired cultural artefacts as a means of asserting control over local populations and representing colonial rule at home through the display of native artefacts.[86] The conquest was both physical and spiritual, a fact particularly evident in the sequestration of Bushongo king's effigies in European museums. By contrast, Sheppard conceived of his collection as a "counter-archive" to oppose colonial and imperialist propaganda alleging the racial inferiority of Africans.[87] The student newspaper of Shepherd's alma mater, the Hampton Institute (now Hampton University) reported in 1911 how Sheppard, after recounting "the story of his trial by the Belgian Government for telling the truth about some of the cruelties and atrocities practiced against the natives by the Kasai Rubber Company, whose stock is controlled by the Belgian Government," immediately thereafter showed them "many curiosities from Africa. . . . The cloth he showed, woven by them on their looms, was most extraordinary."[88] The article was published the very year that Sheppard donated his collection to Hampton, where it would occupy a central place in the curriculum.

Similar ambitions motivated Locke, who as a Rhodes scholar in the first decade of the twentieth century visited African collections in European museums. In 1925, Locke tried to acquire Belgian diplomat Raoul Blondiau's collection of Congolese art for a proposed Harlem Museum of African Art. Although his efforts were thwarted in the short term by white American collectors including Albert Barnes, Locke succeeded in exhibiting the collection at the 135th Street branch of the New York Public Library, the precursor to the Schomburg Center for Research in Black Culture.[89] Like Sheppard, Locke and his associates in Harlem and at Howard University allied the "ancestral arts" to the cause of African Americans' intellectual, economic, and political empowerment. Their accounts were well known to Belgian colonial officials, who assembled the vitrine of Congolese art in the Colonial Section to pacify their American critics and find common ground.

The enormous resources and preparation Belgium had placed in service of its national pavilion paid off, resulting in a steady stream of visitors, even as there is scant evidence that the displays—even of Congolese art—changed the hearts and minds of colonial resistors. In late September Belgium became the first country to agree to stay for a second season, despite early concern about whether it could shoulder the costs at a time when the outbreak of World War II had already engulfed Poland, which Germany had invaded on the first day of that month.[90] Having welcomed six million visitors in the fair's first season, the Belgians, despite making preparations for war, hoped to add a display of lace-making, complete with bringing over female artisans from Belgium to show off their skills. Others stateside, however, questioned how the fair had been organized and the place they had been allotted within it.

African Americans at the Fair

The cover of the April 1939 issue of *The Crisis,* published by the NAACP, featured a photograph of a plaster model of a sculpture entitled *Lift Every Voice and Sing.*[91] Also known as *The Harp,* this work by Augusta Savage was named after the song of that name, which served as an unofficial African American national anthem. Its lyrics were written by Savage's friend, the poet James Weldon Johnson, and set to music by his brother, the composer John Rosamond Johnson, both of whom were, like Savage herself, luminaries of the Harlem Renaissance. The sculpture was specially commissioned to be displayed in the Palace of Contemporary Art at the 1939 Fair, where its depiction of pillar-like young choristers supported on an extended, monumental arm offered compelling evidence of African American talent in both the visual and musical arts. Savage's sculpture was so popular that it was issued as a postcard that demonstrated the monumental presence of the tall, rigid forms of choristers doubling as harp strings (fig. 69). She was one of only two African American artists chosen to present their work. An article in the same issue of *The Crisis* featured the other prominent African American contribution to the fair. A six-minute "symphonic poem with choral finale" by the composer William Grant Still "form[ed] the background and emotional climax" for the "Democracity" exhibition housed in the Perisphere.[92]

There were nonetheless clear limits to African American participation at the fair. The prominent size and location of Savage's sculpture compensated, in part,

Figure 69. Souvenir postcard of *Lift Every Voice and Sing (The Harp)*, Augusta Savage, 1939, as seen on display in the courtyard of the Contemporary Arts Pavilion, New York World's Fair, 1939. The original sculpture was painted plaster, 16 feet high, and was destroyed at the conclusion of the fair. Small, 10 ½ in. bronze replicas of it cast in 1939 as souvenirs persist in public and private collections. (Schomburg Center for Research in Black Culture, Art and Artifacts Division, The New York Public Library)

for the lateness of the commission, as fair officials had contacted the sculptor only at the last minute in an attempt to palliate the public outcry over the absence of African American achievements from the fair's displays—and this at the height of the Harlem Renaissance! Savage's sculpture remained a plaster painted to resemble basalt; she was never able to raise the money to cast it in bronze, and the plaster was eventually destroyed. Miniature metal replicas of it cast during the fair as souvenirs prolonged its life and testify to its wide appeal.[93] This was not the first time Savage had faced the discrimination typically meted out to talented African Americans. In 1923, an offer of a scholarship to study in Paris was withdrawn by a committee that included Whitney Warren, the architect of the University of Leuven's library, and James Gamble Rogers, who designed many of the interwar buildings on the campus of Yale University, because she would have sailed and studied alongside young white women from the South.[94] The composer William Grant Still had received his commission only because the competition had been entirely anonymous.

Despite these headwinds, across the country African Americans joined their fellow citizens in being fascinated by the fair. As far away as the small community of Mileston, Mississippi, an African American teacher drew the striking silhouettes of the Trylon and the Perisphere on the chalk board for the edification of the students in her under-equipped, segregated classroom. Her students may also have glimpsed the remarkable structures in newsreels that they would have watched from the balconies of segregated movie theaters (fig. 70). African Americans, particularly residents of Harlem, remained incensed however, that the few jobs they had been allotted were mostly menial.

The *Pittsburgh Courier* reported with disgust that porter positions were allotted only to "the darkest and the funniest candidates." The *Courier* also noted that Harlem politician William T. Andrews had declared on the floor of the New York State Assembly "that if the Fair's slogan, 'The World of Tomorrow' was fairly illustrated by its employment attitude toward the Negro, then there is no hope for Democracy in America."[95] The most notorious instance of discrimination involved a graduate of the Carnegie Institute of Technology in Pittsburgh, who was initially offered a post as a receptionist rather than as a draftsman.[96] The *New York Age* noted in February 1938 that the application for employment form contained "a box wherein the applicant designates whether he is 'white or Negro,'" which it labeled "an open admission of discrimination."[97] Adam Clayton Powell Jr., who had recently replaced his father in the pulpit of Harlem's Abyssinian Baptist Church and who was later elected to Congress, led protests at the Empire State building. These led to a slight increase in the numbers hired, but they remained in mostly menial positions, and African Americans picketed the fair's opening day.[98]

African Americans also protested that they had not been featured prominently enough in either the displays or the accompanying program of entertainment. As Mabel Wilson has described, "antiblack racism limited access to the key areas of

Figure 70. A teacher in Mileston, Mississippi, explains the Trylon and Perisphere to her students, Marion Post Wollcott, 1939. (Schomburg Center for Research in Black Culture, Photographs and Prints Division, The New York Public Library)

American society that the mainstream world's fairs celebrated: the ability to exercise full rights of citizenship in a democratic republic and the right to earn wages as laborers in the wage economy." Nevertheless, African Americans had for decades fought hard to participate in such events.[99] In 1895 Booker T. Washington delivered his famous "Atlanta Compromise" speech on the grounds of the Cotton States and International Exhibition, in which he advocated for manual over liberal arts education as the path to economic progress. African Americans had also organized their own alternative exhibitions, marking the progress made since Emancipation. Two exhibits, held in Chicago and Detroit in 1940, were intended to counter the degree to which African Americans had been largely excluded from "The World of Tomorrow."[100]

Although segregation was officially banned on the Flushing Meadows fairgrounds, African Americans often felt insufficiently welcome when they attended.

Few hotels in New York would admit them. The *Pittsburgh Courier* reported that racial segregation at the fair was so extensive that even the West Indian subjects of the British king and queen who came to the fair to see George VI and his wife Elizabeth were not allowed to join the audience for their majesties.[101] While there is little to suggest that this discrimination bothered exhibitors, and certainly not the Belgians, this history of exclusion would make the eventual transfer of much of their pavilion to the historically Black Virginia Union University particularly poignant.

The highlight of African American participation at the fair came only midway through its second season when the organizers designated July 23 to 28 as "Negro Week."[102] Although not all African Americans regarded it as a sufficient substitute for a prominent exhibition displaying their social, economic, and political achievements, it did provide an opportunity for them to be recognized in ways that extended beyond the entertainment offered by "The Hot Mikado," where, according to the *New York Age,* "the golden vestments of Bill Robinson [are] attracting all the sightseers"; the paper's columnist Floyd Snelson described the tap dancer, better known as "Bojangles" Robinson, as "our most exquisite showman." Negro Week also featured African Americans who more overtly challenged the status quo.[103] A wall of honor "show[ing] how greatly the Negro has added to the cultural and material wealth of the country" included the painter Henry Ossawa Tanner and the architect Paul R. Williams, alongside such political figures as Henry Highland Garnet and Blanche K. Bruce.[104] W. E. B. Du Bois was among the speakers. The finale was a meeting of the National Council of Negro Women at which its president, Mary McLeod Bethune, led an audience of eight hundred in honoring a group of women who included Savage and the jazz singer Ethel Waters, and also Marian Anderson, who had given her celebrated concert on the steps of the Lincoln Memorial the year before, after being excluded from a segregated venue. Sadie Alexander, the first African American woman to receive a PhD in economics and a prominent lawyer in Philadelphia, also figured among the honorees.

When the New York World's Fair finally closed on October 27, 1940, the United States was still more than a full year away from entering the conflict raging in Europe, Asia, and Africa. In its most popular attractions, such as Futurama, "The World of Tomorrow" presented the future for which its citizens were to mobilize at home and soldiers were to fight abroad. In place of this consumer-driven prosperity, the Belgian Pavilion presented a picture of continuity and stability quite different from the nation's actual experiences in 1940 in particular. The building showcased a measured modernism, in which craft and the representation of the human figure still had a place, as did the exploitation of colonial subjects. In the aftermath of the conflict it would prove challenging to maintain this balance, with African American and Congolese claims for political empowerment ushering in an entirely different political and cultural landscape. The bones of the Belgian Pavilion would make an unexpected contribution to this future, one that would be at times at odds with much of its original purpose at "The World of Tomorrow."

3

DIPLOMACY AND PROPAGANDA AT THE PAVILION AFTER THE FALL OF BELGIUM

On May 10, 1940, the German army invaded Belgium. A photograph shows Belgian commissioner general Joseph Gevaert and deputy commissioner General Jan-Albert Goris tensely listening to the news on the radio in the Belgian Pavilion (fig. 71). The pavilion immediately became a potent symbol of resistance. The next day seventy-five thousand people visited it, as the *New York Times* put it, to "pay their respects to the little nation and express their sympathy over the Nazi invasion." Belgian supporters included most notably New York governor Herbert Lehman, who was accompanied by his wife, their son, and her mother. In an interview, Gevaert declared that the Belgians had "just begun to fight." He declared, "But do not think for one moment that Belgium will be defeated. The army and the people of Belgium are not lost. We can check the invasion and with the help of the Allies thrust back the Nazis who have invaded our country."[1]

Gevaert's optimism proved sadly misplaced. Certain defeat at the Battle of Dunkirk led King Leopold III of Belgium to surrender to Nazi Germany, against the wishes of Prime Minister Hubert Pierlot and his cabinet members, who had urged him to leave the country and continue to fight alongside Belgium's allies France and Britain. Pierlot and French prime minister Paul Reynaud vilified Leopold's action, while British prime minister Winston Churchill denounced his surrender

Figure 71. Belgian officials Joseph Gevaert and Jan-Albert Goris listen to radio news in the Belgian Pavilion opposite a painted portrait of Leopold III, May 1940. (Manuscripts and Archives Division, The New York Public Library)

in a speech to the House of Commons on June 4, 1940, prompting the British press to label Leopold the "Traitor King."

The king's surrender and Belgium's ensuing constitutional crisis caused shock waves that reverberated across the Atlantic, with the Belgian Pavilion, which closed for three days while officials tried to figure out what to do next, emerging as a site of anti-royalist demonstrations.[2] The *New York Times* reported in early June how Marcel Rau's sculpted marble bust of Leopold III in the pavilion's Reception Room had become a focus of protest, provoking the "jeers" of fairgoers denouncing the "treasonous" king (fig. 72).[3] Sensing a mounting crisis, the Belgian ambassador to Washington, Count Van der Straten-Ponthoz, recommended discretely removing the offending sculpture after the building's nightly closure. However, its stealthy disappearance only intensified concerns, especially as the king's monogram remained embedded in the room's inlaid wooden ceiling. With Gevaert suspected of royal-

Figure 72. Marcel Rau's sculpted marble bust of Leopold III, as exhibited in the Belgian Pavilion's Reception Room, New York World's Fair, 1939, Photograph by Robert E. Coates, Obj-0011987. (Flanders Architecture Institute—collection of the Flemish Government, archive of Léon Stynen)

ist sympathies, Goris stepped in to realign the pavilion's reporting structure, away from the king to Pierlot's exile government in London. Pierlot joined Albert de Vleeschauwer, minister of the colonies, in entering the war on the side of the Allies; together they mobilized their full resources, especially those of the Belgian Congo, in the Allied war effort.[4]

The Belgian Pavilion remained open until October 27, when the fair finally closed. The building's fate—it became the most prominent structure from the fair to be reconstituted elsewhere when the site was cleared—emerged out of the specific circumstances in which the government in exile found itself. These included the London government's continued, if somewhat nominal, control of the Belgian Congo and its good standing with the U.S. government. These good relations, combined with Goris's skill, culminated in the alleged "gift" of the pavilion's parts to Virginia Union University, a historically Black institution in Richmond, an "offering" that it was hoped would ameliorate suspicions in the United States, and especially among African Americans, about empire in general and Belgium's in particular.

The Congo in World War II

Despite assiduous planning, none of the government officials could have predicted the importance that the Belgian Pavilion—especially its Colonial Section—would gain upon Germany's invasion of Belgium in May 1940. The political, religious, and racial tensions surrounding Belgium's colonization of the Congo temporarily receded as Belgium was overtaken by the German army. Anti-colonial critiques of Belgium persisted into the war years and beyond, but these were largely replaced by general sympathy for Belgium's wartime plight and a growing awareness of the threat posed by fascism, except among dissenting African Americans.[5] With Belgium under German military occupation for the second time in a little over twenty years, diplomatic and international relations associated with the Belgian Pavilion focused less on the Applied and Industrial Art Section and more on the Colonial Section representing the remaining free Belgian territory. Geopolitical stakes were matched by American commercial, and eventually military, interests in Belgium's resource-rich colony, whose importance would rise in 1942, when Allied colonial possessions in Malaysia and the Dutch East Indies fell to the Japanese.

On July 8, 1940, De Vleeschauwer, Belgium's minister of the colonies, changed the course of the war when he aligned the Belgian Congo with Great Britain.[6] This extraordinary and farsighted decision was enabled by Pierlot's Decree of June 18, 1940, elevating De Vleeschauwer to the rank of administrator general with both executive and legislative powers over the Belgian Congo and Rwanda-Urundi (now Burundi).[7] This decree meant that De Vleeschauwer could unilaterally govern the Belgian Congo, to the point of changing its founding charter or declaring war, without the approval of the Belgian parliament, king, or the council of ministers, whose authority had been suspended following Germany's invasion. These privileges allowed him to act decisively during the summer of 1940, when Belgium's government fell into disarray, with its king imprisoned and its ministers and government officials desperately seeking refuge in France, Portugal, and England. Amid this chaos, De Vleeschauwer met in London with Churchill, who recognized him as a legal delegate of the Belgian government.[8] Churchill had an interest in negotiating with De Vleeschauwer, as Great Britain placed paramount importance on keeping the Congo out of German hands. De Vleeschauwer agreed to supply Britain with resources from the Congo in exchange for wartime protections. In the coming years, the Congo would prove to be one of the Allies' major arsenals, as well as an important base for military operations. Belgium also courted the United States, first in 1939–40 as a friendly, politically neutral trading partner. The efforts of the government in exile to secure its support became more overt and intense after the Japanese bombing of Pearl Harbor in December 1941, which brought the United States into the war on the Allies' side.

Belgium's importance was not lost to the United States; beginning in the fall of 1939, ships from the Congo began arriving in New York with greater frequency. The British and French had placed a naval blockade around Germany that impeded shipping traffic between the Congo and Belgium. Cargo checks at French and British ports, combined with a growing list of trade restrictions, led then-neutral Belgium to seek commercial markets outside Europe.[9] In September 1939, one month before the closing of the World's Fair's first season, Edgar Sengier, director of the Belgian mining company Mining Union of Upper-Katanga, relocated to New York and began seeking U.S. contracts for the processing and sale of copper from his mines, which his company was no longer allowed to ship to Antwerp. In June 1940, Sengier made contact with American atomic engineers; following this meeting, he began transferring uranium from his company's mines in Katanga to a storage site on Staten Island. It would take the U.S. military two years to renew contacts with Sengier, who reported to Georges Theunis, special envoy in New York, in April 1942 that "Uranium has very recently acquired a very significant importance in the eyes of the American authorities and they have asked how quickly our mines in Congo will recover, can be put into operation."[10] These inquiries led to Congolese uranium—by far the richest uranium ore in the world—fueling the top-secret Manhattan Project and the entire U.S. nuclear program throughout the 1950s.[11]

Jan-Albert Goris: Propagandist for Belgium

Although Belgians were not privy to the secrets of the Manhattan Project, representatives of Belgium's government-in-exile were keenly aware of the importance of gaining support for their cause in the United States. Goris would play a key role in this effort and also in postwar Belgian propaganda campaigns. The eighteen months that separated the invasion of Belgium from the Japanese attack on Pearl Harbor were particularly crucial. At a time when many in the United States opposed becoming entangled in the conflict raging across Europe, not to mention Asia and Africa, it was important to present Belgium in the best possible light, especially in view of Leopold III's hasty capitulation and alleged rumors about Belgian civilian complicity with the German military occupation.

Negotiations over war materials were of utmost importance, but the role that cultural, or "soft," diplomacy played in the war effort cannot be overestimated. Goris led a dual existence as Jan-Albert Goris (his given name) and Marnix Gijsen (his pseudonym). He was both writer and civil servant, a poet in the Catholic tradition and atheist, a Flemish nationalist and U.S. resident for twenty years.[12] These contradictions were embraced by Goris, whose novels—including the critically acclaimed *Het boek van Joachim van Babylon* (1947)—recount the struggles of a first-person narrator who wrestles with his faith, sexuality, and morality and with the duty of being a good citizen. In 1974 he was awarded the Dutch Literature Prize, the highest literary award a writer could obtain in the Low Countries. Government work allowed Goris a temporary reprieve from his ceaseless questioning, and his managerial abilities and sure command of languages led him to advance from positions in the Antwerp city administration to Philip van Isacker's cabinet at the Ministry of Economic Affairs in Brussels. Goris's cultural connections and diplomatic skills caused Van Isacker to appoint him secretary to the Technical Committee for the 1937 International Exposition in Paris, and his success in Paris in turn led to his appointment as deputy commissioner general for the Belgian Pavilion in New York.

These experiences nourished Goris's interest in modern design and architecture.[13] In Brussels he lived in one of a bold pair of fifteen-story apartment blocks designed in 1934 by Raphael Verwilghen and Jean-Jules Eggericx, instructors at La Cambre who collaborated with van de Velde on the design of the Belgian Pavilion in Paris in 1937.[14] Goris's presence in design meetings for the New York building is documented in photographs (fig. 23). Although his responsibility to enforce deadlines and balance budgets occasioned some conflicts with van de Velde in the installation of displays in the Belgian Pavilion prior to its opening, Goris smoothed things over upon the architect's departure, pledging his "sympathy and admiration" for his work, which was "in every respect perfect and worthy of our homeland."[15] The stresses accompanying Goris's position were counterbalanced by the privilege of working in offices at 630 Fifth Avenue, otherwise known as the International Building and a part of Rockefeller Center. The Belgian government spared no expense in appointing its offices with stylish furniture manufactured by Belgium's esteemed De Coene firm.

As deputy commissioner, Goris mobilized his considerable literary and administrative abilities to promote a positive image of Belgium, including burnishing its reputation as a colonial power. After the important humanitarian food relief effort coordinated by Herbert Hoover during World War I, Belgium had faded from public view in the United States. Goris's job was formidable, but so too was his resolve. He was both grateful to the United States and dedicated to advancing Belgium's interests abroad, a commitment that he approached with renewed conviction following Germany's invasion in May 1940. Although he would privately acknowledge that Belgium's days as a colonial power were numbered, his private views did not keep him from fulfilling his public duties garnering support for Belgium's "civilizing mission."[16] Furthermore, the cynical side of Goris relished undercutting the moral pretense of anti-colonialism by recalling the U.S. history of slavery and imperialism and the ongoing racial inequalities it enforced in many states through Jim Crow legislation. During the war, Belgian colonial propaganda would occupy an increasing amount of Goris's attention, as the fate of Belgium depended to a large degree on the full mobilization of the Congo, which Belgium sought to defend not only from Germany but also from the encroaching demands of the Allied powers.

The Liquidation of the Pavilion

Not least among Goris's brilliant and Machiavellian maneuvers was his orchestration of the Belgian Pavilion's sale to Virginia Union University, where it became known as the Belgium Friendship Building or simply the Belgian Building. As the already-prolonged fair was coming to an end in October 1940, the Belgian government in exile found itself in a bind, having no budget for the building's dismantling and yet being under contractual obligation to the heavily indebted New York Fair Committee to remove the building and all its components from the grounds of Flushing Meadows within ninety days of the fair's closing. In a letter dated October 17 to the Belgian ambassador in Washington, Van der Straten-Ponthoz, Goris spelled out two possible courses of action: one would be to proceed with the pavilion's dismantling as planned and to sell its materials, which the American government had barred from returning to Occupied Belgium.[17] However, this plan faced certain difficulties, as Goris estimated that the costs of dismantling the building alone would run over $20,000; in addition, import duties in the amount of $15,000 must be paid, as all the building materials to be sold originated in Belgium. It was unlikely, Goris reasoned, that these costs could be covered through the sale of the materials. With the Belgian government already $70,000 in debt to the construction company Debusschere-Tedesco for unpaid bills related to the ongoing maintenance on the pavilion since October 1939, it was unlikely that the company would agree to disassemble the building without prior payment. Furthermore, the government would need to compensate Debusschere-Tedesco for the loss of the building materials, which had been promised the company in 1939 as part of its compensation.

For these reasons, Goris suggested a second and preferrable course of action: the sale of the standing pavilion. The building, Goris reasoned, could be easily transformed into a place of instruction, and its acquisition could even be considered a windfall for a college or university. In effect, the buyer would acquire a building that cost upward of $700,000 for the price of $300,000. He broke down the sale price as follows: $40,000 to dismantle the building with the intention of reconstruction, $200,000 to reconstruct it, $20,000 to reimburse Debusschere-Tedesco for the loss of construction materials, plus the cost of transporting three thousand tons at approximately $10 per ton, depending on the distance and mode of transport. To avoid paying import duties, Goris proposed that the Belgian embassy could ask the State Department in Washington for authorization to repossess the building, which would allow the embassy to arrange for the "donation" of the building to a religious or scientific institution. In this way, a sale could be repackaged as a "gift" to avoid customs duties. The second solution, Goris concluded, was the only one that would allow the Commissariat General to honor its obligations to the fair committee and the construction company. In addition, it was the only course of action that would shield the Commissariat General from litigation and hefty penalties, should it fail to remove the pavilion. Goris reminded the ambassador that the World's Fair would incur a fine of $300,000 if it did not clear Flushing Meadows within ninety days of the closing, a cost that would no doubt be passed on to the offending parties.

A few points bear observing related to Goris's calculations. First, there is no mention of Van Isacker's original plan to return the pavilion to Belgium, where it would house a state-sponsored institute to support Belgian applied arts and manufacturing. Goris's correspondence reveals that the original plan to convert the pavilion from a temporary to a permanent structure had never been developed. Instead, the Belgian government had formed a partnership with Belgian construction companies and manufacturers to save money on the pavilion and its contents. Beyond Debusschere-

Tedesco's ownership of the building materials, the carillon manufacturer Marcel Michiels of Tournai possessed half the value of the carillon.[18] Even though Goris was aware of these financial arrangements, he misleadingly and duplicitously continued to refer to the pavilion's planned reconstruction in Belgium in his dealings with the Americans. He never publicly acknowledged the Belgian government's termination of that program in 1938 and instead presented the pavilion as a permanent structure whose reconstruction in Belgium had only been canceled by Germany's invasion and military occupation.

Since 1940, the "gift" of the Belgian Pavilion has been heralded as a generous gesture of peace and good will, but official and personal Belgian correspondence from the time reveals that the "gift" was in fact a sale that saved the Commissariat General from bankruptcy. When $9,000 sent by De Vleeschauwer from the Belgian Congo to cover the costs of dismantling the Colonial Section failed to arrive in the chaotic month following the German invasion of Belgium, the Belgian ambassador in Washington, Van der Straten-Ponthoz, authorized that $3,000 from his discretionary funds be put toward the building's liquidation.[19] However, these emergency funds sent on June 25 were inadequate, so that on July 1, 1940, the Colonial Commission gave the commissioner general authority over the Colonial Section.[20] On July 17, 1940, De Vleeschauwer sent a telegram to the commissioner general authorizing the sale of the pavilion, carillon, and its contents "to benefit Belgian interests."[21] By this time, however, General Commissioner Gevaert was out of the picture, having ceded his responsibilities to Goris following his fall from grace in May 1940.[22] Goris stepped in to fill the void in leadership, a task that nourished both parts of himself, the civil servant who honored contractual obligations and the cynic who unscrupulously turned an impossible situation to his advantage. Goris wrote to the Belgian minister Frans van Cauwelaert at the beginning of the process: "I try to sell everything here and I succeed: liquidate the carillon (to Galpin-Hoover), masses of gingerbread (to Roosens and Co.), silverware and ceramics, chasubles and books. It looks like a department store, and I hope that at last the spirit of the trade takes hold of me."[23] By October he had gained confidence in his newfound abilities, as he marveled in a letter to his brother René: "I still do budget acrobatics and I succeed to my own astonishment. I've even gotten to the point, brother, that I'm also starting to understand accounting and take pleasure in things that previously seemed Egyptian to me."[24]

To raise the necessary funds, Goris-the-salesman divided the building into discrete sales opportunities. The carillon—consisting of thirty-five bronze bells suspended from an oak framework, along with its keyboard, pedals, and electrically operated steel drum—was sold to the Hoover Institute on October 1, 1940, for $15,000, plus the cost of dismantling, shipping, and reinstalling the carillon.[25] The bells were shipped out of New York in November 1940 and installed at the Hoover Tower on the campus of Stanford University in 1941.[26] Even today, the transfer of the bells continues to be heralded as a gesture promoting world peace, but in practical terms it was a sale allowing the Commissariat General to honor its contractual obligations to the Belgian manufacturer.

A similar dynamic unfolded with the sale of the pavilion to Virginia Union University. In searching for a worthy, tax-exempt buyer for the standing Belgian Pavilion, Goris in October sought the help of the Association of American Colleges, which contacted some thirty of its member schools, only one of which promised to raise the funds on short notice. This school was Virginia Union University. For William J. Clark, its president, the "generous offer" from the Belgian state appeared too good to be true; as for the Belgian government, the opportunity to "assist" an African American institution advanced its broader aims in ways that even Goris could never have anticipated.

The first conversations about the pavilion's transfer to Virginia Union date to late October 1940, when Virginia Union was the only school to respond to the call put out by the Association of American Colleges. Pressed for time, Goris's office followed up immediately with Clark on October 22 to provide details of the building.

> Dear Dr. Clark:
>
> On behalf of Dr. Goris, I wish to thank you for your inquiry, and note that you are interested in our proposition about the Belgian Pavilion at the New York World's Fair. I am glad to give you hereafter some details on this buildings [*sic*].
>
> The total area is about 80,000 square ft. on the first floor and about 16,000 square feet on the second floor. As a school it accommodates 900 students in 30 modern classrooms of 24′ x 26′—it has a large gymnasium 78′ x 52′—general laboratories and offices—a huge library with reading and study gallery 120′ long—a movie theater with 300 seats—an assembly hall with balcony 105′ x

58′ in black marble. The general layout of the building on a plot 350′ x 170′ is on three sides round a large patio, finished on the fourth side by a covered colonnade.

Several points bear mentioning. First, in attempting to sell the building, Goris's office misrepresented it as an already converted school building complete with modern classrooms, library, and gymnasium. Interestingly, no mention is made of the bell tower, but the offer clearly included some luxury items, such as the expanses of black marble. Although the cost of constructing the building in 1939 was $700,000, Goris's office estimated the price of its dismantling, shipping, and rebuilding to amount to $260,000.[27]

The deal moved quickly, with Goris reporting progress of the sale in his personal correspondence to his brother on November 3, 1940: "I succeeded in pressing a college in Virginia so hard," he boasted, "they agreed to buy a considerable part of the building."[28] By December, the college had in fact agreed to purchase the three wings of the Belgian Pavilion (the deal still made no explicit mention of the bell tower). Selling the pavilion to Virginia Union University allowed Goris not only to repay the Commissariat General's debts; Debusschere-Tedesco agreed to cede its portion of the demolition materials, so that the Commissariat General made an unexpected $20,000 profit from the sale. To make matters even better, Goris's budgetary acrobatics were reported in Richmond as a generous "gift" in the spirit of international peace and racial uplift to a worthy and striving institution. Goris underscored the deal's symbolic significance to the Belgian ambassador: "The building will be reconstructed in its integrity in an environment that is extremely aware of our 'generosity' and that accords the building's reconstruction an enormous moral import. It has already provoked enthusiastic commentary in the press and has been the occasion for expressions of sympathy which enhance the standing of our country in the hearts of the American public."[29] To the Belgian Ministry of the Colonies, Goris telegrammed a triumphant statement: "Succeeded in having entire building, including the Congo, reconstructed by Richmond University [*sic*] in Virginia, Baptist seminary for negroes. Attribute very large spiritual importance to our gesture and give it sympathetic publicity."[30] Privately, in a letter to his brother René in Antwerp, Goris commented on the deal with Virginia Union, noting, "We are giving them a Greek surprise, a real Trojan Horse."[31]

To understand the significance of Goris's statement, it bears recalling his circumstances in the fall of 1940: Goris was in between jobs, as he had no clear employment prospects after dismantling the Belgian Pavilion. Ultimately his exemplary service in managing the pavilion and its contents would lead to his appointment as director of a newly created Belgian Information Center (BIC) located in the former fair commission's offices. Special envoy Georges Theunis felt that war-torn Belgium needed a propaganda agency in America, especially as the country's image had been damaged by King Leopold III's capitulation. Funded by the Belgian Ministry of Foreign Affairs, the BIC was charged with promoting Belgium's interests in the United States, including its colonial possessions. At first, it was little more than a specialized documentation service that published a weekly four-page newspaper. However, Goris expanded its purview, so that by the end of 1942, the BIC had grown into a small company with three executives, six secretaries, and an errand boy.

A skilled tactician, Goris knew how to mobilize the media to sway public opinion. In addition to broadcasts on U.S. commercial radio stations and well-timed appearances on *The Voice of America,* he founded a weekly, *News from Belgium,* in April 1941 that addressed Belgian exiles and ordinary Americans. The newsletter, whose circulation would reach one hundred thousand copies weekly in 1943, presented an anthology of newspaper clippings published in occupied Belgium, foreign newspaper articles about Belgium, official statements and messages from the Belgian government-in-exile in London, and documents from the underground Belgian resistance.[32] Goris preceded this reportage with pithy and pointed editorials, in which he praised the courage and resistance of everyday Belgian citizens and excoriated those collaborators, the "one per cent of the Belgian population," who handed over free Belgian institutions to the iron fist of the German military occupation.[33] The violence and indignities Belgians endured under the German Occupation were also passionately reported, in addition to workers' and soldiers' perseverance and valiant defense of their fatherland, as he sought to rally his dispersed countrymen and to convince his American readership of the pressing need to liberate Belgium.

Quite a few editorials by Goris defended Belgium's "civilizing mission" in the Congo. In these he addressed American anti-colonialism. The first phase of colonial settlement is always brutal, he acknowledged, and Leopold II's exploits were certainly no worse than U.S. settlers' near extermination of Native Americans. He then drew a clear line of demarcation between early colonization efforts in the Congo, which were largely the work of private hands, and the Belgian Congo under the governance of the Belgian state. Ignoring Sheppard's charges of forced labor in the Kasai region, Goris, who had yet to set foot in the Congo, asserted that "not a single accusation of cruelty or barbarism has been uttered against the Belgians since the Belgian Government took over responsibility for the administration of the Congo in 1908."[34] He went on to present the Belgian colonial administration as a model of good governance that abolished sickness and raised the standard of living for indigenous populations.

Goris approached his work for the Belgian Pavilion and the Belgian Information Center as one continuous mission. In both capacities, he took it as a point of pride to introduce Americans to some of the lesser-known regions and traditions of Belgium, underscoring the distinct contributions and cultural traditions of Flemish and Walloon populations, which were directly threatened by the German invasion and occupation.[35] In an editorial for *News from Belgium,* he waxed poetic describing the Ghent altarpiece (ca. 1432), which had hung for five hundred years in "a small dusty chapel" in Saint Bavo's Church in Ghent. In 1940, the altarpiece fell into German hands for the second time (it had also been seized during World War I). Just as the Belgian people will survive their present ordeal, Goris maintained, so too will the *Adoration of the Mystic Lamb* endure its abduction by Hermann Göring, "for the spirit has always survived brute force." The work, in all its "majesty and beauty," mirrors the Belgian psyche: "Each of [the people of Belgium] felt as if he had painted it. Nobody was in a position to explain its every detail but everybody felt that this compendium of science and art, harmoniously united, was the very symbol of the national soul."[36] The *Adoration of the Mystic Lamb* would have been familiar to fairgoers, as it was the subject of a short film commissioned by the Commissariat General and projected in the Belgian Pavilion's cinema.

This context helps explain Goris's metaphor of the Trojan Horse in his letter to his brother, as he realized that the pavilion's sale was not only a solution to immediate budgetary problems but a powerful source of state propaganda. At issue in December 1940 was the sale of three wings of the pavilion (Hall of Honor, Applied and Industrial Art wings, and Colonial Section). Beneath the veneer of world peace and racial harmony, tensions simmered, however. Goris's report of the ground-breaking ceremony in Richmond drips with irony: "There was a constant and long prayer, and there were a dozen or so speeches, all of them done by pompous pastors, Baptists and Methodists who were guests, there was also a negress [*negerin*] who was almost white, and one of the speakers was so captivated by our generosity that he almost wept. He apparently never heard of the horse of Troja."[37] Goris's patronizing commentary reveals the deep racial, religious, and cultural divides separating him, an atheist, from Richmond's African American Baptist and Masonic communities. Their rituals struck him as both touching and foreign, and he wrote of them as a European ethnologist might write about Congolese natives in the early twentieth century: "They are really lovely people, unusually gentle with each other, and of a slightly comical courtesy, and formality. They are almost as fond of titles as the Flemish, but of course they are more civilized, I mean on the inside."[38]

Goris's sense of cultural superiority led him to present further "gifts" to Virginia Union that the school did not ask for but could not refuse. In his rush to liquidate the pavilion, Goris sent those contents he could not sell into storage at friendly institutions, including the Hoover Institute.[39] Among these unsaleable items were the pavilion's two monumental bas-reliefs: *Belgium at Work* by Oscar Jespers and Henri Puvrez and *Belgian Congo* by Arthur Dupagne, with the latter being an instrument of colonial propaganda showing the moral and material progress white Belgium purportedly introduced into their African colony.[40] The Belgian Information Center would remain in contact with Virginia Union University throughout the Belgian Friendship Building's reconstruction and delayed opening in 1949.

However, Virginia Union was hardly a passive recipient of these unexpected and sometimes unwanted gifts. On 24 May 1949, the very month of the Vann Memorial Tower's dedication, Goris's office sent Virginia Union's president a letter along with materials for a planned-but-never-realized Congo exhibition. Its contents included Belgian colonial propaganda in the form of books, photographs, and maps. Among the items was a series of photographs and a book by Belgian filmmaker André Cauvin, who had made propaganda films for the Belgian Information Center, including the film *Congo* (1943), which was widely shown at U.S. commercial movie theaters.[41] The book's preface is illustrated with a heroic image of Vincotte's equestrian statue of Leopold II, the very statue that had been on display in the Belgian Pavilion in New York. Undertaken as a joint Belgian-American partnership with the celebrated American lyricist John Latouche, the book documents an expedition to the Congo. Latouche, who was well-known to U.S. audiences as the lyric composer of the popular *Ballad for Americans,* seeks to correct the "erroneous accounts" of the

Congo propagated by so many of his countrymen, who register "only a complaint against the inexorable assembly belt of progress."[42] It is no surprise that Virginia Union never mounted this Congo exhibit supported by the Belgium government, as its ambitions were soon focused on winning civil rights in the United States and never on defending Belgium's "civilizing mission." From the beginning, Goris and his associates had only conceived of racial uplift within the context of Belgium's colonial interests. However, Virginia Union would reinvent the pavilion to serve its own purposes. Over time this reinvention would expand from a fairly conservative approach to African American education to a whole-hearted embrace of the civil rights movement.

4

THE BELGIAN PAVILION'S NEW HOME

African American Richmond

The Belgian government-in-exile's agreement to "donate" their world's fair pavilion to Virginia Union University was not just a Trojan horse that unloaded the cost of disassembling the building onto the historically Black university in Richmond, Virginia. It was also, along with Virginia Union's unusually distinguished turn-of-the-century campus buildings, a testament to the university's high standing within the ecosystem of institutions established to educate freedmen and freedwomen after the Union victory in the Civil War. Moreover, the Baptist-run university contributed to Richmond's emergence in the 1920s as a city where African Americans committed to uplift were able to find a measure of economic success, despite its history as the capital of the Confederacy, and despite the continued oppression imposed by Jim Crow. The gradual economic empowerment of at least some of Richmond's African American residents during the 1920s, despite considerable ground being lost during the Great Depression, nevertheless emboldened the community and informed its efforts to lay the groundwork for what would become the civil rights movement of the 1950s and early 1960s.

There was an inherent tension in the 1930s and 1940s between the goals of Virginia Union's African American students, faculty, and alumni, as well as Richmond's vibrant African American community, on the one hand, and the white philanthropists and academics who funded and governed the university, on the other. Unlike the Tuskegee Institute (now University) founded by Booker T. Washington or, closer to home, the Hampton Normal and Agricultural Institute (now Hampton University), where Washington had trained, both of which focused on vocational education, Virginia Union prided itself on its track record of educating the professionals whom W. E. B. Du Bois termed the "Talented Tenth." Union's graduates were more likely to be pastors, teachers, or even university professors than carpenters and farmers.

Yet by 1940, one of Union's most important funders, the General Education Board (GEB) was hoping to steer the university's curriculum toward manual training aimed at rural African Americans. In exchange, the GEB helped engineer a shift from white to African American leadership that it hoped would also help wean the university from the necessity for white support. However, even as many of Virginia Union's white funders made clear that their contributions to African American educational and economic advancement were not intended to dismantle Jim Crow, Richmond's African American leaders felt increasingly empowered to push for full equality. The university continued to be an incubator for political activism, including the campaign to dismantle segregation. This drive for racial equality coincided as well with the increasing pride African Americans took in African history and culture and with the increasing recognition that white cultural leaders bestowed upon African art, including artifacts from the Congo.

Richmond and Its African American Community

Richmond, Virginia, is located on the falls of the James River on the site of an earlier Powhatan village. English settlers established first a fort; an iron works was built downriver from the falls in 1619, the same year that the first enslaved Africans were imported into the colony. It was well over a century before a real town developed on the site. The community was formally established by the General Assembly only in 1742. In 1779 it replaced Williamsburg, which was more vulnerable to invasion by the British army, as Virginia's capital. The men of European descent who acquired the land on which the city was founded were enslavers, and enslaved men and women were present in the community from its earliest days.[1]

In the first decades of the nineteenth century, Richmond's growth was indivisible from the institution of slavery and, indeed, from its worst horrors. The city was the site of one of the country's largest slave markets, located in Shockoe Bottom, as planters who had grown rich off tobacco in the eighteenth century found their soil depleted and supported themselves instead by selling off enslaved labor, sometimes including even their own progeny.[2] Although the sale of enslaved labor made the largest contribution to the state's economy across most of the first six decades of the nineteenth century, Richmond also industrialized. Established in 1837, the Tredegar Iron Works, which employed both free and enslaved African Americans—in part to avoid paying whites as much as they would have otherwise earned—manufactured much of the material used in the construction of the region's growing rail network. Free and enslaved African Americans working in other skilled roles, including blacksmithing, carpentry, and masonry, also played a major role in constructing the rapidly expanding city, whose population grew from 3761 in 1790 (nearly 40 percent of whom were enslaved, with another 7 percent being free African Americans) to ten times that number by 1860 (of whom 30 percent were enslaved and again 7 percent free African Americans).[3]

Following Virginia's somewhat belated succession from the Union, from 1861 to 1865 Richmond served as the capital of the breakaway Confederate States of America, which was established to preserve slavery. Munitions manufactured by Tredegar helped sustain the Confederate war effort. At the end of the war, retreating Confederate troops set much of the city ablaze shortly before it surrendered to Union troops. Richmond's African Americans gave Abraham Lincoln a tumultuous welcome when he visited the following day.[4]

Reconstruction saw Richmond's now entirely free African American community establish a host of institutions intended to sustain its members' spirits and to enable them to prosper economically. Baptist churches, schools, and businesses clustered in Jackson Ward and on Church Hill—by the late nineteenth century the city's two predominantly African American neighborhoods—were key to these efforts.[5] For more than two decades, across the 1870s and 1880s, African American men, many of them active in the Baptist church, were deeply involved in state and local politics, serving in the General Assembly, the state's legislature, and on the city council.[6] This political progress was quickly rolled back in the century's closing years. Nothing signaled this shift more than the erection in 1890 of an equestrian statue of Robert E. Lee at the base of what became Monument Avenue, to which celebrations of Jefferson Davis, Stonewall Jackson, Matthew Fontaine Maury, and J. E. B. Stuart were later added.[7] A new state constitution, adopted in 1902, disenfranchised most Black and many white voters.[8] Although African Americans initially boycotted the city street cars when they were segregated in 1904, they eventually lost this battle.[9] These measures left Richmond's African American community in the early twentieth century focused on education and business rather than politics alone as the way forward, and dependent upon the church, especially the Baptists, for spiritual sustenance.

Jackson Ward and the Struggle for Justice

Upon its arrival in Richmond, the Belgian Friendship Building was inserted into a campus with a demonstrated history of architectural ambition, and into a neighborhood that was central to the national campaign for African American progress. In the decades after the Civil War, Jackson Ward, located just north of downtown, became a center of Black Richmond's economic and political aspirations, many of which were furthered with the assistance of Virginia Union's faculty and graduates. While in the 1910s and 1920s, African Americans in Richmond had focused on economic advancement, the harsh economic conditions of the Great Depression encouraged an ever-deepening commitment to political change. Jackson Ward was the site of important institutions such as Armstrong High School and Hartshorn College, which educated African American women, and historic churches and the enterprises established by Maggie Walker, the first African American woman to be a bank president. It also hosted the offices of attorneys Oliver Hill and Spottswood W. Robinson, two of the country's leading civil rights lawyers who were also active in local politics. Another way in which the neighborhood had a national impact was through the careers of Virginia Union alumni, such as Robert Vann, the founder and editor of the *Pittsburgh Courier,* and the tap dancer Bill "Bojangles" Robinson, who had starred in *The Hot Mikado* at the 1939 New York World's Fair.

No one embodied the success of Jackson Ward in the first half of the twentieth century better than Maggie Walker. She was born in 1864, as the Civil War was still raging, in the household of Unionist spy Elizabeth Van Lew, for whom her mother worked as a cook. Walker benefited enormously from growing up during Reconstruction, before the imposition of increasingly aggressive forms of Jim Crow discrimination in the 1890s. Because of her marriage, she had to resign from her teaching position. Walker then successfully transformed the Order of Saint Luke, a women-run mutual aid organization, into an engine of African American empowerment. In 1903 Walker opened her bank, which remains in business as the Consolidated Bank and Trust Company. The *Encyclopedia Virginia* describes it as "the oldest Bank in the United States that has been continuously run by African Americans."[10]

The relative prosperity that some inhabitants of Jackson Ward were able to achieve did not result in equal political rights, however. The historian Margaret Edds notes: "Statistically, black Virginians might have less to fear when it came to random violence than their brethren to the south; official violence was another matter. From 1900 to 1935, among southern and border states only Georgia and Texas surpassed Virginia in the number of executions, with African Americans making up a disproportionate number of those put to death." Edds continues, "Virginia's political elite rarely tolerated crushed bodies, but they excelled at breaking spirits."[11] Virginia Union's faculty and alumni helped create the climate in which Jackson Ward's occupants fought back at the state, and even at the federal government.

Walker participated in these efforts. Not just a successful entrepreneur, she was also politically engaged. In 1921, just after women gained the vote in Virginia, she ran for statewide office on an all–Black Republican ticket. This came seven years after she had helped establish the Richmond chapter of the National Association for the Advancement of Colored People (NAACP). She was also a board member of both Hartshorn and Union, from which she received an honorary degree in 1925. The NAACP also established a separate chapter at Union in 1914. Claudrena Harold argues that "the Union branch developed into an important incubator of New Negro thought and political expression for many students, stressing race pride and black cultural awareness, group unity, cross-regional collaboration among young African Americans, and the necessity of consistent political engagement."[12] Historians, including Harold, have increasingly argued for the importance of southern interwar opposition to Jim Crow to the civil rights movement of the 1950s and 1960s.[13]

Two younger and combative figures, Hill and Robinson, did not graduate from Virginia Union, although Robinson, whose father had taught law there, studied on the campus for two years before completing his degree at Howard, which was also Hill's alma mater. In 1942, Hill helped secure an agreement to equalize pay over the next five years for the African American teachers in Richmond's woefully inadequate segregated public schools. Six years later he became the first African American elected since Reconstruction to the Richmond City Council. Working together with Thurgood Marshall for the NAACP's Legal Defense Fund, Hill and Robinson laid the foundations for *Brown v. Board of Education,* the historic 1954 Supreme Court case that ruled that segregated schools were unconstitutional.[14] This was a historic leap forward in dismantling the Jim Crow system that had imposed legal restrictions on the physical and educational mobility of African American residents of the southern United States.

There were finite limits, however, to what even the most ambitious African Americans could achieve in Richmond or the rest of Virginia during the interwar period, and few were ever allowed to forget this. The very definition of who belonged to what race became more restrictive, when between 1924 and 1930 the General Assembly passed a series of laws that prohibited all interracial marriages and defined as white only those who were of completely European descent. This marked a tightening of earlier laws passed in 1910 that defined as "colored" anyone who was at least one-fourth Native American or with one-sixteenth "negro blood." The increased segregation of places of public assembly that accompanied this legislation was generated by a case in which a white woman sat next to African Americans at a concert at Hampton, which in consequence stopped opening its events to the public. This strengthening of Jim Crow further reduced the contexts in which people of different races might possibly mingle, with African Americans relegated to the balconies of such settings as cinemas or the Mosque (now the Altria Theatre), Richmond's principal concert venue, which acquired its original name from its exotic architectural ornament.[15] Nor was this shift in the legal environment restricted to the state level. As early as 1911, the city of Richmond passed the region's first ordinance restricting where African Americans could live. In 1929, a much tougher regulation mandating residential segregation was briefly in effect, although the United States Fourth Circuit Court of Appeals quickly ruled this unconstitutional in an early victory for the NAACP and local activists. Another legal victory of the period opened the state's Republican primary to African American voters, at a time when the party still commanded the loyalty of the relatively small group who could afford to pay the poll tax.[16]

The Great Depression brought further retrenchment as whites reclaimed jobs they had not wanted during boom times. However, assisted by the largest NAACP branch in the South, African Americans living in Richmond nonetheless realized modest gains in their challenges to the city's entrenched patterns of segregation. Marvin Chiles summarizes this progress:

> In 1933, the Richmond branch [of the NAACP] helped secure positions for black principals in black public schools. A year later, they [a group that included Virginia Union students] led a citywide retail boycott that opened up hundreds of downtown jobs to blacks. In 1935, the Richmond branch also became the home of Virginia's NAACP Conference, a consolidated group of smaller branches throughout the state. In 1936, during the Great Depression, the branch compelled Richmond's all-white school board to build a new black school [named for Walker]. In the next five years the branch helped equalize black teachers' and principals' salaries with their white counterparts, as well as integrate YMCAs, city libraries, buses, and other public services.[17]

This track record is particularly notable, considering what was happening elsewhere in the state. For instance, in Norfolk, then Virginia's second largest city, the campaign to equalize teachers' salaries faltered. W. H. Venable, a Norfolk lawyer, summarized the sentiments of all too many Virginia whites when he criticized these attempts in words that are indicative of the hurdles Virginia Union still faced:

> A generation and a half of advancement from the unlettered toward the learned is only a step and a half in the right direction for the Negro race. All right minded white people take pride in the educational progress made by the Virginia Negro race in a short period of 75 years; but don't fool yourself, Mr. or Miss Negro, with the idea that you have, in this short time, caught up with the white race of Virginia who started the climb of civilization's ladder hundreds of generations ahead of you. The white people have got a lot more pulling to do, and you with their assistance, have a good deal more climbing to do before there can be any serious thought given by sensible people of either race, to your far-off dream—social equality in Virginia.[18]

More liberal whites in Richmond, however, understood the cost to both races of maintaining a dual system of higher education. Writing in 1943, Virginius Dabney, the white editor of the *Richmond Times Dispatch,* one of Richmond's two daily papers, noted, "The Southern states devote a larger share of their limited incomes to the public schools, and also towards support of the higher learning, than the states of any other comparable area, but having elected to operate two separate systems, one for the white and the other for the colored, they naturally have trouble making their low revenues stretch the required distance."[19] Such an opinion, however, did not hinder Dabney from later supporting Virginia's state government's strategy of Massive Resistance to school integration, although he had earlier advocated the integration of public transport.[20] It was in this context that Union offered the most ambitious education available to African Americans in the state of Virginia, and indeed one of the best educations that most were able to obtain anywhere in the United States.

Virginia Union: Educating the Talented Tenth

Virginia Union is justifiably proud of its origin story, which was referenced many times in publicity related to the Belgian Friendship Building.[21] The Colver Institute, later known as the Virginia Theological Institute, was established in Richmond in 1865 by the American Baptist Home Mission Society (ABHMS). Founded in 1832, the ABHMS was a northern white Baptist organization that, after the Civil War, committed to educating newly emancipated slaves as well as the city's ambitious community of African Americans who had already secured their freedom before the start of the conflict. In an extraordinary turn of events beginning in 1867, the institute was housed in Lumpkin's Jail in Shockhoe Bottom, where the enslaved had previously been held until such time as they were sold at auction. This property was donated to the institute by Mary Ann Lumpkin. The African American widow of her notorious enslaver appears to have been determined to contribute to the establishment of a new order in the city.[22] In 1885, John D. Rockefeller, the Baptist founder of Standard Oil and for much of his life the country's richest man, inaugurated his family's support for the institution by donating $25,000 to endow a professorship in biblical theology, apparently the first at a Baptist-run HBCU.[23]

The strongly religious character of white support for the university in these years was captured in a declaration in the late 1890s by Thomas Jefferson Morgan, who had led African American troops in the Civil War, in which he was promoted to the rank of brigadier general. Later, as director of the ABHMS, Morgan noted that Virginia's African American Baptists, whom he characterized as "a great host and goodly army now," had already won victories. He continued: "You have vindicated your right to freedom; you have performed in a credible way your duty as citizens; have made for yourselves in many institutions comfortable homes; have built yourself meeting houses for the worship of God; have supported your pastors and done much for your children. All this you have done in circumstances that were in many respects very discouraging."[24]

In 1899 the Virginia Theological Institute merged with another ABHMS-sponsored institution for African American education, Wayland Seminary, which had been based in Washington, D.C. Through the choice of the name Virginia Union University, the founders of the new university clearly expressed their defiance of the veneration of the so-called Lost Cause that was sweeping across the former Confederacy. In 1932 Virginia Union absorbed its neighbor, Hartshorn Memorial College, one of the few HBCUs exclusively for women.

During the first half of the twentieth century, Virginia Union was one of the most prominent of the HBCUs to offer a liberal arts education to African Americans. Its focus in its early years was above all on training clergymen, although it also produced many other professionals, especially educators, and in its early years required manual training of all its students.[25] Moreover, this was a period when the number of students enrolled in these institutions was rapidly growing. In the late 1930s, Virginia Union had an enrollment of five hundred students, double the number who had attended in 1910. They were officially charged $75 a year in tuition, although not all of them could afford to pay this. In 1935, Union was awarded class A accreditation by the Southern Association of Colleges and Secondary Schools, a status that had already been granted to Atlanta University and Fisk.

Union's graduates, including figures such as the journalists Thomas L. Dabney and James Waldo Ivy, were examples of the "New Negro," a term coined by Alain Locke to describe African America's cultural and intellectual leadership, which he identified as being based almost entirely in cities.[26] Harold credits the quality and character of the education Dabney and Ivy received at Union for providing the foundation for their later achievements. She notes: "Despite external pressure to mold its curricular offerings along the lines of Tuskegee Institute, Union claimed a progressive group of faculty members deeply committed to supplying students with the intellectual training necessary to maximize their individual gifts. Of Union's constellation of stellar instructors, no one received greater praise than Joshua Baker Simpson."[27] Simpson taught Greek, Latin, German, and economics, exactly the type of subjects embraced by Du Bois and Locke, but that Washington eschewed at Tuskegee.[28] From 1925 until 1930, Rayford Logan chaired the history department. After being fired from Virginia Union for his radicalism, he earned a doctorate in history from Harvard and taught for nearly three decades at Howard. He was described by Kenneth Janken as "W. E. B. Du Bois's close assistant and one of the principal organizers of the post–World War I Pan-African Congress movement," as well as "a protégé of Carter Woodson."[29]

Virginia Union alumni also included half a dozen university presidents. Samuel H. Archer of Morehouse College in Atlanta, Ferdinand D. Bluford of North Carolina Agricultural and Technical College (now State University) in Greensboro, John Bacoats of Leland College in New Orleans, Robert P. Daniel of Shaw University in Raleigh, Charles S. Johnson of Fisk University in Nashville, and Richard McKinney of Storer College, with which Virginia Union would later merge, were all alumni, as were Eugene Kinckle Jones and T. Arnold Hill, early leaders of the Urban League, founded in 1910 as a more moderate alternative to the NAACP. Benjamin May, the legendary president of Morehouse College between 1940 and 1967, began his college education at Union before transferring to Bates College in Maine. The most celebrated of the many clergymen who studied at the school was Adam Clayton Powell Sr., who was also an alumnus of Wayland. Powell went on to serve as the pastor of Abyssinia Baptist Church in Harlem from 1908 to 1936, which under his stewardship became the largest congregation in the United States. The faculty, some of whom were also alumni, were no less distinguished. In addition to Simpson, they included Abram L. Harris, a Virginia Union alumnus, who later taught economics at the University of Chicago, where he was one of the first African American full professors at a prestigious historically white university.[30] In a 1941 fundraising letter to white Baptist leader Luther Wesley Smith, John Malcus Ellison, by then the university's first African American president, described the university as "the outstanding Baptist educational institution for Negro youth" and cited in support of this claim that it had educated, in addition to many of the figures named above, 1,393 ministers, 1,149 grade school teachers, 156 high school teachers, 35 principals, 65 college professors, 140 physicians, 65 dentists, and 35 lawyers.[31]

In the interwar period the most notable Virginia Union faculty member was arguably the sociologist Gordon Blaine Hancock, who arrived on campus in 1921 after earning his master's degree from Harvard. Hancock was also the pastor of the Moore Street Baptist Church, located just south of the campus. His biographer Gavin Richmond described him as "one of the most articulate and outspoken analysts of race relations and black social problems in the [interwar] South."[32] The author of a widely distributed syndicated column, Hancock was also a frequent contributor to the *Journal and Guide* (Norfolk, Virginia), which was at the time the South's leading African American newspaper, for which Dabney would also write. As a moderate, Hancock kept his distance from the NAACP, instead helping to establish the Richmond chapter of the Urban League. He was also a member of the Commission on Interracial Cooperation.

Although the white members of this group supported segregation, they were nonetheless willing to work to improve the conditions in which African Americans lived. In 1930, Hancock established the Torrance School of Race Relations at Virginia Union, a subject whose teaching he helped pioneer. Hancock strongly encouraged African Americans to spend their money only at businesses that would hire them. He was appalled, however, when Union students began to picket local white businesses in consequence in the 1930s.[33]

Expressing Pride through Built Form: The Noble Nine and Charles Russell

One of the first concerns voiced about the transfer of the Belgian Friendship Building to Virginia Union was that it might not fit into the campus's well-established architectural context, of which the university was justifiably very proud, even as it had come to recognize the limitations of its existing facilities. For instance, Albert Mann, the director of the GEB, worried in November 1940 that the Belgian Friendship Building "would introduce a violent contrast with the existing building on the University campus."[34] It was indeed true that the so-called Noble Nine, the campus's original buildings, were very different—if equally distinctive—in appearance.

The creation of Virginia Union in 1899 had been accompanied by the purchase of a thirty-acre site. A pamphlet issued by the AMBHS announced that "No better location for a large university could be secured adjoining the city of Richmond. It is outside of the city limits [which was no longer the case by 1940] and yet with

Figure 73. Noble Nine, Virginia Union University, John H. Coxhead, Richmond, Virginia, photographed ca. 1909. (Library of Congress)

good electric car connections both teachers and students will enjoy all of the advantages the city affords."[35] Between 1897 and 1901, John H. Coxhead, an architect who was then based in Buffalo, New York, designed a series of buildings whose neo-Romanesque rock-faced granite facades, reflecting the influence across the United States since the 1880s of the architect Henry Hobson Richardson, made them one of the most imposing architectural ensembles of any early twentieth-century southern campus (fig. 73). The largest, Pickford Hall, served as the administration building. Others housed students and faculty, including the university's president. A chapel seating six hundred, a powerplant supplying electricity, a library, a cafeteria, a barn, and an industrial hall for manual training classes rounded out the group.[36]

Morgan spoke at the dedication of these buildings. He characterized them as exemplifying an institution committed to "that broader, nobler conception of education which, while not neglecting the preparation of pupils for the homely duties of life, seeks to train as well for professional careers and also offers to the gifted few an opportunity for the development to its highest form and degree whatever of talent God has entrusted them."[37]

Not just their architectural ambition was extraordinary. The Noble Nine also represented an unusual departure in Virginia from the classical architecture that had dominated high-end building in the state from the eighteenth century up to the Civil War, and again from the end of the nineteenth century until the middle of the twentieth. Classical architectural styles remained particularly popular on college

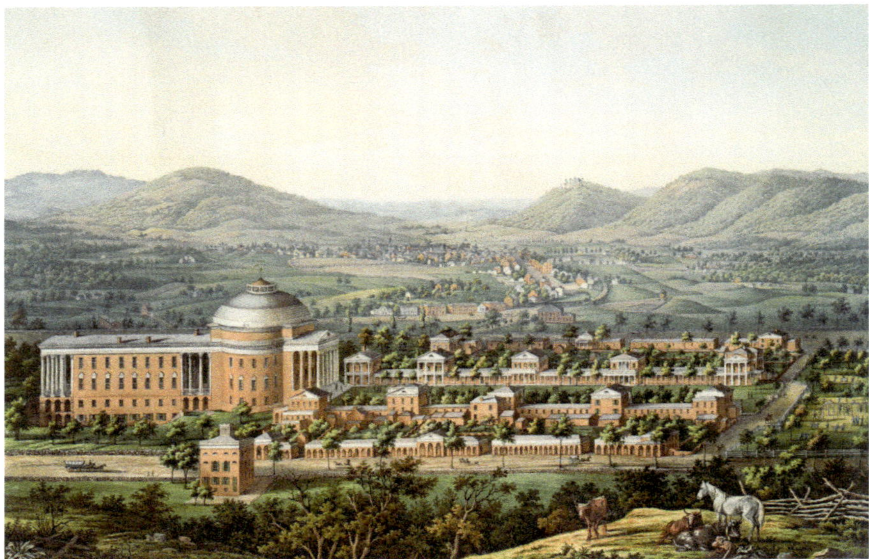

Figure 74. University of Virginia, Thomas Jefferson, Charlottesville, Virginia, 1828. (The Miriam and Ira D. Wallach Division of Art, Prints and Photographs: Print Collection, The New York Public Library)

and university campuses long after their appeal had waned for more commercial uses. Although Richmond's city hall, completed in 1894, is a monumental example of Gothic-inspired design using similarly rusticated stone work, such a break with the approach embodied by Thomas Jefferson's design of the Virginia State Capitol and the campus of the University of Virginia remained unusual (fig. 74).[38] At Virginia Union, the Noble Nine almost certainly spoke to the desire of both the white northern philanthropists who paid for them and the African Americans who studied in them to stand outside of an architecture that many associated with slavery and the more recent imposition of Jim Crow. In the first half of the twentieth century, such a choice remained anomalous among HBCUs, as most instead conformed with local architectural taste for the colonial revival, which was closely associated with the antebellum South.

From the start, the quality of Virginia Union's architecture burnished its reputation. As late as 1917, when Richardsonian Romanesque had gone out of style, the authors of a survey of African American education published by the U.S. Department of Education singled out Virginia Union as the only historically Black institution "developed in accord with a . . . general plan."[39] Adopting environmental determinism, they argued for the importance of high-quality buildings such as the ones they inspected on this campus:

> No educational institutions are more urgently in need of the intelligent application of the principles of sound building than the private and higher schools for Negroes in the United States. The influence of good design, good construction, and attractive surroundings upon character and citizenship is as important in the school as in the home; and the reflex action of the school upon the home is greater and more far-reaching than is generally understood. While the waste in construction is probably not much greater than with other groups of schools, the need for funds is more pressing.[40]

Impressive buildings embodying popular approaches to civic architecture communicated that those who taught and studied within their walls merited being fully integrated into the educated middle class. Early landmarks in the story of HBCU architecture include Virginia Hall at Hampton Institute (now University) in Hampton Roads, Virginia, which was designed by Richard Morris Hunt, the first U.S. citizen to study at the prestigious École des Beaux-Arts in Paris, and Jubilee Hall at Fisk University in Nashville, which was funded by the international concert tours undertaken by the school's famed choir (fig. 75).[41] Both buildings were completed in the 1870s and stood on campuses that were, like Virginia Union, founded by white missionaries from the North. Hampton and Fisk were established by the American Missionary Society, created by abolitionist Congregationalists.

In 1892 Hampton's most celebrated early graduate, Booker T. Washington, hired Robert Robinson Taylor to design buildings on the campus of Tuskegee, which Washington had established in 1881 (fig. 76). Taylor was the first African American to receive a university degree in architecture, having studied at the Massachusetts Institute of Technology, which was also a pioneer in admitting women to its architecture program. At Tuskegee, he trained students in architecture as well as construction.[42] Taylor's many buildings at Tuskegee offered up-to-date colonial revival alternatives to the spiky Gothic Revival–infused designs of Virginia and Jubilee Hall. They were also almost always infused with an awareness of the Italian Renaissance and built on a scale that made them grander than their purported eighteenth-

Figure 75. Virginia Hall, Hampton University, Richard Morris Hunt, Hampton Roads, Virginia, 1879 and 1885. (Douglas W. Reynolds / Wikimedia Commons)

century sources. The 1917 survey of African American education undertaken by the U.S. Department of Education advocated the colonial revival as "the only true American architecture, with variations indigenous and appropriate not only to each section of the original thirteen Colonies but to the whole country."[43] Moreover, as Ellen Weiss, Taylor's biographer, has pointed out, even pillared plantation houses should be understood as examples of the skill of African American artisans, as well as of the oppression of the enslaved. She also argues that African Americans could claim a style associated with power and freedom as their own: "A classical portico could also be best practice for any ambitious institution, never mind that this one sheltered those who could not ride in the white man's railway car, get justice in his courts, or vote in what should have been everyone's election."[44]

The campuses of Hampton and Virginia Union differed in a second way, beyond style, namely siting. As Kenrick Ian Grandison has established, Tuskegee faced inward with buildings sited in relation to difficult topography whose ravines offered some degree of isolation from the white town to which it sat adjacent, and from the hostile white community that surrounded it.[45] By contrast, although a train line buffered it from downtown Richmond, Virginia Union faced proudly outward onto an ample lawn sloping gently down to North Lombard Street, relatively secure in its

Figure 76. Panoramic view of Tuskegee Institute (now Tuskegee University), Tuskegee, Alabama, 1916. (Library of Congress)

position within Jackson Ward. In this, it followed the example set by majority-white campuses, with its open site setting it apart from the less valued settings that, according to Grandison, camouflaged Tuskegee and other more isolated HBCUs.

Virginia Union's campus was further exceptional in not featuring classically inspired structures that continued to be built on HBCU campuses across the first half of the twentieth century. Particularly notable in this regard is Founders Library at Howard University in Washington, D.C., completed in 1939, the same year that "The World of Tomorrow" opened in New York. Here the historic reference is clearly to freedom. Its African American architect Albert Irvin Cassell modeled it on one of the icons of the eighteenth-century architecture of the original thirteen colonies, Independence Hall, which served as Pennsylvania's state house at the time that the Declaration of Independence was signed there in 1776. After earning an architecture degree from Cornell, Cassell taught at Howard, where from 1922 to 1938 he headed the architecture program. He also designed a dormitory for Hartshorn in Richmond. This was in keeping with his commitment to education for African American women; two of his daughters became architects.[46]

Instead of these neoclassical structures, Virginia Union featured its Noble Nine, which by the mid-1930s were showing their age. And, although classicism would remain popular on campuses across the South for another two decades, alternatives were emerging. For the most part, the South's African American elite took a cautious interest in modernism, even as the quest for economic and political progress rightly dominated. Although white funders with conservative taste continued to control decisions about the appearance of buildings on HBCU campuses, there were at least

Figure 77. Milo Cravath Library, Fisk University, Henry Hibbs, Nashville, Tennessee, 1930. (The Peep Holes / Wikimedia Commons)

two noteworthy precedents for Virginia Union's engagement with modern architecture as an optimistic expression of the future.

The largest of these was the Erastus Milo Cravath Library at Fisk University in Nashville, Tennessee, completed in 1930 (fig. 77). In a prominent break with the appearance of new buildings on HBCUs of this time, Cravath Library features Gothic detailing around and above its entrances. Named for the university's first president and designed by Henry Hibbs, the white architect responsible for many buildings just a few miles to the south at Vanderbilt University, which accepted its first African American student only in 1953, the building is otherwise frankly modern. Nine stories tall, it is a miniature version of the ziggurat-like skyscrapers built across the United States in the late 1920s. These in turn were modeled on Eliel Saarinen's unsuccessful but widely admired entry in the Chicago Tribune Tower competition of 1922. Virginia Union academics, however, were probably more impressed that the building, which joined Yale's Sterling Library as one of the country's few high-rise university libraries, could hold 175,000 books.[47] In 1939 their own collection totaled only 27,000 volumes.[48]

The progressive character of Cravath Library was enhanced by the murals contributed by Aaron Douglas, which as works of art commissioned at this time by a historically Black campus rivaled Hale Woodruff's Amistad murals for Talledega College in importance (fig. 78). For Cravath, Douglas employed a style that fused references

Figure 78. *Philosophy,* Aaron Douglas, 1930. Oil on canvas on plaster walls, Cravath Library. (Fisk University Galleries, Nashville, Tennessee, 1991.2147; photograph by Caroline Allison)

to African art with an awareness of recent developments in European painting. The cycle expressed pride in African culture as well as chronicling the history of Americans of African descent.[49] As an artistic achievement, Douglas's Library Murals at Fisk rival *The Epic of American Civilization* that the Mexican artist José Clemente Orozco contributed later in the decade to Dartmouth's Baker Library, which also challenged Eurocentric histories. One of the key artists associated with the Harlem Renaissance, Douglas returned to Nashville in 1939 to found Fisk's art department. His connections prompted Georgia O'Keeffe to make a generous donation to Fisk from the estate of her husband, Alfred Stieglitz, who in 1914 had been the first to mount an art exhibition in the United States composed entirely of artifacts from sub-Saharan Africa.[50] O'Keeffe's gift established the Carl van Vechten Gallery on the university's campus, which immediately became one of the country's foremost venues to see modern art made in Europe and the United States since the end of the nineteenth century, as well as the African masks Stieglitz had collected.

Closer to Richmond was the campus of Virginia State College (now Virginia State University). Located in Petersburg, the state-funded institution was founded in 1882 to train African American teachers; unlike Virginia Union, it originally had Black leadership. Beginning in the 1920s, after it acquired land grant status, its campus buildings were designed by Charles M. Robinson in a Colonial Revival style. Robinson, who worked for publicly funded institutions across the state, as well as the Richmond public school system, was careful not to rock the boat at an institution dependent for funding upon what was from 1891 to 1966 an all-white legislature; the GEB also supported the construction efforts.[51]

Undoubtedly reflecting the wishes of a board of trustees that remained all white until 1964, Virginia State's campus was far more conventional in style than that of Virginia Union. However, by the time the Belgian Friendship Building was reconstituted in Richmond, an awareness of modern alternatives was on clear display in Petersburg. The founder of its art department, Amaza Lee Meredith, although not as well-known an artist as Douglas, had a more obvious commitment to innovative approaches to architecture, which she displayed in Azurest South, the Art Deco house she built in 1938 on the edge of the campus for herself and her partner, Edna Meade Colson (fig. 79). A native of Lynchburg whose white father had been a carpenter, Meredith had studied in New York at Columbia University's Teacher's College, the same institution incidentally attended earlier by O'Keeffe. In New York, Meredith frequented architecture exhibitions, including at the Museum of Modern Art, and furniture displays at the city's department stores. Both while there and at home in Virginia, she also kept abreast of the ideas being published in the shelter magazines intended to educate consumers about the latest ideas in domestic architecture, home decoration, and garden design.[52] While clearly a private commission, Azurest South demonstrated a level of artistic sophistication present in Virginia's African American community at a time when such a choice was highly unusual for white Virginians.

Figure 79. Azurest South, Amaza Lee Meredith, Petersburg, Virginia, 1938. (Devry Becker Jones)

There is no evidence that Virginia Union was already interested in making such a bold architectural statement before the Belgian Building was "offered" to them, but the "gift" was only sent their direction because they had already secured a pledge from the GEB toward the cost of a new library.

Virginia Union's Quest for Improved Facilities

By 1939, in addition to needing renovation, Virginia Union's Noble Nine could no longer fully accommodate the university's increasingly ambitious needs, which included better science laboratories and, above all, a new library. Not surprisingly, the first place it turned for assistance was the GEB. Established by John D. Rockefeller Sr. in 1903, the GEB served as the conduit for many of the contributions he and his son John D. Rockefeller Jr. made to higher education across the United States, as well as to his other charitable activities in the South.[53] In the first half of the twentieth century, the Rockefeller family was the country's most generous philanthropist. The GEB provided the template for professionally managed philanthropy in the United States and also for much of the country's post–World War II involvement in economic development in the Global South. In return for its support, the GEB micromanaged many of the institutions it financed; such oversight was undoubtedly especially strict when it came to HBCUs.

The GEB had long taken an interest in Virginia Union. In the 1920s, it offered the university $350,000, contingent on it raising an additional quarter of a million dollars.[54] By 1936, however, economic conditions meant that many who had pledged support had not delivered the promised sums. The pattern of optimism on the part of Virginia Union, and patient extension on that of the GEB, would be repeated often during the campaign to erect the Belgian Friendship Building. Already in 1935, John D. Rockefeller Jr. was alert to precisely this problem. He wrote Trevor Arnett, then the GEB's president, of the unfulfilled older pledges that were repeatedly submitted to the board of the Executive Committee for extension: "If I may say so quite frankly, I cannot help wondering [...] if it might not be advisable to cancel them and make a new pledge. It seems to me that conditions which existed prior to the depression must frequently have been so altered as to warrant a new type of commitment, if not a complete lapsing of the obligation without renewal."[55]

The more immediate backdrop to the board's eventual contributions toward building the Belgian Friendship Building was an accreditation visit in 1934 of what was by then an undergraduate college with a graduate theology division (many HBCUs did not yet offer accredited bachelor's degrees, but in effect remained only high or "normal" schools, the latter providing teacher training). A poor assessment by the Southern Association of Colleges and Schools resulted in the university being briefly placed in the second tier of higher education institutions in the region because of its low faculty salaries and the poor condition of its library and science facilities.[56] In 1937, the GEB pledged $100,000 toward the cost of a new library, which represented nearly the annual budget of the university, but once again the required matching funds trickled in very slowly, not least because, instead of raising it himself, the president, William J. Clark, initially turned to professional fundraisers, who kept most of the proceeds for themselves.[57] At this point, the cost of a library was estimated at $125,000.

The largest windfall Virginia Union accrued during this effort was originally set aside for the endowment, although it would eventually be transferred, at least temporarily, toward meeting the costs associated with the Belgian Friendship Building.[58] Following Union's absorption of Hartshorn, it no longer needed the land occupied by the former women's college. The university was able to sell Hartshorn's land to the city of Richmond for the princely sum of $50,000. The city built a second segregated high school for African Americans on that site. Named for Walker, the facility, now a magnet school that attracts students of all races, is currently considered one of the best in the entire country.[59]

Once again, however, Virginia Union's fundraising campaign fell woefully short. Poor economic conditions, especially of the African American community from which the GEB had hoped for more support, were just part of the reason. Only in 1938 did Virginia Union hand over the task of soliciting funds from the local white community to board member Egbert Leigh, who did not have significant wealth himself, but who at least threw himself into the task without asking to be paid. His success was only moderate, however. Leigh was careful to cast his approaches to local whites in terms that were as uncontroversial as possible. In May 1938, the *Richmond News Leader* quoted him as saying, "The work done at Virginia Union in the way of training Negroes in the responsibilities of citizenship is a very essential one, not only for the Negroes directly benefitted but for the moral and material welfare of the States as a whole."[60]

Further catering to the prejudices of local whites, the funding appeal for a new library opened with language clearly intended to downplay the threat that educated African Americans might pose to deeply entrenched white supremacy:

> Virginia Union University . . . is one of America's greatest assets in the intellectual training and moral guidance of her colored people.
>
> Over one-tenth of America's population is colored, and in Richmond the proportion is 29 per cent. This presents economical, social, and political problems that must be met.
>
> Experience has proved that freedom from the shackles of illiteracy, superstition, poverty and disease, develops character and good citizenship among Negroes. Given properly trained leadership, the Colored race in America will solve its own problems in a manner satisfactory to all of our citizens. It is the illiterate who clutter our courts, join the Communists and other subversive movements, who threaten our institutions, especially during periods of economic stress. By training leaders in schools such as Virginia Union University, this can be prevented.[61]

The same brochure also reassured its presumably white readers: "Trained professional colored men and women segregate themselves by practicing their respective professions among their own race." And, very unusual for Virginia Union, it claimed Booker T. Washington, who had briefly attended Wayland, as an alumnus.

The university's hopes of a new library remained largely dependent upon the GEB, which in December 1939 gave it a two-year extension to raise the matching funds.[62] In the summer of 1940, Sidney Evans Hening, Virginia Union's white treasurer, was engaged in trying to match these funds.[63] Hening had previously worked for the Young Men's Christian Association, where his roles included leading tours of its building at the New York fair.[64] He probably also knew that the Rockefeller family's previous support for Belgium made it particularly likely that the GEB could be persuaded to release the promised funding in order to pay for the shipment of the Belgian Pavilion to Richmond. John D. Rockefeller Sr. had been among those who had assisted the future U.S. president Herbert Hoover in his efforts to feed Belgians between the German invasion in 1914 and the immediate aftermath of the eventual Allied victory in that war.[65] The family also contributed generously toward Belgium's reconstruction in the 1920s. John D. Rockefeller Jr. was among those, for instance, who helped underwrite the cost of the new library for the University of Leuven (fig. 80), a building that its van de Velde–designed counterpart in Ghent was designed to rival, not least by being executed in a far more obviously modern style.[66]

Moreover, by the time he hatched the scheme to bring the Belgian Building to Richmond, Hening had already shown a strong interest in Virginia Union's architecture. This was accompanied by a demonstration of his tendency to dismiss African American abilities and aspirations. Although Clark had approached Jens Frederick Larson—the Dartmouth College architect who had designed the stylistically conventional Colonial Revival Baker Library that housed the Orozco murals—for a sketch of a new library for Union, the university's preferred architect was usually Charles Thaddeus Russell.[67]

A native of the Jackson Ward neighborhood that Virginia Union bordered, Russell studied carpentry at Hampton before being placed in charge of that division of Tuskegee in 1901. Six years later he returned to Richmond to teach at Union and to become superintendent of its grounds. In 1910, Russell launched his career as an architect by designing new quarters for the Order of St. Luke. For the next three decades, he ran a busy architectural practice in the city, where he designed the busi-

Figure 80. University Library, Whitney Warren, Leuven, Belgium, 1921–28. Leuven, Belgium (Snonwdog / Wikimedia Commons)

nesses, houses, and churches that sheltered the city's leading African American institutions and represented its economic, social, and spiritual ambitions. Among his notable buildings was Huntley Hall, a dormitory for men on the Virginia Union campus, which was completed in 1913. In 1922 Russell became one of the first two African American architects officially licensed to practice in the state.[68]

In the spring of 1940, Hening was particularly concerned about Russell's design for a pair of faculty houses on the campus. In a report on a recent visit to Virginia Union he noted:

> Some of the suggestions made by our office concerning these buildings have been followed, but construction was too far along to make all the changes which seemed to us desirable. While the residences had been constructed rather rapidly and the workmanship seems to be good, I regretted to note that the plans did not seem to take full advantage of the opportunity to demonstrate to the students what can be achieved at the present time in the way of constructing modern, attractive, substantial and convenient residences at moderate cost. Instead, the buildings impressed as being not much out of the ordinary.[69]

Hening's comments appear, however, not simply to have been grounded in an interest in current architectural discussions. Reservations he expressed already a month earlier about the cost of these houses, priced at $8,000 apiece, suggest that he was particularly uncomfortable with the ability of Union faculty to live on the scale of their white counterparts in two-story Colonial Revival structures rather than in more modest bungalows.[70]

The arrival of the Belgian Building at Virginia Union thus coincided with great concern on the part of white Baptists about how to balance their concern for African American education with their uneasiness with African American aspirations for equality and with increasingly African American interest in architecture as a means of expressing these aspirations. Imposing the Belgian Friendship Building—along with a vision of both modern architecture and vocational education—upon Virginia Union was a means of trying to maintain control of a situation that was clearly already beginning to slip out of white hands, not least because they increasingly expected African Americans to provide financial support as well as administrative leadership for it. Modern architecture may not have been a major aspiration of African American southerners, but equal access to the fruits of modernity that it symbolized certainly was.

Dramatis Personae

The white beneficence embodied in the "bestowal" of the Belgian Building upon Virginia Union was intended to ameliorate African American demands for a more equitable society by providing facilities that could supply the economic advancement liberal whites undoubtedly hoped would mute calls for more radical change. The transfer of the Belgian Building was also predicated upon a relationship between Belgium's "civilizing mission" in the Congo and white Baptist paternalism, at a time when African Americans were increasingly reluctant to accept the legitimacy of either. These concerns were more prominent in Belgian propaganda and in fundraising literature, however, than they were in the behind-the-scenes discussions that brought the building to Richmond. These deliberations involved a number of men with often competing interests, including most prominently Hening; Theodore Adams, the chair of Virginia Union's board; Jackson Davis, an official from the GEB; Ellison, who in 1941 became Union's first African American president; and Luther Foster, another African American, who with GEB support became president of Virginia State two years later.

As an outpost of intellectual rather than just economic uplift, Virginia Union continued to be supported through the first half of the twentieth century, albeit within carefully defined limits, by the Northern Baptists who had helped establish it. This situation was particularly complex because Union officially owed its fealty to the ABHMS, which owned its property and determined its governance. This arrangement began to falter already during the Depression, when the ABHMS could no longer raise enough from white Baptists to maintain its previous level of support for Baptist-affiliated HBCUs. In consequence, ABHMS reported to the Board of Education of the Northern Baptist Convention, beginning in 1935.[71] The Northern Baptists had supported a network of denominationally affiliated schools and institutions of higher education for African Americans since the Civil War. In addition to Virginia Union, these included most notably two of the constituents of what became in 1929 Atlanta University: Morehouse College for men and Spelman College for women, the later renamed in 1884 in honor of John D. Rockefeller Sr.'s wife, Laura Spelman Rockefeller, and her staunchly abolitionist family. Although communication between the two Baptist organizations and between them and the GEB funded by the Rockefeller family, who were Northern Baptists, was frequent, the situation was clearly uncomfortable for Virginia Union administrators, who had to balance often conflicting demands.

It was also difficult for the ABHMS, which retained only nominal control after 1935. Officially, Hening, the treasurer of the ABHMS and of Virginia Union, reported to Frank Padelford, who from 1912 to 1941 was the executive secretary for the board, and to Donald Faulkner, who served under Padelford as its director of higher education. Hening, a Richmond native, drew upon his local connections when he conspired with Goris to bring the Belgian Pavilion to Virginia Union. Playing fast and loose with facts as well as money, he clearly exasperated almost everyone else involved.[72] While his motives, which certainly included supporting Goris, remain unclear, in many ways his intervention may be seen as an attempt to exercise renewed ABHMS control over an institution that was otherwise slipping from its grasp.

The university's board was chaired not by a representative of either of these Baptist bodies but by Theodore Adams. Born in New York and educated in the North, Adams nonetheless spent his entire career in Richmond. From 1936 to 1968, he was the pastor of the city's First Baptist Church, a white congregation; from 1955 to 1960 he was also president of the Baptist World Alliance. Until the fundraising campaign for the Belgian Friendship Building, southern white Baptists provided Virginia

Union with only minimal support, a situation Adams worked hard to change. He traveled north to New York to meet with GEB officials much less often than did Virginia Union's presidents, but he clearly commanded the trust of all but Hening among the other white Baptists involved in funding and running Virginia Union.

Not surprisingly, Adams also worked well with Noble Beall, who in 1942 was appointed the field secretary of the Southern Baptist Convention's Board of Education. The Southern Baptists were delighted to assist in the rebuilding of the Belgian Building as a means of finally matching the Northern Baptists in the financial contribution they were making toward an HBCU. They viewed this philanthropy as progress in regard to race relations, but clearly also as a step toward edging Northern Baptists, who were generally more progressive when it came to race, out of their controlling position in regard to these institutions.[73] This was part of a larger pattern of southern whites claiming to "understand" African Americans better than did their northern counterparts and thus deserving, at least in their own eyes, the chance to impose their (typically extremely racist) views. Beall nonetheless was, like Adams, an admirer of Ellison.

Although the Board of Education representing the ABHMS officially ran the university, the GEB was at least as important. The key figure in all of Virginia Union's relations with the New York-based organization was Jackson Davis. Like Hening, Davis was a Virginian, although officially he represented Northern Baptist interests. He joined the GEB in 1915 after five years as Virginia's state agent for Negro rural schools, a post funded by the GEB. He rose through the GEB ranks to briefly become its vice president and in 1946 its director, before dying the following year. Only in 1937 did he move from Richmond to New York. Therefore, although he orchestrated many aspects of the administration of Virginia Union from a distance, he was intimately familiar with the situation on the ground.[74]

Davis played a paternalistic role in the administration of the HBCUs, one that undercut the authority of their boards of trustees and of their faculty. He typically communicated only with leading members of their administrations and with a handful of board members. Moreover, the GEB's support for what were then exclusively white institutions such as Duke (already the best endowed university in the region), Vanderbilt, and the University of Virginia far exceeded what it bestowed upon institutions such as Virginia Union and came with far less interference in their governance. And the support of even these paled beside Rockefeller expenditure on the University of Chicago, which was as a result at mid-century the fourth best endowed university in the country. The historian Marvin Chiles perceptively notes that "Southern state governments and Northern philanthropic foundations ensured that historically black colleges and universities lagged financially behind their white counterparts. White public and private universities had better-trained faculty, more research money, larger departments, and closer access to political power brokers. This disparity helped white universities and scholars maintain their educational supremacy."[75]

For Davis, support for Virginia Union in particular, and African American higher education in general, represented his Christian duty toward his fellow man. In a letter to Ellison in January 1943, he wrote of the Belgian Friendship Building, "A practical undertaking of this sort is certainly a good answer for Christian people to make in a time of great racial tension."[76] Two months later he reported to Adams: "The active cooperation of the white churches [in raising funds for the Belgian Friendship Building] is of great significance, as you say, in this time of racial tension. It is, in my judgement, the best way of dealing with this situation, showing in a practical way the concern of the Christian people of the South for the education and welfare of our colored citizens."[77] That the solution to racial tensions might instead be acceding to the increasing demands of Richmond's African American community for equal treatment had clearly not occurred to Davis who—although he treated individual African Americans with great respect, always addressing them, for instance, with appropriate titles—continued to view Union and the other HBCUs within his remit with a frank sense of his own superiority. In particular, he worked hard to ensure that the shift to African American leadership did not result in Union's presidency being bestowed upon Hancock, whose scholarly focus was race relations, but instead upon Ellison, who was at the time the more moderate of the two.

Ellison is undoubtedly the central figure in the story of the Belgian Friendship Building's reconstitution in Richmond. On April 29, 1941, after a brief stint as executive vice president, he became Virginia Union's first alumnus to be named president. He had long benefited from Rockefeller money, which had funded his doctorate at Drew University in the hopes that he might eventually prove worthy of just such a position.[78] In 1936, Clark, Union's final white president and Ellison's immediate predecessor, requested that the GEB help underwrite the appointment of Ellison at a salary of $3,000 a year. The amount was impressive, as in 1940 no one else on the faculty made more than $2,250.[79] For the next five years, Ellison repeatedly reported to Davis behind Clark's back, often detailing his plans for the reorganization of the university.[80] Although Ellison and Davis both knew that Clark had envisioned Ellison as his successor, the task of pushing Clark discretely aside was not as smooth as either Ellison or Davis might have hoped.[81] The Belgian Friendship Building proved the catalyst for Ellison's historic appointment.

Ellison's ascendancy to the presidency was part of a larger shift across HBCUs from white to Black leadership, although Virginia Union was scarcely in the forefront, as by 1941 forty-seven other such institutions had been led by African Americans.[82] For instance, in 1937 Dwight Oliver Wendell Holmes was appointed president of what was then Morgan College (now Morgan State University) in Baltimore, which had been established by Methodists in 1867. Davis placed particular faith in the judgment and abilities of Luther Foster, the business manager of Virginia State, Virginia's only state-supported HBCU. Undoubtedly with the strong support of the GEB, Foster became president of Virginia State two years after Ellison gained the top post at Union. The GEB also funded the education of Foster's son Luther at the University of Chicago.[83] The younger Foster would follow in his father's footsteps as an HBCU president, leading Tuskegee from 1953 to 1981. The GEB clearly trusted the elder Foster's judgment, especially when it came to money and building. Although one might have expected Virginia Union and Virginia State to be rivals, in the construction of the Belgium Friendship Building Foster operated as Ellison's strongest African American ally.

One reason that so many white Baptists favored Ellison was that they recognized in him someone who could help Virginia Union stand on its own two feet financially. Since their inception beginning in the 1860s, most HBCUs had been funded largely either by northern white philanthropists or southern white legislatures, but—the GEB aside—private northern support was waning and public southern support had not yet begun to grow, as it later would in an unsuccessful effort to stymie integration. The GEB preferred to give monies that would be matched by others and also that would be well managed. They regarded Clark, Ellison's white predecessor who had served as president since 1919, as ineffectual. While this was partly a matter of Clark's inability to raise funds, more was almost certainly at stake. In addition to his unwillingness to engage in fundraising, Clark was also completely unable to effectively manage the university's finances. One of Ellison's first tasks, executed with the support of Davis and Foster, was to put the university at last on a firm and completely sound financial footing. This took several years. In the meantime, Hening exploited the situation to get Virginia Union to cover unanticipated costs involving the transfer of the Belgian Friendship Building.

That Virginia's African American Baptists could play a larger role in supporting Union was of great importance to the GEB, but they also were impressed by the degree to which Ellison proved able to garner unprecedented donations from local and, more broadly, southern whites. Clark and Davis insisted that Ellison demonstrate his worthiness for the presidency by leading the African American side of the fundraising campaign for the Belgian Friendship Building already in the early months of 1941. Ellison agreed only reluctantly, as he had reservations about the project's viability that would prove prescient.[84] In the end, however, no one would prove more crucial to its success.

But there was more to the story. Clark and the GEB were also anxious to have Ellison, a moderate African American, become the next president because they were aware that Virginia Union was a leading HBCU when it came to educating students concerned with race relations, especially due to the presence of Hancock. At this point in his career, Ellison instead focused on the education and economic uplift, as well as the spiritual welfare, of the rural poor. He proposed to reorient Virginia Union more towards vocational education and to place less emphasis on the training of professionals whose leadership of their community might include controversial political advocacy. In April 1941, he wrote Davis in an unthreatening tone that he wanted to "develop Virginia Union so that it can meet the simple but urgent needs of simple people."[85] Ellison was particularly concerned about the political empowerment of women, which he wanted to counter by ensuring that Virginia Union's female students, most of whom were studying to become teachers, "should have the opportunity for training in Home-making, the Christian family, and Christian social service."[86] He anticipated that this instruction could be housed in the Belgian Friendship Building. At the same time, Ellison argued for the importance of private, Christian-run institutions in training effective pastors for the twentieth century. In a 1940 address, he admitted: "The scientific findings of the age have been and are powerful factors in discrediting much that the church has believed and taught. In many cases, our ministers and religious leaders have not been and are not sufficiently trained to adequately defend themselves and the church against the attacks of these liberal thinkers. Religious leadership today must be trained not only in the field of religion but as well in the fields of science, literature, history, and philosophy."[87] Ellison also advocated a preaching style based on such knowledge rather than appeals to emotion. In this way, Ellison commanded the support of shrewd white Baptists who realized that he was their best hope for containing and indeed channeling African American ambitions. In return they treated him with real respect, welcoming him to their New York offices, and, except for Hening, always referring to him very positively in all their correspondence even as, like funders everywhere, they expected a degree of control in return.

With their strong ties to the city, Adams, Davis, and Hening must have been aware and apprehensive of Hancock, not to mention of younger, more radical men such as Hill and Robinson. Replacing Clark with a highly competent African American who still kept a distance from the emergence of what would become the civil rights movement was one step in this direction. Attempting to unite whites and Blacks in a campaign to bring an internationally significant structure to the city as part of an effort to provide Virginia Union with facilities for manual education (a function the building never actually fulfilled) was another.

Bringing the Belgian Building to Richmond: The Baptist Side of the Story

Hening probably met Goris while they both worked at the New York fair, although he may have learned of the Belgian Pavilion's potential availability only through Goris's call to the Association of American Colleges. In the most extensive account of Virginia Union's acquisition of the building published at the time, the Richmond journalist Clarence E. Boykin, writing in *Opportunity: A Journal of Negro Life,* reported in 1941:

> Now it happens that Virginia Union has been turning out able graduates in professional fields—teachers, preachers, and lawyers; it also produces first-rate basketball teams. A young white man, quite a basketball player himself, saw one of Virginia Union's games and was impressed by the skill and deftness of its players. He was disturbed to learn that Virginia Union had no basketball floor of its own—merely a makeshift practice court. Something should be done about it. The young man mentioned the matter to his father, S. E. Hening, of

> the American Baptist Home Mission Society of New York, who is a treasurer of the university's board of trustees. Mr. Hening made a mental note.
>
> Just a few days later, Mr. Hening heard that a number of colleges—27 of them—were asking the Belgian government for the gift of the building . . . The Belgian Commission to the World's Fair had built the pavilion carefully in its native country, then dismantled and shipped it across the ocean. [It] . . . was to be returned to Belgium at the close of the fair. It was one of the few World's Fair structures designed for permanent use . . . [Robert van der] Straten-Ponthoz [the Belgian ambassador to the United States], was authorized to make a gift of the building to some United States college as a gesture of international friendship.[88]

Although some of these details were repeated in an earlier GEB memo dated October 28, 1940, and again in a second of November 4 probably written by Hening, not all of them were true.[89] The myth that Belgium had intended to reconstruct the building for permanent use in Belgium was effective in convincing Hening's superiors at the Northern Baptist Convention, as well as Davis, other GEB officials, and President Clark, in November 1940 of the project's credibility. Moreover, this myth was frequently repeated in the press and in fundraising appeals in the months and years that followed. And yet the claim was nothing more than a subterfuge on Goris's part to present the Belgian Pavilion as a viable structure that would be worth the price of disassembling and reconstructing. It is not even certain that Hening's son actually attended a Panthers basketball match, not least because late October was early for the basketball season to have begun, although the Panthers fielded an excellent team that had won their conference championship the previous year.[90] This was, however, a story that was already circulating in the spring of 1941, when Hancock, who devoted one of his syndicated newspaper columns of "Between the Lines" to it, wrote Hening that it was "evidence of these finer race relations" that "always move me deeply."[91] In his column he wrote, "Although the buildings will fill a pressing [need] for more commodious quarters at Virginia Union, the good will gesture alone would doubly justify everything that is being invested in the great project." It would, he stated, be not only one "of the finest buildings in the world, but one of the finest monuments to interracial and international good will."[92]

Nothing in the Baptist, GEB, or Virginia Union archives from 1940 or even 1941 hints at the pressures Goris actually faced, which, in addition to the clearing of the site at Flushing Meadows, included repaying the Belgian Commission's construction and maintenance debts and providing for the Belgian labor force that had been left stranded in New York by the outbreak of the war. Instead, the earliest mention of the Belgian Friendship Building by the GEB is in a memo of a meeting between Fred McCuistion of the GEB and Hening on October 28, 1940:

> Hening came in to report that he had contacted representatives of the Belgian Building at the World's Fair, and that he thought those in charge would be willing to give Virginia Union University certain units of the structure as a memorial. . . . H. is especially interested in the unit designed as a future library and in sufficient materials to construct a gymnasium. Hening hopes the Board will consider making available the conditional grant of $100,000 which, in addition to the $15,000 raised by Virginia Union, would provide sufficient funds to dismantle the Belgian Building, transport it to Richmond, and reconstruct the library and gymnasium. The necessary new facilities, such as heating, plumbing, lighting would be included in this amount.[93]

Importantly, these figures are much lower than the ones Goris's office had provided Clark just four days earlier. This lower estimate is almost certainly because, at this point, Hening was asking the GEB only for the part of the building that could serve as a library, rather than for the whole thing. Although GEB officials were originally reluctant, Hening was able to convince Northern Baptist officials to pressure the GEB. For instance, Padelford wrote to Mann, the director of the GEB, not even a week later: "I only want to record my feeling that if this fine building can be secured for the library and gymnasium of Virginia Union it will be of great advantage to the college. The college desperately needs a library building. . . . I shall be glad if your Board can see its way clear to help them. I think it is a good investment for the Negro race."[94]

Mann responded cautiously and presciently:

> I confess, however, it raises almost insurmountable difficulties in my own mind. . . . It has vast expanses of glass running to considerable heights, involving serious questions of glare and heating. Furthermore, most of the ceilings are very high and the heating expense for unused spaces would thus be a very large

> continuing cost. While the interior could be rearranged as to room sizes, there are many difficulties connected with the architecture and the materials used in the interior. It is a serious question in my mind whether notwithstanding the acute need of Virginia Union and their grasping at this straw for relief, it would be sensible to aid them in erecting such an unusual and somewhat difficultly adjusted building to their campus.[95]

Mann, a former provost of Cornell University, retained his doubts until almost the end. For one thing, he was distrustful of modern architecture. Moreover, HBCUs comprised only a small part of his brief, as most GEB funding went to predominately—when not exclusively—white institutions. With a stronger eye on the bottom line and fewer personal ties to African Americans, Mann was often the last to be convinced, and he undoubtedly acted as a brake on issuing the crucial second tranche of board funding for the building.

In the meantime, Davis met with Clark, Hening, S. C. Mitchell, and Belgian architect Hugo van Kuyck, who was described in a memo of the meeting as having "been appointed by the Belgian commissioner to dispose of the building." Davis reported that the Belgians would rather donate it to a college, "so that it can be kept together and constitute a visible link between this country and Belgium," than sell it for scrap and pay duty on the proceeds. At this point, the most vocal supporter of the project on behalf of Virginia Union was Mitchell, a professor at the then entirely white University of Richmond, who "hoped that the entire building might be set up on the campus . . . where it would have international significance as a mark of appreciation from the Belgian people for American aid during the World War, and he thought it would have special significance from an interracial point of view." Hening offered two proposals. One, costing $120,000, or less than Virginia Union had budgeted for a library, would include only part of the pavilion and provide "an assembly room and offices" in addition to a library. The other, coming in at $300,000, involved the entire original structure and would also provide "as many classrooms and laboratories as the College would need for many years."[96] Only the first figure represented a potential bargain.

Davis was not yet entirely convinced. Among the points that concerned him was "the suitability of the building to a campus with buildings of an entirely different type," to which Van Kuyck responded "that he had visited the campus at

Virginia Union and he thought it would be possible to fit the building in without any unpleasant architectural effects."[97] Davis was also rightly concerned about the structure's suitability as a library and about the costs of disassembling it in New York and transporting it to Richmond. Davis's suspicions regarding the cost of taking the structure apart would prove correct, as Hening's supervision of precisely this part of the project would result in the first of many overruns of his overly optimistic budget estimates. Although it had been "erected with bolts, rather than rivets," this had not been "in order to make it possible to dismantle it quickly and economically and with a minimum of damage to the materials," but to save on the cost of hiring New York union labor.[98]

To some degree Union and its Richmond supporters were defrauded by Hening and Goris, as the university could have built a new library at a fraction of the cost it ended up paying for the Belgian Friendship Building. At the time, however, excitement over a quick and prestigious fix to one of the university's greatest problems appealed to Clark and his board. The GEB was probably largely swayed by international considerations, which figured prominently in subsequent publicity, even if they are largely absent at this point from the archival record. Although the building's reconstitution would take years to complete, it was already clear at this point that one way to fund the construction was to garner support in Washington, D.C., aligning the Belgian Friendship Building with preparation for the war, which many correctly anticipated the United States would eventually enter. Here again, Van Kuyck proved useful, traveling to Washington to counter criticism in the United States of Belgium's hasty surrender.[99] Clark participated in the effort, writing Davis that he had already consulted with officials in Washington "to offer the use of some of this space for special vocational training classes in connection with defense preparation."[100]

Among the most egregious misunderstandings that arose at this point was the identity of the building's original architect, with Henry van de Velde's role now almost entirely erased, along with any mention of Victor Bourgeois or Léon Stynen. Clark reported to Davis the "desire [of the Belgians] that the building be transferred in its entirety and re-erected under the direction of its own architect and contractor to preserve as far as possible the original design with appropriate adaptation to our campus."[101] This implied that Van Kuyck had designed the original building. Many other readers of publicity for the Belgian Friendship Building, and perhaps even some of those who met Van Kuyck in person, were undoubtedly given this impression, which left him especially well positioned to oversee its reerection in Richmond.

Despite the confidence Van Kuyck inspired, his primary commitment was to the liberation of German-occupied Belgium, which would often distract him from his obligations to Virginia Union. After studying architecture in Antwerp and engineering in Ghent, Van Kuyck worked for four years as an assistant to Victor Horta, van de Velde's archrival in Belgium. In 1937, Van Kuyck, a committed mariner, was a visiting lecturer at Yale University intermittently while sailing around the world on his ship, the *Askov,* before returning to Belgium, where he designed social housing in Antwerp. When the Germans invaded Belgium, he fled to France together with a portion of the Belgian government. Because he was already in possession of a yearlong visa to the United States to take up a lectureship at Yale during the 1939–40 academic year, Van Kuyck was sent by Belgium's minister of foreign affairs, Paul-Henri Spaak, on a diplomatic mission there, which he completed while also delivering lectures at both Yale and the Massachusetts Institute of Technology. In New York, Van Kuyck briefly entered a partnership with architect William Hamby, who had recently attracted national attention for his modestly modern house designs, and George Nelson, who would achieve postwar fame as a furniture designer.[102] Given his range of activities, it is hardly surprising that Van Kuyck found little time to tend to his duties in Richmond.

There were several grounds for why Richmonders obfuscated the identity of the Belgian Pavilion–cum–Belgian Friendship Building's original architect. First and most obviously, Van Kuyck was on the ground in the United States and was more than willing to claim credit for the building's design, especially because his teacher and mentor was the sworn enemy of van de Velde. Van Kuyck's contributions were hardly neutral, even as his architectural qualifications and diplomatic connections had helped convince Davis and undoubtedly also encouraged other support for the building's transfer south. Van Kuyck would continue to undermine van de Velde's reputation in the United States after the war. In a pamphlet he published on modern Belgian architecture in New York in 1955, the Belgian disciple of Horta observed, "If Horta was undoubtedly the leader and pioneer of the whole movement, the most curious figure in the group was probably Henry van de Velde, who was a prophet without honor in his early days."[103]

As Van Kuyck's characterization suggests, there were also political motivations behind the erasure of van de Velde's name from the building in Richmond. As the government in exile was undoubtedly aware, van de Velde had, unlike Van Kuyck, remained in Belgium after the German invasion and had initially served in the Belgian Civil Administration, which was part of the Ministry of Public Works headed by his friend and supporter, the labor politician and fellow Fleming Hendrik de Man. In May 1940, De Man remained loyal to King Leopold III and publicly welcomed the German invaders with open arms. Although De Man later changed his mind, retreated from public life, and took refuge in neutral Switzerland, his reputation was ruined; in 1944 De Man was convicted *in absentia* of collaboration by a Belgian military court.[104] It is likely that Van Kuyck, committed as he was to the liberation of Belgium, contributed to the erasure of van de Velde's and his associates' authorship due to van de Velde's compromising political associations.

Finally, van de Velde, although one of the most influential architects of his generation in Europe and widely admired by key members of the next generation of European modernists, was not well known in the United States. Although Bloemenwerf, the house he designed for himself and his family in the Brussels suburb of Uccle in 1895, had been published in *House Beautiful* in 1898, his work would first appear in a major architectural periodical only when Henry-Russell Hitchcock wrote in 1937 in *Architectural Forum* about the Belgian Pavilion at the Paris fair.[105]

The dissembling was effective. On November 5, Davis and McCuistion joined Hening and Van Kuyck at the fairground to inspect the pavilion, which was already being dismantled. While Davis and Hening would not always see eye to eye in the future, the Rockefeller official reported that Van Kuyck "made a fine impression." "As an architect," Davis reported, "he is resourceful and has an appreciation of the artistic as well as the utilitarian point of view." Furthermore, "he would be available to supervise the removal and re-erection of the building on the Virginia Union campus and he would associate with his several other Belgians who were employed in the building—competent and skilled workmen."[106] Any doubts Van Kuyck might have had regarding the appropriateness of reconstituting the building must have paled in light of the pressing need to provide these men with a livelihood. Van Kuyck's assurances undoubtedly accounted for Davis's eventual conversion to Hening's idea that Virginia Union could raise enough money to take the whole building and thus gain laboratories as well as a library. A week later, however, Davis was still on the fence, while Hening continued to solicit his support and also to encourage Virginia Union officials.[107]

In mid-November, Hening returned to Richmond to lobby the board of Virginia Union. He also met with the mayor, the superintendent of schools, and the city librarian. Goris and Van Kuyck also attended the board meeting. Hening told Davis, "The question of adaptability of this modernistic building to the Virginia Union campus was discussed. Mr. Van Kuyck's suggestions involving rearrangement of units, omitting some of those required for the Fair, satisfied the Trustees."[108] At this point Hening placed the cost of dismantling the building at $83,900. Mann, however, remained skeptical, including about the projected costs. He insisted that Arthur Loomis Harmon, one of the principals of the architecture firm responsible for the design of the Empire State Building, weigh in on its feasibility.

Harmon was extremely tactful. He described the parts of the building that would be taken to Richmond, which did not include the exterior stair, the terrace, the cinema, and the restaurant, as "simple, designed with a dignity and restraint" and made out of "substantial materials." Equally importantly he believed that the Belgian Building would harmonize with the colors and textures of the existing buildings on the campus. He continued with a defense of the modern architectural position it represented:

> This building has received highly favorable comment from the architectural profession over the past two years and is of the type of building expressive of the best contemporary design in scholastic architecture. It should have, in itself, an educative significance. . . . We think that the erection of this building at the University is logical, would be helpful to the University, and in spirit with educational growth.[109]

Tellingly, however, Harmon was not asked to judge the overly optimistic cost estimates, nor was he asked to assess the alleged permanence of the building's construction. Nonetheless, Mann was now convinced.

Harmon's letter was one of the few times when the specific character of the building merited mention, and when it was clearly evaluated by someone well positioned to understand its position in relation to contemporary architecture in Europe and the United States. Although the Belgian Friendship Building was often described in the years that followed as an example of architectural excellence and praised for the high quality of its materials, the names of its architects and their standing in Europe, of which Harmon was undoubtedly well aware, again went unmentioned.

On the positive side, the trio of letters sent to New York from Richmond on a single day in late November 1940 included the claim Clark made to Davis: "In addition to the intrinsic value of this building and the great material aid it would provide, there are other important considerations. One is the international significance, as it is proposed that the building in its entirety be presented to Virginia Union University as a memorial to continuing Belgian-American friendship and as an example of inter-racial good-will."[110] Absent from the GEB's own internal discussions was the role that the Rockefeller family had played already for more than a quarter century in supporting Belgium, which must have helped sway the board's senior officials, most of whom needed more persuading than Davis. The theme of international goodwill would feature prominently in the fundraising campaign, particularly, of course, when Belgians were present.

At the end of November, Virginia Union made an official request through Adams to the GEB to request the transfer of the $100,000 they had pledged toward the library to be applied instead toward the acquisition of the Belgian Friendship Building. Adams sought to reassure the GEB: "Because of the unusual nature of the proposal, we have made careful and extended investigations concerning adequacy, suitability, architectural design, heating, maintenance and operating costs, satisfying ourselves on all these points before presenting this request."[111] In fact, there was little time for detailed examinations. Clark, in particular, proved vulnerable to Hening's blandishments. Adams also suggested that furnishings for the building could be bought from other national pavilions; he made clear that although the structure was Belgian, the plumbing and electrical equipment were entirely American, and that all of it was built to code for New York City. He described the pavilion as being of a higher standard than Virginia Union would otherwise have been able to afford and noted that a surplus of the original components had been imported with the original structure. On December 12 the GEB obliged.[112]

It would take nine long years rather than just a few months to reconstitute the building, proving many of the initial reservations expressed by Ellison and the GEB staff to be entirely correct. The financial challenges involved swept Clark, who had joined Goris and Hening as the biggest supporter of the project, into retirement. Davis died before the building was completed and with him so did most of the pressure to reorient Virginia Union around manual training. The local and national respect Ellison garnered for his success in seeing the building's reerection through to completion would instead be harnessed into support for a civil rights movement that would almost certainly have shocked and appalled Davis. But before these stories can be told, one more aspect of what happened in the autumn of 1940 merits investigation.

African Americans and Africa

Baptist officials, whether white or African American, were not the only target audience that Goris and the Belgian government in exile courted by moving the Belgian Building to Richmond. Even if they did not necessarily monitor the African American press, Goris and, for that matter, also the GEB must have been acutely aware of the challenge that Belgium's record in the Congo posed for African Americans. Although African American editors and journalists were keenly attentive to the threat posed by fascism, many of their readers were not necessarily committed to the fight against it if the combat was not also framed as one against colonialism and segregation.[113] African American opposition to the possible entry of the United States into the war was particularly vocal in the period between the outbreak of the war in Europe in September 1939 and the Japanese attack on Pearl Harbor in December 1941. At a time when their opinions seldom played as strong a role in shaping national politics as they would have liked, the transfer of the Belgian Friendship Building to Virginia Union was an unusual example of a European power seeking to curry their favor. This did not mean, however, that the Belgians understood the difference between the "civilizing mission" of their regime in the Congo or the GEB's patronizing interference in the governance of the HBCUs, on the one hand, and the aspirations of Virginia Union's faculty and students, or of those other African Americans who were beginning to take increasing pride in their African heritage and in the continent's precolonial culture, on the other.

For many African Americans, the Belgian Congo remained in the 1930s and 1940s a useful shorthand for the worst aspects of European imperialism. Readers of the *Pittsburgh Courier,* for instance, were repeatedly reminded of Belgium's exploitation of the Congolese population. They understood, furthermore, that both the Germans and their Afrikaner acolytes in South Africa would like to turn the clock even further backward, were there to be an Axis victory. In September 1939, shortly after the Germans invaded Poland, George S. Schuyler, the writer, journalist, and business manager of the NAACP who had served in the U.S. Army during World War I before going AWOL in 1918 in response to the systematic racism he experienced in the army, wrote an opinion piece for the paper in which he declared:

> So far as the colored peoples of the earth are concerned, it is a toss-up between the "democracies" and the dictatorships. Neither care about the darker folk except to exploit them. What is there to choose between the rule of the British in Africa and the rule of the Germans in Austria? What is there to choose between the Belgians in the Congo and the Russians in the so-called Mongolian Peoples' Republic?[114]

In June of the next year Samuel L. Brooke added: "Before shedding too many tears over the plight of Belgium, Negroes in America should consider that Mississippi is heaven for colored folk compared to the Belgian Congo. There natives must tip their hats even to white missionaries and always go to the back door."[115]

The Belgian government in exile was strongly motivated to counter such arguments. Reaching out to a historically Black university offered one means of doing this. There are undeniable parallels between the emphasis that Virginia Union's white philanthropists placed on manual training and the approach that Belgium took in the Congo, where the focus on educating the Congolese was on basic literacy and numeracy, leaving the local population with almost no access to higher education. In both cases, education was to improve the material conditions of poor Blacks without overturning racial hierarchies. Davis, who traveled during the war to both the Congo and South America, was sympathetic to Belgium's view of its colonial responsibilities. He also sought to export the manual training he favored for rural African Americans to Latin America, in which the Rockefeller family took a strong interest during World War II, not least because of the oil interests they already had in Venezuela.[116]

Such assumptions about white supremacy were increasingly being challenged, not only by African American campaigns for social equality but also in other contexts in which African culture was beginning to be a source of Black pride. One of these was the display in Richmond of both African and African American art at the Virginia Museum of Fine Arts, which opened in 1936. Thomas Colt, its first director, had to contend with donors such as Jessie Ball DuPont, who queried, "Why not let the negro develop to a much higher degree mentally before forcing the arts upon him?"[117] He nonetheless rallied the museum's trustees to support the creation of fellowships that enabled the teaching of art at Virginia Union. Almost from the beginning, the museum exhibited the work of local African American artists.[118] African works were also included in the Walter Chrysler collection that was on view at the Virginia Museum of Fine Arts in the early months of 1941, during the peak of the fundraising campaign for the Belgian Friendship Building. From 1943 to 1960, the museum displayed some of Hampton's collection of works from the Congo that had been amassed by William Henry Shepherd. Although it is not clear how many African Americans had access to this collection there during these years, its presence in the Virginia Museum of Fine Art's galleries would have instructed at least some local whites in the significance of Central African art and heritage.

There is no evidence that the Belgian Friendship Building's presence in Richmond encouraged African American support for Belgium's colonization of the Congo or indeed that it had a major impact on white attitudes toward the unfolding global conflict, at a time when an isolationist stance commanded considerable public support. The U.S. entrance into the war in December 1941, just over a year after the transfer of the Belgian Pavilion to Richmond made front page news in the city, delayed the building's reconstruction. When it was finally dedicated in 1949, the political landscape had changed considerably. The campaign for civil rights staged in Richmond, including in the Belgian Friendship Building itself and across the south of the United States during the 1950s and 1960s, was accompanied by African American support for the Congo's independence. The story of the Belgian Friendship Building at Virginia Union did not adhere to the script of the original "donation" but instead unfolded in ways that Goris, Hening, and Davis could never have imagined.

5

RAISING MONEY AND RAISING STEEL

The Challenges of Reconstituting the Belgian Friendship Building

On December 5, 1940, even before the General Education Board had committed the necessary funds, Virginia Union proudly announced that it was receiving the central portion of the Belgian Friendship Building as a "gift" from the Belgian government in exile. Richmond's two largest newspapers exulted. Repeating the official rhetoric from the Belgian government and Virginia Union on December 6, the *News Leader* described the entire structure as being worth $700,000 and reported that it "was considered one of the most magnificent buildings at the fair."[1] In a front page story published on the same day, its chief rival, the *Times Dispatch,* noted that it was "built on strikingly modern lines" and emphasized the quality of its materials—"the finest products of Belgium."[2] It also noted the inclusion in the "gift" of at least some of the works of art from the pavilion, including the two bas-reliefs, *Congo* and *Belgium at Work,* which still decorate the building today. An editorial in the *News Leader,* also published on December 6, captured the sense of pride that even white Richmonders could take in what it said about Virginia Union:

> Richmond will not fail to see in this new contribution to the school a gratifying evidence of the esteem in which Virginia Union is held by educators. A noble work it has discharged in Negro education. It has supplied to the minis-

> try a large number of sane, earnest ministers. In the field of the social sciences, it has held leadership among Negro institutions. Some of the ablest Negroes in sociology were schooled at Virginia Union.
>
> At one time, as funds from the Northern Baptists diminished, the future of the local school seemed dark. Even now it has some acute problems to solve. In the light of this new gift, the school may feel that new friends are being raised up to help it. The library and assembly hall not only will serve but also will revitalize Virginia Union.[3]

The *Richmond Times Dispatch* instead married boosterism with an eye to the wider reach of the story when its editorial opened with the words, "Virginia and Richmond have been signally honored. A prize of inestimable usefulness and of historic and international significance has been placed within their reach." The writer continued, "Richmond, Virginia, the South, and the nation owe a debt of gratitude to those who have made possible this important advance in the field of Negro education." The editorial concluded:

> There should be rejoicing over the fact that a worthy educational institution in Virginia has this opportunity shortly to multiply its usefulness through the good offices of the Belgians, whose generosity, in this instance, may be regarded as, in some measure, a reciprocation of John D. Rockefeller, Jr.'s munificence in restoring the destroyed university library at Louvain [Leuven, in Dutch], after the first world war, in co-operation with thousands of American school children. We hazard the assertion that Belgium's action in making the central portion of her pavilion available to Virginia Union University under such advantageous terms, will not be forgotten by America when the time comes to restore the liberty of that gallant little nation at the postwar council table.[4]

The story had first been broken by the *Journal and Guide,* an African American newspaper based in Norfolk, in advance of the official announcement. Already in a banner front-page headline on November 23, it reported that the Belgians had offered the structure to Virginia Union. Describing it as "one of the most expensive and elaborate" of the national pavilions, it added that Belgian government officials had already visited the Richmond campus, and that those attending chapel had heard that the building would "house the library, auditorium, classrooms and might also provide gymnasium space."[5]

Other African American newspapers spread the good news throughout the country weeks later. On December 20, the *St. Louis Argus* celebrated that Virginia Union was receiving a "$1,000,000 Xmas Gift," while the short-lived *Phoenix Index* had a particularly insightful article.[6] Its unnamed reporter clearly had extremely good sources, writing on December 14, "The spacious structure which was one of the most beautiful at the recent World's Fair, was designed under the direction of Henry van de Velde, famous Belgian architect, as a model college building." This was the only account to mention the architect, even if the building's original purpose as a national pavilion at the 1939 New York World's Fair was elided. It also established that "before a packed Colburn Chapel audience Friday, two weeks ago, President Clark introduced Mr. S. E. Hening, treasurer of the board of trustees and of the American Baptist Home Mission Society, who hinted at the surprise gift. Efforts were made to keep the news from newspapers since school officials left [*sic*] that premature publicity would endanger [their] chances."[7] This suggests that Hening had not alerted President William J. Clark to the fact that no other institutions were seriously competing for the building. But what is most remarkable about the article is that the writer, who placed a library and a gym for the Panthers at the top of the university's needs, divided the pavilion into ten parts, speculating on how each could be reused. The Hall of Honor, the Arts and Crafts Hall, and the elevated gallery were all suggested for the library, while the industrial gallery was proposed for the gymnasium. The Belgian Congo installation was described as "of interest to the entire Negro race but [its] location might affect usage," with the author noting that Virginia Union was "undecided as to its acceptance," while the restaurant was apparently "not to be accepted."

The "gift" also attracted the attention of papers with larger circulations composed predominantly of white readers. For instance, in January 1941 an editorial in the *New York Post* concluded: "Free Belgium is crushed, for the time being, yet it lives here in the United States as though the disaster had never occurred. George Theunis, the Belgian ambassador [he was in fact a special Belgian envoy], announces that the beautiful Belgian Pavilion from the World's Fair has been given to Virginia Union University, the Negro educational center at Richmond."[8]

Some of the coverage also captured what would turn out to be the wild optimism that Clark, no doubt encouraged by Jan-Albert Goris and Hening, displayed toward to the project. There is no hint of the serious reservations harbored by Clark's successor John Malcus Ellison, and by Luther Foster, then the treasurer and shortly to become the president of Virginia State in nearby Petersburg. The *News Leader* reported that Clark believed the building "would be reconstructed within six to ten months."[9] The costs were originally estimated to be as low as $50,000.[10] Lauded on its fundraising letterhead as "in the interest of international friendship, interracial goodwill," and "Negro Education," the project would gain Virginia Union unprecedented attention and support, but it would also cost far more than anticipated.[11]

A three-pronged campaign raised the money. Even before he was appointed president, Ellison was charged with targeting African American donors; upon his assumption of his new role he also shared the responsibility with Theodore Adams, the chair of the board, for lobbying the General Education Board (GEB) for additional funds. Meanwhile, a separate effort sought to raise money from whites, especially but not only in Richmond. This was originally led by Egbert Leigh, who had earlier taken over the fundraising for the library, although Hening also played a major role in it. The reconstitution of the building, of course, depended on the money available. Therefore it proceeded slowly. One reason that costs quickly escalated was that Virginia Union took the entire pavilion, instead of just the central part, thereby gaining space for science laboratories and an auditorium that doubled as a basketball court. Another obvious factor was the war. Materials were increasingly in scarce supply, as was labor, even in the year before the U.S. entry into the conflict. Renting out the facility's completed portion to the military for use as an induction center for processing new troops provided much of the necessary funding and also enhanced the building's visibility among local whites. But the war also played a role in other ways, including changing the dynamics of local and national race relations, as African Americans insisted that their participation be rewarded with greater democracy at home as well as abroad.

Raising Money

The first challenge for Virginia Union was finding the money to bring the Belgian Building to Richmond and to reconstitute it there. For several months after the announcement, the *News Leader* and *Times Dispatch* regularly featured articles detailing the progress of the fundraising campaign. This, however, was never merely a local one. New York and Pittsburgh's African American communities joined their Richmond counterpart in playing particularly prominent roles in what was intended to be a national effort. Motivations varied. For some, support for Belgium dominated. Interracial goodwill, the second theme of the campaign, took varied forms, as individuals and groups of both races sought to influence Virginia Union's future direction. African American education clearly mattered, too. Union used the campaign to advertise the prominent role it already played in this sphere. As costs skyrocketed, personalities as well as purposes occasionally clashed, especially when some whites sought to control a process that other whites were already willing to acknowledge belonged in largely African American hands.

Although the General Education Board pledged $100,000, this was never going to be enough. By mid-December, efforts led by Leigh were already underway to locate at least $15,000 in Richmond, and $35,000 more in Virginia.[12] Leigh later commented that he "had not found much enthusiasm for higher Negro education among the white men and women on whom he had called," but at the time the local press instead focused on the positive.[13] For instance, students at the then all-white University of Richmond, of which Hening was an alumnus and which his son attended, contributed to the effort, in what the *News Leader* characterized as a "gesture of racial, religious and educational co-operation existing between the two schools."[14] Hening was even more effusive in an article aimed at white Baptists from across the country. He stoutly declared: "Seldom do the horrors and complications of war produce such a happy event whereby a highly cultured and peaceful nation of Europe presents to a minority race in another land a gift of inestimable material and historical value, thus providing the world with a striking and heartening expression of international friendship and interracial good will. The acceptance of this unique gift places Baptist leadership in Christian Negro education on a new high level."[15] Other reputations were also burnished in the process. Goris must have been delighted to see himself described in the *News Leader* as "for many years one of Europe's leading educators and internationally recognized as an authority on art."[16]

Nor did it take long for the campaign to spread northward and to the vibrant African American communities there. The day after Christmas, Adam Clayton Powell Jr., the minister of Abyssinia Baptist Church in Harlem, wrote Hening that he would be able to raise $5,000 from Virginia Union's Alumni Association and other

African Americans within a month. Powell, whose father was a Wayland Seminary and Virginia Union alumnus, described the building in his letter as "the most magnificent [gift] ever made to a colored institution."[17] The elder Powell pledged $1,000 and agreed to be the honorary chair of the Belgian Building Fund.[18]

A notable early success came when Goris and Hening secured the endorsement of First Lady Eleanor Roosevelt, who was a strong supporter of African Americans, much more so than her husband. Hening, accompanied by Goris, paid Mrs. Roosevelt a visit at the White House on January 14.[19] Just three days later, Roosevelt wrote about the campaign in her nationally syndicated newspaper column. Undoubtedly encouraged by Goris and Hening, she addressed all three of their major themes when she wrote: "This gesture of friendship has significance in a world of war. It is not only a gesture of international goodwill but a gesture of interracial goodwill, because it is to be erected on a campus of a college devoted to the higher education of Negroes."[20] She eventually served as the honorary chair of the fundraising committee.[21]

At this point the costs were assumed to be relatively modest, although published and private estimates both varied, in part depending on whether the figure included only the central part of the pavilion or the whole structure, and on whether the estimated value of the "gift" was factored in, or simply the amount of money it would take to rebuild it.[22] Already in November 1940, before the public announcement was made, Goris and Hening had successfully persuaded Clark to try to take the entire building. Clark wrote Jackson Davis of the GEB that to do otherwise would snub the Belgians, who would have to sell the rest for scrap to pay their workers. At that point it appeared that Secretary of State Cordell Hull would officially accept the building.[23]

A hint that Hening knew how much he had underestimated the cost of rebuilding came when he sought the advice of Albert Mann of the GEB in a telephone call made in late February. He wanted to approach David K. E. Bruce (whom he described as a Virginian, although Bruce in fact had been born and raised in Baltimore), to ask him to make an emergency donation of $100,000 to fund the project, a sum that was twice what Richmond's papers were reporting was needed.[24] At the time Hening contacted Mann, Bruce was in London, serving as the chief representative of the Red Cross during the Blitz. There is no record of his response, although Bruce's sympathy for African American education had already led him and his wife,

Ailsa Mellon Bruce, the daughter of the former secretary to the Treasury, Andrew Mellon, to donate eleven Virginia public libraries that, although segregated, were nonetheless the first in the state to be open at least in part to African Americans.[25]

Another breakthrough was nonetheless achieved on March 7, 1941, when the Executive Committee of Union's board was informed that Jessie Vann had pledged to raise $25,000 in order that the building's grace note, its tower, be a memorial to her late husband, Robert Lee Vann, her predecessor as the publisher and owner of the *Pittsburgh Courier* and one of Virginia Union's most prominent alumni.[26] The highly capable Vann, who had earlier worked as a teacher, ran the *Courier* with great success until 1963, when she finally retired. During her tenure at the *Courier,* she served on the boards of both the Urban League and the NAACP.[27]

Hints of her contribution had already come in December following Vann's visit to Richmond, but it took time to secure the promise in writing.[28] Ira Lewis, the general manager of the paper before the death of Robert Vann, and its president afterward, appears to have offered key encouragement.[29] The naming of the tower for Vann was an important step in assimilating the Belgian Friendship Building project into the African American community at both local and national levels. The tower's dedication explicitly tied the building to the cause of racial uplift and civic education, even as it also furthered Belgian propaganda among African Americans. The community's needs included not just improved educational facilities for the state's most intellectually ambitious university to which African Americans had access. They also encompassed monumental commemoration as a counterweight to the central place that Monument Avenue's Confederate's statues occupied in the myth of the Lost Cause, belief in which was in the 1940s by no means limited only to white southerners.

Vann's pledge and the naming of the tower transformed the Belgian Pavilion into a monument to the aspirations and achievements of highly educated African Americans. To be sure, the building had not been designed as a monument but as a national pavilion on a civic scale. However, its architectural language that avoided association with oppressive ideologies of the past and historicist bombast, as well as its employment of valuable durable materials that synthesized handcraft and industry, had undeniable appeal for Vann and her community as they sought to chart a new era in African American higher education. The building's terra cotta and schist cladding lent it weight and permanence, whereas its steel frame and soaring bell tower connoted both technological and spiritual uplift. This was a more fitting language of monumentality than the mobile and lightweight forms that Sigfried Giedion, Josep Lluís Sert, and Fernand Léger would propose in their coauthored position paper on monumentality from 1943. The striking combination of monumentality and asymmetry that van de Velde, Stynen, and Bourgeois achieved on a grand scale in the Belgian Pavilion lent itself to new expressions and new purposes in its adopted home. Equally striking is how its architectural language appealed to Black and white communities alike, each seeing in it a noble form fitting of their aspirations.

Jessie Vann's pledge and the naming of the tower ensured that the campaign remained newsworthy for African Americans. The *Courier* helped organize fundraising efforts in Baltimore, Chicago, Cleveland, Detroit, Nashville, New York, and Philadelphia, as well, of course, as in Pittsburgh. Emmett Scott, who had been an administrator under Booker T. Washington at Tuskegee as well as at Howard University, and who chaired the national committee raising money from African Americans, reminded *Courier* readers that "Mr. Vann was a crusading patriot who refused to compromise any essential rights of his people," and that the tower "will permanently symbolize the fierce passion of a man who ever spoke for equal and exact justice for all elements of our population." Scott praised "particularly his never-ending denunciation of the wrongs and injustices heaped upon those of his own racial group, blood, and tradition."[30]

White Baptists continued to be involved as well. In April 1941, New York's Baptist establishment pulled out all the stops for a fundraising dinner held at New York's Riverside Church, which was, like the GEB, a bailiwick of Rockefeller philanthropy. The event featured an assortment of Belgian dignitaries as well as leading Baptists. At this point the Belgian contribution was valued at $400,000, rather than the $700,000 given in most other early accounts, with $325,000 required for its rebuilding. Of this amount, $100,000 was being provided by the GEB, and $80,000 of the rest had already been raised, leaving the substantial sum of $145,000 still to go.[31] The cost would quickly rise, while the announced total donations may not have been entirely accurate. Less than two months later, the *Pittsburgh Courier* reported that the bill for the rebuilding would come to $380,000, and the *Richmond Times Dispatch* noted that $75,000 had been raised to date.[32]

The fundraising campaign slightly softened racial boundaries in Richmond, without in any way dismantling them. At the end of March the city's mayor, Gordon

Ambler, agreed to speak at the First African Baptist Church in support of the building, the first time that he had addressed its congregation.[33] The groundbreaking ceremonies, which were held on June 9, 1941, provided a far more important occasion for the two races to meet on terms of dignity and respect, if certainly not equality. The proceedings, led by Virginia governor James H. Price, were broadcast on "Wings over Jordon," the country's leading African American–oriented radio program, thus garnering further national attention.[34]

Although Goris privately wrote back to his brother in patently racist terms about the event, the audience he intended to impress responded exactly as he had hoped. Oscar W. Adams, the African American editor of the *Birmingham Reporter*, reported in the *Birmingham News*, the city's white newspaper:

> Declaring the beautiful Belgian Pavilion, which includes the imposing Robert L. Vann Memorial Tower, was the gift of a colonial empire to a Negro university, the gift of a Catholic country to a Baptist school, the symbol of human understanding and goodwill and the negation of racial prejudice of hatred and of violence, Dr. Jan Albert Goris, special delegate of the Belgian Embassy, struck the keynote of the impressive cornerstone laying ceremonies of the Belgian Friendship Building before a distinguished audience of 5,000 at Virginia Union University, Richmond last Monday.[35]

Describing "one of the most significant events in the history of Virginia Union University and of Negro education," Adams also noted that Dr. Goris had "commended the Negro for the contribution he had made to American and European life in loyalty, poetry, and music." Goris also conveyed greetings on behalf of the African inhabitants of the Congo.

Not surprisingly, the occasion was of even more importance in Richmond, where the *Times Dispatch* informed its largely white readership about the details of the event, at least part of which was also broadcast live over the local radio station WRNL. In addition to Goris, whom it quoted as saying, "Every European who travels in the United States is impressed by the contribution of the Negro community to United States culture," the speakers included Douglas Southall Freeman, the editor of the rival *Richmond News Leader,* the city's leading afternoon paper (the *Times Dispatch* appeared in the morning).[36] The author of a hagiographic biography of

Robert E. Lee that won him a Pulitzer Prize, Freeman strongly supported segregation, but as a Baptist, he also took pride in Virginia Union's history of educating African Americans.[37] He furthermore viewed the building as an "augury" of Belgium's eventual victory in a war to which the United States was not yet committed.

The event also provided poignant moments in which to honor Vann. His widow inserted into the cornerstone the Bible his mother had given him when he left Ahoskie, North Carolina, to study in Richmond, as well as the obituary he had written for Booker T. Washington, and the one his own paper had published for him. The University of Pittsburgh, from which he had received his law degree and which was one of the few universities in the country to be housed in its own skyscraper, the so-called Cathedral of Learning, sent a scroll to be placed in the tower's lobby.[38] Without changing the form of the tower, these personal effects and tributes, along with the tower's dedication, remade the Belgian Pavilion, including its colonial and racist imagery, into a commemorative monument to exactly the form of African American leadership that made many of the building's white funders apprehensive.

The most extraordinary aspect of the groundbreaking may have been the way in which white Belgians and African Americans alike equated Belgium's suffering under German occupation with what African Americans had and continued to endure. A follow-up article in the *Courier* by James Edmund Boyack quoted Professor I. W. Taylor, who in his role as past grand master of the Most Worshipful Grand Lodge of Virginia, Ancient Free and Accepted Masons, an African American fraternal association, had participated in the ceremony. Boyack was happy to repeat Taylor's remarks, in which the African American dignitary equated the trials and tribulations of white Belgians under Nazi occupation with the discrimination still faced by African Americans. Taylor told the reporter: "Today the Belgian people are being exploited . . . [African Americans] are a people suffering from both discrimination and disparagement. They are a race which is constantly fighting for equality of opportunity in the pursuit of happiness. This is, therefore, a gift from sufferer to sufferer. It is significant, therefore, that this magnificent building should be presented to Virginia Union University, an institution of higher learning and the cultural development of the Negro, which seeks to inculcate into its votaries the ideals and precepts of virtue, manliness and liberty."[39] Taylor concluded with the hope "that men of whatever nationality or hue, shall all be brothers."

The groundbreaking was not just of interest to African Americans and to white southerners. Eleanor Roosevelt sent a telegram of support.[40] Clark, the university's outgoing president, contributed an article to the *New York Times* on what he termed "a historic milestone in the progress of Negro education."[41] He predicted that the building would enable the university to nearly double the size of the student body to 1,000, noting that it was "divided into four parts: a library providing space for 94,000 books with two reading galleries, an auditorium space for 2,000 persons, a science laboratory, a gymnasium, and the Vann Memorial Tower from which the Virginia Union University Choir will broadcast." Addressing a largely white readership, Clark was careful to state that "we develop our students especially to serve their own people and the communities in which they live" and that "emphasis has always been placed on the dignity of all useful work," while also noting that "since the turn of the century our institution has played a leading role in developing and stimulating Negro leadership. Today, as this group of our citizenry faces both a national emergency and the nation's call to arms, leadership and resourcefulness in the race is more urgently needed than ever before."

Making the airwaves and the papers did not easily convert to raising the necessary funds. An accounting made in July 1941 is notable for the way in which it broke down what had been received by both race and location and for the reference it made for the first time to $90,000 from a previous campaign, probably an earlier one to match the unfulfilled pledge of the General Education Board for a new library. By this point, Richmond whites had given $11,333 and other whites $19,282, while faculty had donated $3,100 and students a further $1,000. In addition, $8,000 had come from New York's African American community and $14,967 from other African Americans, including alumni. The Carnegie book fund gave $4,500, and International Seminary Equipment another $3,000. More than $185,000 was now listed as being in hand, once again calling into question Clark's rosy initial estimate of the price of rebuilding to be $50,000.

Different constituencies pitched the building in different ways. For instance, Hening, writing for a largely white Baptist audience across the country, wrote that "American Baptists should take pride and rejoice in this unusual and generous proposal." He described Virginia Union as "one of the best established and strongest of the dozen or more Negro colleges owing their birth to Northern Baptists." Appeals to local whites were framed much more carefully. A fundraising brochure of the period reassured them that most of the money they donated would stay in the city;

it also pitched educating local African Americans as a means of protecting whites from the threat of radical change. Under the heading "Virginia Union Trains Leadership," it declared:

> One of the great needs of the Negro race is well-trained, sound and dependable leadership. Churches, schools, organizational enterprises must have . . . clear sighted guidance [and] leadership. Industrial and Vocational education, as important as it is, cannot develop the type of leaders that our communities and institutions need and must have if the masses of people are to rightly and properly understand their position as law-abiding, loyal and dependable citizens. For the large masses of industrial workers, agriculturalists, domestic workers, the church and community organizations serve as centers of recreation and inspiration. They furnish the means of appropriate emotional expression. They serve as channels for their thinking and activities. They are the avenues of needed information and direction. Thus, the uncritical thinking masses are saved from the inroads and impositions of the many rising "isms," racial movements and similar propaganda. Here is the special task of the carefully trained and wise community leader. It is he who interprets the meaning of citizenship, loyalties, wholesome attitudes and the methods of expressing them. Virginia Union has through the years of its existence, specialized in the preparation of this important and much needed type of leadership.[42]

The authors of this pamphlet walked a narrow line between advocating for African American leadership and circumscribing it within "acceptable" boundaries. For them, leadership encompassed educational and economic progress, but not challenging Jim Crow.

Even more disturbing were parts of the paragraph that followed on the university and race relations:

> The University supports strongly, wholeheartedly, and in a very concrete way, amicable race relations. The emphasis is not only approached in the classroom, but teachers and students go out into the communities to make their contributions. Opportunities are sought and accepted for face-to-face and tolerant understanding of problems, and methods of expressing good will are worked

> out. The school's choir frequently appears before white groups for musical entertainment. Several of the faculty members serve on the Virginia Commission for Inter-racial Cooperation. One is the chairman of the Commission's Research Committee. Students serve acceptably in the homes of many of Richmond's white families. They are reported as reliable, mannerly, and efficient workers. Many of the students, through this contact, earn their expenses through college.[43]

Examples of the "tolerance" cultivated at Virginia Union are carefully chosen. The definition of "leadership" in this fundraising brochure intended for white audiences in the early 1940s was conservatively calibrated to avoid any hint of disturbance to the existing social and racial order.

Nor was this the only time that the Belgian Friendship Building was defended in this patronizing way. In the spring of 1943, the *Richmond News Leader* wrote that "Long observation of the work of the local school has convinced the officers of the [General Education] Board that Virginia Union is one of the soundest institutions of higher learning available to the Negroes of the South," and that with the completion of the Belgian Friendship Building and the updating of the Noble Nine, it could "continue as an apostle of moderation, of Christian service and of educational progress."[44]

Despite the efforts clearly targeted at whites, it was African Americans who kept the ball rolling. By the end of 1945, the alumni association had raised $37,000. The *New York Age* proudly reported on its front page, "This is probably quite unique among alumni associations of Negro colleges and universities."[45] Even the famous Negro League baseball teams got involved with the Grays, who alternated between Homestead, Pennsylvania, and Washington, D.C., playing the Baltimore Elites in a benefit game in Richmond's Mayo Island Ball Park.[46] Josh Gibson, the Grays' star hitter, probably took to the plate. The Virginia Union Panthers championship basketball team of 1939 also reunited to play a match against the Harlem Globetrotters to raise funds for the building. This unfortunately prompted a six-month penalty for the university meted out by the Central Intercollegiate Athletic Association, the HBCU athletic conference to which it belonged, for competing against a professional team.[47]

By the beginning of March 1941, Ellison had taken charge of the project; the following month he was appointed president. Ellison, like Foster at Virginia State, with whom he would work resolutely to straighten out Virginia Union's finances, had doubts about the wisdom of acquiring the Belgian Building. Ellison and Foster were quick to see through Hening, but they could also tell that executing the project competently would win them crucial white allies. In a meeting Ellison had with Davis in early November 1940, Ellison voiced no opinion on the matter. In a follow-up letter, however, clearly influenced by a recent meeting with Hening, he described local enthusiasm for the scheme.[48] A month later, Ellison wrote to Davis in a more clear-headed vein:

> The matter that disturbs me now as much as anything else is Dr. Clark's almost wild emphasis on an immediate campaign to secure $200,000 to bring the remainder of the Belgian Pavilion to the campus. To me, in light of the rapid deterioration of our present plant even to the danger point such a venture seems most unreasonable. Dr. Clark is not able to get money from any source. He wants to saddle that upon me. I regret that Mr. Hening encourages it by making promises which I fear he cannot realize.[49]

Davis, however, made clear in his response that Ellison had little choice but to fall in line behind the effort. After Ellison was named executive vice president in March, Davis chided him for a plan for the university's reorganization that Davis felt placed more emphasis upon the appointment of new administrators than he believed the scale of the institution warranted. He cautioned, "Frankly, I am puzzled that you should be thinking of these matters when the crying need of Virginia Union is to raise the money required for the completion of the Belgian Pavilion."[50] Other whites agreed that this was the chief task at hand. Reporting later in the year on Ellison's appointment as president, the *Times Dispatch* noted that the "Belgian Friendship Building will provide the university with one of the handsomest and most modern educational units in the South."[51] The struggle for funds must at times have seen interminable to Ellison, but his astute stewardship would see the building through to completion.

Ellison had substantial support from fellow African Americans; the building committee's membership was nearly half African American, and he would have unprecedented success in garnering African American donations to the institution more broadly. African American building committee members included Ellison; the architect Charles T. Russell, who was the university's superintendent of grounds; Everett B. Poole, the university's business manager; and Booker T. Bradshaw, the African American president of the Virginia Mutual Life Insurance Company.

Thomas Parker Ayer, D. Tennant Bryan, C. Braxton Valentine, and Leigh as well as Hening represented the white community on the Belgian building committee.[52] The presence of Ayer and Bryan is particularly notable. Ayer was the director of the Richmond Public Library. Like many southern cities, Richmond was a latecomer to the public library movement, in part because the city was reluctant to fund such facilities. By at least 1936, the city's African American community was clamoring for equal access to this civic institution, which indeed it gained in 1947, long before other public and private institutions in Richmond were integrated.[53] Running the library at Virginia Union as a publicly accessible and particularly large branch of the city library system, as was planned in 1942, was undoubtedly intended to delay the end of segregation.[54] Bryan's family owned the *Times Dispatch*. Despite his support for Virginia Union, he would later be a staunch opponent of the desegregation of the state's public schools.[55] Valentine was a member of the family that established the Valentine Museum, Richmond's first museum, whose collections preserved the city's history, and whose board he eventually chaired.[56] Leigh left Richmond during the war to join the Office of Strategic Services, which sent him immediately after the war to Belgium. He participated in the American occupation of Japan from 1947 to 1950, before joining the Central Intelligence Agency.[57]

Fundraising continued throughout the rest of the year in both New York and Richmond. Although Virginia Union's charter prohibited it from going into debt, the trustees turned to local banks for support, taking out a loan for $130,000, which they would pay off in just four years.[58] An additional $50,000 was found by raiding the endowment of the money obtained from the sale of the Hartshorn College site to the city of Richmond.[59] The *Times Dispatch* ran a cartoon in December that condescendingly showed Ellison in children's clothing hanging up his stocking and requesting from the people of Virginia the final $50,000 needed to complete the building.[60] Between January 1942 and September 1943, another $88,507.17 would indeed be found, with the GEB contributing more than $50,000 of that total. With the exception of $10,000 from the Mission Board of the Southern Baptist Convention, which would eventually donate $25,000, most of the rest of this support the project received appears to have come from African American sources, yet the funding was still insufficient.[61] On June 14, 1942, the *Pittsburgh Courier,* which had not surprisingly followed construction progress carefully, announced that Virginia Union was about to pause work on the reconstruction.[62] It would resume again only after the war. In the meantime, the steel skeleton of the unfinished tower remained on display as a frank illustration of the building's incomplete status.

This did not mean, however, that efforts to find money ceased. As Davis pointed out in a letter he wrote Ellison in January 1943, "Your desire to press the campaign now is sound. People are well employed and are earning good wages."[63] Prodding the GEB to do more proved as important as raising funds from individuals and from organizations. In April 1943 the GEB pledged $158,000, but the money would become available only once Virginia Union raised matching funds, which it would only accomplish in early 1946.[64] S. C. Mitchell, a board member who taught history at the University of Richmond and who had been an early supporter of the project, wrote Davis an effusive letter of thanks.[65] White support also arose from infighting between Baptists. Greatly encouraged by Davis, and possibly also prompted by Hening, both of whom were Virginia-born Baptists, Noble Y. Beall of the Home Mission Board of the Southern Baptist Convention and Blanche White of the Women's Missionary Union, a white Virginian group, both offered the Belgian Friendship Building campaign unprecedented support during this lull. Southern Baptists had previously refrained from contributing to African American campuses largely funded by their northern white counterparts.[66] Although this new assistance was phrased in terms of racial understanding, it undoubtedly also arose from a desire to gain influence over institutions that had long operated outside the orbit of southern whites. The two organizations were not unique. In November 1945, Henry Alford Porter, the white former minster at First Baptist in Charlottesville, bequeathed the bulk of his library and his estate, valued at over $50,000, to Virginia Union, following the death of his widow, which occurred the following year.[67]

What really enabled Virginia Union to begin to stand on its own two feet, however, was the income it began to obtain in February 1943 from renting out the partially completed building as an induction center for those who had been drafted into or had volunteered for duty in the U.S. armed forces. The *Times Dispatch* reported, "Army officers said that they believe this will be one of the most spacious, as well as one of the most beautiful, establishments of its kind in the country."[68] According to the article, the auditorium housed waiting inductees, with offices for each of the services on the same floor. The building was also outfitted with spaces for medical examinations and the other bureaucratic steps necessary to process the men who passed through it. In addition to the $20,000 per year the university received for the space, Virginia Union was allowed to charge 10 cents a meal overhead on the 50-cent meal its canteen offered to the center's staff and to the incoming soldiers.[69] The food was reported to be the tastiest available to inductees in that part of the country. This mattered, as its provision provided much more income than the university had originally expected. Theodore Adams was so encouraged by these developments that he wrote Davis: "Frankly, I feel more encouraged about the situation at Virginia Union than at any time in recent months. . . . The feeding project provides an added source of income which I think assures us of enough to keep the school going during the war emergency even though we shall lose most of our men and will make doubly sure our ability to provide the $20,000 listed as income from the rental of the building."[70]

Also important to the building's eventual completion were the first tranches of money from the United Negro College Fund (UNCF), which was established in 1944. Although the amounts were lower than what Virginia Union received from the GEB, they came with fewer strings attached and less oversight. Already in its first year, the UNCF gave Virginia Union nearly $16,000.[71]

By the end of the decade, however, the GEB had pulled back from its support of the Belgian building, if not of Virginia Union. Davis's death in 1947 undoubtedly played a role, but so did postwar conditions. In 1949, the GEB turned down a request to assist with the equipping of the science laboratories, at an estimated cost of $50,000, once the army finally vacated the premises.[72] Instead, most of the funds were raised from the Old Dominion Dental, Medical and Pharmaceutical Societies, an African American professional society established in 1905. Their pledge arrived "on the condition that office space, including space for [a] medical library can be provided for the Association, and that certain portions of the Unit be a memorial to deceased members of the Association," since at the time African American physicians "have no place with such facilities and offerings for clinics, research, and for filing community health bulletins and other materials and research findings."[73]

In the end, the Belgian Friendship Building cost Virginia Union more than anyone had anticipated and certainly far more than the original scheme for a new library building alone ever would have, even accounting for wartime inflation. Davis admitted as much in a memo in 1943:

> It may be questioned whether Virginia Union got the best building for its purpose that could be had for an expenditure of $600,000. But with the modifications that have been made in the plans, there is no question that the institution will have an excellent library, adequate laboratory facilities, needed classroom space, lecture halls and a large assembly hall which will serve for concerts, plays, and public meetings. The space provided in this building is roughly equal to the rest of the space for teaching purposes in the other buildings of the University. It may be pointed out that the institution had been trying for three years to raise money for a regular building with very little success. The Belgian Pavilion, as a gift from the Belgian Government, has made a public appeal and brought a natural response which seems to secure the completion of the project.[74]

The effort also confirmed the faith that the GEB and Virginia Union's trustees had placed in Ellison's abilities. These encompassed his talent for attracting funds from fellow African Americans, as well as from white Southern Baptists, without alienating the northern white philanthropists upon whose support the university had always relied. It was a delicate balancing act requiring consummate diplomacy. Ellison had proven himself more than up to the task.

Raising Steel: Assembling the Belgian Friendship Building

Long before the first round of fundraising concluded, pieces of the building were on the move. Belgian workers who may have been involved in the building's construction were also engaged in demounting it. They also made modest contributions toward the cost of transporting and reconstituting the structure.[75] It was estimated that it would take eighty to ninety freight cars to transport the pieces from New York to Richmond.[76] The arrival on the campus of the first shipment at the end of February 1941 was met by cheering students, with many joining the faculty in snapping photographs of the occasion. The *Phoenix Index* gave the most complete account of the occasion, noting "that in spite of a piercing wind and wintry sky, practically the entire student body of the University as well as members of the faculty were on hand to witness the unloading. Several young men rushed forward to help with the unloading as the first pieces were taken from the truck, loud cheers and yells filled the air. This attracted others, including several passersby."[77] At this point it was envisaged that "the building is expected to be completed by September and dedicatory exercises are scheduled for October." Although this proved overly optimistic, that it "will house one of the finest library and auditorium combinations to be found in the South" was indeed the case, especially considering the degree to which even most white institutions in the region lagged behind their northern counterparts.[78]

It took more than nine years to complete the reassembly of the pieces once they arrived in Richmond and the fitting out of the new interiors. The entrance of the United States into the war in December 1941 was a principal reason for the delay, even as the war ultimately generated much of the income necessary to complete the project. But there were other factors at work as well. Goris was more concerned about funding Belgians stranded in the United States than about seeing the building finished, and Hening almost certainly assisted him in foisting outstanding costs the Belgians had accumulated during the fair onto Virginia Union. Moreover, Van Kuyck was not always available even before he enlisted in the U.S. Army. The fact that the building was assembled out of materials measured in meters rather than feet and inches and in a construction system unfamiliar to American builders and unsuited to permanence posed additional obstacles. There was also often a racial dimension to these tensions, as Goris and Hening continued to assume that they could exploit Virginia Union, going so far in Hening's case as attempting to oust Ellison, an effort Adams and GEB officials strongly resisted.[79]

The Belgian team of laborers that had assembled the building in New York remained in the United States for the fair's second season. Goris and Van Kuyck engineered their transfer to Richmond. The contractor, the engineer Armand R. Guilmain, was Belgian, as was much of his labor force. Guilmain's bid on behalf of the newly formed Amstel Contracting Company (also sometimes referred to as Amstel Construction Corporation) was the only one solicited, and awarding him the contract for the project was almost certainly an inside job.[80] There were also African Americans on the job site, however, such as Allen Norman Burns, a carpenter who worked on the building until he was drafted in January 1943.[81]

Ellison endured, but another prominent African American did not. In early 1941 and again in April 1942, Virginia Union announced that Charles Russell, the city's foremost African American architect, would help erect the building.[82] In May 1941 a photograph published in the *New York Herald Tribune* showed him overseeing the unloading of one of the bas-reliefs.[83] Other African American newspapers from across the country publicized Russell's role in the project, as reported by Simeon Booker, who graduated from Virginia Union in 1942 and was already on his way to becoming an eminent journalist.[84] Russell served on the building committee and was appointed clerk-of-work on the site in August 1941, when Van Kuyck finally submitted the blueprints needed for the contractors to begin work.[85] By May 1942, however, something had gone terribly wrong. Baptist official Donald Faulkner wrote Ellison urging him to dismiss Russell, whom Faulkner accused of being disloyal to Ellison; in the same letter he also urged Ellison to drop the university librarian, whom he described as being "not your kind of Negro."[86] Faulkner was not operating in tandem with Hening, however, as he also urged that Hening be replaced with Valentine, and that Leigh, who apparently had not yet left Richmond for the OSS, take over Ellison's role as the head of the Building Committee. Tellingly, Faulkner wrote of Leigh, "You know he has the conservativism to project the University, and the ability to direct the construction along proper channels."[87] Clearly, affirming to local whites that Virginia Union posed no challenge to the local racial status quo was key.

It is impossible to reconstruct the circumstances that led to Russell's departure, but certainly Hening was no fan of the African American architect. Moreover, no one would have been better positioned than Russell to understand that Hening and Van Kucyk were being less than honest with Virginia Union, as others, too, would come to suspect. The issues included the cost of bringing the building to Richmond, the questions of whether it was indeed necessary to bring the entire building and whether the Belgians employed on the site were doing an efficient job, not to mention Goris's original deception regarding the building's alleged permanence. Transporting the materials for the entire building quickly pushed the costs well over the $120,000 that Hening had promised only a library would require.[88] The GEB suspected that the disassembling and shipping costs had been inflated.[89] The argument that the entire building had to be acquired in order to reconstruct a section of it also seems spurious.[90] What is not in question is that the sale of all rather than just a portion of it saved Goris the task of offloading the rest. Ellison was among those who were not convinced that Guilmain and his men were working as hard as local labor might have. Certainly, the question for Guilmain's men of what they might do after the job was over must have haunted them.

Hening tried to save face and to shift the blame for selecting Guilmain onto Russell.[91] The conflict boiled over in 1943, when Hening tried to extract additional payments for Van Kuyck and for Guilmain's firm from a highly suspicious board. He also accused Virginia Union of selling off steel and a valuable copper frieze.[92] GEB staff suspected that Hening and Faulkner were making trouble because their organization was not wielding as much authority over Virginia Union as its own Board of Trustees or the GEB.[93] Beall, who represented the Southern Baptists, felt exactly the same way, deeming Hening resistant to proper accounting and auditing procedures.[94] An audit of the university's account in the fall of 1942 had turned up a number of troubling discrepancies, many of which were reported in detail to the GEB.[95]

Russell had apparently clashed with Guilmain and with Van Kuyck, neither of whom had endeared themselves to anyone on the ground in Richmond, nor had they remained in good standing with the GEB, despite their initial good impression. The problems may have begun with the issue of whether the entire building needed to come to Richmond, but trust really began to break down when Van Kuyck was slow to provide the documentation necessary to send the project out to bid. In January 1941 it was announced that Van Kuyck "will design the Belgian building to harmonize with the present structures on the campus," and that he was to come to Richmond, which he had already visited in October and again in December 1940 "to discuss with alumni and friends of the university just what he intends to do about the erection of the building, to give the complete history of the building, and to afford an opportunity for interested persons to ask him questions in regard to the structure and material of the building."[96] Instead, however, Van Kuyck traveled to Bogata, Columbia, so that he could reenter the United States as an applicant for citizenship.[97] In June 1941 neither he nor Hening could provide estimates of what the construction would cost.[98] A month later Ellison sent the first of many missives urging Van Kuyck to make a promised visit. In this one, Ellison stated that visitors to the site "are rather disappointed when they arrive on campus and see materials scattered and no work being done."[99] It took Van Kuyck until August 15 to issue the construction drawings, documents that were necessary to begin to put the building back together.[100] It was in part because of Van Kuyck's absences that in August 1941 the Building Committee appointed Russell, who was already on the university's payroll, as clerk of work.[101]

Until the push to produce the drawings, the Belgian architect's contribution appears to have been limited largely to a drawing and model explaining how "The World of Tomorrow" pavilion could be reconfigured for use in Richmond. The drawing, entitled "Proposed Reconstruction of the Belgian Pavilion for Virginia Union University, Richmond Virginia," shows what was undoubtedly the initial scheme to bring only the central pavilion to Richmond (fig. 81). The entrance facade it illustrates is derived from the Belgian Pavilion's Hall of Honor, which in Richmond was reconstituted to form the auditorium that doubled as a basketball court. In comparison, the model that was frequently illustrated in the fundraising literature makes use of most of the original structure, including the tower (fig. 82).[102] While the pavilion at the fair had been U-shaped, with the tower tucked next to covered gallery enclosing the fourth side of the roughly rectangular plot, Van Kuyck opened up the courtyard, shifting the covered gallery to one end of the rear of the ensemble and placed the tower at the opposite edge of this facade. The library corresponds to the left volume in the model photo, with the science building in the center volume and the auditorium in the tallest volume on the right. A construction drawing shows the science block divided into laboratories for physics, chemistry, and biology, plus a lecture theater (fig. 83).

Van Kuyck arranged the parts of the original structure, opening the composition to face North Lombard Street in a confident and welcoming manner. He also regularized the building, getting rid of the canted volume of the original auditorium and restaurant block as well as the curved end of the section that had housed the Belgian Congo exhibition. Finally, his changes entailed a nearly complete reorganization of the placement of the windows, since especially the auditorium and basketball court no longer required so much glazing.

Once he had drafted this scheme, Van Kuyck remained under-engaged in the building project, which took a back seat to diplomatic and military engagements. In October he had still not signed a contract for his work, for which he was to receive a 4 percent fee for the cost of reconstituting rather than designing the building.[103] His delay in signing was unusual and may have resulted from the fact that he was not licensed to practice anywhere in the United States, let alone in Virginia.[104] For this

Figure 81. Proposed reconstruction of the Belgian Pavilion for Virginia Union University, Richmond Virginia, presumably Hugo van Kuyck, 1940 or 1941. (Virginia Union University Archives and Special Collections)

Figure 82. Model of Belgian Friendship Building, Hugo van Kuyck, 1941. (Virginia Union University Archives and Special Collections)

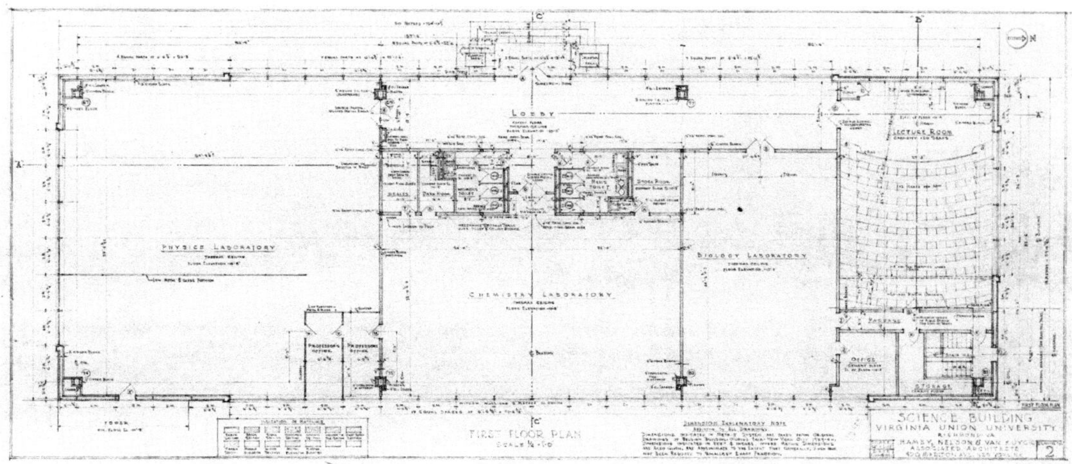

Figure 83. Plan of science block, including physics, chemistry, and biology laboratories and a lecture room, Belgian Friendship Building, Hamby, Nelson, and Van Kuyck, 1941. (Library of Virginia)

reason, the final drawings for the Belgian Friendship Building were signed by the New York architectural office of Hamby and Nelson for which Van Kuyck served as a consultant, and evidence suggests that Hamby contributed to the Belgian Building's redesign.[105]

Beyond architectural consulting, Van Kuyck juggled a number of engagements. He had been sent to the United States on a diplomatic mission by Belgium's government-in-exile and made several trips to Washington, D.C., to reassure the U.S. government of Belgian opposition toward the Germans, King Leopold III's hasty surrender notwithstanding. Van Kuyck also delivered lectures on new techniques of camouflage at MIT, which led to his hire in December 1940 as a consulting engineer for the U.S. Army.[106] In July 1942, he formally enlisted in the U.S. Army at the rank of lieutenant, thanks to an agreement signed between Belgian prime minister Hubert Pierlot and Belgian minister of foreign affairs Paul-Henry Spaak and the American government.[107] Van Kuyck's work on amphibian transport vehicles with General Motors led him to study the terrain of French beaches, and in 1943 the army sent him to England to prepare for the Allied invasion of Nazi-occupied Europe to which he would make a crucial contribution both by helping to choose and by mapping its site. He was awarded a Legion of Merit, an Air Medal, and a Bronze Star for his achievements.[108]

One solution to Van Kuyck's absence from Richmond was to rely instead upon Armand Vermaelen, a Belgian civil engineer. Vermaelen had played a role in the construction of the Belgian Pavilion at the Paris fair in 1937, which, built entirely with Belgian labor, had been the first pavilion to be finished.[109] Under the direction of Paul Célis, the chief engineer for the Belgian government who had helped van de Velde develop designs for the 1937 and 1939 Belgian Pavilions, Vermaelen had also supervised both the construction and the demolition of the New York fair building. The August 1941 Virginia Union press release that announced Vermaelen's role noted that construction would get underway once plans had been approved by Richmond's building inspector, C. Stuart Duggins.[110]

On October 15, 1941, Guilmain finally signed a contract for the reassembly.[111] The cost was given as $231,016.64, which did not include the amount already expended on disassembling the building and shipping its parts to Richmond. The contract encompassed the entire fitting out, complete with electricity, plumbing, and painting of the library, science building tower, and a covered gallery. The "main hall," to be used as an auditorium and basketball court, was at this point to be "completed only for limited use," until more money could be raised.[112]

Among the many challenges associated with the project was the fact that many of the Belgian construction workers did not speak English. The *Richmond Afro American* proudly announced already in July 1941 that George Ellis, a Virginia Union senior from Brooklyn, was translating from German (Dutch, the native language of many of the Flemings, was not taught at Virginia Union) and presumably also from French into English for them.[113] Another hurdle was that the entire structure was dimensioned metrically, making it to this day an outlier for a building in the United States, where inches and feet still prevail.

Despite these problems, progress was indeed made, even after the United States entered the war (fig. 84). By January 1942, the *Times Dispatch* reported that "the library already is virtually complete," although the sheets of glass along one side of the space remained taped, "a precaution against the possibility of bombing" (fig. 85).[114] The steel frame was in place, and three-quarters of the tower's slate revetment had been reinstalled (fig. 86 probably dates to the spring of 1942). The roofing of the science section was also underway. The same article apportioned credit for the

Virginia Union Moves Forward

These pictures of a building in the rough—strong steel girders, slate, tile, plate glass and marble—represent the material out of which shall come increased facilities—a new library, holding 94,000 volumes, an auditorium-gymnasium seating 2,000 persons, and twenty new class rooms.

Truly, VIRGINIA UNION MOVES FORWARD in preparing our youth for useful lives in many fields. . . . .

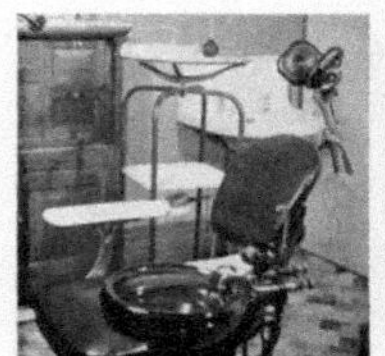

Figure 84. *Virginia Union University Bulletin*, 1941. (Virginia Union University Archives and Special Collections)

Figure 85. Construction photo, Belgian Friendship Building, probably 1942. (Virginia Union University Archives and Special Collections)

progress that had been made to date. Guilmain and electrician Maurice Buysmans were singled out along with two locals, Fred McRae, the construction superintendent, and Norman Mugford, the steel foreman. That month Van Kuyck wrote Ellison for permission to confirm details required to finish the exterior walls and roof of the science building and main hall.[115] Economy remained foremost in Ellison's mind, especially in wartime conditions, as did opportunities to earn income. In April 1942 he wrote to Van Kuyck suggesting that the ceiling in the Vann Memorial Vestibule might be simplified.[116] He also worried that same month that the proposed ventilation system appeared to operate completely independently of the heating system, a matter that was troubling the Building Committee.[117] In an early sign of trouble in March, however, an article in the *Journal and Guide* (Norfolk, Virginia) noted that the basketball arena with space for 1,200 fans might not be ready in time for the next season "because of a lack of funds for completion and equipment."[118] A report issued in September 1942, three months after the decision to pause construction was made, described a recording of the Westminster Chimes peeling forth from the still unfinished tower, whose carillon had been sold separately to Herbert Hoover.[119] By that point the library and science sections were ready for use, although they were not yet heated.[120]

Opinions regarding the building's unfinished state depended, in part, on the particular person's initial outlook on the project. Just before construction was largely

Figure 86. Construction photo, Belgian Friendship Building, probably 1942. (Virginia Union University Archives and Special Collections)

halted in June 1942 due to wartime shortages of funds, materials, and labor, 2,500 people attended commencement in the unfinished main hall.[121] By this point the exterior was largely complete, and the library was being kitted out with tables and stacks. Davis was pleased with the progress, noting "that the temperature inside the Building was lower than that outside." Even on the building's western side, he observed, "with the battery of windows unshaded, the temperature was hardly up to that outdoors. Apparently the excellent insulation of the ceiling and sides offsets the radiation through the unusual amount of window surface."[122] In April 1943, Hening wrote Mrs. Wilfred W. Fry, the widow of a businessman who had supported many educational institutions, to give a positive report on what progress had and could still be made.[123] Meanwhile, the building, instead of being occupied by the university, had been rented, including to store automobiles. The following year Mann, who had been skeptical about the project from the beginning, toured the campus. He wrote in November 1944 that it was difficult for him "to see how [the Belgian Friendship Building] can ever serve academic needs in proportion to funds invested in it. There is a vast amount of space but there are many structural peculiarities."[124] At this point the $65,000 needed to convert the main hall into an auditorium had been raised, but it would not be spent until the war was over (see fig. 87 for the original blueprint of the proposed configuration). Plans for the library and the appearance of the tower were also finalized (figs. 88 and 89).

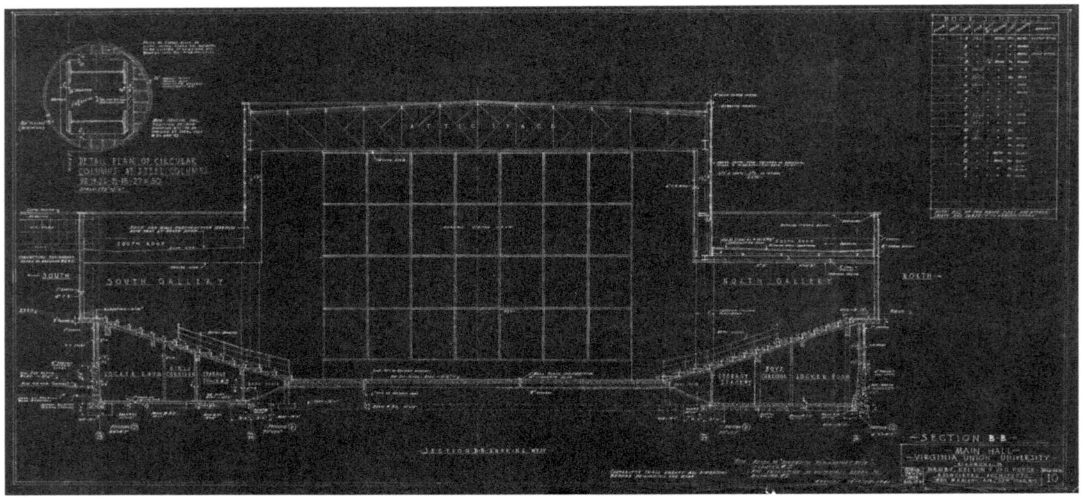

Figure 87. Blueprint cross section of auditorium, Belgian Friendship Building, Hamby, Nelson, and Van Kuyck, 1941. (Library of Virginia)

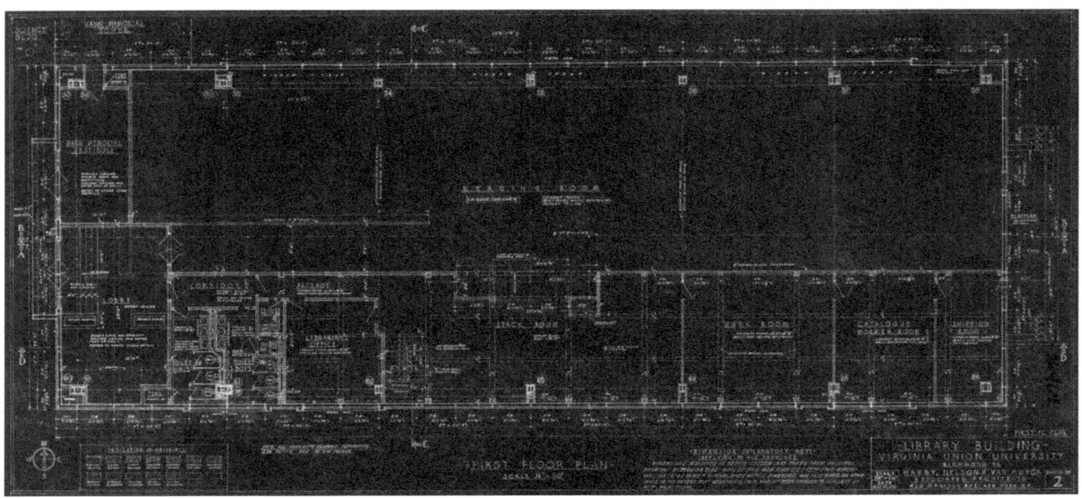

Figure 88. Blueprint plan of the library, Belgian Friendship Building, Hamby, Nelson, and Van Kuyck, 1941. (Library of Virginia)

Figure 89. Blueprint elevation of the Vann Memorial Tower, Belgian Friendship Building, Hamby, Nelson, and Van Kuyck, 1941. (Library of Virginia)

It took time for the army to move out after the war's end. One of the first signs of progress was when the basketball season began in the building on January 11, 1947, with Virginia Union edging out Hampton University 49–45.[125] This was the first time the team had ever played on campus.[126] The interior fitting out of the auditorium was completed in 1949, by which time the GEB had committed over $250,000 in funding for the project; a year later the science facilities were finally ready for use.[127]

The Backdrop of the War

Although designed in peacetime, the Belgian Friendship Building's appearance today is very much an artifact of World War II. The conflict prompted the transfer of the Belgian Pavilion from New York to Richmond, where it then hindered its reconstitution before eventually helping fund its completion. The war also transformed the aspirations of the African American community, many of whom were no longer willing to fight for liberty for others without demanding better conditions for themselves. Although meaningful change was painfully slow to arrive, whites as well as African Americans were also cognizant of the challenges wartime conditions posed to the status quo.

Early opponents of fascism, African Americans enlisted in large numbers following the bombing of Pearl Harbor, even though they were fighting for an ideal of democracy that they did not yet enjoy at home. By April 1942, Virginia Union had contributed at least 234 current students and alumni to the U.S. armed forces, including three captains, a lieutenant colonel, and thirty-one lieutenants. Among those who had fallen by that date were Sargent Gilbert Frazer, the captain of the 1941 basketball team, and Lieutenant Clemenceau McAdee Givings, a fighter pilot who was one of the Tuskegee Airmen.[128]

The war placed many additional burdens on the university. Poole, its finance manager, later described the 1942–44 academic years as "the most trying in the financial history of Virginia Union University."[129] Enrolment fell by one-third, as male students enlisted or were drafted, as were faculty and staff. Poole also noted many additional challenges: "Operating costs soared 25% above budget estimates. Necessary equipment and supplies were unobtainable. Labor was at a premium. Several teachers resigned to accept more lucrative jobs, and the rate of turnover among non-teaching employees and service workers was unbelievable."[130] It was a testament to Ellison and Poole that even before victory was achieved in first Europe and then Japan, Virginia Union's financial situation had stabilized, and that across the years 1941–46, the university raised half a million dollars to improve its facilities. Not all of this was expended on the Belgian Friendship Building, as some of it went to landscaping and retrofitting the Noble Nine.

As an induction center for the U.S. military, the Belgian Friendship Building replaced Blues' Armory, which was too small, now that inductees were also enlisting in the navy, the marine corps, and the coast guard. The building's use for this purpose was particularly extraordinary as it meant that both white and African American serviceman were coming onto Virginia Union's campus, although they used the facility on different days. Even though the U.S. armed forces would not be integrated until Harry Truman issued his executive order in 1948, some 161,000 men, many of them white, were processed on the campus of Virginia Union. Stepping onto the campus must have been an extraordinary experience for them, in a state where most public facilities remained firmly segregated until the 1960s. While in many other parts of the country the army erected purpose-built induction centers, often out of temporary materials, its rental of the Belgian Friendship Building tied the structure even more firmly to the effort to liberate Belgium, a goal achieved by Allied troops between September 1944 and February 1945. By 1946, the Belgian Building was also "being used for storage purposes by a division of the War Assets Corporation, a government agency for the handling and disposal of surplus property."[131]

Political developments on the home front also elevated the Belgian Friendship Building's symbolic importance. In January 1942, the *Pittsburgh Courier* began the Double V campaign, in which it called for victory not only in the war but also in the campaign to abolish Jim Crow and other forms of discrimination against African Americans.[132] One of those whose public support it promptly enrolled was none other than Hening.[133] Although the press campaign proved short-lived, the intensified demands for equality persisted and grew. An example was the Durham Manifesto. Issued in October 1942, following a meeting of African American leaders from across the South, it represented a significant acceleration in the demands made in relation to what would soon be termed civil rights. One of the organizers was Virginia Union professor Gordon Blaine Hancock. Previously considered a moderate, Hancock was now ready to condemn a wide variety of strategies employed to circumscribe his community's political rights, as were the other southern-based African American leaders who attended the meeting. Individuals like Hancock pushed the boundaries of "acceptable" leadership, as it was conservatively defined in the Belgian Friendship Building's early fundraising brochures. Instead, Hancock and proponents of the Durham Manifesto adopted a more oppositional stance by protesting "the poll tax, the white primary, police brutality, voter intimidation, and exclusion from juries and unions."[134] Prior to the Durham gathering, Hancock arranged for many of the attendees, including W. E. B. Du Bois, to attend a secret planning meeting at Virginia Union.[135]

While Ellison did not support Hancock's efforts, he, too, recognized the challenges that the war posed for race relations. Writing in April 1944, Ellison noted:

> As we plan the post-war services that Virginia Union can render, it is important to anticipate and explore some of the problems and needs that will inevitably arise. We know that vast numbers of men will return to civilian life mentally and physically broken—disappointed, distrustful, cynical. These conditions and attitudes will be due partly to the experience of the armed forces, both on the field of battle and off, and partly to what will happen when they come back home. Many people in all sections of the country entertain great fear that interracial tension will reach the tragic breaking point in the post-war days. I am of the opinion that what will happen will be determined largely by how much democracy will be accorded to the Negro veteran who, along with the white soldier, gave up everything to fight that democracy might be available to all people.[136]

Even local whites realized that change was in the air. Virginius Dabney, for instance, helped organize a meeting in 1943 of liberal whites held in Atlanta to garner support for the Durham Manifesto. This was followed by a Richmond meeting of the attendees of both earlier events who gathered to affirm whites' acceptance of the Manifesto. That very year Dabney acknowledged: "Americans must candidly admit that the democratic ideal is at war with the thesis that American citizens can be placed in separate pigeonholes and given varying educational and social advantages, depending upon the color of their skins. Any discrimination among citizens of this country for reasons of race or religion, is undemocratic." He continued, however, in words that foreshadowed how difficult real progress would be: "Yet sight must not be lost of the fact that the modern South inherited a problem of tremendous complexity and difficulty at the end of the Civil War. Moreover, if the South is to be blamed for the system of slavery upon which is built its economy and its society prior to that war, what are we to say of the eminent New Englanders who made vast sums out of the uniformly barbarous slave trade?"[137] A few pages later Dabney noted that Virginia Union "has just acquired its first Negro president, as well as a fine new library building, formerly the Belgian pavilion at the New York World's Fair," as examples of African American progress in higher education.[138]

This was one of the many increasingly anxious references that whites close to the Belgian Friendship Building project made regarding race relations as the war continued. Unwilling to support the dismantling of Jim Crow, they instead found in the Belgian Friendship Building a more moderate way of improving the lives of their African American neighbors. Already in 1942, white Virginia Baptists voted to oppose racial discrimination in defense programs and to pay African American teachers the same salaries as their white counterparts. These ameliorative measures were passed at the same convention in which Adams, the chair of Virginia Union's board, encouraged white Baptists to contribute to the reconstruction of the Belgian Friendship Building.[139] Another positive development came when Virginia Union's School of Religion was admitted into the American Association of Theological Schools.[140]

Efforts to promote interracial goodwill continued in the United States in 1943 as part of a larger defense of democracy in the fight against fascism. In March 1943, Adams wrote to Davis in the context of Virginia Union's soon to be successful plea for more funds with which to complete the Belgian Building: "I feel very keenly that if the General Education Board will give us the amount we are asking, it will not only enable us to meet our obligation and complete our program, but that it will also be a very genuine help in promoting better race relations in Virginia in this critical hour."[141] In a memo he wrote a week later following Ellison's appointment as president, Davis noted, "The colored people feel that [Virginia Union] is their own and it gives them a sense of responsibility and gives the institution an opportunity to influence their religious and cultural life to an increasing extent." He continued, "It is felt that this type of cooperative work for a building which stands as an international symbol in a time of racial tension in which the white people of the North and

South are working with Negroes in providing increased facilities for higher education is the best answer that responsible citizens can make."[142] Once the GEB made the grant, the *Richmond News Leader* observed that the Belgian Building's completion would allow the university to "continue as an apostle of moderation, of Christian service and of educational progress."[143] Baptist official Donald Faulkner, who was considerably less comfortable with African American leadership than Davis, nonetheless wrote Davis in January 1945 to thank him for the support he had provided, not just to Virginia Union, but also to other HBCUs:

> The members of the Board of Education and all those who are interested in Negro Education realize the splendid generosity and indispensable help which the General Education Board has given to the development of this great race of people. The colleges which your Board has aided in establishing stand as a bulwark against ignorance, racial misunderstanding, and prejudice, which if not partially controlled by an intelligent trained leadership among the Negroes could easily destroy our democracy.[144]

Democracy, as it was understood by members of the GEB and white Baptists, depended on improving educational institutions for African Americans as a means of staving off more radical solutions. This is the context for understanding the rhetoric of "friendship" in expressions of support for the Belgian Building. In the face of Nazi xenophobia, it became imperative to align democracy with racial uplift and to downplay the antidemocratic character of Belgium's colonial regime.

The war cast a shadow not just in the United States and Europe, but also in the Congo, where the Belgians ensured that there was not yet any chance of democracy. There was much less sympathy for Belgium in the United States in 1940 than there had been in 1914, largely because of Leopold III's swift capitulation. Much of the support that the government in exile was able to command came because of its continued control of the Congo. At about the same time that Goris was organizing the transfer of the pavilion to Virginia Union, Belgian leaders, including Van Kuyck, traveled to Washington to garner support for their cause.[145] In the face of their country's capitulation, these Belgian officials regained footing among the Allies by offering them troops and materials from its richest and largest colony. In January 1941, the government in exile signed an agreement with the British, and early the next month Congolese soldiers fought off the Italians in East Africa alongside the British.[146] At the groundbreaking, Goris was careful to mention the recent participation of these troops in a victorious campaign in Ethiopia, which remains Belgium's most important military triumph to date. He stretched the truth, however, when he reassured his audience that the Belgian king "would continue to resist Hitler's efforts to restore him as the puppet king of a puppet state."[147]

By 1941, a small contingent of American troops was stationed in the Belgian colony to facilitate a lend-lease agreement that saw the Congo provide the Allied war effort with tin and rubber. The Belgians, who were reluctant to cede even a small degree of control of a territory they regarded as entirely theirs, were particularly incensed when the United States included African Americans among the soldiers they sent to Africa; they successfully demanded their removal, and the experiment was not repeated.[148] Meanwhile, under pressure to contribute to a war effort that took Congolese soldiers across Africa, as well as to Asia and Europe, Congolese civilians suffered from heightened pressure to increase harvests and to work in mines and factories, at a time when the buying power of stable wages rapidly waned.[149]

Of particular importance to the war effort, although known to relatively few people at the time, was uranium sourced from the Congo. The Shinkolobwe mine, located near what was then Elizabethville (now Lubumbashi) in the Haut-Katanga province, in the far southeast of the colony, was reopened to provide the uranium that was key to the Manhattan Project and used in the atomic bombs dropped in August 1945 on Japan. Although most of those engaged in sourcing this highly dangerous material had no idea of why it was needed (even Vice President Truman was entirely unaware of the project until President Franklin Roosevelt's sudden death), the American presence in the colony greatly increased as a result, with the Office of Strategic Services sending its own men and women to supplement the embassy staff, who were to ensure that this and other key materials did not fall into Axis hands. This American presence was critical, as many Belgian residents in the Congo were suspected of having Nazi sympathies, especially in the early years of the conflict when it appeared that the Germans would win. There is no reason, however, to believe that any care was paid to the health and welfare of those who mined the highly radioactive material, which was found in much purer concentrations here than anywhere else in the world. Uranium and atomic technology would be central to relations between the United States and Belgium for years after the war, with the United States insisting on a monopoly of the valuable resource, which Belgium wanted to claim as its own. This pattern continued until the United States eventually depleted the Shinkolobwe mine and located other useful sources. Although African Americans often labored in appalling conditions during the war and even died in catastrophic industrial accidents, such as the Port Chicago explosion in Contra Costa County, California, that killed 320 sailors, they undoubtedly never faced anything as deplorable as the situation in Shinkolobwe.[150]

The war did little to transform Belgian attitudes toward the Congo, especially as they were represented by Belgian propaganda in the United States. In 1945 Goris edited a volume on Belgium published as part of a United Nations series "dedicated to the task of mutual understanding among the Allies and to the achievement of successful cooperation in this war and in the coming peace."[151] The book is notable for rehabilitating van de Velde. Georges Philippart wrote of him: "Comparable perhaps with Frank Lloyd Wright and several Austrian architects, Henry van de Velde has contributed more than anyone else to the triumph of the esthetic revolution in modern architecture. . . . Today the most brilliant Belgian modernists consider him their master."[152] But it is the writing about the Congo that demonstrates that the war had done little to alter patronizing attitudes toward the Congolese on the part of the white authors, regardless of whether they were Belgians or from the United States. Six different contributors went out of their way to praise Belgium's role in the colony, although Melville J. Herskovits, a professor of anthropology at Northwestern University, where he founded a pioneering program in African studies, did acknowledge the high quality of Congolese sculpture.[153]

The end of the war did, however, bring a spirit of optimism about the possibility that peace would transform social relations in the United States. The January 1947 issue of the *Virginia Union Bulletin* included the text of a speech that the Rev. William P. Hayes, a member of the class of 1907, had given at a recent Founders Day. In it he declared:

> The herculean task of winning the war has precluded the possibility of drawing blueprints for the world of tomorrow. All that any man dare say at the present time is that the world of tomorrow will be different from the world of today. This present global conflict is something more than ordinary warfare; it is indeed a revolution of the first magnitude. Many social and political structures

> that have served mankind in the past will be swept into oblivion by the impact of this revolution; and many other structures more basic and fundamental will be salvaged and used as foundation material for the new world a-coming. There must be a conservativism of moral and spiritual values in the world of tomorrow, or else we shall only succeed in building a Frankenstein monster that will turn on us and destroy us. We must build a new world in which human personality shall be supreme. We must build a new world in which every boy and girl, every man and woman, regardless of race, color, or creed shall have equal opportunity for education, for economic security, and political and religious freedom.[154]

Hayes's appropriation of the fair's theme "The World of Tomorrow" is telling, especially because he likely delivered his address within or in the shadow of the Belgian Friendship Building, whose tower was completed by 1945 but which would not be dedicated until 1949. Hayes pairs revolution with conservatism of values, a pairing that was mirrored in the building's synthesis of new technologies and familiar materials, all on a civic scale. Just one year earlier, the *Virginia Union Bulletin* had summed up the new administration's "keynote" in precisely these terms. "The age which the students of VUU are to serve is sure to require an artistic touch in keeping with advanced architecture and landscape developments," the editors noted. They continued: "Dr. Ellison believes that beauty is not necessarily a term applied to that which is old. We have fine old granite buildings, but in a new age they must be shown off to their best advantage." After enumerating improvements made to the rest of the campus, the editors proudly observed that the Belgian Building was "the most modern school building in the country."[155]

The "world of tomorrow" Hayes envisioned would prove far from easy to create, but Virginia Union students and alumni can certainly share the credit for the extent to which it was achieved in word, in deed, and in the built environment. The financial burden of reconstituting the building, the editors of *Virginia Union Bulletin* noted, compelled the university to "find friends" to support the effort. Far from the diversion that Ellison initially perceived it to be, the building, over the nine years it took to reconstitute it, would become the cornerstone of the administration's preparations for the future. "In keeping with the general theme of student development for a contribution to a new age, they are directed by word and action to think of and appreciate the elegant and the beautiful. Taste necessarily has to be developed for art appreciation. . . . Make things beautiful and similar lives will be the inevitable result," the editors of *Virginia Union Bulletin* observed in 1946, as progress towards the building's completion accelerated.[156] Such sentiments crystallized during the war years, with both the Belgian Friendship Building and the Belgian Congo contributing to the war effort in ways that foreshadowed the roles they would play in the postwar years. In the 1950s and 1960s, Virginia Union students would be leaders in the campaign for civil rights, even as the Congo's rebirth as an independent nation would be marred by continued white efforts to control its natural resources.

The Finished Building

In June 1949, two thousand people assembled inside the auditorium of the Belgian Friendship Building to celebrate the graduation of 176 students, the fiftieth anniversary of Virginia Union's establishment following the merger of the Richmond Theological Institute and Wayland Seminary, and the completion of the building.[157] Goris, incorrectly described in the *Richmond Times-Dispatch* as the former Belgian ambassador to the United States, was once again on hand to celebrate the result as "a symbol of friendship between nations and equality between races," as was Colgate Darden, a former governor of Virginia and current president of the then still all-white University of Virginia.[158] The library, which the *Pittsburgh Courier* described as featuring "tall windows more than two stories in height" that "brighten the blue and gold and pale green walls," was dedicated to William J. Clark, Virginia Union's former president who had agreed to take the Belgian government's "gift," while the prayer room was dedicated to Adam Clayton Powell Sr. and the tower, of course, to Robert L. Vann.[159] Jessie Vann and Powell were both present, as probably was Clark, although the African American press failed to single him out.

More than a decade after the Belgian Pavilion had opened its doors for the first time to visitors to "The World of Tomorrow," the Belgian Friendship Building that now contained the Clark Library, the Powell Chapel, and the Vann Tower was only in part the same structure. Gone were the lavish interior finishings and the splendid displays. Gone as well were the cinema and the restaurant. But in many other ways this was recognizably the same building, albeit one with a new purpose. Only

Figure 90. Clark Library, Belgian Friendship Building. (Virginia Union University Archives and Special Collections)

someone with behind-the-scenes access could see the "Made in Belgium" lettering stenciled in white onto many of the steel beams, but the Ardennes slate and Courtrai terra cotta were in full view, if not as securely fixed onto concrete backing and brick infill as they ought to have been. The new interiors, if now more pragmatic and cost-efficient, impressed observers as being handsome, although one might wonder what students studying in the library thought looking out onto Dupagne's bas-relief of Congolese life before and after colonization. (fig. 90).

Toki Schulk Johnson, a social columnist for the *Pittsburgh Courier,* oscillated between lauding Vann for "bravely reading the dedicatory address in her own fashion, that of simplicity and human warmth, bringing the tears to the eyes of all who listened," and praising "the austere beauty of the Robert L. Vann memorial room" in which she held forth. Johnson noted its oak paneling and the indirect lighting that fell "on the glass enclosed model of the S. S. Robert L. Vann, which was given to his widow by the ship company which made the Liberty Ship during the war"—one of the first U.S. naval vessels to be named for an African American.[160] Elsewhere in the same issue another reporter for the *Courier* even more obviously elided the architecture of the building with the goals of the institution on which it stood, describing it as having "a feeling of spaciousness [and] of freedom [as] the dominant note throughout the building."[161]

On this occasion, Ellison wrote the GEB to thank them:

> Today the library of Virginia Union and the Vann Tower, both of which are housed in the Belgian Building, are among the most beautiful and inspiring pieces of architectural equipment that are to be found in any of our colleges. I assure you that these achievements are of inestimable educational value.
>
> Your gifts have not only inspired the students and faculty of the University, but have inspired many other people to make significant contributions to the University.[162]

The level of trust between Ellison and the board had indeed been confirmed through the process of reassembling the Belgian Friendship Building in Richmond, even if no more Rockefeller funds would go toward its completion. Ellison was successful, however, in persuading the GEB to donate $75,000 to a campaign that focused on increasing the institution's endowment. Despite having been depleted by nearly $80,000 for the construction of the Belgian Friendship Building, the endowment had risen as a result of Ellison's efforts. Combined with the GEB's contribution, it rose to one million dollars in the very month of the building's dedication. This sum represented an increase of over $250,000.[163] This success empowered the university on all fronts. "I believe the Negro in America is headed for a great political awakening in both the North and the South," Cecil L. Rowlett noted in his "Founders Day Address" held at Virginia Union in 1947, concluding, "Continued and intelligent participation can be furthered by our institutions of higher learning."[164]

Not surprisingly, the links between Virginia Union and Belgium stretched into the postwar period. In July 1945, after the war had ended in Europe but while it was still being fought in Asia, Ellison presented Prof. William J. Goodwin, the director of the University Choir, with a mahogany baton with ivory tips, which Davis had acquired during a wartime visit to the Congo.[165] Davis wrote, "Since Virginia Union now has on its campus the Belgian Friendship Building, I felt that it would be very appropriate for the University to have a baton from the Belgian Congo, especially one that came from an area in which the Baptists are doing such a fine work."[166] Four years later, in the peaceful conditions of June 1949, a group of Virginia Union students set off for Europe. The *Pittsburgh Courier* reported that the Belgian ambassador to the United States had arranged for them to "present to the college students of Belgium a library of books concerning the life of the colored people in the United States and Virginia, biographies of outstanding men such as George Washington Carver; a giant 4-foot long color photograph of the Belgian World's Fair Building, now at VUU, with the whole of the campus, and another photograph of Union students." These gifts, the article explained, "will be made to the students of the 'Université Coloniale' at Antwerp," an institute established in 1920 to prepare the Congolese for careers as functionaries in Belgium's colonies, which the paper incorrectly described as being the original post-fair destination of the building.[167]

Today Dupagne's bas-reliefs proclaiming the progress Belgium had purportedly bestowed on the Congolese wrap around two facades of the Vann Tower. Nearby is the even larger architectural sculpture *Belgium at Work* created by Oscar Jespers and Henry Purvez that traveled from New York to Richmond with the rest of the building. Despite the presence of the building on Virginia Union's campus and the racist assumptions of many of the white Baptists who had supported its reconstruction there, the Belgian Friendship Building did not moderate African American demands for a "double victory." Instead, it provided Virginia Union and the African American community in Richmond with space from which to continue the campaign.

6

POSTWAR CAMPUS ARCHITECTURE, CAMPUS ACTIVISM, AND CITY PLANNING

On November 10, 1956, the *Richmond Afro American* informed its readers that the 69th annual convention of the Virginia Teachers Association had attracted a record six thousand teachers to the Belgian Friendship Building on the campus of Virginia Union. One reason for the high attendance was undoubtedly the urgent conversations necessitated by the state's recent adoption of an official policy of Massive Resistance to the integration of its schools mandated in 1954 by the *Brown v. Board of Education* decision of the United States Supreme Court. Another reason, however, was certainly the presence of Dr. Martin Luther King Jr. (fig. 91). The *Afro American* described him as "the celebrated boycott leader," a reference to the events in Montgomery, Alabama, triggered less than a year earlier when Rosa Parks refused to give up her seat on a local bus. King informed the teachers, "Racial segregation is on its death bed but history has proven that social systems have a great last minute breathing power, and the guardians of the status quo are always on hand with their oxygen tents to keep the old order alive."[1] That this speech took place in the former national pavilion of a major colonial power only four years before the Belgian Congo would win its independence and eight years before the passage of the Civil Rights Act in the United States testifies to the ability of a building to take on new meanings,

Figure 91. Martin Luther King Jr. after speech at Virginia Union University, surrounded by faculty and students. (Virginia Union University Archives and Special Collections)

beyond the intentions of its original designers or even those of the administrators and officials who reconstituted it in Richmond.

The story of the Belgian Friendship Building in Richmond is important for many reasons. It is the largest object surviving from an event that mesmerized tens of millions. It is a key example of Belgian architecture from a decade in which that small country produced some of the most compelling modern buildings in Europe. And it testifies to the presence already in Richmond of a vibrant African American community that was highly engaged in building the foundations for what would become the civil rights movement. In the postwar years, the Belgian Friendship Building supported the cultural and sporting—but above all the political—aspirations of both Virginia Union and this larger community. Thanks in part to the activism of Virginia Union students, Richmond would indeed integrate. And as African Americans in Richmond well knew, the peak of local civil rights activities coincided almost exactly with the Congo achieving its independence in June 1960. By this time, the Belgian Friendship Building no longer appeared startling; the 1950s and early 1960s saw a building boom on publicly funded HBCU campuses as southern state legislatures sought to forestall the integration of their flagship campuses by providing African Americans with facilities they could argue were "separate but equal." Some, if not all, of the new buildings were erected in a modern style.

The relationship between modern architecture and progressive politics has often been exaggerated. Yet despite the intentions of its architects, the Belgian Friendship Building played a far greater role as a staging ground for civil rights activities than did any of the far better-known exponents of modern European architecture erected across the 1940s on overwhelmingly white campuses in the North. Paradoxically, the opening salvo in the importation of interwar European architecture to universities across the United States nurtured the destruction of exactly the kind of white suprematism it was originally designed in part to support. This powerful reorientation of its original purpose distinguishes the Belgian Friendship Building from its better-known counterparts. Buildings erected on the campuses of the Illinois Institute of Technology, the Massachusetts Institute of Technology (MIT), and Harvard University in the 1940s, along with slightly later ones at Yale University, designed in all but one case by architects who greatly admired Henry van de Velde, instead laid the groundwork for the utility of modern architecture in the United States to Cold War politics. While struggles against fascism and communism enhanced pressure on the United States to live up to its democratic ideals and assist in precipitating the dismantling of Europe's overseas empires, student activism at these northern institutions and in their surrounding communities came much later than it did at Virginia Union.

By the time protests erupted in Chicago, Cambridge, and New Haven, largely because of opposition to the Vietnam War, the issue confronting African American communities was as likely to be urban renewal as civil rights. Integration did not bring equality of opportunity to Virginia Union or to the African American community directly to its west. Instead, the campus was severed from the rest of the city when Interstate 95 ripped the heart out of Jackson Ward. Urban renewal displaced many of Richmond's African American residents and businesses and crippled the vitality of the neighborhood to which Virginia Union had contributed so much. Meanwhile, integration also provided new opportunities at majority white campuses for small numbers of African American students and faculty, a development that further drained HBCUs of the resources they needed to continue to operate effectively as engines of African American social and economic mobility.

The Belgian Building in Use: Culture, Sports, and Civil Rights

The Belgian Building provided Virginia Union with the facilities for many extracurricular activities, including art exhibitions, classical music concerts, and basketball games, as well as addresses by King and other civil rights meetings. Although the building still bore the marks of its colonial origins in the form of Arthur Dupagne's bas-reliefs of the Congo, it proved to be a place that helped fulfill African American aspirations for cultural as well as political empowerment. As the largest facility available to African Americans in Richmond on their own terms, the Belgian Friendship Building provided Union with enhanced educational facilities, but it also served much of the city's thriving African American community.

Art exhibits were held in the Clark Library, while plays and musical events were staged in the auditorium.[2] The university began an annual Fine Arts Festival in 1954, which in 1958 included a performance of the ancient Greek drama *Oedipus Rex.* The previous year the annual concert series staged a production of Johann Strauss II's operetta *Die Fledermaus.* Whether mounted by students or touring groups, and often featuring white artists, such events made European high culture accessible to Virginia Union students and the wider African American community in Richmond who otherwise had limited local access to it.[3] The African American jazz great Duke Ellington performed at the Belgian Friendship Building as well, charming an audience of over two thousand for more than two and a half hours in May 1958.[4] Other celebrated musicians heard here included Count Basie, Lionel Hampton, Etta Moten, and William Warfield.[5]

No account of the Belgian Building's history would be complete without mention of the Panthers basketball teams, who play in what has been known since 1959 as Barco-Stevens Hall. In a perfect balance of the celebration of academics and athletics, the auditorium-cum-gymnasium was named for Dr. John W. Barco and Dr. Wesley A. Stevens.[6] Barco, class of 1902, subsequently studied at the University of Chicago, returning to his alma mater to teach Latin and Hebrew. He cofounded the Central Intercollegiate Athletic Association, the league of HBCUs, of which Virginia Union was a founding member, and also served as vice president of the university from 1929 to 1947.[7] Stevens was a professor of mathematics who taught at Virginia Union for more than half a century.

Barco-Stevens Hall has been the site of many an athletic triumph. The men won the National Collegiate Athletic Association (NCAA) Division II championship in 1980, 1992, and 2005, and the women in 1983 (fig. 92). During Dave Robbins's thirty-year tenure as coach, which began in 1978 and ended in 2008, the men advanced to the division's final four an additional four times. Eight Panthers have

Figure 92. Charles Oakley playing for the VUU Panthers, 1985. (Virginia Union University Archives and Special Collections)

gone on to the NBA, including most famously Ben Wallace, a Hall of Fame player for the Detroit Pistons, and Charles Oakley, who played for several teams including the New York Knicks. In a city without any first division professional sports franchise, these successes are a matter of enormous pride. Generations of Richmonders have been thrilled by their performances on the Belgian Friendship Building's court.

The building also provided the backdrop for much of the university's engagement with the civil rights movement, hosting many events that were open to the public. Even before the landmark Supreme Court ruling in *Brown v. Board of Education* and the Montgomery bus boycott, Virginia Union's student body included outspoken opponents of segregation. In February 1954, months before the Brown decision was announced, the front page of the *Richmond Afro American* described the reaction when Walter Fauntroy, who later served as the District of Columbia's first (nonvoting) member of the U.S. House of Representatives, intervened in an unexpected way at an integrated fundraising event held at a local hotel for a new baseball park for the city:

> The applause was polite but several times faces turned crimson red Friday night at an unsegregated banquet to raise funds for rebuilding Parker field after a Virginia Union student's speech took an unexpected turn.
>
> When Walter E. Fauntroy, Union junior and a baseball player, rose to speak, it was expected that he would merely utter a few polite words.
>
> Throats were cleared . . . as Mr. Fauntroy spoke of "the very important matter of providing for accommodation and arrangements for spectators in Richmond in keeping with the tradition of other Triple A parks. However, in my opinion, this mistake can be offset to a considerable degree by the satisfactory solution to the issue of seating arrangements. It will take courage and cooperation to operate our park under the same [integrated] general conditions as Griffith stadium in Washington. But it can be done, and Richmond, I believe, will accept it just as readily as we accepted "Cannonball" Cooper [the Virginia Union alumnus who was the star halfback of the Richmond Rebels football team]."
>
> Although he had been asked not to say anything "controversial," his speech has been highly praised by many of those who attended the affair.[8]

Fauntroy may have been inspired in part by having met King already in the summer of 1953, during King's first visit to Virginia Union.[9]

The following year another Virginia Union graduate, the distinguished journalist Simeon Booker, class of 1942, broke the story of Emmett Till's murder in the pages of *Jet Magazine*. It was illustrated with the gruesome photographs of the boy's corpse that Till's mother Mamie Till-Mobley insisted the entire nation should have to confront.[10]

HBCUs have been criticized for having timidly tried to restrain rather than encourage the student activism that was central to the success of the civil rights movement, but this was never the case at Union, where John Malcus Ellison's successor Samuel Proctor, a mentor of King's, welcomed students expelled from other

HBCUs for their political activities.[11] HBCUs were the incubators of change long before the establishment of the Student Nonviolent Coordinating Committee (SNCC) in 1960.[12] Already in 1947, during Ellison's presidency, Cecil L. Rowlett gave a Founder's Address at Virginia Union that he entitled "The College as Preparation for the Exercise of Citizenship Rights." In a speech that focused on the importance of voting rights, he noted, "If political activity were not so important, the South would not go to such lengths to disenfranchise its Negro citizens."[13] Nor was this commitment to political activism entirely new even then. Virginia Union alumnus Henry Allen Bullock, who in 1969 became the first African American on the arts and sciences faculty at the University of Texas after winning the Bancroft Prize the previous year for his book *The History of Negro Education in the South,* wrote in the preface to that volume of his own education at Virginia Union, from which he graduated in 1928:

> During the early years of my college days at Virginia Union University, there developed within me the feeling that segregated education has some accidental purpose. The rather orthodox value system that Union imposed upon its students—not to smoke; not to play cards; not to drink; and, above all, not to refer to ourselves by that vulgar term with which racists were wont to identify Negroes—was selectively internalized, but the more fundamental belief that the system inculcated was embraced in full. It was the doctrine that the Negro college was to develop the leadership for the emancipation of the Negro American as a person. I shared this faith and sought its justification in a common denominator applicable to the development of all peoples. This was not a very diligent search, some intellectual crusade, that I waged; it was only a gnawing need to preserve and foster my self-respect.[14]

The same crusade to instill self-respect and leadership in Virginia Union's students motivated the care and expense to which the university went to beautify and update its campus grounds and facilities, beginning with the Noble Nine and continuing through the acquisition of the Belgian Friendship Building and the dedication of its memorial tower.

When a cross was burned on the campus in September 1958, the *Richmond Afro American* reported, "Police were unable to explain why the cross was burned at Virginia Union as the university has not been involved in the current school segregation controversy."[15] This was disingenuous to say the least, as already, the previous year, Virginia Union's advertisement in the annual schools and colleges section of the *Afro American* featured a photograph of King, who, it stated, "typified prominent speakers at Virginia Union."[16]

Following his initial appearances on campus, King returned to Richmond three more times over the next four years, and on two of these occasions he spoke in the Belgian Building.[17] In March 1957 he delivered three sermons to packed crowds as part of the university's Department of Theology's Annual Week of Prayer.[18] Again, attendance soared because of his presence. Although it was meant to be a religious occasion, King did not shy away from political statements, declaring, "I am concerned not only about milk and honey flowing in the streets of heaven, but about people on earth having to go to bed hungry; not only about mansions of gold in heaven, but the hundreds of thousands of persons forced to live in slums here on earth."[19] In perhaps his most prescient remarks, he stated, as noted in the *Richmond Afro American,* that "life should have length, breadth, and depth." He explained that length does not mean longevity but "the determination with which you do your life work."[20] In early January 1960, "the modern Moses," as the local paper now termed him, addressed the second annual Pilgrimage of Prayer for Public Schools at the Mosque (now known as the Altria Theatre), before leading a prayer pilgrimage from there to the state capitol.[21] The purpose of the 2,700 people who attended the meeting, many of whom subsequently joined the march, was to pressure Prince Edward County to reopen its public schools, which it had closed rather than integrate. Among those present was Ellison, who had by now leapfrogged over his former opponent Gordon Blaine Hancock to offer his whole-hearted support for the movement. That November, fresh from his release from Georgia State Prison, King once again addressed the teachers' union in the Belgian Building.[22] He returned one final time to Union and to the Belgian Building in September 1963 to give the keynote at the seventh annual conference of the Southern Christian Leadership Conference, of which he was president.

King's presence helped inspire Virginia Union's students and Richmond's larger African American community, but they achieved plenty independently of it as well. Other inspiring speakers included sports heroes Jackie Robinson and Muhammad Ali, as well as civil rights leaders Julian Bond, Shirley Chisolm, and Coretta Scott

King.[23] Students and faculty were involved in voting rights efforts, with meetings of the Voters League held in the Belgian Friendship Building.[24] Most famously on February 22, 1960, Virginia Union students led the city's first lunch counter sit-ins, following the lead of their counterparts from North Carolina A & T in Greensboro and Fisk and Tennessee State in Nashville, as well as closer to home in Portsmouth, Virginia.[25] Sit-ins were not a new tactic that year, as college students, including a group from Morgan State who successfully desegregated Read's Drug Store counters in and around Baltimore in 1955, had been among those who had already implemented them. Nevertheless it was the actions of students in Greensboro and in Nashville, including John Lewis and Diane Nash, that sparked further activism across the South in 1960.

Thirty-four Virginia Union students, including Marise and Joseph Ellison, out of a group that was estimated to have numbered two hundred, were arrested on February 22 after they sat down to eat at the lunch counter at Thalheimer's, one of the city's leading department stores. When the students continued this demonstration by picketing the store the following week, Ruth Tinsley, whose husband was the president of a local bank and of the local chapter of the NAACP, was also arrested, although she had not actually been among the protesters (fig. 93).[26] Her arrest further enraged the community, leading thousands of local African Americans to join the picket lines and mass meetings at several local Baptist churches as well as at the Belgian Friendship Building.[27] President Proctor, who would later voice strong support for the students, declared that "no disciplinary action is planned against the participants . . . but those who cut classes will have it charged against them."[28] Civil rights lawyer Oliver Hill, who represented the protestors in court, urged the community not to buy new Easter finery, but instead to continue its boycott of stores that would not serve them as equals.[29] By the end of April, several lunch counters in the city's Church Hill neighborhood had integrated; in August the first African Americans were admitted to historically white public schools.[30] Hill eventually got the charges against the students dismissed, as it was clear that the students were not trespassing. Indeed, the *Richmond News Leader,* a white-run paper that did not support integration, was embarrassed to admit: "Many a Virginian must have felt a tinge of regret. . . . Here were the colored students, in coats, white shirts, ties, and one of them was reading Goethe and one was taking notes from a biology text. And

Figure 93. Ruth Tinsley being carried away from Thalheimer's department store, Richmond, by city police, 1960. (Library of Congress Prints and Photographs Division, Washington, D.C.; photograph by Malcolm O. Carpenter)

here on the sidewalk outside, was a gang of white boys come to heckle, a ragtail rabble, slack jawed, black-jacketed, grinning to kill, and some of them, God save the mark, were waving the [Confederate] flag."[31]

Virginia Union students had dignity long before the Belgian Friendship Building arrived in Richmond, but the shift that the building's presence helped engender toward African American leadership on campus turned out to be more empowering than the GEB and other white philanthropists could ever have imagined. Ellison and Proctor, along with Union's faculty and, above all, its students, used the Belgian Building's space for a wide variety of activities that fostered individual and community pride. As the *Virginia Union Bulletin* noted:

> This building, housing the library, laboratories in physics, chemistry, and biology, and an auditorium which will be a community center for service, will make possible a fuller training for students who are to lead in a new age. Grounds which are beautiful and buildings which are grand and artistic will so influence the thinking of young men and women that they will brighten the dark and beautify the unsightly wherever they find them, whether in things material or in things moral.[32]

The Panthers' many victories in the Belgian Friendship Building's auditorium justifiably generated a great deal of excitement, but it was the public gatherings held in the same space that provided the inspiration and staging ground for real political change.

The Congo as Seen from Richmond

Change was also afoot nationally; when King spoke in the Belgian Building's auditorium in 1957, he did not limit his remarks to the situation in the United States. Instead, he also described "the rumblings of discontent in Africa and Asia" as "the revolt against imperialism and colonialism perpetuated by the Western Civilization for so many years."[33] Africa and Asia, to which he was about to travel for the first time at the invitation of Kwame Nkrumah and Jawaharlal Nehru, the first prime ministers of Ghana and India, respectively, were very much on his mind.[34] In Ghana, he would witness the country's independence ceremonies. Yet Belgian awareness that the Congo's colonial regime could not be a source of ongoing pride was extremely slow to develop.

For Jan-Albert Goris and Sidney Hening, it had undoubtedly been completely appropriate to include Arthur Dupagne's bas-relief sculptures celebrating Belgian rule in the Congo in the shipment of the Belgian Friendship Building to Richmond. A photograph of part of the work showing nearly naked Congolese men and boys at work and learning to read appeared on the cover of an issue *La revue coloniale belge* devoted to recounting the colony's participation in the war effort when the journal resumed publication in 1947.[35] A decade later, when the Belgians dedicated their first purpose-built chancery in Washington, D.C., the situation had not noticeably altered. Not surprisingly, the new structure was designed by Hugo van Kuyck, who worked in collaboration with the New York firm of Vorhees, Walker, Smith & Smith. Like the Hall of Honor of the Belgian Pavilion, the lobby of the new embassy featured black Belgian marble. A tapestry originally on view in the 1939 Belgium Pavilion in New York was also loaned from its new home at the New York Historical Society. And like the Belgian Pavilion, the chancery served once again to highlight materials from the Congo, the source of the korina wood panels in the entrance hall.[36] Such celebrations of colonialism were, however, soon to come to an end.

Interleaved in the pages of the *Richmond Afro American* with accounts of local civil rights activities in 1960, which culminated in King's address to Virginia teachers that November, was international coverage of the situation in the Congo. The Richmond paper was part of a chain, based in Baltimore, that also included newspapers in Washington, Philadelphia, and Newark. Taken collectively, these had by this point replaced the *Pittsburgh Courier* as the African American newspaper with the largest circulation.[37] The *Afro American*'s international coverage underscores the ways in which the civil rights movement in the United States dovetailed with independence movements in the Global South, especially Africa. With the possible exception of Ghana, the first Sub-Saharan African country to be granted independence by a European colonial power, and Liberia, where the descendants of people who had been enslaved in the United States played a decisive role, the story of the Congo filled the most column inches in the chain's reporting on the continent.

Most of this coverage was extremely critical of Belgium. In December 1958, for instance, William Gordon noted in an article entitled "Belgian Congo Sees Promise of Freedom": "The Belgian government is facing criticism, both from the native population and the people in Brussels. Some Belgians feel that steps toward preparation for independence for the Congo have been too slow. . . . Others feel that more should be done to give Africans in the Congo more economic and political freedom."[38] The following month the paper announced that the Congo was demanding more self-government. "This delay," its anonymous journalist noted, "coupled with visible progress towards independence and self-rule in other African countries, has added to the impatience of the Congo's nationalists."[39] A month later, reporting on riots in the colony, the *Richmond Afro American* reminded its readers that Belgian King Leopold II

> was as ruthless and cruel a tyrant as ever lived. He is only mentioned here because there is talk of handing the Congo again to the Belgian Royal Family, to be ruled by ex-King Leopold III as the direct Viceroy of his son, King Baudouin with the assistance of six African Princes. It has been suggested that such a plan would meet with considerable resistance from the Africans, in the light of the Congo's early harsh history under the hand of the earlier King Leopold II. The Belgians are willing to give the natives anything they want, except freedom. But freedom is what the natives want, and they want it now.[40]

More news of the Congo filled the very same February 1960 issues of the paper that were dominated by reporting on the sit-in campaign. Once the struggles for Congolese independence and African American civil rights were even coupled on the same front page.[41] After the Congo achieved independence that June, the *Afro*'s reports continued to criticize Belgium and predicted that the Congolese would emerge to control their own destiny.[42] When things went badly, the newspaper placed the blame squarely on the Belgians. In July it editorialized:

> The real culprit, it appears, is the Belgian Government, its soldiers and the brute policy they have and are seeking to enforce. All but pushed out of the Congo by the Africans' sheer determination to run their own affairs, the government in Brussels is seeking to cling to the last shreds of empire—even if it means substituting brute force for fawning paternalism. But to do this, they need a protest—a smoke-screen. This need explains the screaming headlines of rioting, looting, rape and murder which for the past weeks have been front-paged in the Western World by a press that's either gullible or prostituted.[43]

The tone did not change as the Congo situation worsened. The paper was equally forthright in criticizing American policy in the Congo.[44] It interpreted the death of Patrice Lumumba as an "effort to 'wipe out' Congo's 'articulate leadership.'"[45] As these press reports demonstrate, the "gift" of the Belgian Friendship Building did nothing to encourage African American support for colonialism, including in the Congo. Instead, African Americans, in Richmond as elsewhere in the United States, understood their own demands for full civic rights to be inextricably intertwined with the demise of empire, including Belgian rule in the Congo.

Historically Black Campuses Envision the New

Following their independence, a number of former colonies, including perhaps most notably India and Ghana, were forthright in adopting modern architecture as a symbol of their break with a colonial past. Use of a modern style also liberated them from employing their own architectural heritage in ways that might be seen to empower precolonial elites.[46] Understanding modern architecture as inherently emancipatory, however, overlooks the use to which colonizers put it in the 1950s, whether in the Congo or elsewhere.[47] It also disregards the reasons that it flourished on the campuses of many HBCUs by the late 1950s.

The modernization of the architecture of historically Black college and university campuses was closely tied to changes in funding for higher education that followed World War II. The GI Bill made college unprecedently affordable, especially for white, male veterans, while the Manhattan Project that produced the atomic bomb provided the precedent for the federal provision of research funding, albeit through channels almost always open only to majority white universities.[48] The result, along with the increasing if disproportionate prosperity of both races during the 1950s, fueled an unprecedented increase in college and university enrollment that was accompanied by new construction. Much of the new building showcased styles of architecture that were increasingly associated, especially by university professors and their most aesthetically engaged students, with aspirations for more democratic societies as well as other forms of social and technological progress.[49] The industrial aesthetic pioneered by the International Style particularly suited the latter, especially when expressions of engineering prowess provided the excitement that the style often otherwise lacked.

The political circumstances surrounding modern architecture's increasing presence on HBCU campuses by the 1950s parallel those that made it popular with European colonial officials in Africa, including the Congo, at this time. It could stand for "progress" even in situations designed to preserve racial inequality. An insidious reason why new construction flourished on state-funded HBCUs was that it was intended to subvert demands for the desegregation of exclusively white "flagship" universities. Although no state-supported HBCUs received their fair share of public money, in the first two decades after the war many enjoyed unprecedented support from legislatures anxious to preclude African American applications to all white public universities that offered degree programs the HBCUs lacked. This strategy of attacking segregation, launched by the NAACP legal defense fund, began to succeed even before *Brown v. Board of Education* sounded the eventual death knell for legally segregated public schools. In 1938, the court ruled for Lloyd Gaines, who had been denied admission to the only public law school in Missouri.[50] Twelve years later the University of Virginia's law school was forced to accept the enrollment of Gregory Swanson on the same grounds.[51]

Throughout the 1950s, the most effective means of avoiding real integration at the college and university level was to introduce more graduate programs on public HBCU campuses and to otherwise upgrade their clearly substandard facilities. Under the headline, "Trying to Ward Off Integration," the *Richmond Afro American* described a "new and modern academic building at South Carolina State College [now University], Orangeburg, with its many conveniences," as being "typical of the many new buildings being erected in the vast building program now under way at the college. State is clinging desperately to 'Separate but Equal' theory in face of inevitable integration in its public schools and colleges."[52]

Such efforts improved the situation of state-funded HBCUs but had little impact upon private institutions such as Virginia Union. Meanwhile the white philanthropic support upon which private HBCUs had long depended was drying up. The General Education Board concluded its activities in 1954. The United Negro College Fund (now UNCF), established in 1944, was seldom able to close the gap left by the GEB's departure. Located in a rapidly growing city that branded itself as "too busy to hate," although in fact it was often slower to desegregate than Richmond, and with a college named after the grandmother of a new generation of Rockefeller philanthropists, Atlanta University, another private, Baptist-supported HBCU, continued to thrive.[53] However, the situation was more difficult in Richmond, not least because Virginia's policy of Massive Resistance to integration discouraged outside investment.

Modern architecture remained the exception on HBCU campuses and in their immediate environs, however, until the late 1950s. When the *Afro American* affiliates ran a college special issue in August 1953, many institutions included photographs of their signature buildings in their advertisements.[54] None was in an obviously modern style. Two years later, however, the situation had already changed. For instance, Howard, "called [the] leader of education in [the] nation" in an accompanying headline, highlighted its $2,225,000 engineering and architecture facilities, completed in 1952, and a $3,000,000 school of dentistry, both designed in a modern style (fig. 94).[55] The first, now known as Lewis K. Downing Hall, was designed by Paul R. Williams and Hilyard Robinson, who held bachelor's and master's degrees from Columbia University and who taught architecture at Howard in a program established in 1911.[56] An understated brick box with ribbon windows enlivened by a projecting volume perpendicular to the main block, it is appropriately factory-like for an engineering school. The month before it featured the Howard buildings, the

Figure 94. Engineering and Architecture Building, Howard University, Hilyard Robinson and Paul R. Williams, Washington, D.C, 1952. (Theodor Horydczak Collection, Library of Congress Prints and Photographs Division, Washington, D.C.; photograph by Theodor Horydczak)

newspaper's Richmond edition had also profiled the new library, recently completed at the cost of over a million dollars, at what was then the Negro Agricultural and Technical College of North Carolina (now North Carolina Agricultural & Technical State University) in Greensboro, which, although less obviously modern in appearance, must have excited the envy of Virginia Union's faculty and perhaps also students.[57] Upon its opening in 1955, it was the largest library on an HBCU campus.

By 1964, the shift toward the new was largely complete. While Fisk still showed a photograph of Jubilee Hall (the Cravath Library no longer appeared so new, and the other modern buildings on its campus were not as central to the institution's identity), Morgan State chose the Carter Grant Wilson Administration Hall, completed only the year before, to represent it.[58] The drawing gave only an inkling of the building's exceptional quality (fig. 95). A dark glass box was wrapped in stone-

Figure 95. Carter Grant Wilson Administration Hall, Gaudreau and Gaudreau, Morgan State University, Baltimore, Maryland, 1963. (Courtesy of Morgan State University)

faced piers supported on reinforced concrete pilotis. The shallow V-shape of the piers and the texture and color of the stone gave a sense of warmth and scale that made this one of Baltimore's earliest and finest Brutalist buildings. That Morgan showcased it, rather than Holmes Hall, its Colonial Revival predecessor completed as late as 1952, which remains today the campus's iconic structure, says a great deal about the forward-looking image it now chose to present. Nor was this the campus's first experiment with modernism. The less imposing and more pragmatic Milton L. Calloway Hall, for science instruction, was built already in 1953 at a cost of $1.5 million. What was most unusual for Morgan, a campus with buildings by nationally known African American architects Albert Cassell, Hilyard Robinson, Louis Fry, and Leon Bridges, was that Wilson Hall was instead the work of the local white firm of Gaudreau and Gaudreau, architects best known for their Catholic churches. They had also designed the Refectory and Murphy Auditorium on the Morgan campus.[59]

Bluefield State College, Knoxville College, LeMoyne College, Lincoln University, Miles College, Norfolk State College, and Talledega College were among the other HBCUs that presented a public image in 1964 defined by distinctively modern buildings. Southern University advertised itself as "ultra-modern," boasting that its one-and-a-half million-dollar student union, opened in 1959 and designed by August Perez and Associates, featured a "cafeteria, game room, bowling alley, post office, bookstore, barber and beauty shops, guest bedrooms, snack bar, offices for student organizations, program director, union director, TV area, listening and browsing rooms." Such a wide array of facilities mattered for students, especially in cities such as Baton Rouge, where restaurants and cinemas were among the many locales that remained segregated when the building was dedicated.[60] The building was later named the Smith Brown memorial union after two students, Leonard Brown and Denver Smith, were killed by law enforcement responding to peaceful protests by students demanding that Southern University receive funding equal to that accorded to the majority white Louisiana State University.[61]

Virginia Union participated in this shift. In 1954, it ran an advertisement in the *Richmond Afro American* timed to coincide with commencement ceremonies at Armstrong High School, one of the city's two all-Black high schools. Alongside the banner, "Prepared, Confident, Secure," it illustrated one of the Noble Nine rather than the Belgian Friendship Building, in order to communicate how well established the university was.[62] However, in 1964, Virginia Union paired a drawing of the Vann Memorial Tower with text reading, "Our size, our location in a dynamic urban setting, the diversity of our student body, our faculty-student fellowship, our rich traditions and the outstanding achievements of our graduates provide incentive for personal and intellectual maturity."[63] The following year the Vann Tower was featured on the cover of a Virginia Union publication entitled "For Our New Day" (fig. 96). The building also still appeared modern to the city's African American community. In 1961, for instance, it provided the background for an advertisement for Richmond Motor, which showed a well-dressed African American couple posing in front of their Ford convertible.[64] That the Belgian Friendship Building could still convey a balance between an established identity and forward thinking a quarter century after the opening of "The World of Tomorrow" demonstrates how well the design had held up as an idea, if not always as a structure.

Although the prominence of modern architecture on historically Black campuses cannot always be tied directly to the civil rights advances made in the period, many HBCUs, including Virginia Union, encouraged both. Talladega's 1964 advertise-

Figure 96. "For Our New Day," Virginia Union University publication, 1965. (Virginia Union University Archives and Special Collections)

ment paired a photograph of Ish Hall, a dormitory for women completed the previous year at a cost of $450,000 and designed by Talley W. Piper of the Atlanta firm of Godwin and Beckett, with a description of the Alabama college, the state's oldest HBCU, as a place "where leaders of a free society affirm an ideal" (fig. 97).[65] Part of the turn toward modernism was also simply part of a larger shift in style happening across the United States and indeed around the world. Here, a projecting concrete skeletal frame established a rhythm not dissimilar to that of the bays of the campus's Colonial Revival buildings, but with larger windows and in a distinctly modern idiom. At the same time, however, the economies that helped propel an unornamented approach to architecture do not explain much of what happened on these campuses, nor the use many of them made of resources granted to them in exchange for what was supposed to be a continued acceptance of segregation. Real-

Figure 97. Ish Hall, Talladega College, Goodwin and Beckett, Talladega, Alabama, 1963. (Courtesy of Talladega College, photo credit Perry H Trice)

izing really ambitious architecture remained a challenge on campuses when white funders and neighbors did not approve. Even the form that the Colonial Revival had earlier taken on most HBCU campuses had been quite inexpensive, with solid red brick structures often embellished with the bare minimum of ornamental trimmings. Furthermore, although HBCUs almost always lacked the financial resources of comparable exclusively or predominantly white institutions, their administrators and the African American public they served took enormous pride in the often substantial cost of postwar modernist buildings, finding in them an expression of progress that African Americans could and would, it was hoped, continue to make through higher education. This took place at a time when new doors were increasingly opening to at least the college-educated middle class, if not necessarily to all African Americans.

If not inherently progressive, modern architecture and design nevertheless appealed to at least some African Americans who could choose how they lived. In the 1960s, houses built for HBCU faculty also served as a locus for African American patronage of the new. The Pearl and Isiah Thornton Creswell House, completed on the edge of the Fisk campus in 1963, is an outstanding example of such sponsorship and also demonstrates how closely aesthetics and politics could be intertwined (fig. 98). In addition to being a Fisk alumna, Pearl Creswell was until 1991 the inaugural curator of the Van Vechten Art Gallery, established as a result of Georgia O'Keeffe's donation of part of her husband Alfred Stieglitz's estate. Creswell was also a board member of the local NAACP. Her husband, Fisk's comptroller from 1945 until 1967,

Figure 98. Pearl and Isiah Thompson Creswell House, Robert M. Anderson Jr., for Donald E. Stoll & Associates, Nashville, Tennessee, 1963. (Robbie D. Jones)

was the first African American on the local school board and the first to chair it. Their house, designed by Robert M. Anderson Jr. when he was employed by Donald E. Stoll & Associates, was profiled in *Jet* in 1964. The single-story dwelling, which fills most of the lot, is arranged around an internal courtyard rather than fronting a garden. A partially screened projecting porch supported on brightly painted pillars provides a degree of privacy for the extensively glazed brick box. Stephen Ferris was the interior decorator; the house also showcased local displays of modern art.[66]

The position of modern architecture within the African American community was thus ambivalent. It symbolized economic progress, although it was often relatively inexpensive per square foot to build. It was associated with political equality and the empowerment of the previously disenfranchised as well, both at home and abroad, although in fact it often arrived on the campuses of HBCUs in lieu of meaningful integration. The situation was even more complex when one considers how and why modern architecture and urbanism were being deployed on overwhelmingly white campuses and in African American neighborhoods, including Jackson Ward, in the 1940s and 1950s.

The Politics of Modern Architecture: Northern Campuses and the Cold War

In 1946, an article in the *Virginia Union Bulletin* declared: "The Belgian Building is the most modern school building in the country. There is nothing else quite like it anywhere. One artist said that it is fifty years ahead of its time."[67] By the time these words were written, however, other European architects, including admirers of van de Velde, had begun to contemplate and even to build International Style structures on overwhelmingly white campuses in the North. Attracting far more attention nationally and internationally than the Belgian Friendship Building had, these buildings would come to define the story of the arrival of European modernism on American shores. Although consumers in the United States often made far more conventional choices, these modern buildings helped pave the way for the political and cultural elite to champion the architecture of Bauhaus émigrés and their acolytes as the face of the democratic capitalism the United States claimed to want to export internationally. By 1952, Philip Johnson, the inaugural curator of architecture and design at New York's Museum of Modern Art, could declare, "The battle of modern architecture has long been won."[68] "The World of Tomorrow" had finally arrived, and it now looked less like the Belgian Building or almost anything else on display in Flushing Meadows in 1939 or 1940 than any visitor to the New York fair had reason to expect.

The pioneering role of the Belgian Friendship Building was overlooked because it was not an example of the International Style, but also because of confusion about who had designed it. Furthermore, van de Velde's career during his last years in Belgium did not fit neatly into postwar narratives about modern architecture. The Belgian Building's location in a southern city and on an HBCU campus were additional factors that led to its omission from modern architectural narratives. At the same time, its capacity for supporting African American Richmond's quest for political equality distinguished it from International Style buildings lauded for their ability to symbolize democratic values. These celebrated buildings stood on northern campuses that did little in the immediate postwar years to welcome African Americans and that hosted very little campus activism until the anti-Vietnam War protests of the 1960s.

The misunderstanding about who had designed the Belgian Friendship Building was useful for Van Kuyck and the Belgian government in exile in 1940, but it eventually hindered the structure from gaining the widespread recognition it deserved. After being charged—but cleared—of collaboration with the Germans in his wartime role in reconstruction planning, van de Velde moved for a second time to Switzerland in 1947, where he spent the last decade of his life.[69] In these years, he defined his own contribution largely in terms of his contributions to Art Nouveau and the related design reforms that had flourished at the turn of the nineteenth into the twentieth centuries, rather than on his more recent and far more controversial role as an arbiter of modern art, architecture, and urbanism in interwar and particularly wartime Belgium.[70] The book tower of his library at Ghent University, completed in 1942, remains one of that city's most visible structures, but it did not feature in postwar accounts of modern architecture. These narratives instead stressed modern architecture's purportedly socialist origins and democratic present in order to create a usable past for an approach that was now widely seen as offering a useful alterative to classical styles tainted by their associations with fascism and communism. Just over the border from Belgium in West Germany, for instance, many architects who had built successful careers during the Third Reich reinvented themselves as politically acceptable after the war by working in what they described as a Bauhaus style.[71] Van de Velde's reputation grew over the course of the 1950s and 1960s, but few of those who admired his contributions to Art Nouveau paid much if any attention to his late work or were aware that the fruit of one of his most significant final design collaborations actually stood in the United States.[72]

Victor Bourgeois, Léon Stynen, and Van Kuyck all fared better in postwar Belgium, where there were few challenges left to the International Style, to which all three were now committed. Bourgeois's most prominent work was a new city hall for the beach community of Ostend. With one short wall devoted to the name of the building and the city's heraldic shield, and a symmetrical procession of two stories of tall windows set deeply into the main facade and above a recessed ground story, this is a building that regularizes and monumentalizes the more experimental architecture of the architect's youth. Stynen's BP tower in Antwerp remains one of the most elegant Belgian office buildings of its day (fig. 99). It was the first European building to have its facade literally hung from the roof, and its daring structural system anticipates the high-tech architecture of the following generation, as well as allowing entirely uninterrupted interiors. Van Kuyck also returned to Belgium, where he renewed his friendship with Egbert Leigh, who briefly worked for U.S. intelligence in Antwerp.[73] Van Kuyck was not as talented an architect as Bourgeois or Stynen, but, possibly because of his work for the Belgian government in exile and the U.S. military, he was extremely good at getting very large commissions. He shared credit for several Brussels office towers. He and Stynen collaborated, for instance, with Marcel Lambrichs on the design of the Finance Tower (1968–82) in Brussels, which

Figure 99. BP Building, Léon Stynen, Antwerp, 1963. (Paul Hermans / Wikimedia Commons)

is one of the country's largest and tallest, if not necessarily handsomest structures.[74] None of the men, however, gained any real recognition in the United States, despite Van Kuyck's design of the Belgium embassy in Washington.

Meanwhile, back in the United States, national and international politics also played a part in the Belgian Building's relative obscurity. The United States emerged from the ashes of war as one of the world's two superpowers. Richmond lay well outside of the national discussion of new approaches to architecture. Championing the International Style as an inherently democratic alternative to fascist monumentality and Soviet socialist realism to advance the U.S. side in the Cold War was unconvincing, as communists were quick to point out, if African Americans were denied full political equality. Of the forty-three buildings Henry-Russell Hitchcock selected for inclusion in the exhibition "Built in USA: Post-War Architecture" held at the Museum of Modern Art (MoMA) in New York in 1952, only eight were located in the former Confederacy. None was in Virginia, and none was credited to an architect who was not a white man.[75]

Hitchcock proved to be an ardent Cold War warrior, even organizing a lecture series for the Voice of America to be broadcast to Communist Eastern Europe.[76] In his introduction to the catalog "Built in USA," he boasted of the United States, "In architecture, as in many other things, we are the heirs of Western civilization."[77] Hitchcock's definition of civilization assiduously overlooked the fact that van de Velde was not the only supporter of modern architecture to have made politically questionable decisions, above all under Germany's military occupation of Belgium when he sought above all else to continue his work for the Belgian civil administration and to protect his school. International Style architects Walter Gropius and Ludwig Mies van der Rohe were also compromised by their contributions to Nazi-sponsored exhibitions in the 1930s, even if, like van de Velde, they never joined the Nazi Party nor professed Nazi ideology.[78] Even Alvar Aalto, the architect whose Finnish pavilion made such a positive impression upon American visitors to the fair and whose international reputation soared after World War II, had visited the Third Reich in 1943.[79]

These contacts with Hitler's Germany notwithstanding, Gropius, Mies, and Aalto designed buildings at Harvard University, the Illinois Institute of Technology, and the Massachusetts Institute of Technology, respectively, that did a great deal to win support for the International Style in the United States—an approach to architecture that became associated with liberal democratic ideology in Cold War architecture historiography. First out of the starting blocks was Mies. The third and final director of the Bauhaus arrived in the United States in 1938 to direct the architecture program at what was then the Armour Institute of Technology in Chicago, which after a merger with the Lewis Institute in 1940 rebranded itself as the Illinois Institute of Technology (IIT). In 1943, Mies completed the Minerals & Metals Building, his first of a total of thirteen low-slung buildings he designed for IIT's new South Side campus. An understated metal framed box with glass and brick infill, it established the template for the pavilions with which he would eventually fill the campus. Indeed, the relatively unremarkable structure initially drew relatively little attention; only when he began to more clearly express his buildings' steel frames, beginning with Alumni Memorial Hall, completed in 1946, did Mies begin to provide a much-imitated template for postwar architecture on both sides of the Atlantic (fig. 100). Although not strictly modular, the exquisite proportions and details of this building suggested a logic that would attract international attention when showcased in 1947 at an exhibition of Mies's work that Johnson curated at MoMA.[80] Arthur Drexler, the third contributor to the catalog of "Built in USA," wrote in it that Mies, "excluding from his architecture whatever is not directly related to structure, makes structural clarity a value independent of the specific buildings that occasion it."[81] There was little about the rigid lean lines of these buildings that suggested Mies's long-standing admiration for van de Velde, whose theater building for the Werkbund exhibition held in Cologne in 1914 he insisted be included in a display of

Figure 100. Alumni Memorial Hall, Illinois Institute of Technology, Ludwig Mies van der Rohe, Chicago, Illinois, 1946. (© Scott Gilchrist / archivision.com, 1A1-MVR-II-E1)

recent architecture held at the Bauhaus in 1923.[82] While van de Velde could serve as a touchstone for the modern movement then, his work for Hendrik de Man's Ministry of Public works in Belgium in the 1930s and his defense of his friend and ally throughout the 1940s and 1950s, after de Man had been convicted of collaboration with the German military occupation, placed him well outside the postwar narrative of modern architecture as inherently democratic.

Van de Velde's shortcomings notwithstanding, it would be his only building in the United States, the Belgian Friendship Building, that would do more to embody the goals of the civil rights movement, however unwittingly, than the campus buildings by Mies, Gropius, and Aalto. The expansive lawns on which Mies's IIT buildings sit so lightly are deceptive. This was not previously open prairie; rather these blocks had been developed already in the late nineteenth century and had been throughout the 1930s a part of Bronzeville, a predominantly working-class neighborhood densely populated by African Americans who had participated in the Great Migration from the South in order to find jobs and escape segregation. Although public facilities in the northern city were integrated, housing was not, ensuring that African Americans crowded into the neighborhoods to which they were confined. Crown Hall, the building housing the architecture school that is perhaps the most admired of all of Mies's contributions to the IIT campus, sits on the site of the Mecca Flats, once a Bronzeville landmark. The clearance of part of the neighborhood for IIT and the Michael Reese Hospital complex for which the urban planning was done by Gropius and his biographer Reginald Isaacs, was an early example of why the

African American novelist James Baldwin would later term urban renewal "Negro removal."[83] The appellation was apt, as modern urban planning principles that broke with established street patterns to clear space around buildings were repeatedly used in the postwar period to displace working-class and lower-middle-class African Americans in order to turn land over to predominately white and middle-class institutions and residents.

Nevertheless, despite its participation in urban renewal or because of its proximity to Bronzeville, IIT was relatively open to African Americans. During Mies's tenure there his most notable African American students included Georgia Louise Harris Brown, who would later practice in Brazil; Henry Clifford Boles, who practiced in Monrovia, Liberia, before moving to Massachusetts; Jerome Campbell, the first president of the National Organization of Minority Architects; and John Warren Moutoussamy, who went on to design the Chicago headquarters of the Johnson Publishing Company, whose periodicals included *Ebony* and *Jet.* Moutoussamy's daughter, the photographer Jeanne Moutoussamy-Ashe, married Richmond-born tennis legend Arthur Ashe.[84]

African American students were less welcome in the immediate postwar years on the campuses of the other showcases of European modern architecture, MIT and Harvard, both located in Cambridge, Massachusetts. Two showcase dormitory complexes, Aalto's Baker House at MIT and the Harvard Graduate Center, the work of The Architects Collaborative (TAC), completed in 1949 and 1950, respectively, undoubtedly included relatively few African Americans among their early residents (figs. 101 and 102). Although a pioneer already at the end of the nineteenth century in training both women and African Americans to be architects, MIT admitted only a few African Americans a year before the late 1960s.[85] The Graduate School of Design at Harvard enrolled African Americans, including IIT graduate Boles, but they were not always made to feel welcome. In 1952, when the architect Max Bond was a freshman, he had to endure a cross being burned in front of his dormitory room on the Harvard Yard. There is no record of any faculty member having spoken out about the incident.[86]

Although van de Velde's late work fell out of narratives of modern architecture for political reasons, his designs from the 1930s continued to exert an influence on architectural practice, especially his privileging of organic form and materials. Baker House and the Harvard Graduate Center, located a short stroll across Cam-

Figure 101. Baker Hall, Massachusetts Institute of Technology, Alvar Aalto, Cambridge, Massachusetts, 1949. (Gunnar Klack / Wikimedia Commons)

Figure 102. Harvard Graduate Center, The Architects Collaborative, Cambridge, Massachusetts, 1950. (John Phelan / Wikimedia Commons)

bridge from one another, were designed by architects with very different views of van de Velde and very different approaches to the International Style. Yet that Aalto could be inspired by van de Velde would hardly surprise any close observer of Baker House.[87] Its gentle curves that ensure each student room a panoramic view of the Charles River and the highly textured brick that helps integrate it into its surroundings were both choices that van de Velde would have appreciated. In many ways Aalto's approach to plastic form and tactile materials kept key concerns of van de Velde's interwar architecture alive in the postwar period, when Aalto was one of Europe's most admired architects. The Finnish architect took a very different approach to the International Style than Mies had at IIT. While both eschewed ornament, Aalto was, like van de Velde before him, more interested in line as an expression of structural and physical forces latent in materials than he was in an industrial aesthetic, which was among Mies's chief concerns.[88] Although Aalto took no consistent approach to the International Style, the same could be said of many of the contributions that Eliel Saarinen's son Eero Saarinen made to the MIT and Yale campuses in such structures as the MIT Chapel, completed in 1956; the Ingalls Rink, finished two years later in New Haven; and Samuel Morse and Ezra Stiles Colleges, which opened on the Yale campus in 1962 (fig. 103).

In contrast, the Graduate Center was antiseptic. Even Hitchcock, a resolute champion of the International Style, had trouble defending the postwar work of Gropius, TAC's most notable partner, as equal to the best buildings he had designed in Germany.[89] Consisting of a series of seven low-rise slabs—five of them set perpendicularly to one another to define a courtyard and further mid-block spaces, plus a dining hall with a slightly curved facade intended to animate the composition—these are workmanlike structures with little of the compositional verve or the meticulous detailing found at the Dessau Bauhaus. To the degree to which it is present, visual interest was instead provided by works of art, many of them executed by former Bauhaus students.[90]

While Baker House has always been more widely admired than the Graduate Center, Gropius was a much more powerful figure, and it was his narrative of modern architecture, from which van de Velde was deliberately excluded, that won out in the end. From 1937 to 1952, Gropius chaired the Department of Architecture at Harvard's Graduate School of Design. His former students, including Edward Larrabee Barnes, I. M. Pei, Paul Rudolph, Hugh Stubbins, and Anne Tyng, contributed prominently to architectural culture in the United States and far beyond for the next half century; Pei, for instance, added the pyramid to the Louvre Museum in Paris.[91] Unlike Mies, who had been the school's third and final director and who was busier building, Gropius spent much of his retirement tending to the Bauhaus's reputation and equating modern architecture with the democratic side of the Cold War that had divided his native city of Berlin. Gropius had long begrudged van de Velde his role in establishing what became the Bauhaus in Weimar. Now he frequently

Figure 103. Ingalls Memorial Rink, Yale University, Eero Saarinen, New Haven, Connecticut, 1958, renovated, 2009. (Yale University)

wrote would-be historians of the Bauhaus to deter them from crediting the older architect with laying the foundations upon which the school had been built.[92] At a time when Gropius's advocacy of modern architecture was rooted in his ability to tie it to democracy, van de Velde was best forgotten.[93] But democracy was incomplete as long as African Americans did not have equal political rights, equal economic opportunities, and equal access to these campuses.

Urban Renewal and the Evisceration of Jackson Ward

Cold War claims that modern architecture and urbanism were inherently democratic faltered even more notably when juxtaposed with the reality of how their aesthetics were imposed upon established African American neighborhoods across the country, including in Richmond. The civil rights movement's eventual achievements in obtaining voting rights and access to public space were offset here, as elsewhere, when urban renewal proved devastatingly effective in clearing the neighborhoods that had sustained African Americans in their search for economic and spiritual sustenance as well as justice. While middle-class whites gained access in the postwar period to single-family suburban homes designed with little if any concern for the International Style, their African American counterparts often had to settle for cast-offs, moving into the no longer fashionable neighborhoods that whites with wider consumer choice had abandoned. Meanwhile, in cities such as Richmond much of the African American working class was shunted into bare-bones public housing that did little to live up to modernism's utopian promises.[94] Gropius declared that "nothing promotes an understanding of environmental planning better than active participation in it," but planning decisions were something to which working-class African Americans seldom had full access. In Richmond, they did not enjoy full voting rights until 1964, when the poll tax was finally outlawed thanks to the adoption that year of the Twenty-Fourth Amendment to the U.S. Constitution.[95]

Modern planning principles eroded a respect for the street while prioritizing high-speed automobile traffic in ways advocated at "The World of Tomorrow" by Futurama, its most popular attraction. Dense urban neighborhoods where dwellings often lacked such basic amenities as adequate indoor plumbing were particularly vulnerable to being either replaced by facilities serving the white middle class, as had happened when IIT built upon a former section of Bronzeville, or by public housing that was seldom properly maintained by city housing authorities. Richmond never warehoused its poor in high-rise towers, whose height was intended to accommodate residents in more modern conditions supplemented by light, air, and access to green space. Such buildings proved particularly problematic, however, not least because their construction was seldom accompanied by the provision of the shops and other neighborhood facilities present in neighborhoods such as Jackson Ward.[96] Instead, the most destructive action taken in Richmond was the location of the Richmond–Petersburg Turnpike, which opened in 1958. Now Interstate 95, this multilane highway sliced through Jackson Ward and cut Virginia Union off from the center of the city. Across the United States, interstate highways of this kind were often deliberately located to destroy African American neighborhoods.[97]

Even before the interstate highway system tore through African American communities, in many cases displacing not only their residents but also the institutions that had nurtured solidarity between the working and the middle classes, these neighborhoods faced challenges rooted in racial discrimination. For instance, already in 1917, the authors of a study of African American education published by the U.S. Department of Education noted:

> Hartshorn [College] and Virginia Union, Richmond, Va., have recently had to suffer from a new railroad bordering their grounds. Hartshorn is being hard pressed by factories and other manufacturing plants, the water supply is inadequate, the buildings are too high, and the location is no more central to students than other sites more appropriate.[98]

Virginia Union students and graduates gradually benefited from opportunities for which they had vigorously campaigned, but new threats quickly developed. Virginia Union nurtured the African American politicians who gained real political power in Richmond and across Virginia, but this occurred too late to save Jackson Ward. Two of Union's most distinguished alumni are Douglas Wilder and Henry Marsh, who graduated in 1951 and 1956, respectively. In 1969 Wilder became the first African American elected to the Virginia State Senate since Reconstruction; two decades later he became the first African American to be elected a governor in the United States.[99] In 1977 Marsh, a prominent civil rights lawyer, became Richmond's first African American mayor.[100]

The route that the turnpike took as it linked Maine to Miami was first discussed in 1946 but only fixed in 1957, a year after the state officially committed to a policy of Massive Resistance to public school integration (fig. 104). K. Ian Grandison wrote that the road "not only blocked, physically and symbolically, Virginia Union University's access to Richmond's official civic and commercial centers; it also devalued sites of other important black institutions—schools, churches, banks, funeral homes, fraternal lodges—by razing them or razing their surroundings or squeezing their fronts and backs up against the highway."[101] The original plan for the highway pushed it to the east of the university, but as white opposition to African American aspirations became more openly hostile, its location was adjusted to plough through Jackson Ward, leaving Virginia Union severed from the neighborhood that had been its lifeblood. Furthermore, the area to the east where the highway had originally been located was rezoned for industry, attracting unwelcome neighbors, including many servicing truck travel on the new road. Grandison noted as well what may

Figure 104. Richmond's North Side in 1956, prior to the construction of I-95, with the campus of Virginia Union in the foreground. Within two years I-95 would bend slightly into this view from the left, separating Virginia Union from the Jackson Ward neighborhood to the southeast. (Library of Virginia)

have been a backlash against the prominence of the Belgian Building, as the "Vann Bell Tower also raised the university's physical and symbolic profile to new heights, becoming a landmark visible far beyond the campus borders."[102] As a result of the highway construction, Virginia Union became increasingly geographically isolated, even as the number of people who glimpsed the Vann Tower as they sped along the new highway rose far beyond what anyone could have imagined in 1940.

The highway displaced seven thousand Jackson Ward residents, severely diminishing the consumer base for the neighborhood's Black-owned businesses, many of which closed. It cannot be blamed for all of the neighborhood's decline, however. Following the actions of the Richmond Thirty-Four, African American consumers enjoyed better access to formerly segregated businesses. Improved political rights, coupled with economic opportunities, also enabled Jackson Ward's middle-class residents to move to more modern houses in less crowded neighborhoods elsewhere in the metropolitan area.[103]

Integration proved a two-edged sword for HBCUs as well. It expanded African American students' access to majority white institutions, which now also began to hire African American faculty. Integration also diminished pressure on both philanthropists and legislatures to fund HBCUs, even as, in the words of a *Richmond Afro American* article reporting on the Founder's Day celebration at Virginia Union, "They relate and understand our needs and aspirations. They have the best track record for producing black leadership. They prepare you better to face problems in a society where racism remains a problem for black people."[104] The financial challenges that Virginia Union continued to face limited its ability to maintain the Belgian Building, even as the Vann Memorial Tower became a widely recognized, if still underappreciated, landmark to the many motorists who sped by or were stuck in traffic alongside it. Meanwhile, awareness that it commemorated Vann and of his importance to the interwar history of the United States faded as the building aged. While IIT, MIT, and Harvard sponsored scholarships that enhanced the appreciation of their roles in nurturing modern architecture, Virginia Union was left simply struggling to maintain its equally innovative facilities.[105]

7

THE TEMPORARY BECOMES PERMANENT

The Challenge of Extending the Life of Impermanent Construction

Today Virginia Union's staff and students no longer see the Belgian Friendship Building as it appeared in 1950, following the completion of its reconstruction on the Richmond campus (fig. 105). Time has not been kind. In part, the problem is that the building, which was designed to be temporary, was not rebuilt in Richmond in a way that fully addressed its conversion into a permanent structure. The building's current state is also the result of the persistent discrimination against African Americans that continues to ensure that HBCUs such as Virginia Union remain under-resourced. Consequently, their architecture is not always well maintained, even when it is widely admired and a source of institutional pride. The poor condition of the architectural heritage of many of these campuses is due to a lack of resources, including access to specialized professional knowledge in historic building conservation, a field not taught at many HBCUs.

The Belgian Friendship Building was never forgotten, especially in Richmond, but it also has never garnered the level of attention that would generate the funding necessary to conserve it properly. It lies instead in a precarious limbo, suspended between appreciation and abandonment, continuing to deteriorate even as it also serves important functions for the university, among them providing the basketball court for a team that in the 2022–23 season won three-quarters of its games,

Figure 105. Vann Memorial Tower, 2021 (Richmond Times-Dispatch)

including the Freedom Classic against arch-rival Virginia State.[1] It also houses lively dance, theater, and music programs. Although far from invisible, the Vann Memorial Tower has been stripped of its most distinctive features, while the rest of the building suffers from the difficulty of keeping it in good repair.

Problems Caused by the Original Reconstruction

The Belgian Friendship Building is a unique building, and unique buildings fail uniquely. The very conditions of its construction that made it such an exemplary display of Belgian construction, first in New York and then Richmond, are also what make it a particular challenge to conserve. Distinctively Belgian materials were entirely appropriate for the fair, but this feature of the building makes it almost impossible to easily replace tile or slate that is chipped or broken, although in the 1950s Newport Bricks, credited in a plaque on the building, imported Courtrai ceramics into the United States.[2] The proper repair of a broken tile requires that an indi-

Figure 106. Cracked tiles revealing chicken wire backing and space between tiles and cement masonry unit wall, 2022 (Katherine M. Kuenzli)

vidual mold be made and a custom piece of terra cotta tile be fired (fig. 106). There is no premanufactured tile that can be substituted, and the costs for producing new ones are steep. And while skeletal frame construction was well established on both sides of the Atlantic in 1939, metrically dimensioned materials remain unusual in the United States, which almost singularly retains its commitment to inches, feet, and yards. Even routine maintenance becomes much more difficult under such conditions.

A second major problem is that the Belgian workforce simply reerected the same construction system in Richmond that it had employed in New York (fig. 107). This

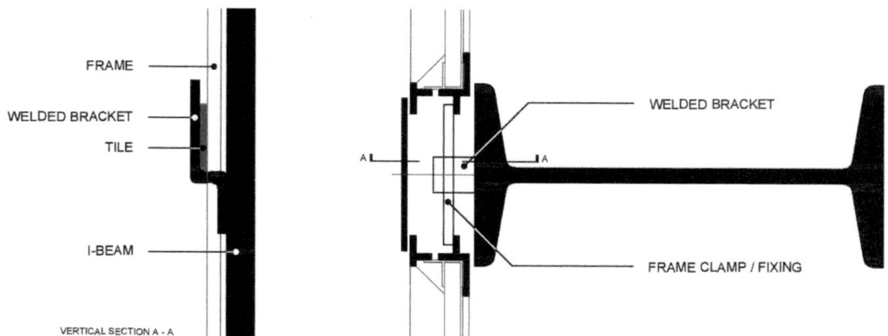

Figure 107. Section of construction detail (Niall Howard)

system of steel bolts and beams had been developed for Belgium's earlier contribution to the Paris fair of 1937. Repeating it in Richmond overlooked the fact that an additional layer of waterproofing needed to be added between the steel frame and the revetment in order for the building to work well as a permanent structure. A guide to ceramic material systems, published in 2015, confirms construction practices that were already standard practice in the 1930s:

> Adhered tiles require a well-finished, flat surface. Masonry and concrete walls are the preferred, traditional base for adhering tiles, and are widely used, especially in Europe and Asia. . . . North American steel construction often connects tiles to rigid building boards carried by metal stud wall systems—these are good base surfaces that tend to be flat and dimensionally stable . . . Certain sub-surfaces are less suited for adhered tile construction. Steel is generally not recommended because any water penetration will lead to corrosion and expansion—quickly loosening the tiles.[3]

These best practices were employed by van de Velde in his Technical School in Leuven, where similar terra cotta tiles were affixed to a thin coat of concrete applied to brick infill. Although that building has undergone a major renovation and is in excellent condition today, the general state of the terra cotta demanded less attention than it now requires in Richmond.[4] By contrast, the Belgian Friendship Building's cladding system consists of horizontal steel channels into which the tiles are set, all wired to a concrete masonry unit (CMU) backing and then mortared into place.

This makeshift solution has allowed water ingress that has cracked many more of the terra cotta tiles and slate cladding than would have been the case had the methods employed in Leuven been repeated here.

After Integration: Challenges Remain

The history of the Belgian Friendship Building over the last six decades has oscillated between increasing local, national, and even international recognition of its importance and the continued deterioration of the actual structure. Most buildings require little more than routine maintenance for their first forty to sixty years. At that point they are particularly vulnerable because elements such as roofs and mechanical systems, as well as many types of flooring, generally need replacing. By 1966, Virginia Union was already considering demolition. The Belgian Friendship Building was spared largely because the university could not yet afford a replacement. Yet the same financial challenges continue to impede its conservation; a building purportedly given as a "gift" eventually became a burden. Like HBCUs across the United States, Virginia Union struggles with a limited endowment, modest budgets, and challenges faced by student recruitment and retention, all of which render the maintenance of a building that is already of limited use both a financial liability and a management conundrum.

Paradoxically, the success of the civil rights movement did not always help the institutions that had done so much to nurture it. In the 1950s, publicly funded HBCUs benefited from increased funding, as states sought to stave off the integration of their flagship campuses, but private HBCUs benefited less during what were otherwise boom times for higher education in the United States. Northern white Baptist philanthropy, already on the wane during the Depression, did not substantially increase. After Jackson Davis's death, the role of the General Education Board drastically diminished. White Southern Baptist support for HBCUs, of the kind Virginia Union received for the erection of the Belgian Building, also proved short-lived, as the paternalistic approach to interracial relations that had generated it became less common in the wake of *Brown v. Board of Education.* The establishment of the United Negro College Fund provided a conduit for donations from all racial groups and parts of the country, but it was not always enough to make up the deficit.[5] The mid-1980s were particularly tough on Virginia Union, but after a rebound in the 1990s, the twenty-first century has not always been much kinder.[6] That alumni often face racist discrimination that hinders their ability to earn enough to donate generously has been a further impediment.

Integration also opened new opportunities for many of the best-prepared African American students and faculty. By the late 1960s, almost all majority white colleges and universities had opened their doors to African Americans, and many eventually went a step further and adopted affirmative action policies.[7] Later, often in response to student pressure, they also diversified their course offerings. Today students at the previously all-white University of Richmond, the University of Virginia, and Virginia Commonwealth University can major in African and African American studies. Although throughout the first half of twentieth century a handful of African Americans had been able to earn advanced degrees from majority white institutions in the North and West, most were never considered for faculty positions at even the universities that were willing to accept them as students.[8] By the 1960s this situation was changing, too. Not surprisingly, many of the pioneers were Virginia Union alumni, including Abram Lincoln Harris at the University of Chicago and Henry Allen Bullock at the University of Texas.

These changes made it difficult for Virginia Union to maintain its position as a premiere institution for African Americans seeking a liberal arts education and an entrée into the professions, even as it, like all HBCUs, retains its importance as a ladder into the middle class, including for many from disadvantaged backgrounds who are unable to pay the tuition that private, majority-white institutions can charge.[9] This has meant that the university has struggled to maintain its historic structures, including the Belgian Friendship Building, even as it has added new facilities and degree programs. The Belgian Friendship Building has always been an object of pride on campus and across the city of Richmond, but the very factors that make it such a visible symbol for the university also make it a special challenge to preserve.

Recognition versus Repair

Across the decades, the Belgian Building remained newsworthy in Richmond and occasionally further afield as well. Attention focused both on the structure's unusual history as a relic of the fair and on efforts to maintain it, including following repeated storm damage. Increased appreciation began to come at precisely the same time that the Belgium Friendship Building's deterioration became serious. It was listed individually on the Virginia Landmarks register in 1969 and on the National Register of Historic Places the following year.[10] Both of these designations were created only in 1966, making it a very early entrant on each list. Clearly at a time when historic preservation efforts were just being institutionalized and the preservation of mid-century modernism was extremely unusual, concerned locals in Richmond knew what a treasure it was. In 1975, it was added as a single building in Richmond's Old and Historic District; this recognition came in advance of protection for the campus as a whole. The Noble Nine joined the Virginia Landmarks register only in 1981 and were subsequently added to the National Register in 1982.[11] These designations offer a significant degree of protection, without, however, translating into wider national recognition of the significance of these structures or adequate provision for their continued maintenance. Already in 1970, the National Register nomination described the Belgian Building as being in only fair condition.[12] What the nomination described as "a slender slate-faced campanile-like tower, one corner of which is ornamented with glass blocks while the top is crowned with a distinctive louvred lantern" lost much of its architectural character when in the winter of 1971–72 the tower shaft was clad in aluminum siding donated by Richard S. Reynolds Jr., the president of the Reynolds Metals company, which between 1938 and 2000 had its headquarters in Richmond (fig. 108).[13] This well-intentioned gesture by a major manufacturer had unfortunate consequences, as aluminum siding was an entirely inappropriate material for the tower, which in the process lost the interplay of slate and glass that had given it much of its character.[14] Moreover, the new cladding lasted less than twenty-five years.

The need for further repairs was highlighted in 1986, when then president of Virginia Union Dallas Simmons told the *Richmond Times Dispatch* that the building was in need of a complete renovation.[15] The interview was prompted by the interest that Barbara Capitman, an enthusiast for Art Deco who had spearheaded preservation efforts in Miami Beach, had shown for the building and for raising the funds necessary to restore it. By 1990, Simmons estimated that restoration would cost $10 million. Instead, the university was only able to manage a "facelift" of the tower in 1994, on which it spent a far more modest $300,500.[16]

Virginia Union took a huge step forward in 1997 when the library moved into a new purpose-built structure named for former Virginia governor and Union

Figure 108. Belgian Friendship Building with aluminum siding on Vann Memorial Tower, early 1970s. (Library of Congress; Historic American Buildings Survey; photograph by Walter Smalling Jr.)

alumnus Douglas Wilder. At that time, plans for a new basketball arena were also mooted, as the university contemplated an expensive move into the NCAA's Division I, a jump many of its long-time HBCU rivals had already made.[17] The city and the university hoped that the Belgian Friendship Building could be converted into a museum once these two functions had been moved into new facilities. The proposed "Hard Road to Glory African-American Sports Hall of Fame" was inspired by the title of a four-volume book series authored by tennis great Arthur Ashe, a Richmond native.[18] Instead, skeptical that the museum would be realized, Virginia Union's trustees opted to renovate the building for the performing arts, as well as for classroom and office spaces.[19] This function seemed particularly appropriate, considering the presence of the two 1939 bas-reliefs, *Belgium at Work* and *The Belgian Congo.* Shorn from its context of celebrating Belgian colonialism, even the latter could serve as a source of inspiration for student artists. Arthur Blackwell, who graduated from Virginia Union at the age of forty-nine in 1999, reported that he was impressed by seeing "blacks excelling in fishing, construction, dancing, music and science." "How," he asked, "can you pass by this piece of art every day and not be inspired? How can you not strive for perfection?"[20] In 1998 the university received an award from the Historic Richmond Foundation for its work on this and two other buildings.[21]

The performing arts remained the focus in 2000, when Union president Bernard Franklin announced a campaign to raise $1.5 to $2 million for a thorough renovation.[22] The Mary Morton Pierson Foundation, a Richmond-based philanthropy, pledged half a million dollars toward the effort, but like earlier grants from the General Education Board, it came on the condition of the university raising more, in this case not just matching funds but doubling the amount.[23] Although portions of the former library were converted to a theater and rehearsal space, funding ran short, and the repair of portions of the first floor and the entire second floor of the library remained incomplete.[24] As had been the case in the 1930s, Virginia Union was once again unable to fulfill its aspirations for improved facilities.

Furthermore, not all renovation efforts had an entirely positive impact. Instead, lack of funds encouraged stopgap measures that continued detrimentally to impact the building's historic integrity and architectural performance. In September 2003, Hurricane Isabel struck Richmond, causing serious property damage across the city and tearing the roof off the Belgian Building.[25] Left unrepaired, this led to massive water infiltration and the eventual abandonment of parts of the complex. The tower, which was in the middle of a $2 million restoration, was clad in an exterior insulation finishing system (EIFS) in order to repair it as expeditiously and inexpensively as possible (fig. 109).

Recognition for the building continued apace, however. In 2004 John Malcus Ellison's niece Dianne Watkins, who had lived with her aunt and uncle on the campus of Virginia Union during the 1940s, launched "Bells for Peace," a campaign whose focus was to add a carillon to the Vann Memorial Tower.[26] More than that, it also aimed to draw attention to the Belgian Friendship Building and Virginia Union's history, while also promoting the humanitarian purpose the building had once been purported to serve. The goals of the organization included "to promote excellence at Virginia Union University through the visual representation that a preserved Belgian Friendship Building" offered, to commemorate Ellison and his wife Elizabeth Balfour Ellison, and "to continually recognize the need to bring about

Figure 109. Vann Memorial Tower with EIFS cladding. (Bryan Clark Green)

peace for the benefit of all mankind." The effort, which lasted over a decade, drew considerable attention to the tower in Belgium as well as across the United States.

One of the most interesting aspects of this campaign was its focus on Henry van de Velde, to whom for the first time the building in its entirety was attributed. This emphasis was undoubtedly in part because he was by far the most famous of the architects involved in its design. In 2006, Watkins wrote of Bells for Peace: "It highlights this unique structure in Richmond and the history of its designer, Henry Van de Velde (1863–1957), one of the greatest architects of his time. The Belgian Building is his only masterpiece in America; its majestic tower can be seen from many areas of the Richmond community."[27]

Bells for Peace had an impact, even if it proved unable to commission a new set of bells. In 2011 an electric carillon was installed in the tower; the organization also experimented with lighting effects. In 2013 Bells for Peace funded the conservation of the *Belgium at Work* and *The Belgian Congo* bas-reliefs.[28] Once again, however, matching funds were an issue. In 2007, the Belgian government pledged to pay for four bells if the tower was restored. This prompted Bells for Peace to commission a study that showed that the tower required $300,000 of repairs before it could support the weight of new bells. Three years later Congress pledged $150,000 towards the effort on the condition that the financially strapped university match it.[29]

In 2005 Barco-Stevens Hall was named by the National Collegiate Athletic Association (NCAA) as one of a baker's dozen of athletic facilities from across the United States that were "unique." Others receiving this distinction included Eero Saarinen's famed Ingalls ice hockey rink at Yale University, whose curved profiles descended directly from van de Velde's 1914 Werkbund Theatre in Cologne, Germany (fig. 103). The article quoted NCAA staff member Michelle Brutlag Hosnick as saying, "While some institutions are tearing down the old to make way for the new others are celebrating the uniqueness by restoring or renovating older facilities."[30] In fact, two years earlier Virginia Union had once again proposed building new facilities for the storied Panthers. For nearly a decade the team had been using Barco-Stevens Hall, which at that time sat only 1,800 (it now holds 2,500), mostly as a practice court, while playing most of its home games off campus.[31] When the new facility proved too expensive, Virginia Union instead renovated Barco-Stevens, adding new bleachers, a new floor, and a new roof.[32] Yale, by contrast, hired the Pritzker Prize–winning firm of Kevin Roche and John Dinkeloo to undertake a renovation and expansion of Ingalls. The acclaimed result was completed in 2009, with Yale spending $23 million on the project.[33]

Virginia Union has never had access to such generous funding. By 2023 the National Trust's African American Cultural Heritage Action Fund had raised a relatively modest $91 million in its first five years, which it had used to support 242 different projects.[34] In 2007, the Getty Foundation provided Virginia Union with $120,000 with which it hired Commonwealth Architects, a Richmond firm, to develop a historic master plan for the entire campus.[35] This followed the renovation at a cost of $500,000 of the middle part of the Belgian Friendship Building, which had formerly served as science laboratories, into regular classrooms and offices.[36] The plan aspired to "serve as an inspiration for other historically black institutions of higher education as they seek to retain their own historic campuses while encouraging future growth and prosperity."[37] Instead, the Belgian Friendship Building's fate only illustrated how difficult it was for such institutions to care adequately for their built heritage. The recommendations developed by Bryan Clark Green were never fully funded. Only a series of relatively minor repairs, including to the steel frame of the tower and windows on one elevation, were realized. A fitness center was slotted into the building in 2009, but the inability to fulfill a comprehensive plan was all too evident.[38]

Bells for Peace and the Getty grant failed to achieve what they had hoped, but they did spur further research. In 2010, *Belgium at the Fair: Exhibition on Main Street,* a book edited by Mil De Kooning that addressed Belgium's participation in the Paris and New York fairs, as well as the construction of the Belgian Friendship Building in Richmond, was published with the assistance of a number of Belgian civic and commercial organizations.[39] Meanwhile, the building continues to be a site of civic activism. When in September 2015 the NAACP organized a march from Selma, Alabama, to Washington, D.C., its Richmond stop was at the Belgian Building.[40]

Yet the pride of place stimulated by these many efforts did not slow the gradual decay of the structure itself. In 2010, the National Park Service supplied Virginia Union with a grant of $340,000 in return for assurances that the university would not allow the Belgian Friendship Building to be altered. In 2019 it supplied another $500,000 through its African American Civil Rights Grant Program.[41] This was intended to supply a new heating, ventilation, and air-conditioning (HVAC) system, which, however, was a very modest sum for such a goal. The following year the university breached the terms of the agreement when it added seventeen-foot illuminated school logos to each side of the tower (fig. 105). The ensuing conflict between Virginia Union's administration—which was willing to pay a $35,000 annual fee to keep the signs that purportedly "provide a lasting bright-shining symbol of justice, hope, and equality"—and preservation officials who worried about the added weight, exposes a divergence of visions for how the building may best fulfill its symbolic purpose. The university administration values branding, while the state's Department of Historic Resources prioritizes the building's historic appearance.[42] Neither commands the necessary resources to fund a proper restoration.

Most recently, on April 1, 2023, yet another storm damaged the tower, breaking windows and causing water to pour into its interior. According to the city government, the university originally began repairs without obtaining the required building permit and then waited two months to file the necessary application. The damage occurred in part because of the poor quality of the replacement siding. Ironically, had it been properly attached—or subsequently reattached—to the building's structural frame, the original slate might have fared much better because, unlike the EIFS, it does not absorb water.[43]

Virginia Union has a distinguished past and is making a real difference as well in the present. There is no doubt that the presence of the Belgian Friendship Building on its campus has contributed mightily to its local prominence and reputation. Especially in its early years, the building also made a real difference in the education of its students, providing the university with facilities it would have otherwise lacked. Moving forward, however, requires envisioning the building as having sufficient international architectural significance to merit funding its renovation in ways that enhance rather than diminish the campus of current and future Virginia Union students and staff and honor its alumni's storied achievements.

CONCLUSION

Christina Sharpe has argued that "in the face of Black people's continued eviction from the category of the human, we should not mistake the erection of the monument or memorial for repair, or for the end horizon of something like justice or the fulfillment of something like liberation." She continues:

> No matter the intention, every monument or memorial to atrocities against Black people already contains its failure. Because they are projects of reform and not radical projects, they do not imagine new worlds. They stage encounters. But for whom? Who is the subject seen to be coming to terms with an ongoing brutality imagined as past and then reimagined as an aesthetic project? Who are the subjects imagined as witness and participant in the encounter, and who is imagined by being moved by the encounter and to what end? How is such movement facilitated or inhibited by its architectures? The monument or memorial is a staged encounter in which the terrible grammars of the past, though disrupted, still remain.[1]

The Vann Memorial Tower is not, of course, a memorial to an atrocity but a monument to one of the most prominent African Americans of his day. At the same time, the Belgian Friendship Building of which it is a part also contains a misplaced celebration of a deeply exploitive colonial regime, whose effects continue to hamper living conditions in the Democratic Republic of the Congo today. The working conditions for the Congolese men, and possibly also women, who mined uranium at Shinkolobwe were scarcely as benevolent as those depicted in the bas-reliefs of Congolese and Belgians at work that still decorate the Belgian Friendship Building on Virginia Union's campus. More than six decades after their country achieved independence, workers in the Congo continue to be exploited by corrupt politicians and foreign mining companies.[2] As it stands today in Richmond, the Belgian Friendship Building encapsulates both the oppression that continues to characterize too many Black lives and exceptional achievement in the face of that oppression. As Sharpe makes clear, there are limits to what memorials can achieve, but that has not prevented Richmonders from continuing to struggle with how to find physical forms through which to celebrate African American courage, leadership, and accomplishment.

Today the Vann Memorial Tower's original commemorative purpose is not well remembered in Richmond. The connection is occasionally mentioned in local newspaper coverage, but it is not highlighted on Virginia Union's website, where it is noted only in the history of the university, and not on commemorative signage on the campus itself.[3] Significantly, on a campus that abounds with plaques noting the historic importance of its handsome buildings, the panel corresponding to the Belgian Building has been removed, diminishing awareness of its significance among those who regularly enter or pass by it. Students educated in the building's shadow continue, however, to make notable contributions of which the Vanns would both be proud. To name only a few of them: Leontine Kelly, class of 1960, was one of the first women in the United States to become the bishop of a major Protestant denomination; Randall Robinson, class of 1967 and founder of TransAfrica and the Free South African Movement, led demonstrations in Washington against the Apartheid government in South Africa;[4] Roslyn Brock, class of 1987, was the first woman to chair the board of the NAACP.

How does a physical form come to recognizably embody such achievements? This has not yet happened in Richmond, despite the addition of the university's logo to the four sides of the tower. To be effective, a memorial's original commemorative purpose needs to be remembered. This is easiest when it is more obviously representative of the figure it honors. The transposition of a memorial purpose into an architectural element, such as a tower, presents a greater challenge, especially if the name drops out of regular use, as has happened at Virginia Union. Memorialization requires investment, not simply in signage, but in cherishing a story and repeating it enough so that it becomes inseparable from the culture of the institution. One can contrast Virginia Union's emphasis on the logo of the university, rather than on Vann, with the memorial culture associated with the Hoover Tower at Stanford University in Palo Alto, California, from which some of the original bells from Belgium's pavilion at the New York World's Fair continue to ring. In 2021, the carillon and the tower's observation deck were named for Stanford alumna Lou Henry Hoover, President Hoover's wife.[5] This naming expanded, rather than diminished, the association of that university's signature building, which, like the Belgian Building, was a mid-century addition to an already architecturally distinguished turn-of-the-century campus.

Another contrasting strategy is with a memorial in Richmond. Sixty years after the Belgian Friendship Building was dedicated in the presence of Robert Vann's widow, Jessie, the Virginia Civil Rights Memorial was installed behind the Virginia State Capitol on a site adjacent to the Governor's Mansion (fig. 110). The work of the sculptor Stanley Bleifeld, it is not as distinguished a sculpture as the Belgian Building is a piece of architecture, but its role as a memorial is much more easily comprehensible. A bronze plaque near ground level spells out clearly that it commemorates the protest that Barbara Johns, an African American high school student in Farmville, Virginia, launched in 1951, against the segregation of her school system. Her Richmond lawyers, Oliver Hill and Spottswood Robinson, folded her case into what became the landmark United States Supreme Court decision *Brown v. Board of Education,* which in 1954 finally struck down the idea that separate could ever be equal. The monument consists of a rectangular stone slab, reminiscent of an oversized gravestone, to which figures are affixed. The long side, greeting people approaching from the Capitol, features bronze statues of Johns and her contemporaries engaged in protesting. Also visible from here, on the short side, are Hill and Robinson (fig. 111). The other short end is anchored by the figures of the Reverend L. Francis Griffin and one of his daughters, another plaintiff in the case. On the other long end, facing east toward Shockoe Bottom and the site of Lumpkin's Jail, are a group of what are intended to be contemporary figures, only some of whom

Figure 110. Virginia Civil Rights Memorial, Stanley Bleifeld, Richmond, Virginia, 2008. (WomenArtistUpdates / Wikimedia Commons)

are clearly identifiable as African American. Their presence challenges viewers to engage in the struggle the memorial celebrates. They are assembled below a quote from Thurgood Marshall that reads, "The legal system can force open doors and sometimes even knock down walls but it cannot build bridges. That job belongs to you and me."

In comparison with the more prominently situated but often overlooked Vann Memorial Tower, the purpose of the 2008 memorial is clear to anyone who knows anything about the history of Virginia's civil rights movement or simply reads the plaque and the lettering that clearly identify the historical figures. Today, most visitors to the Civil Rights Memorial who want to know more about the struggle for civil rights in Virginia and throughout the nation can usually look it up on their phones. The location of the memorial in such close proximity to the executive and legislative branches of the commonwealth's government, as well as to city hall, makes it easily accessible to visiting school groups and to other tourists, as well as to

Figure 111. *Oliver Hill and Spottswood Robinson*, Virginia Civil Rights Memorial. (WomenArtistUpdates / Wikimedia Commons)

the many state and city employees who work there. Moreover, it is part of an early twenty-first-century ensemble of memorials on the Capitol grounds that also features commemorations of the state's original inhabitants and of its women leaders, among them Maggie Walker.

These attempts to be inclusive are particularly significant in the context of the Capitol building and the older statuary that lines the path to the Civil Rights Memorial. In recent years, Virginia has oscillated between Democratic and Republican governors and legislative majorities. The tussles between them have been marked by considerable conflict over how history should be taught in publicly funded schools and universities.[6] From the time the Capitol was constructed in the 1780s according to the designs of Thomas Jefferson, by a labor force that included both enslaved and free African American men and probably also women, there has been tension on this site between the ideas of political liberty and the inability of the nation's leaders to fully implement these ideals.[7] Jefferson's legacy embodies these tensions most dramatically. An enslaver who wrote the Declaration of Independence, he modeled the Capitol upon an ancient Roman temple from the Republican rather than the Imperial era. Many of the statues of enslavers who contributed to the establishment of the United States and of prominent supporters of the Confederacy still stand nearby, although the one depicting Harry Byrd, the architect of the state's policy of Massive Resistance to desegregation, was removed in 2021.

While the meaning of the Civil Rights Memorial is clear and inescapable, the importance of the Vann Memorial Tower and the Belgian Friendship Building across town are more subtle because they are so much less didactic. It would have been dangerous in the 1940s to spell out the degree to which they subverted the pro-Confederate message conveyed by the statues on Monument Avenue. Even Arthur Dupagne's relief sculpture *The Belgian Congo* can and has been reinterpreted in terms of Black pride rather than of Belgian colonialism. The Belgian Friendship Building, however, is also far more original and unusual than Bleifeld's memorial, as is its conversion into what remains one of the most imposing memorials to an African American anywhere in the United States. It is a testament to the talent of its Belgian architects and to the fortitude of those at Virginia Union who have trained generations of African Americans to be leaders, not by learning management skills as is popular today, but by empowering them to speak out and become agents of real and meaningful change, across the twentieth century and into our time.

The abstract way in which Vann is honored at Virginia Union should not detract from an appreciation of what the dignified and monumental Vann Tower and the Belgian Friendship Building represented at the time and still should mean today. This, too, is complex, because, although all the whites involved in bringing the building to Richmond believed in furthering African American education and interracial dialogue, none appears to have been committed to abolishing Jim Crow. Nonetheless, the building's presence on Virginia Union's campus brought the university national attention and helped instill pride in the cohort of students who studied in its library, conducted experiments in its science labs, and played or cheered for the

Panthers in a space that doubled as the auditorium where they heard Martin Luther King and many others exhort them and the rest of Virginia's African American community to join the struggle to claim their legal rights and strategize about how to do so.

Some forty years before Maya Lin's Vietnam Memorial (1982) and in a very different way, the abstract nature of the Belgian Friendship Building's architecture allowed it to embody divergent values and goals, beginning with those of the Belgian government and its racist colonial administration of the 1930s, followed by the ambitions of white Southern Baptists looking to enhance African American educational facilities as a bulwark against integration, and finally of African Americans seeking racial uplift and empowerment, culminating in the civil rights movement of the 1960s. In the process of being physically reconstituted, the Belgian Friendship Building was also socially redefined in relationship to the new, African American leadership at Virginia Union and to the resourcefulness and pride of its African American community, in Richmond and throughout the United States. In New York, the Belgian Pavilion showcased Belgian and Congolese artefacts and ingenuity; at Virginia Union, it became a setting for African American empowerment by providing enhanced facilities for a liberal arts education, hosting landmark cultural and sporting events, and bringing together the local community with leaders of the civil rights movement who urged African Americans to join together to obtain their full rights as citizens. Like Americans of all backgrounds, African Americans saw in their service to the country during World War II an opportunity to expand educational opportunities along with the political and cultural power of their community. That the Belgian Friendship Building could embody these new aspirations speaks to the flexibility of architecture to take on new meanings, even ones diametrically opposed to the ideologies they once served.

The nondidactic and non-illustrative nature of modern, abstract architecture has enabled the Belgian Friendship Building to endure into the twenty-first century, unlike the tired monuments to Confederate heroes that have been torn down. Restored to their original appearance, the Robert L. Vann Memorial Tower and the Belgian Friendship Building can continue to be a beacon of pride for Virginia Union and its larger community. For unlike the self-effacing form of the Vietnam Memorial, the Vann Tower triumphantly soars. It belongs to a significant architectural complex that deserves to be celebrated as an emblem of international friendship, interracial collaboration, and, above all, African American achievement, in spite of as much as because of its complicated history. The building's historical origins at the New York World's Fair are significant but do not limit or define its importance for Virginia Union University, whose administration, faculty, students, and alumni worked tirelessly to transform them into the towering memorial they have become.

NOTES

Foreword

1. Leroy Davis, *A Clashing of the Soul: John Hope and the Dilemma of African American Leadership and Black Higher Education in the Early Twentieth Century* (Athens: University of Georgia Press, 1998). Davis's definitive biography examines the life of John Hope, the first African American president of Morehouse College in 1906 and Atlanta University in 1929. Davis describes the conflict inherent in Hope's dual roles of serving as a Black college president and as a national leader of his race.

Introduction

1. "Laying Cornerstone at Va. Union University for Belgian Building," *Pittsburgh Courier,* June 21, 1941, 18.
2. Kirk Savage, *Standing Soldiers, Kneeling Slaves: Race, War, and Monument in Nineteenth-Century America* (Princeton, N.J.: Princeton University Press, 1999); Sarah Shields Driggs, Richard Guy Wilson, and Robert P. Winthrop, *Richmond's Monument Avenue* (Chapel Hill: University of North Carolina Press, 2001); and *Monument Avenue Commission Report,* prepared for the Office of the Mayor and City Council, Richmond, Va., July 2, 2018, https://static1.squarespace.com/static/597a220f579fb3cca0ab3454/t/5efe3aee34e2691d9e4c8390/1593719571758/Monument+Avenue+Commission+Report.pdf.

3. See the JXN Project, https://thejxnproject.org; Jackson War Collective, https://members.jacksonwardcollective.com.

4. Adam Hochschild, *King Leopold's Ghost: A Story of Greed, Terror, and Heroism in Congo* (Boston: Houghton Mifflin, 1998); David van Reybrouck, *Congo: The Epic History of a People* (New York: Ecco, 2014); Ira Dworkin, *Congo Love Song: African American Culture and the Crisis of the Colonial State* (Chapel Hill: University of North Carolina Press, 2017).

5. The longstanding connections tying the United States to the Congo are detailed in a brochure from the fair; see Gaston Denys Périer, *Stanley Goes Back to America* (Belgium: n.p., 1939).

6. "Mrs. Roosevelt Backs Memorial for Robt. Vann," *St. Louis Argus,* April 4, 1941, 15.

7. "Vann Tower Will Be Erected," *Pittsburgh Courier,* March 22, 1941, 4.

8. Andrew Buni, *Robert L. Vann of the Pittsburgh Courier: Politics and Black Journalism* (Pittsburgh: University of Pittsburgh 1974). See also Patrick Scott Washburn, *The African-American Newspaper: Voice of Freedom* (Evanston, Ill.: Northwestern University Press, 2006).

9. Andrew Shanken, "Planning Memory: Living Memorials in the United States during World War II," *Art Bulletin* 84 (2002): 130–47.

10. Andrew M. Shanken, *The Everyday Life of Memorials* (New York: Zone Books, 2022).

11. Danny Lewis, "The White House Was, in Fact, Built by Enslaved Labor," *Smithsonian Magazine,* July 26, 2016, https://www.smithsonianmag.com/smart-news/white-house-was-fact-built-slaves-180959916/.

12. This literature includes Irene Cheng, Charles L. Davis II, and Mabel Wilson, eds., *Race and Modern Architecture: A Critical History from the Enlightenment to the Present* (Pittsburgh: University of Pittsburgh Press, 2020); Walter Hood and Grace Mitchell Tada, *Black Landscapes Matter* (Charlottesville: University of Virginia Press, 2020); Sean Anderson and Mabel Wilson, eds., *Reconstructions: Architecture and Blackness in America* (New York: Museum of Modern Art, 2021); Charles L. Davis II, *Building Character: The Racial Politics of Modern Architectural Style* (Pittsburgh: University of Pittsburgh Press, 2021). Dreck Spurlock Wilson, ed., *African American Architects: A Biographical Dictionary, 1965–1945* (London: Routledge, 2004) is an older, invaluable source.

13. Melanee C. Harvey, "Alma Thomas and St. Luke's Episcopal Church," in *Alma W. Thomas: Everything Is Beautiful,* ed. Seth Feman and Jonathan Waltz (Columbus, Ga.: Columbus Museum of Art, 2021), 128–35; Kymberly Pinder, *Painting the Gospel: Black Public Art and Religion in Chicago* (Urbana: University of Illinois Press, 2016); Angel David Nieves, *An Architecture of Education: African American Women Design the New South* (Rochester, N.Y.: University of Rochester Press, 2018); Ellen Weiss, *Robert R. Taylor and Tuskegee: An African American Designs for Booker T. Washington* (Montgomery, Ala.: NewSouth Books, 2011); Amber Wiley, "The Dunbar High School Dilemma: Architecture, Power, and African American Cultural Heritage,"

Buildings & Landscapes 20, no. 1 (2013): 95–128; E. James West, *A House for Struggle: The Black Press and the Built Environment in Chicago* (Urbana: University of Illinois Press, 2022).

14. For a notable exception see Jacqueline Taylor, *Amaza Lee Meredith Imagines Herself Modern: Architecture and the Black Middle Class* (Cambridge, Mass.: MIT Press, 2023); for African American interjections into debates over urban renewal and public housing see Brian D. Goldstein, *The Roots of Urban Renaissance: Gentrification and the Struggle over Harlem* (Cambridge, Mass.: Harvard University Press, 2017).

15. Susan Earle, ed., *Aaron Douglas: African American Modernist* (New Haven, Conn.: Yale University Press, 2008), 36,40, 70, 97, 170, 176, 186, 199, for illustrations of works with this motif, which Douglas employed across the course of three decades.

16. Oliver Wendell Holmes, "The Chambered Nautilus," Poetry Foundation, https://www.poetryfoundation.org/poems/44379/the-chambered-nautilus.

17. Mil de Kooning, ed., *Belgium at the Fair: Exile on Main Street, Paris, New York, Richmond* (Ghent: wzw Editions & Productions, Department of Architecture and Urban Planning, Ghent University, 2010); Karen Vanhercke, "Drei Latere Werken van Henry van de Velde: Het Rito in Leuven 1936–44, Het Tentoonstellingspavilijoen voor Paris 1937, Het Tentoonstellingspavilijoen voor New York 1939," master's thesis, KU Leuven, 1996; Léon Ploegaerts and Pierre Puttemans, *L'oeuvre architecturale de Henry van de Velde* (Brussels: Atelier Vokaer, 1987); Léon Ploegearts, "Henry van de Velde's Only Work in the USA," *DOCOMOMO Newsletter* 7 (June 1992): 56–59.

18. Robin Schuldenfrei, *Objects in Exile: Modern Art and Design across Borders, 1930–1960* (Princeton, N.J.: Princeton University Press, 2024).

19. We have adopted the Dutch editorial convention of printing family names beginning with "van" or "de" in lower case when the name is preceded by a proper name, and capitalizing them when they appear without a proper name or with a title. The one name that is an exception to the rule is Henry van de Velde's, where we always maintain the lowercase "van," in keeping with the artist's own preferences. As a Fleming who wrote in French, and as a committed internationalist, he disregarded national and ethnic capitalization conventions.

20. Katherine M. Kuenzli, *Henry van de Velde: Designing Modernism* (New Haven, Conn.: Yale University Press, 2019); Richard Hollis, *Henry van de Velde: The Artist as Designer, from Art Nouveau to Modernism* (London: Occasional Papers, 2019).

21. Seldon Richardson, *Built by Blacks: African American Architecture and Neighborhoods in Richmond* (Charleston, S.C.: History Press, 2008).

22. *Belgian Pavilion Official Guide Book* (New York: New York World's Fair, 1939).

23. Raymond Pierre Hylton, *Virginia Union University* (Charleston, S.C.: Arcadia, 2014).

24. Susan Williams, *Spies in the Congo: America's Atomic Mission in World War II* (Washington, D.C.: PublicAffairs, 2016).

25. Matthew F. Delmont, *Half American: The Epic Story of African Americans Fighting World War II at Home and Abroad* (New York: Viking, 2022).

26. Raymond Gaines, *The Perils and Prospects of Southern Black Leadership: Gordon Blaine Hancock* (Durham, N.C.: Duke University Press, 1993); Glenda Elizabeth Gilmore, *Defying Dixie: The Radical Roots of Civil Rights, 1919–1950* (New York: W. W. Norton, 2008).

27. Bobby L. Lovett, *America's Historically Black Colleges and Universities: A Narrative History, 1837–2009* (Atlanta: Mercer University Press, 2011); Claudrena N. Harold, *New Negro Politics in the Jim Crow South* (Athens: University of Georgia Press, 2016); Jelani M. Favors, *Shelter in a Time of Storm: How Black Colleges Fostered Generations of Leadership and Activism* (Chapel Hill: University of North Carolina Press, 2020); Eddie R. Cole, *The Campus Color Line: College Struggles for Black Freedom* (Princeton, N.J.: Princeton University Press, 2022).

1. Belgian Modernism

1. "Belgium 1st Nation to File Fair Plans," *New York Times,* February 13, 1938, 43; "Sketch of Proposed Belgian Pavilion for New York World's Fair," clipping reproduced in De Kooning, *Belgium at the Fair,* 104.

2. John Tauranac, *Empire State Building: The Making of a Landmark* (New York: Scribners, 1995).

3. "Belgium 1st Nation to File Fair Plans"; "Sketch of Proposed Belgian Pavilion," 104.

4. Morris Dickstein, "From the Thirties to the Sixties: The World's Fair in Its Own Time," in *Remembering the Future: The New York World's Fair from 1939 to 1964,* ed. Robert Rosenblum (New York: Queens Museum, 1989), 22.

5. Sidney M. Shalett, "Rush as Fair Ends Brings Out 537,952, Its Biggest Crowd," *New York Times,* October 28, 1940, 1.

6. "Sketch of Proposed Belgian Pavilion," 104.

7. "New York World's Fair," *Architectural Forum* 70 (June 1939): 452.

8. "Belgium 1st Nation to File Fair Plans"; "War Held No Curb to World Fair Here," *New York Times,* September 29, 1938, 27.

9. Thomas Coomans, "Progress Exhibition, Chicago 1933," *Revue belge d'archéologie et de l'histoire de l'art,* 89 (November 2020): 141–72; Tom Packet, *Horta in Amerika: Het verblijf van Victor Horta in de Vereinigde Staten van 1915 tot 1919* (Brussels: ASP-Academic and Scientific, 2021).

10. On Victor Horta, see Franco Borsi and Paolo Portoghesi, *Victor Horta,* trans. Marie-Hélène Agüieros (New York: Rizzoli, 1991); Michèle Goslar, *Victor Horta, 1861–1947: L'homme, l'architecte, l'art nouveau* (Brussels: Fondation Pierre Lahaut/Fonds Mercator, 2012). On Henry van de Velde, see Kuenzli, *Henry van de Velde;* Katherine M. Kuenzli, "'Clearing the Terrain of

Art': Henry van de Velde and an Art Theory for the Twentieth Century," in Henry van de Velde, *Selected Essays, 1889–1914,* ed. Katherine M. Kuenzli (Los Angeles: Getty Research Institute, 2022), 1–34.

11. See, for instance, Henry van de Velde, "Declaration of Principles" (1902) and "The New Style" (1906), in van de Velde, *Selected Essays,* 186–207, 252–73.

12. C. L. Davis II, *Building Character,* 119.

13. Van de Velde, "William Morris: Artisan and Socialist," in van de Velde, *Selected Essays,* 137.

14. For the most recent accounts, see Sammy Baloji, Silvia Franceschini, Nikolaus Hirsch, and Estelle Lecaille, eds., *Style Congo: Heritage & Heresy* (Brussels: CIVA and Spector Books, 2023); Ruth Sacks, *Congo Style: From Belgian Art Nouveau to African Independence* (Ann Arbor: University of Michigan Press, 2023).

15. Guy Vanthemsche, *Belgium and the Congo, 1885–1980,* trans. Alice Cameron and Stephen Windross (Cambridge: Cambridge University Press, 2012).

16. Dworkin, *Congo Love Song,* 19–76.

17. Reprinted in John Hope Franklin, *George Washington Williams: A Biography* (Chicago: University of Chicago Press, 1985), 243–63.

18. Dworkin, *Congo Love Song,* 59–60. Sheppard's legal defense was mounted by the Belgian socialist lawyer and van de Velde supporter, Émile Vandervelde.

19. See Debora L. Silverman, "'Percer les ténèbres': Traces of the Congo in Victor Horta's Art Nouveau," in *Horta and the Grammar of Art Nouveau,* ed. Iwan Strauven and Benjamin Zurstrassen (Brussels: Bozart Books, 2023) 131–40, for the most recent discussion of Van Eetvelde's patronage of Horta.

20. Herman Balthazar and Jean Stengers, eds., *La Dynastie et la Culture en Belgique* (Antwerp: Fonds Mercator, 1990); Michèle Goslar, *Victor Horta, 1861–1947* (Brussels: Fondation Pierre Lahaut and Fonds Mercator, 2012), 170–71, 237–53; M. Luwel and M. Bruneel-Hye de Crom, *Tervueren 1897* (Tervuren, Belgium: Musée Royal de l'Afrique Centrale, 1967); Kuenzli, *Henry van de Velde,* 36–41; Amy Ogata, *Art Nouveau and the Social Vision of Modern Living* (Cambridge: Cambridge University Press, 2001), 51–58.

21. Debora L. Silverman, "Henry van de Velde: Art Nouveau and Style Congo, 1895–1897," in Baloji et al., *Style Congo,* 12, confuses these friezes with a figural mural of the Congo. This essay reprises the arguments she made in "Art Nouveau, Art of Darkness: African Lineages of Belgian Modernism, Part I," *West 86th: A Journal of Decorative Arts, Design History, and Material Culture* 18, no. 2 (Fall–Winter 2011): 139–81, where she equates van de Velde's "whiplash curves" with the colonial whip and identifies elephant imagery in much of his early work. This interpretation misattributes figurative elements to ornaments that were designed explicitly to be nonobjective, elemental forces. Closely affiliated with both pro- and anti-colonial factions in Belgium, van de Velde, who insisted on separating art from politics, remained silent on the question of

colonialism and heralded the 1897 exhibition only as a triumph of good exhibition design in "The Colonial Exposition at Tervuren," reprinted in van de Velde, *Selected Essays,* 131–34. See also Debora L. Silverman, "Art Nouveau, Art of Darkness: African Lineages of Belgian Modernism, Part II," *West 86th: A Journal of Decorative Arts, Design History, and Material Culture* 19, no. 2 (September 2012): 175–95; and "Art Nouveau, Art of Darkness: African Lineages of Belgian Modernism, Part III," *West 86th: A Journal of Decorative Arts, Design History, and Material Culture* 20, no. 1 (March 2013): 3–61.

22. Hippolyte Fierens-Gevaert, *Nouveaux essais sur l'art contemporain* (Paris: Félix Alcan, 1903), 60, terms Art Nouveau "style Congo."

23. Ploegaerts and Puttemans, *L'oeuvre architecturale de Henry van de Velde.* See also the first three volumes of the catalogue raisonné of van de Velde's applied art: Thomas Föhl and Antje Neumann, eds., *Henry van de Velde: Raumkunst und Kunsthandwerk, ein Werkverzeichnis in sechs Bänden,* vol. 1: *Metallkunst,* vol. 2: *Textilien,* vol. 3: *Keramik* (Leipzig: E. A. Seemann, 2009–15).

24. Packet, *Horta in Amerika.*

25. Iwan Strauven, *Victor Bourgeois, 1897–1962: Modernity, Tradition, & Neutrality* (Rotterdam: nai010, 2021). On Belgian interwar architecture, see also Jos Vandenbreden and France Vanlaethem, *Art Déco et modernisme en Belgique: Architecture de l'entre deux-guerres* (Brussels: Éditions Racine, 1996), 64–70.

26. See Victor Horta's letter to Émile Vandervelde, January 8, 1923, elucidating his role signing an artists' petition protesting van de Velde's nomination to the position of commissioner general of the Belgian pavilion at the Paris 1925 Exposition. Van de Velde file, X5.1–4, Victor Horta Museum Archives (VHMA), Brussels. We thank Tom Packet for sharing a copy of this letter. On Horta's design for Belgium's national pavilion at the 1925 Paris exhibition, see Werner Adriaenssens, "Een studie van de Belgische bijdrage aan de Exposition internationale des Arts décoratifs et industriels modernes de Paris, 1925" (master's thesis, Vrije Universiteit Brussels, 1997).

27. Adriaenssens, "Een studie van de Belgische bijdrage."

28. L. Pierard, "L'Exposition des Arts décoratifs va s'ouvrir," *Le peuple,* April 22, 1925; cited in Adriaenssens, "Een studie van de Belgische bijdrage," 89. Unless otherwise indicated, all translations from French to English are by Katherine M. Kuenzli.

29. For example, the Giaconda Room designed by Philippe Wolfers for the 1925 Belgian Pavilion was deemed suitable for millionaires by G. Verdavaine, "L'Ensemble 'Gioconda,' de Philippe Wolfers," *Le home* 2 (nouvelle série), nos. 7–8 (1925): 119; cited in Adriaenssens, "Een studie van de Belgische bijdrage," 158. See also "Pavillons d'Honneur, la servitude du luxe, Belgique et Hollande," *7 Arts* 3, no. 25 (April 30, 1925): 2–3; cited in Strauven, *Victor Bourgeois,* 46.

30. Émile Vandervelde, "Lettre de la Haye. Vincent van Gogh et Henry van de Velde," *Le peuple,* December 17, 1922. We thank Werner Adriaenssens for this reference.

31. Strauven, *Victor Bourgeois,* 48–50.

32. Van de Velde's work and residency in Germany from 1901 to 1917 proved to be a real liability for the artist's career in Belgium. His enemies misrepresented his artistic motives for residing in Germany, instead portraying him as a traitor to his country. Van de Velde's doubts and worries about remaining in Germany, as well as his desire to open an art school in Brussels that would be comparable to that in Weimar and enable him to support his family, are expressed in letters to the engineer Charles Lefébure, beginning on October 2, 1910. See FSX 534, Henry van de Velde Archive, Archives et Musée de la Littérature (VDV/AML), Brussels. After finally resigning as school director in Germany in 1915, van de Velde was issued a German passport by the German government that acknowledged his Belgian citizenship, which rendered him a foreigner and enemy combatant in both countries. See his correspondence with Weimar officials regarding his travel documents, beginning in 1914, FSX 168 VDV/AML. Van de Velde's difficulties were eased when he gained passage to neutral Switzerland in 1917, but it would take him another ten years and the support of King Albert I to clear his name and return to Belgium. See the dossier van de Velde presented to Belgian officials in 1926 to obtain the right to return, FSX 181, VDV/AML.

33. The school would undergo several name changes and is known today as the École Nationale Supérieure des Arts Visuels (ENSAV). Because of this, it is most commonly referred to by its location, "La Cambre." See Jacques Aron, *La Cambre et l'architecture: Un regard sur le Bauhaus belge* (Brussels/Liège: Mardaga, 1982); Strauven, *Victor Bourgeois,* 295–328; Vandenbreeden and Vanlaethem, *Art déco et modernisme en Belgique,* 146–47.

34. On the curriculum of La Cambre, see the special issue on the Institut Supérieur des Arts Décoratifs in *Cahiers de Belgique* 6 (1931): 211–54; Robert Delevoy, ed., *La Cambre, 1928–1978* (Brussels: Archives d'Architecture Moderne, 1979).

35. Virginie Devillez, *Le retour à l'ordre: Art et politique en Belgique* (Brussels: Labor, 2002), 56.

36. De Man was heralded by modern architects, beginning in the 1920s, for supporting ambitious projects in architecture and urbanism that had languished on drafting boards for decades. The sums he placed at the disposal of modern architects and urbanists were unprecedented in Belgium and throughout Europe. See Pierre-Louis Flouquet, "Entreprise, Courage, Foi," *Bâtir* 35 (October 1925): 385–86. See also De Man's appeal to modern architects and urbanists in *L'équerre,* as reported in Pierre-Louis Flouquet, "Pour le mieux être de la masse: Travaux d'utilité publique," *Bâtir* 32 (July 15, 1935): 257.

37. Van de Velde had earlier served as artistic adviser to Van Isacker in 1932 when he was minister of transportation. See Devillez, *Le retour à l'ordre,* 98; Henri Moreau, "Quand collaborent artistes et ingénieurs," *Bâtir* 15 (February 15, 1934): 573–75; Victor Bourgeois, "Les nouvelles voitures métalliques de la Société nationale des Chemins de fer belges," *L'ossature métallique* 3 (March 1936): 107–26.

38. Philip van Isacker, "Een bestendig Comité voor Esthetische Zorg," *Elckerlyck,* July 22, 1939,

3–4. Unless otherwise indicated, translations from Flemish into English were done by Ruben Mantels.

39. See van de Velde's essay, "Art and Industry" (1910) in van de Velde, *Selected Essays,* 307–20. See also Kuenzli, "'Clearing the Terrain of Art.'"

40. Jean Delville, "À propos d'une dictature esthétique," *La province de Mons,* January 27, 1938, press clipping 30 from the VHMA.

41. "La guirlande d'H. van de Velde," *Pourquoi pas?,* February 4, 1938, press clipping 29 from the VHMA; "La guirlande d'H. van de Velde," *Pourquoi pas?,* March 4, 1938, press clipping 25 from the VHMA.

42. Devillez, *Le retour à l'ordre,* 100.

43. P.-L. Flouquet, "Architecture et décoration au Heysel. Originalité de la section belge. Interview de M. le Comte Adrien van der Burch, Commissaire Général du Gouvernement," *Bâtir* 30 (May 15, 1935): 176.

44. Franco Borsi, *The Monumental Era: European Architecture and Design, 1929–1939* (New York: Rizzoli, 1987); Jean-Louis Cohen, ed., *Les années 30: L'architecture et les arts de l'espace entre industrie et nostalgie* (Paris: Musée des monuments français, 1997). For the fair itself see Bertrand Lemoine, ed., *Cinquantenaire de l'Exposition internationale des arts et des techniques dans la vie moderne* (Paris: Institut Français d'Architecture, 1987).

45. This perceived lack would be addressed by José Sert, Fernand Léger, and Sigfried Giedion in their 1943 position paper, published as "Nine Points on Monumentality," in *Architecture Culture, 1943–1968,* edited by Joan Ockman (New York: Rizzoli, 1993), 27–30.

46. Henry van de Velde, "Les arts et la réalité contemporaine," in *L'art et la réalité, l'art et l'état* (Paris: League of Nations, International Institut of Intellectual cooperation, 1934), 178–95.

47. Jan-Albert Goris, as interviewed in H.B., "De Belgische deelneming aan de Tentoonstelling te Parijs," *De Standaard,* March 12, 1937.

48. Ploegaerts and Puttemans, *L'oeuvre architecturale de Henry van de Velde;* Anne van Loo, "Belgique: Henry van de Velde," in Lemoine, *Cinquantenaire de l'Exposition internationale des arts,* 140–43.

49. Marcel Schmitz, *L'architecture moderne en Belgique* (Brussels: Éditions de la Connaissance, 1937), as quoted in Geert Bekaert, *Operating Instructions for Architecture: A Century of Planning in Belgium* (Ghent: University of Ghent, Department of Architecture and Urban Planning, 2001), 20.

50. For example, Henry van de Velde, "Art and Industry" (1910), in van de Velde: *Selected Essays,* 307–20. See also Kuenzli, "'Clearing the Terrain of Art.'"

51. De Kooning, *Belgium at the Fair;* Ploegaerts and Puttemans, *L'oeuvre architecturale de Henry van de Velde,* 209–13, 405–6, 412–14. The tiles were donated by the Comptoir Tuilier de Courtrai, which also sponsored its own display at the Paris 1937 Exposition.

52. Ploegaerts and Puttemans, *L'oeuvre architecturale de Henry van de Velde,* 404; Steven Jacobs, Yves Schoonjans, Jan van Vaerenbergh, and Luc Verpoest, *Tweebronnen: De reconversie van de Technische School van Henry van de Velde tot Openbare Bibliotheek en Archief van Leuven* (Leuven, Belgium: Openbare Bibliotheek Leuven, 2000); Luc Verpoest, "Henry van de Velde, A Welcome Home: The Technical School in Leuven," *DOCOMOMO,* July 2002, 101–12. We thank Luc Verpoest for sharing his knowledge of the Technical School in Leuven with us.

53. Henry van de Velde, letter to James Welles, August 19, 1937. FS X 963, VDV/AMI, cited in Devillez, *Le retour à l'ordre,* 110.

54. "M. Van Isacker annonce que le pavillon belge à l'Exposition de Paris sera reconstruit au Heysel," *La libre Belgique,* October 1, 1937.

55. Devillez, *Le retour à l'ordre,* 110–11; Ploegaerts and Puttemans, *L'oeuvre architecturale de Henry van de Velde,* 211.

56. In November 1937, the Liberal politician Paul-Émile Janson succeeded the Catholic Paul van Zeeland as prime minister of Belgium, causing the Catholic Van Isacker to resign from his position as minister of economic affairs nearly three months later. Although Janson withdrew the plan to reerect the New York pavilion in Brussels weeks after Van Isacker's resignation, Van Isacker held out hope that the pavilion's success could lead to more permanent initiatives in Brussels. See Van Isacker, "Een bestendig Comité voor Esthetische Zorg," 3–4. We thank Ruben Mantels for his help in reconstructing this series of events.

57. Jan-Albert Goris, "De Belgische deelname aan de Wereld-tentoonstelling van New York 1939," *Economische Tijdingen* 3, no. 8 (April 25, 1938): 126–30. Goris noted here how evolving construction methods have narrowed the cost differential for temporary versus permanent structures, resulting in the preservation of more and more fair buildings. He associated the Belgian Pavilion with long-term government efforts to elevate the quality and design of products in Belgium. In this way, he kept alive the idea of a permanent building by blurring the boundaries between temporary and lasting construction.

58. Van Loo, "Belgique"; Johan Lagae, "Displaying *Authenticity* and *Progress:* Architectural Representation of the Belgian Congo at International Exhibitions in the 1930s," *Third Text* 50 (Spring 2000): 21–32; Jean-Pierre De Rycke, *Africanisme et modernisme: La peinture et la photographie d'inspiration coloniale en Afrique centrale (1920–1940)* (Brussels: Peter Lang, 2010), 83–108.

59. Strauven, *Victor Bourgeois;* Eric Mumford, *The CIAM Discourse on Urbanism, 1928–1960* (Cambridge, Mass.: MIT Press, 2000).

60. Dirk Laureys, ed., *Léon Stynen: A Life of Architecture, 1899–1990* (Antwerp: Vlaams Architectuurinstituut, 2018); Ania Wolski and Luc Vincent, eds., *Léon Stynen: Architecte* (Ghent: Snoek, 2023).

61. Box LS 3.3.9, Doos 832, Léon Stynen Archives, Vlaamse Architectuur Archieven, Antwerp.

62. Many of these drawings from the Stynen archive have been republished in De Kooning, *Belgium at the Fair,* 94–103, as well as in Wolski and Vincent, *Léon Stynen,* 72–77.

63. Stanislaus von Moos, *Le Corbusier: Elements of a Synthesis* (Cambridge, Mass., MIT Press, 1979), 239–43; Claude Schnaidt, *Hannes Meyer: Bauten, Projekte und Schriften* (Stuttgart: Verlag Gerd Hatje, 1965), 22–37.

64. Luc Rombouts, *Singing Bronze: A History of Carillon Music* (Leuven, Belgium: Leuven University Press, 2014). For the Dutch side of the story see Diederik Oostdijk, *Bells for America: The Cold War, Modernism, and the Netherlands Carillon in Arlington* (University Park: Pennsylvania State University Press, 2019).

65. Rombouts, *Singing Bronze.*

66. "Carillons Sound Religious Theme," *New York Times,* May 1, 1939, 1.

67. Robert Moses, letter to Grover A. Whalen, March 7, 1938, MAD/NYPLDC, https://digitalcollections.nypl.org/items/86950858-62ab-0593-e040-e00a18060f80. See this same website for a drawing in the same collection related to Moses's suggestion.

68. Glen Jeansonne, *Herbert Hoover: A Life,* with David Luhrssen (New York: New American Library, 2016); Kenneth Whyte, *Hoover: An Extraordinary Life in Extraordinary Times* (New York: Alfred A. Knopf, 2017).

69. Laureys, *Léon Stynen,* 19, 271.

70. For the first see Kuenzli, *Henry van de Velde,* 162–67; for the second see Jacobs et al., *Tweebronnen.*

71. Henry van de Velde, *Récit de ma vie, 1917–1957,* ed. Anne van Loo (Brussels: Brepols, 2023), 1: 491.

72. J. W. B., "La Belgique à l'Exposition de New York: Le pavillon de la Belgique connaît un immense succès," Supplément économique et social de *L'indépendance belge,* June 24, 1939: I–II.

73. Vandenbreeden and Vanlaethem, *Art déco et modernisme en Belgique.*

74. For example, "Hilversum," *L'équerre* 2, no. 6 (January 1931) : 1–2. For his impact in Britain see Gary A. Boyd, *Architecture and the Face of Coal: Mining and Modern Britain* (London: Lund-Humphries, 2022).

75. Ministère des Travaux Publics et de la Résorption du Chômage, *Concours d'urbanisme et d'architecture en vue de l'aménagement du Mont des Arts à Bruxelles. Rapport du jury* (Brussels, 1937).

76. Axel de Backer and Herman Mennekens, *Joseph Diongre 1878–1963: Le style beaux-arts à l'épreuve du modernisme* (Brussels: Bitbook, 2021) 82–95.

77. Cohen, *Les années 30s.* See also Stylianos Giamarelos, *Resisting Postmodern Architecture: Critical Regionalism before Globalisation* (London: UCL Press, 2022).

78. Léon Stynen's letter to the editor is printed in "La guirlande de M. van de Velde," *Pourquoi pas?,* May 20, 1938. Press clipping 28 from the VHMA.

79. *Belgian Pavilion Official Guide Book,* 17. See also "Exposition Internationale New York 1939," *L'équerre* 10, no. 2 (1938): 25, which gives full credit to van de Velde, while "Le pavillon de la Belgique à l'Exposition de New-York 1939," which begins on the following page, credits Bourgeois and Stynen working under van de Velde's supervision.

80. These charges were leveled in two articles in *Pourquoi pas?:* "La guirlande de M. H. van de Velde," February 25, 1938; and "Van de Velde à l'Exposition de New-York," May 13, 1939, press clippings 28 and 22, VHMA.

81. Stynen, quoted in "La guirlande de M. van de Velde," *Pourquoi pas?,* May 20, 1938.

82. Erich Mendelsohn, *Amerika: Bilderbuch eines Architekten* (Berlin: Rudolph Mosse Verlag, 1926).

83. Van de Velde, *Récit de ma vie, 1917–1957,* 1: 485–87.

84. Van de Velde, *Récit de ma vie, 1917–1957,* 1: 497–99.

85. Van de Velde, *Récit de ma vie, 1917–1957,* 1: 511–12; Michael Meeuwis, "The Furthest Escape of All: Darkness and Refuge in the Belgian Congo," *Graham Greene Studies* 1 (2017): 58–59.

86. Van de Velde, *Récit de ma vie, 1917–1957,* 1: 512. See also Henry van de Velde, *Les mémoires inachevés d'un artiste européen : Édition critique,* ed. Léon Ploegaerts, 2 vols. (Brussels: Académie royale de Belgique, 1999), I: 492–93.

87. Jan-Albert Goris, "Souvenirs of a Great World's Fair," *Belgian Trade Review* 12, no. 7 (July 1957): 9–10.

88. Johan Lagae and Paoletta Holst, "'Objects That Are Dear to Him': The Colonizer's House and the *mise en valeur* of the Belgian Congo," *e-flux Architecture,* May 2023, https://www.e-flux.com/architecture/appropriations/533163/objects-that-are-dear-to-him-the-colonizer-s-house-and-the-mise-en-valeur-of-the-belgian-congo/. See also Itohan Osayimwese, *Colonialism and Modern Architecture in Germany* (Pittsburgh: University of Pittsburgh Press, 2017).

89. "Le pavillon belge à l'Exposition Internationale de New-York 1939," *L'ossature métallique* 8 (1939): 347–49; advertisement for Usines de Braine-Le-Compte S.A., *Bâtir* 79 (June 1939): 244.

90. De Kooning, *Belgium at the Fair,* 106.

2. Displaying Modern Belgium

1. E. L. Doctorow, *World's Fair* (1985. London: Michael Joseph, 1986), 238.

2. P.-L. Flouquet, "À l'exposition du 'Monde de demain': Pavillon de la Belgique," *Bâtir* 79 (June 1939): 245.

3. Robert W. Rydell and Laura Burd Schiavo, eds., *Designing Tomorrow: America's World's Fairs of the 1930s* (New Haven, Conn.: Yale University Press, 2010); Robert W. Rydell, *World of Fairs: The Century of Progress Expositions* (Chicago: University of Chicago Press, 1993).

4. Adnan Morshed, "The Aesthetics of Ascension in Norman Bel Geddes's Futurama," *Journal of the Society of Architectural Historians* 63 (2004): 74–99.

5. Terry Smith, *Making the Modern: Industry, Art, and Design in America* (Chicago: University of Chicago Press, 1993).

6. James J. Fortuna, "Fascism, National Socialism, and the 1939 New York World's Fair," *Fascism* 8 (2019): 179–218.

7. "L'Exposition de New-York a été officiellement inaugurée dimanche par le président Roosevelt," *L'indépendance belge,* May 2, 1939; Flouquet, "À L'exposition du 'Monde de demain,'" 245–52.

8. *Belgian Pavilion Official Guide Book,* 17–18. For an example of press coverage that closely follows the guidebook, see "Belgian Minister Inspects Pavilion," *New York Times,* June 13, 1939: 21.

9. E. L., "Het Belgisch Paviljoen te New York," *Vooruit,* June 25, 1939: 8.

10. "Ancien pavillon du Comptoir tuilier de Courtai," Inventaire du patrimoine architectural, https://monument.heritage.brussels/fr/buildings/38319.

11. Ru-ber-oid ad, *Architectural Forum* 70 (June 1939): 31. Note that this roof leaked, necessitating repairs before the opening of the fair's second season.

12. Goris, "De Belgische deelname," 126–30.

13. "Belgian Minister Inspects Pavilion."

14. "New York World's Fair 1939," *Architectural Forum* 70 (June 1939): 452.

15. Lewis Mumford, "The Sky Line in Flushing," *New Yorker,* June 17, 1939, 45.

16. Robert Wojtowicz, ed., *Sidewalk Critic: Lewis Mumford's Writings for the New Yorker* (New York: Princeton Architectural Press, 1998); Robert Wojtowicz, *Lewis Mumford and American Modernism: Eutopian Architecture and Urban Planning* (Cambridge: Cambridge University Press, 1996).

17. "Europe Comes to the Fair," *House Beautiful,* Summer 1939, 18.

18. Kathleen James-Chakraborty, "Expanding Agency: Ethel Power, *House Beautiful,* and the Writing of the History of American Architecture," in *Rereading Women and Architecture: Female Agency and the Discourses of Architectural History,* ed. Dana Arnold (London: Routledge, 2024) 152–68.

19. "Europe Comes to the Fair," 18.

20. "New York World's Fair 1939," 444. See also Nikolas Glover and Andreas Mørkved Hellenes, "A 'Swedish Offensive' at the World's Fairs: Advertising, Social Reformism and the Roots of Swedish Cultural Diplomacy, 1935–1939," *Contemporary European History* 30, no. 2 (2021): 284–300, doi:10.1017/S0960777320000533.

21. Talbot Hamlin, "Sven Markelius," *Pencil Points* 20 (1939): 357–66.

22. "À l'Exposition Internationale de New-York: L'inauguration du pavillon belge," *La gazette,*

May 2, 1939; "Le pavillon belge à l'Exposition de New-York a été inauguré lundi," *L'indépendance belge,* May 2, 1939 ; and "Le pavillon belge à l'Exposition de New-York," *La nation belge,* May 7, 1939; press clippings from Victor Horta Museum Archives (VHMA), Brussels.

23. "La Belgique à New York," *Pourquoi pas?,* May 5, 1939, press clipping 7, VHMA.

24. Jacques Sorbets, "Le Monde de demain vue par l'Amérique," *L'illustration,* June 10, 1939; G. F., "Die Paviljoens van eenige buitenlandsche deelnemers op de New York World's Fair 1939," *Bouwkundig Weekblad Architectura* 60 (1939): 359–53, Fonds Henry van de Velde, FSX 967/1, Archives et Musée de la Littérature (AML), Brussels.

25. "Beligë op de Wereldtentoonstelling an New York. Amerkaansche indrukken en persstemmen," *Gazet van Mechelen,* July 20, 1939, press clipping, VHMA.

26. Kuenzli, *Henry van de Velde,* 194–95.

27. Metropolitan Museum of Art, *Design in America: The Cranbrook Vision, 1925–1950* (New York: Harry N. Abrams, 1983).

28. Richard Guy Wilson, "High Noon on the Mall: Modernism versus Traditionalism, 1910–1970," *Studies in the History of Art* 30 (1991): 142–67.

29. Katherine M. Kuenzli, "Architecture, Individualism, and Nation: Henry van de Velde's 1914 Werkbund Theater Building," *Art Bulletin* 94, no. 2 (2012): 251–73.

30. "New York World's Fair," 443. See also Stanford Anderson, Gail Fenske, and David Fixler, eds., *Aalto and America* (New Haven, Conn.: Yale University Press, 2012).

31. Eimear O'Connor, *Art, Ireland, and the Irish Diaspora: Chicago, Dublin, New York, 1893–1939; Culture, Connections, Controversies* (Dublin: Irish Academic Press, 2020); Fabiola López-Durán, "Food Capital: Fantasies of Abundance and Nelson Rockefeller's Architecture of Development in Venezuela, 1940s–1960s," in *Architecture in Development: Systems and the Emergence of the Global South,* ed. Aggregate (London: Routledge, 2022), 303–5.

32. Wojtowicz, *Lewis Mumford,* 91–95. See also Greg Castillo, "German Lessons," *Places,* August 2022, https://placesjournal.org/article/philip-johnson-catherine-bauer-and-modernism-at-moma/.

33. Wojtowicz, *Sidewalk Critic,* 160.

34. "John D. Rockefeller, Jr., 1874–1960," Rockefeller Archive Center, https://rockarch.org/resources/about-the-rockefellers/john-d-rockefeller-jr/.

35. Carol Herselle Krinsky, *Rockefeller Center* (Oxford: Oxford University Press, 1978).

36. [Philip Johnson], "History of Machine Art," in *Machine Art* (New York: Museum of Modern Art, 1934), n.p.

37. James Johnson Sweeney, ed., *African Negro Art* (New York: Museum of Modern Art, 1935), 50–57.

38. Suzanne Preston Blier, *Picasso's Demoiselles: The Untold Origins of a Modern Masterpiece* (Durham: Duke University Press, 2019).

39. Zilah Quezado Deckker, *Brazil Built: The Architecture of the Modern Movement in Brazil* (London: Spon, 2001); Patricio del Real, *Constructing Latin American Architecture: Architecture, Politics, and Race at the Museum of Modern Art* (New Haven: Yale University Press, 2022).

40. See the brochure that was sent to manufactures, soliciting their contributions, *Exposition Internationale de New York 1939: Appel aux producteurs belges* (Brussels: Commissariat Générale du Gouvernement, 1938), FSX 967/3, VDV/AML. See also Goris, "De Belgische deelname." The main pavilion's exhibits are reconstructed here on the basis of press reports and photographs from the time, including Flouquet, "À l'exposition du 'Monde de demain,'" 245–52; *L'illustration,* June 10, 1939, a special issue devoted to the New York World's Fair; J.W.B., "La Belgique à l'Exposition de New York,", I–II; J.W.B., "Le pavillon belge," Supplément économique et social de *L'indépendance belge,* June 24, 1939, II–III; E.L., "Het Belgisch Paviljoen te New York," *Vooruit,* June 25, 1939, 8; G. F. "Die Paviljoens van eenige buitenlandsche deelnemers op de New York World's Fair 1939," *Bouwkundig Weekblad Architectura* 60, no. 36 (September 9, 1939): 349–53.

41. Norbert Poulain, "De Belgische Wandtapijten op de wereldtentoonstellingen tijdens het interbellum, in het bijzonder te Parijs in 1937 en te New York in 1939," in *Liber Memorialis Erik Duverger: Bijdragen tot de Kunstgeschiedenis van de Nederlanden,* ed. Henri Pauwels, André van den Kerkhove, and Leo Wuyts (Wetteren, Belgium: Universa, 2006), 221–54.

42. René Lyr in the commemorative volume published on the Belgian pavilion at the 1937 Paris Exposition Internationale, *Industries et métiers d'art en Belgique* (Brussels, 1937), n.p.

43. Jean Buyck, *Floris & Oscar Jespers: De Moderne Jaren* (Antwerp: Pandora, 1996).

44. At least some of Floris Jespers's tapestries were sent to the Hoover Institute in 1940 for safekeeping. *The Relationship between Belgium and America During and After the First World War* was given to Stanford University by the Belgian ambassador, Baron Robert Silvercruys, in 1953. See "Tapestry Honors Hoover," *New York Times,* March 11, 1953. See also Clifton B. Parker, "Picture at an Exhibition," *Hoover Digest* 3 (Summer 2014): 192–97. Another tapestry, *Belgian Settlers Landing on Manhattan Island in 1623,* was given to the New York Historical Society, also in 1953. See "Flemish Tapestry on View at the New-York Historical Society," Flanders in the USA, https://flandersintheusa.org/FlemishTapestry. Two other tapestries, *Traditional Belgium* and *Modern Belgium,* were returned to Belgium after the war and are in the collection of the Musée d'Art et d'Histoire in Brussels.

45. Lauren Kroiz, *Creative Composites: Modernism, Race, and the Stieglitz Circle* (Berkeley: University of California Press, 2012), 182–83.

46. Jan-Albert Goris, *Modern Sculpture in Belgium,* 2nd rev. ed. (New York: Belgian Government Information Center, 1951), 16–17, 64–65.

47. For example, "La guirlande de M. H. van de Velde," *Pourquoi pas?,* February 25, 1938 ; press clipping 28 from VHMA.

48. For a full list of exhibitors, see *Belgian Pavilion Official Guidebook.*

49. *Exposition Internationale de New York 1939: Appel aux producteurs belges.*

50. G. F., "Die Paviljoens van eenige buitenlandsche deelnemers."

51. "Belgian Congo Movies Shown," *New York Times,* June 16, 1939, 18.

52. Rydell, *World of Fairs,* 6–7. See also Mark Crinson, *Modern Architecture and the End of Empire* (London: Routledge, 2003); Patricia Morton, *Hybrid Modernities: Architecture and Representation at the 1931 Colonial Exposition, Paris* (Cambridge, Mass.: MIT Press, 2000).

53. Lagae, "Displaying *Authenticity* and *Progress,*" 21–32; De Rycke, *Africanisme et modernisme,* 83–108.

54. The Belgian Pavilion joined an unprecedented number of buildings at the World's Fair that were air-conditioned. See Joseph Siry, *Air-Conditioning in Modern American Architecture, 1890–1970* (University Park: Pennsylvania State University Press, 2021), 54–55. The contents of the Colonial Section's exhibits are reconstructed here on the basis of newspaper articles and photographs from the period, including "Le Congo à l'Exposition de New York," *L'illustration congolaise* 213 (June 1939): 7352–53; "Le mois colonial," *L'illustration congolaise* 213 (June 1939): 7404–5; "Le Banquet du Cercle Royal Africain: Discours de M. le Ministre des Colonies De Vleeschauwer," *L'illustration congolaise* 213 (June 1939): 7417; "Le Congo à l'Exposition de New York," *L'iIllustration congolaise* 215 (August 1939): 7439–42.

55. Mary Jo Arnoldi, "Art colonial: Les sculpteurs belges au Congo," in *Le Congo et l'art belge, 1880–1960,* ed. Jacqueline Guisset (Tournai, Belgium: La Renaissance du Livre, 2003), 225–52.

56. "Le Congo à l'Exposition de New York." Photographs of the bas-reliefs show an earlier stage of the first panel in Dupagne's studio, in which the rightmost figure appears as a carver of figurines; Dupagne later changed this figure into a hunter-warrior.

57. Jacqueline Guisset, "Art déco, modernisme et expositions internationales," in *Le Congo et l'art belge,* 171–252.

58. De Rycke, *Africanisme et modernisme,* 30–35.

59. "Contrastes," *L'illustration congolaise* 212 (May 1939): 7330.

60. "Contrastes," 7327.

61. Guisset, *Congo et l'art belge,* 171–224.

62. Périer, *Stanley Goes Back to America,* 5. On Périer, see De Rycke, *Africanisme et modernisme,* 29–54.

63. Périer, *Stanley Goes Back to America,* 9–10.

64. Périer, *Stanley Goes Back to America,* 22.

65. Vanthemsche, *Belgium and the Congo,* 29. On Belgium's evolving colonial policies in the twentieth century, see also Idesbald Goddeeris, Amandine Lauro, and Guy Vanthemsche, eds., *Le Congo colonial: Une histoire en questions* (Waterloo, Belgium: Renaissance du Livre, 2020).

66. Vanthemsche, *Belgium and the Congo,* 29–30.

67. Vanthemsche, *Belgium and the Congo,* 28.

68. Bert Govaerts, *Ik alleen! Een biografie van Albert De Vleeschauwer (1897–1971)* (Antwerp: Houtekiet, 2012), 158.

69. Ruben Mantels, *Geleerd in de tropen: Leuven, Congo, & de wetenschap, 1885–1960* (Leuven, Belgium: Leuven University Press, 2007).

70. Vanthemsche, *Belgium and the Congo,* 26–27.

71. "Le mois colonial," *L'illustration congolaise* 213 (June 1939): 7404–5.

72. Jean-Luc Vellut, *Congo: Ambitions et désenchantements, 1880–1960* (Paris: Karthala, 2017), 405.

73. "Le mois colonial."

74. "Le mois colonial." At the top of the list of allegedly misinformed white Americans are the views of newspaper editor William Randoph Hearst, whom Belgian colonial officials quoted in 1939 as remarking, "The Congo is practically useless to Belgium, whose colonial administration has always been an embarrassment and a scandal for the entire world." See "Le mois colonial," 7404–5. Hearst made these comments in support of a plan to remake Central Africa—including former German colonies that now belonged to Belgium—into an international territory for the settlement of Jewish refugees. This plan was widely publicized in the American press. See, for instance, "Former German Colonies Urged as Jewish Home: Hearst Sees Chance for Creation of Another Great Nation," *New Orleans Times Picayune,* 21 November 1938, 15.

75. In a letter to the general administrator of the colonies in Brussels, December 30, 1937, OC 546 AE, Foreign Affairs Archive (FAA), Brussels, Gaston Denys Périer, president of the Commission for the Protection of Indigenous Arts, observes that "Americans' interest in the art and artisanry of our colony [featured in] partial exhibitions showcasing Congolese art, [and] the contributions of black descendants from Central Africa to American art would seem to justify our Commission's intervention in a committee charged with preparing Belgian colonial contributions to the World's Fair across the Atlantic."

76. Thanks to Dr. Julien Volper, curator at the Royal Museum of Central Africa, for his assistance in identifying these sculptures. On display practices at the Royal Museum of the Belgian Congo, see Sarah van Beurden, "The Value of Culture: Congolese Art and the Promotion of Belgian Colonialism (1945–1959)," *History and Anthropology* 24, no. 4 (2013): 472–92.

77. Gaston Denys Périer and J. M. Jadot, *Native Arts & Craftsmanship in Belgian Congo* (Brussels: Commission for the Protection of Native Arts and Crafts, 1939), 2.

78. Périer and Jadot, *Native Arts & Craftsmanship,* 13–16.

79. Périer and Jadot, *Native Arts & Craftsmanship,* 2.

80. Jacqueline V. Falkenheim, *Roger Fry and the Beginnings of Formalist Art Criticism* (Ann Arbor, Mich.: UMI Research Press, 1980); Christopher Green, ed., *Art Made Modern: Roger Fry's Vision of Art* (London: Courtauld Institute of Art, 1999); Christopher Reed, *A Roger Fry Reader* (Chicago: University of Chicago Press, 1996).

81. Roger Fry, "Negro Sculpture," *Athenaeum,* April 16, 1920, 516; reprinted in Roger Fry, *Vision and Design* (New York: Meridian, 1956), 99–103; Cited in Périer and Jadot, *Native Arts & Craftsmanship,* 14.

82. For example, in 1929, Robert S. Abbott observed in the *Chicago Defender* how indigenous handicraft at the Royal Museum of Central Africa undercut colonial narratives purveyed by the museum alleging the helplessness of the natives prior to their encounter with Europeans. See Robert S. Abbott, "My Trip Abroad V: The Congo Museum," *Chicago Defender,* December 7, 1929, 1, 4. These displays would be amended by Frans Olbrechts. See Van Beurden, "Value of Culture."

83. Alain Locke, "The Legacy of the Ancestral Arts," in *The New Negro* (New York: Albert & Charles Boni, 1925; repr., New York: Atheneum, 1992), 259.

84. Locke, "Legacy of the Ancestral Arts," 259–61.

85. Périer and Jadot, *Native Arts & Craftsmanship,* 18–19.

86. The impressive collection of objects amassed for the Congolese pavilion at the 1897 Brussels International Exposition laid the basis for the Royal Museum of Central Africa, with construction of a permanent building beginning in 1902. On Belgian collectors' prioritization of wooden sculpture and especially *ndop* figures, see Van Beurden, "Value of Culture."

87. Ira Dworkin, *Congo Love Song: African American Culture and the Crisis of the Colonial State* (Chapel Hill: University of North Carolina Press, 2017) 163–200.

88. "Dr. Sheppard on Africa," *Hampton Student* 2, no. 23 (February 15, 1911): 4, cited in Dworkin, *Congo Love Song,* 176. Up through at least the 1920s, the Hampton Museum was the only museum in the South regularly open to African Americans. See Jeanne Zeidler, "The Hampton University Museum Collections," *International Review of African American Art* 11, no. 4 (1994): 46–54; Jeanne Zeidler and Mary Lou Hutgren, "'Things African Prove to Be the Favorite Theme': The African Collection at Hampton University," in *Art/Artifact: African Art in Anthropology Collections,* ed. Susan Vogel (New York: Center for African Art, 1988), 97–111.

89. Jeffrey Stewart, *The New Negro: The Life of Alain Locke* (New York: Oxford University Press, 2018), 420–30, 545–66; Dworkin, *Congo Love Song,* 180–81. The Blondiau-Theater Arts Collection of African Art was exhibited at the Brooklyn Institute of Arts and Sciences (now Brooklyn Museum) in 1923. In 1927, the collection was on display at the New Art Circle in New York City. Alain Locke wrote the introduction to the 1927 exhibition catalogue, *Blondiau-Theater Arts Collection of Primitive African Art* (New York: New Art Circle, 1927), n.p.

90. Frank S. Adams, "Turkish Exhibit May Stay at Fair," *New York Times,* September 21, 1939, 29; Sidney M. Shalett, "Belgium to Stay in the 1940 Fair," *New York Times,* October 20, 1939, 16.

91. Cover, *The Crisis* 46, no. 4 (April 1939).

92. "Music for 50 Million," *The Crisis* 46 (1939): 107.

93. See "World's Fair Promotes One after Protest," *New York Amsterdam News,* January 8, 1938,

10; Helen Harrison, *Dawn of a New Day: The New York World's Fair, 1939/40* (New York: New York University Press, 1980), 86–88. We thank Wesleyan student Sophie Raiskin-Wood for sharing her work on this sculpture.

94. "Negress Denied Entry to French Art School," *New York Times,* April 24, 1923, 8.

95. Edgar T. Rouzeau, "Candidates for World's Fair Jobs Must Qualify as Blackface Comedians," *Pittsburgh Courier,* April 1, 1930.

96. "Charge World's Fair Head Discriminates against Negroes in Employment," *New York Age,* November 13, 1937, 2.

97. "World's Fair Discrimination," *New York Age,* February 19, 1938, 6.

98. Rydell, *World of Fairs,* 181–83.

99. Mabel Wilson, *Negro Building: Black Americans in the World of Fairs and Museums* (Berkeley: University of California Press, 2012) 8.

100. M. Wilson, *Negro Building;* Rydell, *World of Fairs,* 157–92.

101. "West Indian Citizens Segregated at Fair When Royalty Was Welcomed," *Pittsburgh Courier,* June 24, 1939, 2.

102. Rydell, *World of Fairs,* 186–87.

103. Floyd G. Snelson, "Harlem: The Capitol of the Nation," *New York Age,* July 1, 1939, 7.

104. "Talent of Race Recognized in Inscription on Wall of Honor at N. Y. World's Fair," *Pittsburgh Courier,* July 20, 1940, 4.

3. Diplomacy and Propaganda at the Pavilion after the Fall of Belgium

1. "Talks to Antwerp during Air Raid," *New York Times,* May 12, 1940, 38.

2. "Belgium's World Fair Pavilion Is Closed," *Troy (Ala.) Messenger,* June 1, 1940, 3.

3. Milton Bracker, "Leopold's Statue Removed at Fair," *New York Times,* June 5, 1940, 31. See also Jonathan E. Helmreich, *United States Relations with Belgium and the Congo, 1940–1960* (Newark, Del.: University of Delaware Press, 1998), 16–18.

4. Helmreich, *United States Relations with Belgium,* 19–20.

5. Articles in the *Pittsburgh Courier* maintained a staunch anti-colonialist stance in 1940. See, for instance, Samuel L. Brooke, "The World This Week," *Pittsburgh Courier,* June 1, 1940, 4.

6. De Vleeschauwer's decision was both principled and pragmatic. On June 18, Great Britain had seized the entire Belgian merchant marine to keep it from falling into Germany's hands.

7. Govaerts, *Ik alleen!,* 221–22.

8. Govaerts, *Ik Alleen!,* 230–31; Vanthemsche, *Belgium and the Congo,* 126.

9. Govaerts, *Ik Alleen!,* 191–92.

10. Govaerts, *Ik Alleen!,* 283.

11. Vanthemsche, *Belgium and the Congo,* 134–35.

12. Bert Govaerts, *Dubbelman. Een Biografie van Marnix Gijsen/Jan-Albert Goris* (Antwerp: Houtekiet, 2021).

13. Govaerts, *Dubbelman,* 121–22.

14. Strauven, *Victor Bourgeois.*

15. Jan-Albert Goris, letter to Henry van de Velde, May 20, 1939; see FSX 968/7, Henry van de Velde Archive, Archives et Musée de la Littérature (VDV/AML), Brussels.

16. Jan-Albert Goris, letter to Gerard Walschap, December 14, 1950, W 213, Marnix Gijsen/Jan-Albert Goris papers, Letterenhuis, Antwerp (J-AG/Letternhuis), in which he expresses his disgust for the colonial regime and support for Jozef van Bilsen's plan for the long-term independence of the Belgian Congo.

17. Jan-Albert Goris, letter to Count Van der Straten-Ponthoz, Belgian ambassador, October 17, 1940. G994/B2, J-AG/Letternhuis. We thank Ruben Mantels and Bert Govaerts for tracking down this file.

18. Omer Michaux, letter to representative of Charles Somers (manufacturer of carillon mechanisms) and Mr. Michiels (owner of bell foundry), to the Commissariat General, January 21, 1938, Box 13, 1316, folder 119, Department of Economic Affairs, Commissariat of the Belgian section, 1939, Algemeen Rijksarchief, Brussels; Jan-Albert Goris, letter to Count Van der Straten-Ponthoz, December 19, 1940, G994/B2, J-AG/Letternhuis.

19. Van der Straten-Ponthoz, telegram to the Belgian Legation in Lisbon, June 25, 1940, Albert de Vleeschauwer Archive, KADOC Documentation and Research Centre on Religion, Culture, and Society, Leuven Belgium (KADOC).

20. Lichtervelde, telegram to Gevaert, July 1, 1940, De Vleeschauwer Archive, KADOC.

21. De Vleeschauwer, telegram to Gevaert and Goris, July 17, 1940, OC 546 AE, Foreign Affairs Archive (FAA), Brussels.

22. In his letters to his brother René in 1940, Goris wrote scathing accounts of Gevaert, whom he viewed as a pompous figurehead with little involvement in the pavilion's day-to-day operations. See G 994/B1, J-AG/Letternhuis.

23. Jan-Albert Goris, letter to Frans van Cauwelaert, no date but likely the late summer or early fall 1940, FVC, B2, J-AG/L. Goris referred to Perrin C. Galpin, secretary of the Belgian American Education Foundation, who represented Herbert Hoover in the negotiations to purchase the Belgian Pavilion's carillon for the Hoover Tower then under construction at Stanford University. He also mentioned Clement Roosens of St. Albert's Church (Belgian Division) in New York City.

24. Jan-Albert Goris, letter to René Goris, October 21, 1940. G 994/B1, J-AG/Letternhuis.

25. Hoover first learned of the carillon's availability in May 1939, as ground was being broken on the Hoover Tower at Stanford University. In a telegram dated May 19, 1939, he relayed the asking price of $15,000 (not including the costs of import duties, dismantling, or transportation)

to Ray Lyman Wilbur, Stanford's president. See Elena S. Danielson, *Images of America: Hoover Tower at Stanford University* (Charleston, S.C.: Arcadia, 2018), 65–67. For the bill of sale, see the documentation filed under Carillon Sale 31-BAEF, B317-f06 at the Herbert Hoover Presidential Library, West Branch, Iowa.

26. With the carillon weighing 18,000 pounds, architect Arthur Brown had to reconfigure the top of the tower to support the weight and size of the bells and to adjust the acoustic qualities of the belfry.

27. Dr. Goris's office, letter to Dr. William J. Clark, October 22, 1940, MS-110, J.M. Ellison Papers, Subject Files, Belgian Building, Folder 95, Virginia Union University Special Collections and Archives, Richmond.

28. Jan-Albert Goris, letter to René Goris, November 3, 1940, G 994/B1, J-AG/Letternhuis.

29. Jan-Albert Goris, letter to Count Van der Straten-Ponthoz, December 19, 1940. G994/B2, J-AG/Letternhuis.

30. Goris, telegram to the Ministry of the Colonies in London, November 20, 1940, G994/B2, J-AG/Letternhuis.

31. Jan-Albert Goris, letter René Goris, June 6, 1940, G 994/B1, J-AG/Letternhuis.

32. Govaerts, *Dubbelman*, 153–69.

33. Goris's editorials were so popular that a selection of them was republished in a stand-alone volume, *Belgium in Bondage* (New York: L. B. Fischer, 1943). See Goris, "In Flanders' Fields," in *Belgium in Bondage*, 19. He singled out Henrik De Man for special scorn in "The Bitter Draught of Slavery," in *Belgium in Bondage*, 45–46.

34. Goris, "What Is a Colony?," in *Belgium in Bondage*, 178.

35. Goris was a Flemish nationalist who sought to ensure that Flemish demands for equal rights for their language would not be diminished or set aside due to the war. In a letter to Belgian politician Frans van Cauwelaert dated August 4, 1942, Goris noted: "Now that I am trying to set up a radio program with Detillieux, I am once again experiencing how much there is to do to inform the Americans and the English about the Flemish problem. Whenever I succeed in accomplishing something, it is only after much effort and painful, repeated declarations and conferences to make it appear that Flemish does not necessarily mean suspicious or German." FVC, B2, J-AG/Letternhuis.

36. Goris, "The Brute and the Lamb," in *Belgium in Bondage*, 160–61.

37. Jan-Albert Goris, letter René Goris, April 20, 1941, G 994/B1, J-AG/Letternhuis.

38. Jan-Albert Goris, letter to René Goris, May 13, 1941. G 994/B1, J-AG/Letternhuis.

39. The entire collection of Congolese art was housed for the duration of World War II at the Buffalo Museum of Science (created in 1861 by the Buffalo Society of Natural Sciences) before being returned to the Royal Museum of Central Africa. In Buffalo, the Belgian artifacts were put on display in the "Hall of Primitive Art" installed in 1941 with support from the Rockefeller

Foundation. For the history of the collection, see "The Buffalo Museum of Science Collection," in *Art/Artifact: African Art in Anthropology Collections,* ed. Susan Vogel (New York: Center for African Art, 1988), 41–96.

40. The bas-reliefs are visible in a photograph of the partially reconstructed pavilion in Richmond dated April 20, 1942. See 950.FF21 and 950.FF22, Photographs, Series 1054, Rockefeller Archive Center, Sleepy Hollow, New York. In 1948, Dupagne's bas-reliefs would be formally given to Virginia Union on behalf of the Ministry of the Colonies as a continuation of the Belgian State's ongoing colonial propaganda in North America. See R. Bagage, letter to the minister of the colonies, November 10, 1948, OC 546 AE, FAA.

41. Florence Gillet, "La Mission Cauvin ou la propagande coloniale du government belge aux Etats-Unis pendant la Seconde Guerre mondiale," *Cahiers d'histoire du temps présent* 15–16 (2005): 357–83.

42. John Latouche and André Cauvin, *Congo* (New York: Willow, White, 1945), 11. Cauvin knew what he was doing by partnering with Latouche, a popular and established American lyricist who had the approval of the U.S. government. President Franklin Delano Roosevelt had praised Latouche's *Ballad for Americans* as a potential new national anthem, and it had gained added popularity thanks to a performance by African American singer Paul Robeson broadcast on CBS radio in 1939. Latouche's name and credentials staved off suspicions that Cauvin's work was simply colonialist. Howard Pollack, *The Ballad of John Latouche: An American Lyricist's Life and Work* (New York: Oxford University Press, 2017), 171–79.

4. The Belgian Pavilion's New Home

1. Virginius Dabney, *Richmond: The Story of a City* (Charlottesville: University Press of Virginia, 1990).

2. Kathleen E. Bruce, *Virginia Iron Manufacture in the Slave Era* (New York: Century, 1931); Charles B. Dew, *Joseph Reid Anderson: Ironmaker to the Confederacy* (Richmond: Virginia State Library, 1999).

3. Ada May Land, "The Migration into Richmond (1775 to 1860)" (master's thesis, University of Richmond, 1949), https://scholarship.richmond.edu/cgi/viewcontent.cgi?article=1042&context=masters-theses.

4. Ann S. Holder, "The Terrain of Politics: Race, Space, and Vernacular Citizenship," in *In Search of African American Space: Redressing Racism,* edited by Jeffrey Hogrefe and Scott Ruff with Carrie Eastman and Ashley Simone (Zurich: Lars Müller, 2020), 28–59.

5. S. Richardson, *Built by Blacks.*

6. Nicole Myers Turner, *Soul Liberty: The Evolution of Black Religious Politics in Post-Emancipation Virginia* (Chapel Hill: University of North Carolina Press, 2020).

7. Kathy Edwards and Esmé Howard, "Monument Avenue: The Architecture of Consensus in the New South, 1890–1930," *Perspectives in Vernacular Architecture* 6 (1997): 92–110, doi:10.2307/3514365.

8. J. Morgan Krauser, *The Shaping of Southern Politics: Suffrage Restriction and the Establishment of the One-Party South, 1880–1910* (New Haven, Conn.: Yale University Press, 1974), 171–81.

9. Marvin Chiles, "'Down Where the South Begins': Activism before the Modern Civil Rights Movement, 1899–1930," *Journal of African American History* 105 (2020): 56–82, doi/10.1086/705534.

10. Muriel Miller Branch, "Maggie Lena Walker (1864–1934)," *Encyclopedia Virginia,* https://encyclopediavirginia.org/entries/walker-maggie-lena-1864-1934/. See also Gertrude Woodruff Marlowe, *Right Worthy Grand Mission: Maggie Lena Walker and the Quest for Black Empowerment* (Washington, D.C.: Howard University Press, 2003).

11. Margaret Edds, *We Face the Dawn: Oliver Hill, Spottswood Robinson, and the Legal Team That Dismantled Jim Crow* (Charlottesville: University of Virginia Press, 2018), 113, 115.

12. Harold, *New Negro Politics,* 104.

13. See, in particular, Gilmore, *Defying Dixie.*

14. Edds, *We Face the Dawn.*

15. Brendan Wolfe, "Racial Integrity Laws (1924–1930)," *Encyclopedia Virginia,* https://encyclopediavirginia.org/entries/racial-integrity-laws-1924-1930/.

16. Chiles, "'Down Where the South Begins.'"

17. Chiles, "'Down Where the South Begins,'" 81.

18. W. H. Venable, as cited in Earl Lewis, *In Their Own Interests: Race, Class, and Power in Twentieth-Century Norfolk, Virginia* (Berkeley: University of California Press, 1991), 156.

19. Virginius Dabney, *Below the Potomac: A Book about the New South* (New York: D. Appleton Century, 1943), 152.

20. Raymond Gavins, *The Perils and Prospects of Southern Black Leadership: Gordon Blaine Hancock, 1884–1970* (Durham, N.C.: Duke University Press, 1993) 143; Marie Morris Nitschke, "Virginius Dabney (1901–1995)," *Encyclopedia Virginia,* https://encyclopediavirginia.org/entries/dabney-virginius-1901-1995/.

21. See, for instance, James Edmund Boyack, "Notables Attend Ground Breaking at Union University," *Pittsburgh Courier,* May 24, 1941, 5; William J. Clark, "Virginia Union Expands Work," *New York Times,* June 15, 1941, 72; "Belgian Friendship Building Takes Root at Virginia Union with Cornerstone Ceremonies," *Richmond Times Dispatch,* June 10, 1941, 8; W. T. Booker, "A Bit of Belgium Comes Here," *Richmond Times Dispatch,* January 25, 1942, 43, which in part plagiarizes Clarence E. Boykin, "A Gift from Belgium," *Opportunity: A Journal of Negro Life* 19 (1941): 55, 63.

22. Kristin Green, *The Devil's Half Acre: The Untold Story of How One Woman Liberated*

the South's Most Notorious Slave Jail (New York: Seal Press, 2022). The story is hardly untold, however, as it has consistently figured prominently in Virginia Union's self-portrayals. See, for instance, Clark, "Virginia Union Expands Work," 72; Hylton, *Virginia Union University.*

23. Virginia Union Endowment Funds, April 30, 1940, updated December 15, 1942, American Baptist Historical Society Archives (ABHSA), Mercer University, Box 12, Folder 14.

24. J. T. Morgan, "Virginia Union University: To the Colored Baptists of Virginia," Virginia Union Scrapbook, Box 9, Folder 9, ABHSA. See also Adolph H. Grundman, "Northern Baptists and the Founding of Virginia Union University: The Perils of Paternalism," *Journal of Negro History* 63, no. 1 (January 1978): 26–41, doi:10.2307/2717358.

25. George Sale, "One Part in the Solution of a Great Problem," in *An Era of Progress and Promise, 1863–1910: The Religious, Moral, and Educational Development of the American Negro since His Emancipation,* ed. W. N. Hartshorn (Boston: Priscilla, 1910), 71; George Rice Horvey, "Virginia Union University, Richmond, Va.," in Hartshorn, *Era of Progress and Promise,* 99. We thank George Francis-Kelly for this reference.

26. Locke, *New Negro.*

27. Harold, *New Negro Politics,* 106.

28. Harry Jared McGuinn, "Phylon Profile, V: Joshua Baker Simpson," *Phylon* 6 (1945): 219–24.

29. John Hope Franklin, "Rayford Whittingham Logan (1897–1982)," *Hispanic American Historical Review* 63 (1983): 596–97; Kenneth R. Janken, "African-American Intellectuals Confront the 'Silent South': The 'What the Negro Wants' Controversy," *North Carolina Historical Review* 70 (1993): 155.

30. Gavins, *Perils and Prospects,* 23–32, 183.

31. J. M. Ellison, letter to Luther W. Smith, September 3, 1941, ABHSA, Box 184, Folder 4.

32. Gavins, *Perils and Prospects,* 20.

33. Gavins, *Perils and Prospects;* Marvin T. Chiles, "'A Period of Misunderstanding: Reforming Jim Crow in Richmond, Virginia, 1930–1954," *Virginia Magazine of History and Biography* 129 (2021), 244–78.

34. A. R. Mann, letter to Frank Padelford, November 8, 1940, Folder 5617, General Education Board Records, Rockefeller Archive Center (GEBR/RAC), Sleepy Hollow, New York.

35. Virginia Union and Affiliated Societies, undated pamphlet, Box 9, Folder 10, ABHSA.

36. Richard Guy Wilson and contributors, *Buildings of Virginia: Tidewater and Piedmont* (New York: Oxford University Press, 2002), 284–85. See W. N. Hartshorn, *Era of Progress and Promise,* 102–4.

37. "VUU: What It Signifies: An Address Delivered by T. J. Morgan, LL. D., at the Dedication of the New Granite Buildings on May 18, 1900," *Virginia Union Bulletin,* 70 (October 1969): 6–16, as quoted in Gavins, *Perils and Prospects,* 23.

38. R. G. Wilson et al., *Buildings of Virginia,* 179–80.

39. Thomas Jesse Jones, ed., *Negro Education: A Study of the Private and Higher Schools for Colored People in the United States* (Washington, D.C.: Bureau of Education, Department of the Interior, 1917), 207.

40. T. J. Jones, *Negro Education,* 203.

41. Paul Baker, *Richard Morris Hunt* (Cambridge, Mass.: MIT Press, 1980), 192–95; Joe M. Richardson, *A History of Fisk University, 1865–1946* (Tuscaloosa: University of Alabama Press, 2002).

42. Maura Lucking, "Self-Suggestion in the Tuskegee Machine: Technical Drawing under Jim Crow," *Grey Room* 87 (2022): 6–43.

43. T. J. Jones, *Negro Education,* 215.

44. Weiss, *Robert R. Taylor and Tuskegee,* xviii.

45. Kenrick Ian Grandison, "From Plantation to Campus: Progress, Community, and the Lay of the Land in Shaping the Early Tuskegee Campus," *Landscape Journal* 15 (1996): 6–22; Kenrick Ian Grandison, "Negotiated Space: The Black College Campus as a Cultural Record of Postbellum America," *American Quarterly* 51 (1999): 529–79.

46. William Lebovich, "Albert Irvin Cassell (1896–1969)," in *African American Architects: A Biographical Dictionary, 1865–1945,* ed. Dreck Spurlock Wilson (New York: Routledge, 2004), 125–32.

47. I am grateful to George Francis Kelly, who is engaged in writing about the Cravath Library, for this information about it.

48. D. F. Freeman, letter to Jackson Davis, November 20, 1939, Folder 5617, GEBR/RAC.

49. Amy Helene Kirschke, "The Fisk Murals Revealed: Memories of Africa, Hope for the Future," in *Aaron Douglas: African American Modernist,* ed. Susan Earle (New Haven, Conn.: Yale University Press, 2007), 114–35.

50. Yaëlle Biro, "African Art, New York, and the Avant-Garde," *African Arts* 46, no. 2 (Summer 2013): 88–97.

51. Bryan Clark Green and Lisa Meador Bricker, "Intensive Level Survey of Eleven Buildings, Virginia State University, Chesterfield County, Virginia," unpublished report for Virginia State University, June 17, 2013. For an aerial view published in 1955, see the advertisement in *Afro American,* August 6, 1955, 26.

52. Jacqueline Taylor, "Amaza's Azurest: Modern Architecture and the 'New Negro' Woman," in *Suffragette City: Women, Politics, and the Built Environment,* ed. Elizabeth Darling and Nathaniel Robert Walker. (Abington, UK: Routledge, 2019), 33–56; Taylor, *Amaza Lee Meredith Imagines Herself Modern.*

53. Ron Chernow, *Titan: The Life of John D. Rockefeller, Sr.* (New York: Random House, 1998), 482–500.

54. "To Members of the Executive Committee of the General Education Board, Inter-office Correspondence, 10 July 1936," Folder 1595, The Rockefeller Foundation Archives (TRFA), Rockefeller Archive Center.

55. John D. Rockefeller 2nd, letter to Trevor Arnett, 1 August 1, 1935, Folder 1595, Office of the Messrs. Rockefeller records, Educational Interests, Series G/RAC.

56. Walter B. Hill, interview memo, October 1934, Folder 4669, GEBR/RAC.

57. W. W. Brierley, letter to William J. Clark, April 18, 1937; Jackson Davis, interview memo, October 17, 1939; D. F. Freeman, letter to Jackson Davis, November 20, 1939, all in Folder 5617, GEBR/RAC.

58. Jackson Davis, interview memo, January 3, 1946, Folder 5616, GEBR/RAC.

59. Maggie L. Walker Governor's School for Government and International Studies, https://mlwgs.com/welcome-to-mlwgs/.

60. "Leigh to Head Union U. Drive," *Richmond News Leader,* date stamped May 24, 1939, Folder 5625, TRFA.

61. Fundraising brochure, Folder 1595, GEBR/RAC.

62. W. W. Brierley, letter to William J. Clark, December 14, 1939, Folder 5617, GEBR/RAC.

63. S. E. Hening, letter to William J. Clark, August 9, 1940, Box 184, Folder 3, ABHSA.

64. "'Y' Plans to Sponsor Fair Trips," *Lansing State Journal,* February 16, 1930, 30.

65. "Praises Rockefeller Offer," *New York Times,* November 3, 1914, 5.

66. The Rockefeller Foundation's assistance to Belgium began already in 1914. See Tammy M. Proctor, "The Louvain Library and US Ambition in Interwar Belgium," *Journal of Contemporary History* 50, no. 2 (2015): 147–67, doi:10.1177/0022009414552867.

67. William J. Clark, letter to General Education Board, June 18, 1936, Folder 5617, GEBR/RAC.

68. S. Richardson, *Built by Blacks,* 74–78, 97–98, 105; Thomas Tyler Potterfield Jr., "Charles Thaddeus Russell," in D. S. Wilson, *African American Architects,* 510–13.

69. S. E. Hening, Report on Visit to Virginia Union University, June 4, 1940, Box 184, Folder, 2, ABHSA.

70. S. E. Hening, memo to Dr. Dinsmore, May 10, 1940, Box 410, "Virginia Union Univ '39–'43 Financial Correspondence," ABHSA.

71. Sherman John Curl, "John M. Ellison within the Veil: Confronting the Challenges of Leadership in the Age of Jim Crow" (PhD diss., William and Mary College, 2007).

72. For instance, J. M. Ellison, letter to Jackson Davis, May 4, 1942, and Jackson Davis, interview note, April 9, 1945, both in Folder 1596, TRFA; Donald Faulkner, letter to J. M. Ellison, May 22 1942, Box 184, Folder 5, ABHSA.

73. Noble Beall, letter to Jackson Davis, July 21, 1943, Folder 5622, GEBR/RAC.

74. William A. Link, "Jackson Davis and the Lost World of Jim Crow Education," Albert and Shirley Small Special Collections Library, University of Virginia, https://small.library

.virginia.edu/collections/featured/jackson-davis-collection-of-african-american-educational-photographs/related-resources/jackson-davis-and-the-lost-world-of-jim-crow-education/.

75. Chiles, "' Period of Misunderstanding,'" 249. Southern white academics often felt much the same relative to their northern white counterparts. See Dabney, *Below the Potomac,* 139–76.

76. Jackson Davis, letter to John Malcus Ellison, January 6, 1943, Box 5621, GEBR/RAC.

77. Jackson Davis, letter to Theodore F. Adams, March 3, 1943, Box 5621, GEBR/RAC.

78. Arthur D. Wright, letter to Jackson Davis, June 11, 1941, Folder 1596, GEBR/RAC.

79. William J. Clark, letter to Jackson Davis, April 30, 1936, Box 4544, GEBR/RAC. For the salary figures see L. H. Foster, report on Virginia Union University for Jackson Davis, December 3, 1940, 2, Folder 5625, GEBR/RAC.

80. For instance, J. M. Ellison, letter to Jackson Davis, January 22, 1939, Folder 4544, TRFA; Jackson Davis, confidential interview with J. M. Ellison, November 12, 1940, Folder 1596, GEBR/RAC.

81. Jackson Davis, memo of meeting with William Clark, October 17, 1939, Folder 5617, GEBR/RAC.

82. Sherman John Curl, "John M. Ellison within the Veil: Confronting the Challenges of Leadership in the Age of Jim Crow" (PhD diss., William and Mary College, 2007), 4. This was something for which Carter Godwin Woodson had called already in *The Mis-Education of the American Negro* (1933; repr., Washington, D.C.: Associated Publishers, 1969), 27.

83. Foster and Davis were in constant touch between 1940 and 1942 about the finances of Virginia Union and about the Belgian Building. Davis and Ellison, as well as other GEB officials, were clearly dependent upon Foster's judgment and accounting expertise. See Luther Foster, letter to Jackson Davis, July 18, 1941, Folder 5618, GEBR/RAC, for the more personal tone his letters could take and for the funding of his son's doctorate.

84. J. M. Ellison, letter to Jackson Davis, December 5, 1940, Folder 1596, GEBR/RAC.

85. J. M. Ellison, letter to Jackson Davis, April 1, 1941, Folder 5618, GEBR/RAC.

86. J. M. Ellison, annual report, March 24, 1942, Box 184, Folder 5, ABHSA.

87. J. M. Ellison, "The Church of our Times and her Inescapable Challenges," 1940, pamphlet, Box 9, Folder 11, ABSHA.

88. Boykin, "Gift from Belgium," 55.

89. Fred McCuistion, memo of October 28, 1940, Folder 5617, GEBR/RAC; Memorandum to the General Education Board concerning Virginia Union University, from Virginia Union University Board of Education and the American Baptist Home Mission Society of the Northern Baptist Convention, November 4, 1940, Folder 5617, GEBR/RAC.

90. "Great Court Battle Looms between Va. State and Va. Union," *Pittsburgh Courier,* February 15, 1941, 18.

91. Gordon B. Hancock, letter to S. E. Hening, October 29, 1941, Box MS-001, Folder 96, John Malcus Ellison Papers, Archives, Virginia Union University (VUUA), Richmond, Virginia.

92. Gordon Blaine Hancock, "Starting Something," *Black Dispatch,* April 19, 1941, 7, and *Phoenix Index,* April 12, 1941, 8.

93. Fred McCuistion, memo of October 28, 1940, Folder 5617, GEBR/RAC.

94. Frank W. Padelford, letter to A. R. Mann, ovember 2, 1940, Folder 5617, GEBR/RAC.

95. A. R. Mann, letter to Frank W. Padelford, November 8, 1940, Folder 5617, GEBR/RAC.

96. Jackson Davis, interview memo, November 4, 1940, Folder 5617, GEBR/RAC.

97. Davis, interview memo, November 4, 1940C.

98. Davis, interview memo, November 4, 1940.

99. Charles E. Schelfhout, *Hugo van Kuyck, le belge qui conquit les plages normandes avant les armées alliées* (Deurie: Éditions de la Dyle, 2004), 70.

100. William J. Clark, letter to Jackson Davis, November 27, 1940, Folder 5617, GEBR/RAC.

101. Clark, letter to Davis, November 27, 1940.

102. Schelfhout, *Hugo van Kuyck;* see "American Modern," *House Beautiful,* October 1938, 66–67, and "American Modern," *House Beautiful,* Summer 1939, 30–31, for two houses codesigned by Hamby.

103. Hugo van Kuyck, *Modern Belgian Architecture: A Short Survey of Architectural Developments in Belgium in the Last Half Century* (New York: Belgian Government Information Center, 1955), n.p.

104. Kuenzli, *Henry van de Velde,* 167–77. See also Peter Dodge, *Beyond Marxism: The Faith and Works of Hendrik de Man* (The Hague: Martinus Nijhoff, 1966), 192–98.

105. V. C. "A Simple Dining Room," *House Beautiful,* February 1898, 96–97; Henry Russell Hitchcock, "Paris 1937: Henri van de Velde, archit.," *Architectural Forum* 67 (September 1937): 168.

106. Jackson Davis, interview memo, November 5, 1940, Folder 5617, GEBR/RAC.

107. Jackson Davis, interview memo, November 13, 1940, Folder 5617, GEBR/RAC.

108. Jackson Davis, interview memo, November 18, 1940, Folder 5617, GEBR/RAC.

109. A. Harmon, letter to Albert R. Mann, November 23, 1940, Folder 5617, GEBR/RAC.

110. Harmon, letter to Mann, November 23, 1940.

111. Theodore Adams, letter to Jackson Davis, November 27, 1940, Folder 5617, GEBR/RAC.

112. W. W. Brierley to William J. Clark, December 11, 1940, Folder 5617, GEBR/RAC.

113. Gilmore, *Defying Dixie,* 226.

114. George S. Schuyler, "Views and Reviews," *Pittsburgh Courier,* September 9, 1939, 10.

115. Samuel L. Brooke, "The World This Week," *Pittsburgh Courier,* June 1, 1940, 4.

116. Jackson Davis, letter to Luther Foster, November 13, 1942, Folder 5620, TRFA. For Nelson

Rockefeller and Latin America during this period, see Darlene Rivas, *Missionary Capitalist: Nelson Rockefeller in Venezuela* (Chapel Hill: University of North Carolina Press, 2002).

117. Susannah Colt, *Thomas C. Colt, Jr.: The Man Who Launched the Virginia Museum of Fine Arts* (West Lebanon, N.H.: Warner: R. C. Brayshaw, 2021), 230–31, 291–96.

118. Christopher C. Oliver, "Clashing Currents: Contemporary Art Exhibitions and Modernism in Richmond, 1933–1970," in *Southern/Modern: Rediscovering Southern Art from the First Half of the Twentieth Century,* ed. Jonathan Stuhlman and Martha R. Severens (Chapel Hill: Mint Museum in association with University of North Carolina Press, 2023), 360–86.

5. Raising Money and Raising Steel

1. "Union U. Gets Fair Pavilion," *Richmond News Leader,* December 6, 1940.

2. "University Here Given World's Fair Pavilion," *Richmond Times Dispatch,* December 6, 1940, 1, 10.

3. "The Gift to Virginia Union," *Richmond News Leader,* December 6, 1940, Folder 5625, GEBR/RAC.

4. "Belgium to Virginia," *Richmond Times Dispatch,* December 7, 1940, 10.

5. "Union Given Fair Building," *Journal and Guide* (Norfolk, Va.), November 23, 1940, 1.

6. "$1,000,000 Xmas Gift," *St. Louis Argus,* December 20, 1940, 3.

7. "Belgium's World's Fair Building Is Given to Virginia Union Univ.," *Phoenix Index,* December 14, 1940, 4.

8. "Belgian Gift," clipping dated January 19, 1941, Folder 95, Box MS-001, John Malcus Ellison Papers, Archives, Virginia Union University (VUUA), Richmond, Virginia. See also "Gets Belgian Pavilion," *New York Times,* December 6, 1940, 10; "Given to Virginia Union," *Baltimore Sun,* December 9, 1940, 10.

9. "Union U. Gets Fair Pavilion," 10.

10. "To Use Tower for Programs," *Richmond News Leader,* December 19, 1940, 4.

11. S. E. Hening, letter to Albert Mann, March 5, 1941, Folder 5618, GEBR/RAC.

12. "Architect Confers on Plans for Housing Belgian Pavilion," *Richmond Times Dispatch,* December 15, 1940, 30.

13. Minutes of the Executive Committee of Virginia Union University, April 29, 1941, Box 184, Folder 4, ABHSA.

14. "U. of R. Gives Va. Union Aid," *Richmond News Leader,* January 31, 1941, Box 5625, GEBR/RAC.

15. Sidney E. Hening, "A Glorious Conclusion to the World's Fair," *Missions,* February 1941, 82.

16. "Dedication Plans Made," *Richmond News Leader,* December 15, 1940, Folder 5625, GEBR/RAC.

17. A. Adam Clayton Powell, to S. E. Hening, December 26, 1940, Folder 96, Box MS-001, VUUA.

18. "Virginia Union University Alumni Here to Give Testimonial Dinner for Rev. Powell, Sr.," *New York Age,* March 22, 1941, 4.

19. S. E. Hening, letter to JBH, January 14, 1941, photocopy, Folder 96, Box MS-001, VUUA.

20. Eleanor Roosevelt, "My Day," January 17, 1941, clipping, Vertical File, Belgian Building, VUUA.

21. William J. Clark, "Virginia Union Expands Work," *New York Times,* June 15, 1941, 72.

22. For instance, "Architect Confers on Plans for Housing Belgian Pavilion" gave the total costs as $800,000, of which $520,000 had already been raised, while only $300,000 was required according to "Belgian Gift."

23. W. J. Clark, letter to Jackson Davis, November 27, 1940, Folder 5617, GEBR/RAC.

24. Jackson Davis, memo of February 26, 1941, of a meeting with S. E. Hening and Tennant Bryan, Folder 5618, GEBR/RAC. Bruce may have come to Hening's attention because in 1937 Leigh had married Lucinda Kinsolving, whose mother was Bruce's first cousin. Bruce's parents lived just blocks from the Kinsolvings in Baltimore.

25. Nelson D. Lankford, *The Last American Aristocrat: The Biography of Ambassador David K. E. Bruce, 1898–1955* (Boston: Little, Brown, 1996). Bruce's daughter Audrey and son-in-law Stephen Currier later used her Mellon inheritance to fund the Taconic Foundation, which supported voter registration and other aspects of the civil rights movement. See Evan Faulkenbury, *Poll Power: The Voter Education Project and the Movement for the Ballot in the American South* (Chapel Hill: University of North Carolina Press, 2019).

26. Minutes of the Executive Committee of Virginia Union University, April 29, 1941.

27. "Mrs. Jesse Vann, Publisher, Was 82," *New York Times,* June 8, 1967, 47.

28. Jackson Davis, memo of meeting with S. E. Hening and Hugo van Kuyck, December 20, 1940, Folder 5617, GEBR/RAC.

29. Donald Faulkner, letter to Theodore Adams, September 14, 1942, Folder 5620, GEBR/RAC. See also "Ira F. Lewis Dies; Negro Publisher," *New York Times,* August 29, 1948, 59.

30. "Widespread Interest in R. L. Vann Memorial," *Pittsburgh Courier,* June 7, 1941, 18; James Edmund Boyack, "Tower Stone Laid by Masons," *Pittsburgh Courier,* June 21, 1941, 12, for Scott's role.

31. "Program, Dinner at Riverside Church, Tuesday, 15 April 1941," Vertical File, Belgian Building, VUUA.

32. "Widespread Interest in R. L. Vann Memorial," 18; "Ceremonies to Be Today at V. U. U.," *Richmond Times Dispatch,* June 9, 1941, 4.

33. "Work on Belgian Building to Begin," clipping stamped March 29, 1941, Vertical File, Belgian Building, VUUA.

34. "Va. Governor Accepts Bldg. for Union," *Chicago Sunday Bee,* May 4, 1941, 7; "Virginia Governor to Accept Pavilion on 'Wings over Jordan,'" *The Call* (Kansas City), April 25, 1941, 12; "Virginia Governor Speaker on 'Wings' Program Sunday," *Phoenix Index,* April 26, 1941, 7; "Gov. Prince to Accept Belgium Building for Virginia Union University in Radio Talk," *New York Age,* April 26, 1941, 5.

35. Oscar W. Adams, "What Negroes Are Doing," *Birmingham (Ala.) News,* June 10, 1941, 28.

36. "Belgian Friendship Building Takes Root."

37. "Douglas Southall Freeman," *Encyclopedia Virginia,* https://encyclopediavirginia.org/entries/freeman-douglas-southall-1886-1953/.

38. "Belgian Friendship Building Takes Root."

39. Boyack, "Tower Stone Laid by Masons."

40. James Edmund Boyack, "Notables Attend Ground Breaking at Union University," *Pittsburgh Courier,* May 24, 1941.

41. Clark, "Virginia Union Expands Work."

42. Virginia Union University fundraising brochure, date stamp March 15, 1940, Folder 5624, GEBR/RAC.

43. Virginia Union University fundraising brochure.

44. "Va. Union Is Challenged," *Richmond News Leader,* April 13, 1943, Folder 5625, GEBR/RAC.

45. "Virginia Union University's General Alumni Holds Annual Conference: Reports $37,000," *New York Age,* December 8, 1945, 1.

46. "Elites-Grays to Aid Bldg. Fund," *Chicago Bee,* May 4, 1941, 10.

47. Jim Junot, "Barco-Stevens Hall—80 Years of History," Virginia Union University, https://vuusports.com/news/2019/5/1/general-barco-stevens-hall-80-years-of-history.aspx.

48. Jackson Davis, memo of a meeting with J. M. Ellison, November 4, 1940; J. M. Ellison, letter to Jackson Davis, November 17, 1940, both in Folder 5617, GEBR/RAC.

49. J. M. Ellison, letter to Jackson Davis, December 5, 1940, Folder 1596, GEBR/RAC.

50. Jackson Davis, letter to J. M. Ellison, March 11, 1941, Folder 1596, GEBR/RAC.

51. "Belgian Gift Will Enlarge Virginia Union," *Richmond Times Dispatch,* August 3, 1941.

52. W. T. Booker, "A Bit of Belgium Comes Here," *Richmond Times Dispatch,* January 25, 1942, 43.

53. "RPL History," Richmond Public Library, https://rvalibrary.org/about/history/.

54. Booker, "Bit of Belgium Comes Here."

55. Edward Wyatt, "D. Tennant Bryan, 92, Chief of Newspaper and TV Empire," *New York Times,* December 12, 1998, 19.

56. "Mrs. Robin Reeder McLagan Wed to C. Braxton Valentine Jr.," *New York Times,* February 22, 1970, 82.

57. Eric Quinones, "'Accidental Tourist' Exhibition Provides Views of Postwar Japan," Princeton University, July 6, 2009, https://www.princeton.edu/news/2009/07/06/accidental-tourist-exhibition-provides-views-postwar-japan?section=featured; personal reminiscences that his son Catesby shared with the author.

58. Milton L. Randolph, "Union Trustees Get Report; $130,000 Debt Liquidated," *Journal and Guide* (Norfolk, Va.), May 19, 1945, clipping, Folder 1598, TRFA.

59. S. E. Hening, letter to T. Justin Moore, Esq., March 18, 1942, Box 185, Folder 3, GEBR/RAC.

60. "Hanging Up His Stocking," *Richmond Times Dispatch,* December 18, 1941.

61. "Contributions to Virginia Union's Development Program from January 1, 1942 to September 20, 1943," Folder 95, Box MS-001, VUUA; Jackson Davis, interview memo, January 3, 1946, Folder 5616, GEBR/RAC

62. "Union U Halts Work on Belgian Building," *Pittsburgh Courier,* June 14, 1942. See also "Virginia Union Gymnasium Takes Shape," *Pittsburgh Courier,* December 4, 1941, 24; "Vann Memorial Tower Nears Completion," *Pittsburgh Courier,* March 14, 1942, 1.

63. Jackson Davis, letter to John M. Ellison, January 6, 1943, Folder 5621, GEBR/RAC.

64. Jackson Davis, letter to Luther Foster, April 8, 1943, Folder 561, TRFA; J. M. Ellison, letter to the General Education Board, March 14, 1946, Folder 5616, GEBR/RAC.

65. S. C. Mitchell, letter to Jackson Davis, April 26, 1943, Folder 5621, GEBR/RAC.

66. Noble Y. Beall, letter to Jackson Davis, July 21, 1943, Folder 5622, TRFA; Theodore Adams, letter to Hening, May 4, 1942, Folder 5619, GEBR/RAC.

67. "Will Provides Virginia Union Endowment," *Richmond Times Dispatch,* November 15, 1945, clipping, Folder 5616, GEBR/RAC

68. "City Induction Center Moved to New Site," *Richmond Times Dispatch,* 1943 clipping, Folder 5625, GEBR/RAC.

69. Albert R. Mann, interview note, November 14, 1944, Folder 1596, TRFA; Jackson Davis, interview note, July 30, 1945; Jackson Davis, memo of March 12 and 13, 1943, trip to Virginia Union, Folder 5621, GEBR/RAC; financial situation as of September 30, 1942, Folder 1598, GEBR/RAC, for the sum of $20,000/year; John M. Ellison, letter to Local Board #5, June 12, 1944, Folder 142, Ellison Papers, VUUA; Harry Kollat Jr., "Building Virginia Union," *Richmond Magazine,* March 25, 2015, https://richmondmagazine.com/news/news/virginia-union-university/.

70. Theodore Adams, letter to Jackson Davis, March 3, 1943, Folder 5621, GEBR/RAC.

71. Randolph, "Union Trustees Get Report."

72. Robert W. July, letter to J. E. Ellison, February 23, 1949, Folder 1596, GEBR/RAC.

73. J. M. Ellison, letter to Fred McCuistion, February 7, 1949, Folder 1596, GEBR/RAC.

74. Jackson Davis, memo of March 10, 1943, Folder 5621, GEBR/RAC.

75. Clipping stamped January 25, 1941, Vertical File, Belgian Building, VUUA.

76. "C. T. Russell to Help Erect Union Building," and "To Supervise Erection of Fair Building," clippings stamped February 8, 1941, and April 26, 1941, Vertical File, Belgian Building, VUUA.

77. "Part of Belgian Building Moved," *Phoenix Index,* March 1, 1941, 2.

78. "Belgian Building Arriving in Trucks," clipping stamped March 1, 1941, Vertical File, Belgian Building, VUUA.

79. W. W. Brierley, memo of meeting with S. E. Hening and Donald Faulkner, October 6, 1942, Folder 5620, GEBR/RAC.

80. Luther Foster, letter to Jackson Davis, November 12, 1941, Folder 5618, GEBR/RAC; S. E. Hening, letter to E. B. Poole, March 20, 1942, Box 410, Folder "Virginia Union Univ. '39–43/Financial Correspondence," ABHSA.

81. "Burns, Allen Norman," *Richmond Times Dispatch,* February 8 2008, B6.

82. "Russell Aide to Van Kuyck," *Richmond News Leader,* January 29, 1941, Folder 5625, TRFA; "C. T. Russell to Help Erect Union Building."

83. "Fair's Belgian Pavilion Shipped to Negro School," *New York Herald Tribune,* May 4, 1941, clipping, Folder 5625, GEBR/RAC.

84. Simeon Booker Jr., "Negro to Supervise Erection of World's Fair Belgian Building at Virginia Union University," *The Call* (Kansas City), May 2, 1941, 5; Simeon Booker Jr., "Negro to Supervise Actual Belgian Building Construction at Union," *Dayton Forum,* April 25, 1941, 1; Simeon Booker Jr., "Negro to Supervise Belgian Building Assembly at Union," *Phoenix Index,* April 26, 1941, 4.

85. Minutes of the Meeting of Building Committee of the Belgian Friendship Building, August 26, 1941, Vertical File, Belgian Building, VUUA.

86. Donald Faulkner, letter to J. M. Ellison, May 22, 1942, Box 184, Folder 5, ABHSA.

87. Faulkner, letter to Ellison, May 22, 1942.

88. S. E. Hening, letter to GEB, attn. Brierley, January 7, 1941, Folder 5618, GEBR/RAC.

89. They certainly fluctuated. See A. R. Mann, memo of phone conversation with Hening, March 7, 1941, Folder 5618, GEBR/RAC.

90. Jackson Davis, memo of a meeting with S. E. Hening and Tennant Bryan, Febrary 26, 1941, Folder 5618, GEBR/RAC.

91. Luther Foster, letter to Jackson Davis, November 12, 1941, Folder 5618, TRFA; Hening, letter to Poole, March 20, 1942.

92. W. W. Brierley, memo of a conversation with S. E. Hening, August 25, 1943; A. R. Guilmain, letter to S. E. Hening, August 19, 1943, both Folder 5622, GEBR/RAC.

93. Jackson Davis and W. W. Brierley, interview memo of October 7, 1943, Folder 5622, GEBR/RAC.

94. Jackson Davis, memo of September 7, 1943, Folder 5622, GEBR/RAC.

95. W. W. Brierley, memo of meeting with S. E. Hening and Donald Faulkner, October 6, 1942, Folder 5620, GEBR/RAC

96. "Half-way Mark Is Passed in Union's Building Campaign," clipping stamped January 18, 1941, Vertical File, Belgian Building, VUUA.

97. Jackson Davis, memo of meeting with S. E. Hening and Hugo van Kucyk, December 30, 1940, Folder 5617, GEBR/RAC.

98. W. W. Brierley, memo of meeting with Luther Foster, June 27, 1941, Folder 5618, GEBR/RAC.

99. John M. Ellison, letter to Hugo van Kuyck, July 16, 1941, Folder 98, Box MS-001, VUUA; "Paris Fair Delays Lead to Labor Rows," *New York Times,* May 21, 1937, 6.

100. Jackson Davis, memo of July 13, 1941, trip to Virginia Union, Folder 5618, GEBR/RAC. The date is on the full set of blueprints preserved in the Library of Virginia.

101. Minutes of the Meeting of Building Committee of the Belgian Friendship Building, August 26, 1941, Vertical File, Belgian Building, VUUA.

102. A slightly different arrangement, with the tower at the opposite corner, was published in *The Watchman,* January 2, 1941.

103. E. B. Poole, letter to S. E. Hening, October 29, 1941, Box 184, Folder 4, ABHSA.

104. D. Andrew Welch, letter to Hugo van Kuyck, June 4, 1942, Folder 98, Box MS-001, VUUA. Note that Van Kuyck obtained an M.A. in architecture from the University of Richmond, Hening's alma mater, on July 9, 1941 (diploma number 458). See Schelfhout, *Hugo van Kuyck,* 68. However, there was no School of Architecture at the University of Richmond at the time, so the viability of the degree is in doubt.

105. William Hamby, letter to John M. Ellison, April 23, 1942, on firm letterhead, Folder 98, Box MS-001, VUUA.

106. Booker, "Bit of Belgium Comes Here."

107. Schelfhout, *Hugo van Kuyck,* 73–75. See also Hugo van Kuyck, letter to S. E. Hening, August 26, 1943, Folder 5622, GEBR/RAC.

108. Schelfhout, *Hugo van Kuyck.* Several reconnaissance missions led Van Kuyck, an expert mariner, to recommend the Normandy coast as a propitious site for a military landing. Assigned to the Mapping and Aerial Photo Section of the Engineer Amphibian Command as of 1943, Van Kuyck developed technologies of aerial photography in addition to creating precise maps of the coast based on intelligence of German coastal defenses and on the close study of tidal charts. This meticulous and laborious work provided the groundwork for the naval landing at Omaha Beach in preparation for the invasion of Normandy in June 1944 in which Van Kuyck participated.

109. "Belgian Engineer to Confer with Building Inspector," press release, August 7, 1941, Folder 95, Box MS-001, VUUA.

110. Belgian Engineer to Confer with Building Inspector, press release, August 7, 1941, Folder 95, Box MS-001, VUUA.

111. Donald Faulkner, letter to J. M. Ellison, May 22, 1942, Box 184, Folder 5, ABHSA.

112. "Situation: Virginia Union University—Amstel Contracting Corp.," March 25, 1942, Folder 5619, GEBR/RAC.

113. "Knew German, Got Job," *Richmond Afro American,* July 5, 1941.

114. Booker, "Bit of Belgium Comes Here."

115. Hugo van Kuyck, letter to John M. Ellison, January 26, 1942, Folder 98, Box MS-001, VUUA.

116. John M. Ellison, letter to Hugo van Kuyck, April 15, 1942, Folder 98, Box MS-001, VUUA.

117. John M. Ellison, letter to Hamby, Nelson, and Van Kuyck, April 21, 1942, Folder 98, Box MS-001, VUUA.

118. "Part of Belgian Building Nears Completion," *Journal and Guide* (Norfolk, Va.), March 14, 1942.

119. "A Summary Report of the Administration of Virginia Union University: 1942–1943," leaflet, Folder 1598, GEBR/RAC.

120. "Summary Report of the Administration of Virginia Union University."

121. Hamby, letter to Ellison, April 23, 1942, Folder 98, Box MS-001, VUUA, for the shortage of sheet metal needed for the roofing.

122. Jackson Davis, interview notes, June 30, 1942, Folder 1596, GEBR/RAC.

123. S. E. Hening, letter to Mrs. Wilfred W. Fry, April 2, 1945, copy, Vertical File, Belgian Building, VUUA. See also "Wilfred W. Fry," *New York Times,* July 28, 1936, 18.

124. Albert R. Mann, interview note, November 14, 1944, Folder 1596, GEBR/RAC.

125. Jim Junot, "Barco-Stevens Hall—80 Years of History," *Virginia Union University Sports,* May 1, 2019, https://vuusports.com/news/2019/5/1/general-barco-stevens-hall-80-years-of-history.aspx.

126. John Alvin Bacoats, "Our College and University Presidents," *Virginia Union Bulletin* 47 (January 1947): 4–11.

127. Robert W. July, interview memo, January 12, 1949, Folder 1596, GEBR/RAC; J. M. Ellison, "Your Contribution Is Needed," *Virginia Union Bulletin,* November 1949.

128. J. M. Ellison, Annual Report, April 24, 1944, Box 410, Folder "Virginia Union Univ. '44-'46," ABHSA. Clemenceau McAdee Givings was named in honor of Georges Clemenceau, prime minister of France during World War I.

129. Everette Battan Poole, "A Review of Virginia Union University's Finances during the War Period," *Virginia Union Bulletin* 46 (January 1946): 8.

130. Poole, "Review of Virginia Union University's Finances," 8.

131. "Questions and Answers," *Richmond News Leader,* March 15, 1946, 14.

132. Washburn, *African-American Newspaper,* 143–63.

133. "Baptist Head Endorses 'VV,'" *Pittsburgh Courier,* July 4, 1942, 15.

134. Gilmore, *Defying Dixie,* 486.

135. Gavins, *Perils and Prospects;* Chiles, "'Period of Misunderstanding,'" 244–78.

136. J. M. Ellison, Annual Report, April 24, 1944, ABHSA, Box 410, Folder "Virginia Union Univ. '44–'46," ABHSA.

137. Dabney, *Below the Potomac,* 224.

138. Dabney, *Below the Potomac,,* 227.

139. "Baptists Want Racial Equality in War Effort," *The Virginian-Pilot* (Norfolk), February 26, 1942, 7.

140. Minutes, Virginia Union University Board Meeting, April 24, 1944, Folder "Virginia Union Univ. '44–'46/Minutes," Box 410, ABHSA.

141. Theodore Adams, letter to Jackson Davis, March 3, 1943, Folder 5621, GEBR/RAC.

142. Jackson Davis, memo of March 10, 1943, Box 5621, GEBR/RAC.

143. "Va. Union Is Challenged," *Richmond News Leader,* April 14, 1943.

144. Donald Faulkner, letter to Jackson Davis, January 8, 1945, Folder 5621, GEBR/RAC.

145. Helmreich, *United States Relations with Belgium,* 21–24.

146. "British in Trade Pact with Belgian Congo," *New York Times,* January 22, 1941, 5; "Belgian Army of 90,000 to Help British in Africa," *New York Times,* February 6, 1941.

147. Adams, "What Negroes Are Doing"; "Belgian Friendship Building Takes Root."

148. Helmreich, *United States Relations with Belgium,* 25, 38.

149. Van Reybrouck, *Congo.*

150. Helmreich, *United States Relations with Belgium,* 29–61; Gabrielle Hecht, *Being Nuclear: Africans and the Global Uranium Trade* (Cambridge, Mass.: MIT Press, 2012), 183–84, 192–93; Vanthemsche, *Belgium and the Congo,* 134–35; Williams, *Spies in the Congo.*

151. Jan-Albert Goris, ed., *Belgium* (Berkeley: University of California Press, 1945).

152. Georges Philippart, "Architecture," in Goris, *Belgium,* 284.

153. Melville J. Herskovits, "Peoples and Culture," in Goris, *Belgium,* 363.

154. Rev. William P. Hayes, "Virginia Union University: Yesterday, Today and Tomorrow; Founders Day Address," *Virginia Union Bulletin* 46 (January 1947): 7, Folder 1598, TRFA.

155. "The Physical Improvements," *Virginia Union Bulletin* 46, no. 2 (January 1946): 6.

156. "The Physical Improvements."

157. The fitting out of some science classrooms would not be completed until the following year.

158. "Virginia Union Graduates Hear Darden," *Richmond Times Dispatch,* June 8, 1949, 5.

159. "Dedicate R. L. Vann," *Pittsburgh Courier,* June 18, 1949, 4.

160. Toki Schulk Johnson, "Blue Skies of Virginia," *Pittsburgh Courier,* June 18, 1949, 8.

161. "Tower, Library, Prayer Room, Building Dedicated at Virginia Union University," *Pittsburgh Courier,* June 18, 1949, 4.

162. J. M. Ellison, letter to General Education Board, June 23, 1949, Folder 5616, GEBR/RAC.

163. Jackson Davis, interview memo, January 3, 1946; J. M. Ellison, letter to Jackson Davis, January 25, 1946; W. W. Brierley, letter to J. M. Ellison, April 4, 1946, all Folder 5616, GEBR/RAC.

164. Cecil L. Rowlett, "Founders Day Address VUU: The College as Preparation for the Exercise of Citizenship Rights," *Virginia Union Bulletin* 49, no. 2 (January 1948): 9.

165. Photo caption, *Journal and Guide* (Norfolk, Va.), July 7, 1945.

166. Jackson Davis, letter to J. W. Barce, June 8, 1945, Folder 1596, GEBR/RAC.

167. "Unique Foreign Tour Hailed at Va. Union U," *Pittsburgh Courier,* June 5, 1949, 2.

6. Postwar Campus Architecture, Campus Activism, and City Planning

1. Rufus Wells, "'God Walks with Us,' King Tells Teachers," *Richmond Afro American,* November 20, 1956, 1–2.

2. "Union Holds Fifth Fine Arts Festival," *Richmond Afro American,* April 26, 1958, 3.

3. "Va. Union Concert Series Opens," *Richmond Afro American,* November 2, 1957.

4. "Calm under Fire," *Richmond Afro American,* May 31, 1958, 12.

5. Junot, "Barco-Stevens Hall."

6. Junot, "Barco-Stevens Hall."

7. "About Us," John W. Barco Alumni Chapter, VUU, http://www.johnwbarcoalumnichapter.org/about-us/.

8. "Union Student Raps Segregated Seating," *Richmond Afro American,* February 6, 1954, 1.

9. Walter Fauntroy, letter to Martin Luther King, Jr., June 10, 1960, Martin Luther King, Jr., Research and Education Institute, Stanford University, https://kinginstitute.stanford.edu/king-papers/documents/walter-e-fauntroy#fn3. See also "King in Richmond," Dr. Martin Luther King Jr. Memorial Commission, http://mlkcommission.dls.virginia.gov/kinginvirginia/richmond.html.

10. Simeon Booker, *Shocking the Conscience: A Reporter's Account of the Civil Rights Movement* (Oxford: University of Mississippi Press, 2013).

11. "Alcorn Protests? Leaders at VUU," *Richmond Afro American,* April 6, 1957, 1.

12. Eddie R. Cole, *The Campus Color Line: College Struggles for Black Freedom* (Princeton, N.J.: Princeton University Press, 2022); Favors, *Shelter in a Time of Storm.*

13. Cecil L. Rowlett, "Founders Day Address Virginia Union University: The College as Preparation for the Exercise of Citizenship Rights," *Virginia Union Bulletin* 49, no. 2 (January 1948): 5.

14. Henry Allen Bullock, *A History of Negro Education in the South: From 1619 to the Present* (Cambridge, Mass.: Harvard University Press, 1967), vii.

15. "Police Are Investigating Cross Burning at VUU," *Richmond Afro American,* September 20, 1958, 1.

16. Virginia Union University advertisement, *Richmond Afro American,* June 15, 1957, D.

17. All but the 1960 visit are documented in "King in Richmond," Dr. Martin Luther King Jr. Memorial Commission, http://mlkcommission.dls.virginia.gov/kinginvirginia/richmond.html.

18. "Dr. King Draws Thousands to Union," *Richmond Afro American,* March 2, 1957, 1.

19. "Bus Protest Leader Draws 12,000 to VU Religious Fete," *Richmond Afro American,* March 9, 1957.

20. "Bus Protest Leader Draws 12,000."

21. Ruth Jenkins, "Dr. King Advises Schoolless Pupils to Shun Private Offer," *Richmond Afro American,* January 9, 1960.

22. "Dr. King in Favor of 'Social Maladjustment' in Struggle," *Richmond Afro American,* November 13, 1960, 1.

23. Junot, "Barco-Stevens Hall."

24. "Voters League Hits Massive Resistance," *Richmond Afro American,* October 4, 1958, 1.

25. Ruth Jenkins, "40 Cheered to Jail," *Richmond Afro American,* February 27, 1960, 1.

26. "Flash!," *Richmond Afro American,* February 27, 1960, 1. See also Dale Brumfield, "Refused to Move," *Commonwealth Times,* February 9, 2015, Virginia Commonwealth University, https://commonwealthtimes.org/2015/02/09/refused-to-move/.

27. "Pickets Bolstered," *Richmond Afro American,* March 5, 1960, 1.

28. Jenkins, "40 Cheered to Jail"; Chester M. Hampton, "Sit-Downs New Crusade," *Richmond Afro American,* March 12, 1960.

29. "Bibles on Sit-In," *Richmond Afro American,* April 2, 1960, 1.

30. "Pickets Pay Off in Church Hill," *Richmond Afro American,* April 30, 1960, 1; "Chandler High to Be Integrated," *Richmond Afro American,* August 20, 1960, 1.

31. Hampton, "Sit-Downs New Crusade."

32. "Physical Improvements."

33. "Bus Protest Leader Draws 12,000."

34. "King Shuns Doctors to Speak at Union," *Richmond Afro American,* March 2, 1957.

35. *La revue coloniale belge* 31 (15 January 1947): cover.

36. Fredie Floré, "Serving a Double Diplomatic Mission: Strategic Alliances between Belgian and American Furniture Companies in the Postwar Era," *Design and Culture* 9, no. 2 (2017): 167–85, doi:10.1080/17547075.2017.1325625.

37. "More People Buy Afro-American Newspapers Than Any Other Colored Weeklies," *Richmond Afro American,* December 31, 1955, 12.

38. William Gordon, "Belgian Congo Sees Promise of Freedom," *Richmond Afro American,* December 6, 1958.

39. "Congo Asks More Self-Government," *Richmond Afro American,* January 17, 1959, 3.

40. "Belgian Congo Riots Show Freedom Urge," *Richmond Afro American,* February 14, 1959, 5.

41. "Lunchroom 'Sit Downs' Spread to Durham, Winston Salem," and "Congo Freedom," *Richmond Afro American,* February 13, 1960. This situation was repeated on August 20, when the news that Chandler Junior High was to be integrated was announced at the same time as the latest development in the Congo.

42. "A New Nation Is Born," *Richmond Afro American,* July 9, 1960, 4.

43. "Real Culprit in the Congo," *Richmond Afro American,* July 23, 1960, 4.

44. "The Congo No Longer in Existence," *Richmond Afro American,* January 7, 1961, 19.

45. Charles P. Howard, Sr., "In Wake of Political Slayings Observers See Effort to 'Wipe Out' Congo's 'Articulate Leadership,'" *Richmond Afro American,* March 4, 1961. See also Dworkin, *Congo Love Song.*

46. Kathleen James-Chakraborty and Rachel Lee, "*Marg* Magazine: A Tryst with Architectural Modernity; Modern Architecture as Seen from an Independent India," *ABE Journal: Architecture Beyond Europe* 1 (2012), doi:10.4000/abe.623; Janet Berry Hess, *Art and Architecture in Postcolonial Africa* (Jefferson, N.C.: McFarland, 2006); Lukasz Stanek, *Architecture in Global Socialism: Eastern Europe, West Africa, and the Middle East in the Cold War* (Princeton, N.J.: Princeton University Press, 2020).

47. Crinson, *Modern Architecture;* Sofie Boonen and Johan Lagae, "Ruashi, a Pessac in Congo? On the Design, Inhabitation, and Transformation of a 1950s Neighborhood in Lubumbashi, Democratic Republic of Congo," in *The Politics of Housing in (Post-)Colonial Africa: Accommodating Workers and Urban Residents,* ed. Martina Barker-Ciganikova, Kirsten Rüter, Daniela Waldburger, and Carl-Philipp Bodenstein (Oldenbourg: De Gruyter, 2020), 66–97, doi:10.1515/9783110601183.

48. Roger L. Geiger, *American Higher Education since World War II: A History* (Princeton, N.J.: Princeton University Press, 2021).

49. For a critical view of this phenomenon, see Reinhold Martin, *Knowledge Worlds: Media, Materiality, and the Making of the Modern University* (New York: Columbia University Press, 2021).

50. Gilmore, *Defying Dixie.*

51. Tauj'ullah X. Sky Lark, "Unlocking Doors: How Gregory Swanson Challenged the University of Virginia's Resistance to Desegregation. A Case Study," *Spectrum: A Journal on Black Men* 5, no. 2 (Spring 2017): 71–84, doi:10.2979/spectrum.5.2.04.

52. "Trying to Ward Off Integration," *Richmond Afro American,* March 2, 1957.

53. For an astute account of events in Atlanta see Tomiko Brown-Nagin, *Courage to Dissent: Atlanta and the Long History of the Civil Rights Movement* (Oxford: Oxford University Press, 2011).

54. *Afro American,* August 8, 1953.

55. Howard University advertisement, *Afro American,* August 6, 1955, 19.

56. Glan B. Leiner, "Hilyard Robert Robinson (1899–1986)," in D. S. Wilson, 492–99.

57. "A & T Moves into Modern $1 Million Library," *Richmond Afro American,* July 9, 1955, 20.

58. Fisk University and Morgan State College advertisements, *Afro American,* 14 March 1964.

59. "Morgan Gets $1 Million for Two New Buildings," *Richmond Afro American,* April 29, 1961; George P. Matysek Jr., "William Gaudreau, Leading Post–Vatican II Architect Dies at 84," *Catholic Review,* July 9, 2015, https://www.archbalt.org/william-gaudreau-leading-post-vatican-ii-architect-dies-at-84/; "Maryland's Largest Historically Black College Named a National Treasure," Morgan State University, May 3, 2016, https://www.morgan.edu/news/morgan-state-national-treasure.

60. Southern University advertisement, *Afro American,* March 14, 1964.

61. Thomas Aiello, "Violence Is a Classroom: The 1972 Grambling and Southern Riots and the Trajectory of Black Protest," *Louisiana History: The Journal of the Louisiana Historical Association* 54, no. 3 (Summer 2012): 261–91.

62. Virginia Union University advertisement, *Richmond Afro American,* June 12, 1954, 3.

63. Virginia Union advertisement, *Richmond Afro American,* March 14, 1964.

64. Richmond Motor advertisement, *Richmond Afro American,* September 2, 1961, 12.

65. Talladega advertisement, *Richmond Afro American,* March 14, 1964. The names of the architects are given in the National Register of Historic Places Nomination form, https://npgallery.nps.gov/NRHP/GetAsset/NRHP/90001316_text.

66. "Pearl and I. T. Creswell House: International-Style at Fisk University," Tennessee Architecture, https://tennessee-architecture.com/pearl-and-i-t-creswell-house-international-style-at-fisk-university/. For other examples of African American architectural patronage, see Margaret Ruth Little, "Getting the American Dream for Themselves: Postwar Modern Subdivisions for African Americans in Raleigh, North Carolina," *Buildings & Landscapes: Journal of the Vernacular Architecture Forum* 19 (Spring 2012): 73–86; Kofi Boone, "Enabling Connections to Empower Place: The Carolinas," in *Black Landscapes Matter,* ed. Walter Hood and Grace Mitchell Tada (Charlottesville: University of Virginia Press, 2020), 53–73.

67. "Physical Improvements," *Virginia Union Bulletin* 46 (January 1946): 6.

68. Philip Johnson, preface to *Built in USA: Post-War Architecture,* ed. Henry-Russell Hitchcock and Arthur Drexler (New York: Museum of Modern Art, 1952), 8.

69. Kuenzli, *Henry van de Velde.*

70. These memoirs were introduced to anglophone audiences in 1952, when P. Morton Shand

reproduced excerpts from them, selecting passages related to the artist's Art Nouveau period. See Henry van de Velde, "Extracts from His Memoirs, 1891–1901," *Architectural Review* 112, no. 669 (September 1952): 143–55. The publication history of the full memoirs is much more complicated, as they remained incomplete at the time of van de Velde's death in 1957 and have been published in various states of completion in three different posthumous editions. First, there is one single volume completed and translated from French into German by a friend and confidant five years after van de Velde's death. See Henry van de Velde, *Geschichte meines Lebens,* ed. Hans Curjel (Munich: Piper Verlag, 1962). Second, a scholarly, critical edition of van de Velde's memoir presents a typescript of the entirety of the known, incomplete French manuscripts. See Henry van de Velde, *Les mémoires inachevés d'un artiste européen: Édition critique,* ed. Léon Ploegaerts, 2 vols. (Brussels: Académie royale de Belgique, 1999). Third, a four-volume annotated edition offers an edited and revised selection of van de Velde's French manuscripts, along with a scholarly apparatus. See Henry van de Velde, *Récit de ma vie, 1863–1900,* ed. Anne van Loo (Paris: Flammarion, 1992); Henry van de Velde, *Récit de ma vie, 1900–1917,* ed. Anne van Loo (Paris: Flammarion, 1995); and Henry van de Velde, *Récit de ma vie, 1917–1957,* ed. Anne van Loo, 2 vols. (Turnhout, Belgium: Brepols, 2023).

71. Werner Durth, *Deutsche Architekten. Biographische Verflechtungen 1900–1970* (Basel, Switzerland: Vieweg & Teubner, 1986).

72. Ploegaerts, "Henry van de Velde's Only Work," 56–59.

73. His son Catesby has confirmed to James-Chakraborty that the two men remained in touch.

74. Schelfhout, *Hugo van Kuyck,* 146–80.

75. Hitchcock and Drexler, *Built in USA.*

76. Henry-Russell Hitchcock, letter to Louis I. Kahn, March 13, 1960, in "Voice of America—Louis I. Kahn, Recorded November 16, 1960," Box LIK 55, Louis I. Kahn Collection, University of Pennsylvania and Pennsylvania Historical and Museum Commission, Philadelphia. See also Kathleen James-Chakraborty, "From Isolationism to Internationalism: American Acceptance of the Bauhaus," in Kathleen James-Chakraborty, ed., *Bauhaus Culture from Weimar to the Cold War* (Minneapolis: University of Minnesota Press, 2006), 153–70.

77. Henry-Russell Hitchcock, introduction to Hitchcock and Drexler, *Built in USA,* 10.

78. Michael Tymkiw, *Nazi Exhibition Design and Modernism* (Minneapolis: University of Minnesota Press, 2018).

79. Nader Vossoughian, "Alvar Aalto, Ernst Neufert, and Architectural Standardization in Germany and Finland, 1933–45," *Journal of the Society of Architectural Historians* 79, no. 2 (June 2020): 202–12. See also Eeva-Liisa Pelkonen, *Alvar Aalto: Architecture, Modernity, and Geopolitics* (New Haven, Conn.: Yale University Press, 2009).

80. Philip Johnson, *Mies van der Rohe* (New York: Museum of Modern Art, 1947).

81. Arthur Drexler, "Post-War Architecture," in Hitchcock and Drexler, *Built in USA,* 20.

82. Ludwig Mies van der Rohe, letter to Henry van de Velde, September 29, 1923, Folder Private 1923–50/v, Box 2, Ludwig Mies van der Rohe papers, Library of Congress Manuscript Division, Washington, D.C.

83. Daniel Bluestone, "Chicago's Mecca Flat Blues," *Journal of the Society of Architectural Historians* 57 (1998): 382–403, doi:10.2307/991458. James Baldwin said this in "A Conversation with James Baldwin," a television interview broadcast on June 24, 1963, and archived at American Archive of Public Broadcasting, https://americanarchive.org/catalog/cpb-aacip-15-9m03xx2p.

84. Anat Falbel, "Georgia Louise Harris Brown," Pioneering Women of American Architecture, https://pioneeringwomen.bwaf.org/georgia-louise-harris-brown; Margaret M. Grubiak, "Henry Clifford Boles (1910–1979)," in D. S. Wilson, *African American Architects,* 61–65; "Esteemed Chicago Architect, Wendell Campbell, Dies," *Chicago Defender,* July 15, 2008; Andrew Connor, "Making History and a Landmark," *Illinois Tech Magazine,* Summer 2020, https://magazine.iit.edu/summer-2020/making-history-and-landmark.

85. Alice Waugh, "The BSU at 50," October 30, 2018, *MIT News,* https://news.mit.edu/2018/mit-black-students-union-50th-anniversary-1030. See also Kate Zernike, *The Exceptions: Nancy Hopkins, MIT, and the Fight for Women in Science* (New York: Scribner, 2023).

86. Simon J. Levien, "The Crimson Klan," *Harvard Crimson,* March 25, 2021, https://www.thecrimson.com/article/2021/3/25/harvard-klan-scrut/.

87. Kuenzli, *Henry van de Velde,* 1; Anderson, Fenske, and Fixter, *Aalto and America.*

88. See Henry van de Velde, "Giving Life to Matter as a Principle of Beauty" (1903) and "The Line" (1908), both in Henry van de Velde, *Selected Essays,* 222–35, 279–299.

89. Hitchcock, introduction to Hitchcock and Drexler, *Built in USA,* 12. See also Drexler, "Post-War Architecture," 30–31.

90. Laura Muir, ed., *Object Lessons: The Bauhaus and Harvard* (New Haven, Conn.: Yale University Press, 2021).

91. Anthony Alofsin, *The Struggle for Modernism: Architecture, Landscape Architecture, and City Planning at Harvard* (New York: W. W. Norton, 2002); Klaus Herdeg, *The Decorated Diagram: Harvard Education and the Failure of the Bauhaus Legacy* (Cambridge, Mass.: MIT Press, 1983).

92. Kathleen James-Chakraborty, "Fragile Allianz: Über die Beziehung zwischen Henry van de Velde und Walter Gropius," in *Mythos Bauhaus: Zwischen Selbsterfindung und Enthistorisierung,* ed. Anja Baumhoff and Magdalena Droste (Berlin: Reimer, 2009), 35–52.

93. This argument would culminate in Walter Gropius, *Apollo in the Democracy: The Cultural Obligation of the Architect,* ed. Ise Gropius (New York: McGraw Hill, 1968).

94. Christopher Silver, *Twentieth-Century Richmond: Planning, Politics, and Race* (Knoxville: University of Tennessee Press, 1984); Christopher Silver and John Moeser, *The Separate City: Black Communities in the Urban South* (Lexington: University of Kentucky Press, 1995).

95. Gropius, *Apollo in the Democracy,* 26.

96. D. Bradford Hunt, *Blueprint for Disaster: The Unraveling of Chicago Public Housing* (Chicago: University of Chicago Press, 2009).

97. This was pointed out already in June Manning Thomas, "Urban Displacement: Fruits of a History of Collusion," *The Black Scholar* 11, no. 2 (1979): 68–77. For another example of the harm done to HBCUs see Bobby L. Lovett, *A Touch of Greatness: A History of Tennessee State University* (Atlanta: Mercer University Press, 2013), 171. We thank George Francis-Kelly for the reference.

98. *Negro Education: A Study of the Private and Higher Schools for Colored People in the United States* (Washington: Department of the Interior, 1917), 212.

99. L. Douglas Wilder, *Son of Virginia: A Life in America's Political Arena* (Guilford, Conn.: Lyons Press, 2015).

100. The HistoryMakers Video Oral History interview with The Honourable Henry L. Marsh III, November 18, 2003, HistoryMakers African American Video Oral History Collection, https://www.thehistorymakers.org/sites/default/files/A2003_277_EAD.pdf.

101. K. Ian Grandison, "The Other Side of the 'Free' Way: Planning for Separate but Equal in the Face of Massive Resistance," in *Race and Real Estate,* ed. Adrienne R. Brown and Valerie Smith (Oxford: Oxford University Press, 2016), 209–10.

102. Grandison, "Other Side of the 'Free' Way," 215.

103. Dawn S. Bowen, "The Transformation of Richmond's Historic African American Commercial Corridor," *Southeastern Geographer* 43 (2003): 260–78.

104. "Importance of Black Colleges Stressed," *Richmond Afro American,* February 17–21, 1976, 5.

105. Rolf Achilles, Kevin Harrington, and Charlotte Myhrum, eds., *Mies van der Rohe: Architect as Educator* (Chicago: Illinois Institute of Technology, 1986); Anderson, Fenske, and Fixter, *Aalto in America;* Muir, *Object Lessons.*

7. The Temporary Becomes Permanent

1. "2022–23 Men's Basketball Schedule," Virginia Union University, https://vuusports.com/sports/mens-basketball/schedule/2022-23.

2. F. Vandermeersch, letter to Marcel Breuer, September 27, 1954, Marcel Breuer Archive, Syracuse University, Syracuse, New York.

3. Martin Bechthold, Anthony Kane, and Nathan King, *Ceramic Material Systems: In Architecture and Interior Design* (Basel, Switzerland: Birkhäuser, 2015), 48.

4. Jacobs et al., *Tweebronnen.*

5. Marybeth Gasman, *Envisioning Black Colleges: A History of the United Negro College Fund* (Baltimore: Johns Hopkins University Press, 2007).

6. Bonnie Winston, "Even President Isn't Sure of Deficit's Size," *Richmond Times Dispatch*, January 26, 1982, 1.

7. Terry H. Anderson, *In Pursuit of Fairness: A History of Affirmative Action* (Oxford: Oxford University Press, 2005).

8. John Hope Franklin, *Mirror to America: The Autobiography of John Hope Franklin* (New York: Farrar, Straus and Giroux, 2005).

9. In 2022–23, Virginia Union University's tuition and fees amounted to $14,230, a cost significantly less expensive than the national average cost of tuition of $45,713. See "Virginia Union University Tuition & Financial Aid," U.S. News & World Report, https://www.usnews.com/best-colleges/virginia-union-university-3766/paying#:~:text=Virginia%20Union%20University's%20tuition%20is,to%20as%20the%20sticker%20price.

10. "Belgian Building," Virginia Department of Historic Resources, https://www.dhr.virginia.gov/historic-registers/127-0173/.

11. "Virginia Union University," Virginia Department of Historic Resources, https://www.dhr.virginia.gov/historic-registers/127-0354/.

12. National Register of Historic Places Inventory—Nomination Form, Belgian Building, https://www.dhr.virginia.gov/VLR_to_transfer/PDFNoms/127-0173_Belgian_Building_1970_Final_Nomination.pdf.

13. National Register of Historic Places Inventory—Nomination Form, Belgian Building; "VCU Building to Be Given Covering," *Richmond News Leader*, December 7, 1971, 19.

14. This loss is noted by Léon Ploegaerts and Pierre Puttemans, who regretfully observed the "pretty dilapidated" state of the building. See Ploegaerts and Puttemans, *L'oeuvre architecturale de Henry van de Velde*, 413.

15. Virginia Churn, "Art Deco Preservationist Focusing on VUU," *Richmond Times Dispatch*, October 19, 1986, 1, G4.

16. Gordon Hickey and Michael Paul Williams, "Renaissance in Richmond?," *Richmond Times Dispatch*, August 31, 1996, 6.

17. Tim Pearrell, "Union Weighs Costly Move to Division I," *Richmond Times Dispatch*, February 13, 1997, 33, 35.

18. Hickey and Williams, "Renaissance in Richmond?," 1, 6; See also Arthur Ashe, *A Hard Road to Glory: A History of the African-American Athlete* (New York: Warner Books, 1998).

19. Gordon Hickey, "VUU Has Rejected Sports Hall of Fame," *Richmond Times Dispatch*, January 7, 1997, 1, 12; Lindsay Kastner, "Repackaging the Gift," *Richmond Times Dispatch*, December 24, 2000, 71.

20. David S. Brooks, "Teaching Found Him Midcareer," *Richmond Times Dispatch,* May 8, 1999, 18.

21. Virginia Churn, "The Short List," *Richmond Times Dispatch,* March 1, 1998, B7.

22. Kastner, "Repackaging the Gift."

23. "Notable Minority-Related Grants to Higher Education," *Journal of Blacks in Higher Education* 28 (Summer 2000): 141.

24. "Theater," *Richmond Times Dispatch,* April 6, 2003, 6.

25. "Tower Takes Hit, Spruces Up," *Style Weekly,* November 19, 2003, 8.

26. Tom Nash, "Restoration Group Draws Focus to Virginia Union's Landmark Bell Tower," *Style Weekly,* December 16, 2014, https://m.styleweekly.com/richmond/restoration-group-draws-focus-to-virginia-unions-landmark-bell-tower/Content?oid=2158235.

27. Dianne Watkins, "Will There Be Bells in the Tower? Yes!," *Richmond Times Dispatch,* July 31, 2006, A7.

28. "Bells for Peace," https://bellsforpeace.org.

29. Dianne Watkins, "Sweet Sounds Will Again Ring Out from VUU's Tower," *Richmond Times Dispatch,* September 20, 2010, A13.

30. Quoted in James S. Junot, e-mail to Selicia Gregory, June 28, 2005, VUUA.

31. "Basketball Complex Planned for Va. Union," *Richmond Times Dispatch,* July 1, 2003, E2; Michael Paul Williams, "Building Shipped from Belgium," *Richmond Times Dispatch,* August 31, 1996, 6.

32. "VUU to Visit Los Angeles for Holiday Hoops Tourney," *Richmond Times Dispatch,* June 29, 2005, E1.

33. Julie Stitely-Moore and Emily Chace Morash, "David S. Ingalls Rink," [New Haven, Conn.], *SAH Archipedia,* ed. Gabrielle Esperdy and Karen Kingsley (Charlottesville: University of Virginia Press, 2012), https://sah-archipedia.org/buildings/CT-01-009-0074.

34. African American Cultural Heritage Action Fund, https://savingplaces.org/african-american-cultural-heritage.

35. Amy Biegelsen, "VUU Wins Grant to Preserve Historic Buildings," *Style Weekly,* July 11. 2007, https://www.styleweekly.com/richmond/vuu-wins-grant-to-preserve-historic-buildings/Content?oid=1374366; Gary Robertson, "Preserving a Source of Pride," *Richmond Times Dispatch,* July 30, 2007, B1–2.

36. "Return," *Richmond Times Dispatch,* August 20, 2006, B2; "School and College Guide," *Richmond Times Dispatch,* October 15, 2006, S31.

37. Commonwealth Architects, "Historic Master Plan: Virginia Union University," 1.

38. "VUU Plans Fitness Center, AC in Newman Hall Rooms," *Richmond Times Dispatch,* February 17, 2009, B3.

39. De Kooning, *Belgium at the Fair.: Exile on Main Street* (Ghent: wzw Editions & Productions, Department of Architecture and Urban Planning, Ghent University, 2010).

40. Laura Kebede, "NAACP March from Selma to D.C. Will Stop in Richmond," *Richmond Times Dispatch,* September 10, 2015, B5.

41. "Virginia Union University Receives $500,000 Grant for Historic Preservation of the Belgian Building," September 19, 2019, https://www.vuu.edu/news/virginia-union-university-receives-500000-grant-for-historic-preservation-of-the-belgian-building.

42. Eric Kolenich, "Virginia Union Tower Waits for Repair After Storm Damage," *Richmond Times Dispatch,* July 11, 2023.

43. Kolenich, "Virginia Union Tower Waits for Repair after Storm Damage."

Conclusion

1. Christina Sharpe, "Black Gathering: An Assembly in Three Parts," in *Reconstructions: Architecture and Blackness in America,* ed. Sean Anderson and Mabel O. Wilson (New York: Museum of Modern Art, 2021), 27.

2. Eric Lipton and Dionne Searcey, "Fight over Corruption and Congo's Mining Riches Takes a Turn in Washington," *New York Times,* April 2, 2023. See also Lydia Polgreen, "15 and Broke in a Cut-Throat Congo Mining Town," *New York Times,* November 15, 2008.

3. "Lighted VUU Tower Enhances City Skyline," *Richmond Free Press,* March 8, 2016, https://richmondfreepress.com/news/2016/mar/08/lighted-vuu-tower-enhances-city-skyline/; Raymond Hylton, "University History," Virginia Union University, https://www.vuu.edu/about-union/history.

4. Sam Roberts, "Randall Robsinon, Anti-Apartheid Catalyst, Is Dead at 81," *New York Times,* March 28, 2023.

5. Elena S. Danielson, *For Peace Alone Do I Ring: The History of the Lou Henry Hoover Carillon and Its Restoration* (2002; repr. Stanford: Hoover Institute, 2021).

6. Margaret Edds, *What the Eyes Can't See: Ralph Northam, Black Resolve, and a Racial Reckoning in Virginia* (Columbia: University of South Carolina Press, 2022).

7. Lloyd DeWitt and Corey Piper, eds., *Thomas Jefferson, Architect: Palladian Models, Democratic Principles, and the Conflict of Ideals* (New Haven, Conn.: Yale University Press, 2019).

BIBLIOGRAPHY

Archives

Albert de Vleeschauwer Archive, Documentation and Research Centre on Religion, Culture, and Society, Leuven Belgium (KADOC).

American Baptist Historical Society Archives (ABHSA), Mercer University, Atlanta, Georgia.

Department of Economic Affairs, Commissariat of the Belgian section, 1939, Algemeen Rijksarchief, Brussels.

Foreign Affairs Archive (FAA), Brussels.

General Education Board Records, Rockefeller Archive Center (GEBR/RAC), Sleepy Hollow, New York.

Henry van de Velde Archive, Archives et Musée de la Littérature (VDV/AML), Brussels.

Herbert Hoover Presidential Library, West Branch, Iowa.

Jan-Albert Goris papers, Letternhuis, Antwerp (J-AG/Letternhuis).

John Malcus Ellison Papers, Archives, Virginia Union University (VUUA), Richmond, Virginia.

Léon Stynen Archive, Vlaamse Architectuur Archieven, Antwerp.

Louis I. Kahn Collection, University of Pennsylvania and Pennsylvania Historical and Museum Commission, Philadelphia.

Manuscript and Archives Division, The New York Public Library Digital Collections (MAD/NYPLDC).
Marcel Breuer Digital Archive, Syracuse University, Syracuse, New York.
The Rockefeller Foundation Archives (TRFA), Rockefeller Archive Center, Sleepy Hollow, New York.
Victor Horta Museum Archive (VHMA), Brussels.
Virginia Union Special Collections and Archives, Virginia Union University, Richmond, Virginia.

Frequently Cited Serial Publications

Afro American (1941–64)
Architectural Forum (1937–39)
Argus (1941)
Bâtir (1925–39)
The Call (Kansas City) (1940–41)
Chicago Defender (1929, 2008)
Chicago Sunday Bee (1941)
The Crisis (1939)
House Beautiful (1930–39)
Journal and Guide (Norfolk, Va) (1940–45)
L'équerre (1931–38)
L'illustration (1939)
L'illustration congolaise (1939)
L'indépendance belge (1939)
L'ossature métallique (1936–39)
Le peuple (1922–1925)
New York Age (1939–45)
New York Herald Tribune (1938–41)
New York Times (1938–2023)
Ohio Daily Express (1941)
Opportunity: A Journal of Negro Life (1941)
Phoenix Index (1940–41)
Pittsburgh Courier (1930–1949)
Pourquoi pas? (1938–39)
Richmond Afro American (1941–1961)
Richmond News Leader (1939–1971)

Richmond Times Dispatch (1940–2023)
St. Louis Argus (1940–41)
Style Weekly (2003–14)
Virginia Union Bulletin (1946–49)

Primary and Secondary Sources

"About Us—John W. Barco Alumni Chapter." Virginia Union University. http://www.johnwbarcoalumnichapter.org/about-us/.

Achilles, Rolf, Kevin Harrington, and Charlotte Myhrum, eds. *Mies van der Rohe: Architect as Educator.* Chicago: Illinois Institute of Technology, 1986.

Adams, Oscar W. "What Negroes Are Doing." *Birmingham News,* June 10, 1941.

Adriaenssens, Werner. "Een studie van de Belgische bijdrage aan de Exposition Internationale des Arts Décoratifs et Industriels Modernes de Paris, 1925." Master's thesis, Vrije Universiteit Brussels, 1997.

"African American Cultural Heritage Action Fund." National Trust for Historic Preservation. https://savingplaces.org/african-american-cultural-heritage.

Aiello, Thomas. "Violence Is a Classroom: The 1972 Grambling and Southern Riots and the Trajectory of Black Protest." *Louisiana History: The Journal of the Louisiana Historical Association* 53, no. 3 (Summer 2012): 261–91.

"À l'Exposition Internationale de New-York: L'inauguration du pavillon belge." *La gazette,* May 2, 1939.

Alofsin, Anthony. *The Struggle for Modernism: Architecture, Landscape Architecture, and City Planning at Harvard.* New York: W.W. Norton, 2002.

Anderson, Sean, and Mabel Wilson, eds. *Reconstructions: Architecture and Blackness in America.* New York: Museum of Modern Art, 2021.

Anderson, Stanford, Gail Fenske, and David Fixler, eds. *Aalto and America.* New Haven, Conn.: Yale University Press, 2012.

Anderson, Terry H. *The Pursuit of Fairness: A History of Affirmative Action.* Oxford: Oxford University Press, 2005.

Aron, Jacques. *La Cambre et l'architecture: Un regard sur le Bauhaus belge.* Brussels/Liège: Mardaga, 1982.

Arnoldi, Mary Jo. "Art colonial: Les sculpteurs belges au Congo." In *Le Congo et l'art belge, 1880–1960,* edited by Jacqueline Guisset, 225–52. Tournai, Belgium: La Renaissance du Livre, 2003.

Ashe, Arthur. *A Hard Road to Glory: A History of the African-American Athlete.* New York: Warner Books, 1998.

Backer, Axel de, and Herman Mennekens. *Joseph Diongre, 1878–1963: Le style beaux-arts à l'épreuve du modernisme.* Brussels: Bitbook, 2021.

Baker, Paul R. *Richard Morris Hunt.* Cambridge, Mass.: MIT Press, 1980.

Baloji, Sammy, Silvia Franceschini, Nikolaus Hirsch, and Estelle Lecaille, eds. *Style Congo: Heritage & Heresy.* Brussels: CIVA and Spector Books, 2023.

Balthazar, Herman, and Jean Stengers, eds. *La dynastie et la culture en Belgique.* Antwerp: Fonds Mercator, 1990.

"Baptists Want Racial Equality in War Effort." *The Virginian-Pilot* (Norfolk), February 26, 1942, 7.

Bechthold, Martin, Anthony Kane, and Nathan King. *Ceramic Material Systems: In Architecture and Interior Design.* Basel: Birkhäuser, 2015.

Bekaert, Geert. *Operating Instructions for Architecture: A Century of Planning in Belgium.* Ghent: University of Ghent, Department of Architecture and Urban Planning, 2001.

Belgian Pavilion Official Guide Book. New York: New York World's Fair, 1939.

"Belgium's World Fair Pavilion Is Closed." *Troy (Ala.) Messenger,* June 1, 1940, 3.

"Beligë op de Wereldtentoonstelling an New York: Amerkaansche indrukken en persstemmen." *Gazet van Mechelen,* July 20, 1939.

"Bells For Peace." https://bellsforpeace.org/.

Biro, Yaëlle. "African Art, New York, and the Avant-Garde." *African Arts* 46, no. 2 (2013): 88–97.

Blier, Suzanne Preston. *Picasso's Demoiselles: The Untold Origins of a Modern Masterpiece.* Durham, N.C.: Duke University Press, 2019.

Bluestone, Daniel. "Chicago's Mecca Flat Blues." *Journal of the Society of Architectural Historians* 57, no. 4 (December 1, 1998): 382–403. doi:10.2307/991458.

Booker, Simeon. *Shocking the Conscience: A Reporter's Account of the Civil Rights Movement.* Oxford: University of Mississippi Press, 2013.

Booker, Simeon, Jr. "Negro to Supervise Actual Belgian Building Construction at Union." *Dayton Forum,* April 25, 1941, 1.

Boone, Kofi. "Enabling Connections to Empower Place: The Carolinas." In *Black Landscapes Matter,* edited by Walter Hood and Grace Mitchell Tada, 53–73. Charlottesville: University of Virginia Press, 2020.

Boonen, Sofie, and Johan Lagae. "Ruashi, a Pessac in Congo? On the Design, Inhabitation, and Transformation of a 1950s Neighborhood in Lubumbashi, Democratic Republic of Congo." In *The Politics of Housing in (Post-)Colonial Africa: Accommodating Workers and Urban Residents,* edited by Martina Barker-Ciganikova, Kirsten Rüther, Daniela Waldburger, and Carl-Philipp Bodenstein, 66–97. Oldenbourg: De Gruyter, 2020. doi:10.1515/9783110601183.

Borsi, Franco. *The Monumental Era: European Architecture and Design, 1929–1939.* New York: Rizzoli, 1987.

Borsi, Franco, and Paolo Portoghesi. *Victor Horta.* Translated by Marie-Hélène Agüeros. New York: Rizzoli, 1991.

Bowen, Dawn S. "The Transformation of Richmond's Historic African American Commercial Corridor." *Southeastern Geographer* 43 (2003): 260–78.

Boyd, Gary A. *Architecture and the Face of Coal: Mining and Modern Britain.* London: Lund-Humphries, 2022.

Branch, Muriel Miller. "Maggie Lena Walker (1864–1934)." *Encyclopedia Virginia.* https://encyclopediavirginia.org/entries/walker-maggie-lena-1864-1934/.

Brown-Nagin, Tomiko. *Courage to Dissent: Atlanta and the Long History of the Civil Rights Movement.* Oxford: Oxford University Press, 2011.

Bruce, Kathleen E. *Virginia Iron Manufacture in the Slave Era.* New York: Century, 1931.

Brumfield, Dale. "Refused to Move." *Commonwealth Times,* February 9, 2015. https://commonwealthtimes.org/2015/02/09/refused-to-move/.

"The Buffalo Museum of Science Collection." In *Art/Artifact: African Art in Anthropology Collections,* edited by Susan Vogel, 41–96. New York: Center for African Art, 1988.

Bullock, Henry Allen. *A History of Negro Education in the South: From 1619 to the Present.* Cambridge, Mass.: Harvard University Press, 1967.

Buni, Andrew. *Robert L. Vann of the Pittsburgh Courier: Politics and Black Journalism.* Pittsburgh: University of Pittsburgh Press, 1974.

Buyck, Jean. *Floris & Oscar Jespers: De moderne jaren.* Antwerp: Pandora, 1996.

Castillo, Greg. "German Lessons." *Places* (August 2022). https://placesjournal.org/article/philip-johnson-catherine-bauer-and-modernism-at-moma/.

Cheng, Irene, Charles L. Davis II, and Mabel Wilson, eds. *Race and Modern Architecture: A Critical History from the Enlightenment to the Present.* Pittsburgh: University of Pittsburgh Press, 2020.

Chernow, Ron. *Titan: The Life of John D. Rockefeller, Sr.* New York: Random House, 1998.

Chiles, Marvin. "'Down Where the South Begins': Black Richmond Activism before the Modern Civil Rights Movement, 1899–1930." *Journal of African American History* 105, no. 1 (January 2020): 56–82. doi:10.1086/705534.

———. "'A Period of Misunderstanding': Reforming Jim Crow in Richmond, Virginia, 1930–1954." *Virginia Magazine of History and Biography* 129 (2021): 249.

Cohen, Jean-Louis ed. *Les années 30: L'architecture et les arts de l'espace entre industrie et nostalgie.* Paris: Musée des monuments français, 1997.

Cole, Eddie R. *The Campus Color Line: College Presidents and the Struggle for Black Freedom.* Princeton, N.J.: Princeton University Press, 2022.

Colt, Susannah. *Thomas C. Colt, Jr: The Man Who Launched the Virginia Museum of Fine Arts.* West Lebanon, N.H.: Warner: R. C. Brayshaw, 2021.

Connor, Andrew. "Making History—and a Landmark." *Illinois Tech Magazine,* Summer 2020. https://magazine.iit.edu/summer-2020/making-history-and-landmark.

"A Conversation with James Baldwin." Boston: WGBH, June 24, 1963. American Archive of Public Broadcasting (GBH and the Library of Congress). http://americanarchive.org/catalog/cpb-aacip-15-9m03xx2p.

Coomans, Thomas. "Progress Exhibition, Chicago 1933." *Revue belge d'Archéologie et d'Histoire de l'Art* 89 (November 2020): 141–72.

Crinson, Mark. *Modern Architecture and the End of Empire.* London: Routledge, 2003.

Curl, Sherman John. "John M. Ellison within the Veil: Confronting the Challenges of Leadership in the Age of Jim Crow." PhD diss., William and Mary College, 2007.

Dabney, Virginius. *Below the Potomac: A Book about the New South.* New York: D. Appleton Century, 1943.

———. *Richmond: The Story of a City.* Charlottesville: University Press of Virginia, 1990.

Danielson, Elena S. *For Peace Alone Do I Ring: The History of the Lou Henry Hoover Carillon and Its Restoration.* Stanford, Calif.: Hoover Institute, 2021.

———. *Images of America: Hoover Tower at Stanford University.* Charleston, S.C.: Arcadia, 2018.

Davis, Charles L., II. *Building Character: The Racial Politics of Modern Architectural Style.* Pittsburgh: University of Pittsburgh Press, 2021.

Davis, Leroy. *A Clashing of the Soul: John Hope and the Dilemma of African American Leadership and Black Higher Education in the Early Twentieth Century.* Athens: University of Georgia Press, 1998.

De Kooning, Mil, ed. *Belgium at the Fair: Exile on Main Street: Paris, New York, Richmond.* Ghent: wzw Editions & Productions, Department of Architecture and Urban Planning, Ghent University, 2010.

Delevoy, Robert. *La Cambre, 1928–1978.* Brussels: Archives d'Architecture Moderne, 1979.

Delmont, Matthew F. *Half American: The Epic Story of African Americans Fighting World War II at Home and Abroad.* New York: Viking, 2022.

del Real, Patricio. *Constructing Latin American Architecture: Architecture, Politics, and Race at the Museum of Modern Art.* New Haven, Conn. : Yale University Press, 2022.

Delville, Jean. "À propos d'une dictature esthétique." *La province de Mons,* January 27, 1938.

De Rycke, Jean-Pierre. *Africanisme et modernisme: La peinture et la photographie d'inspiration coloniale en Afrique centrale, 1920–1940.* Brussels: Peter Lang, 2010.

Devillez, Virginie. *Le retour à l'ordre : Art et politique en Belgique.* Brussels: Labor, 2002.

Dew, Charles B. *Joseph Reid Anderson: Ironmaker to the Confederacy.* Richmond: Virginia State Library, 1999.

DeWitt, Lloyd, and Corey Piper. *Thomas Jefferson, Architect: Palladian Models, Democratic Principles, and the Conflict of Ideals.* New Haven, Conn.: Yale University Press, 2019.

Dickstein, Morris. "From the Thirties to the Sixties: The World's Fair in Its Own Time." In *Remembering the Future: The New York World's Fair from 1939 to 1964,* edited by Robert Rosenblum. 21–43. New York: Queens Museum, 1989.

Doctorow, E. L. *World's Fair.* London: Michael Joseph, 1985.

Dodge, Peter. *Beyond Marxism: The Faith and Works of Hendrik de Man.* The Hague: Martinus Nijhoff, 1966.

"Douglas Southall Freeman (1886–1953)." *Encyclopedia Virginia.* https://encyclopediavirginia.org/entries/freeman-douglas-southall-1886-1953/.

Drexler, Arthur. "Post-War Architecture." In *Built in USA: Post-War Architecture,* edited by Henry-Russell Hitchcock and Arthur Drexler, 20–37. New York: Museum of Modern Art, 1952.

Driggs, Sarah Shields, Richard Guy Wilson, and Robert P. Winthrop. *Richmond's Monument Avenue.* Chapel Hill: University of North Carolina Press, 2001.

"Dr. Sheppard on Africa." *Hampton Student* 2, no. 23 (February 15, 1911): 4.

Durth, Werner. *Deutsche Architekten. Biographische Verflechtungen 1900–1970.* Basel, Switzerland: Vieweg & Teubner, 1986.

Dworkin, Ira. *Congo Love Song: African American Culture and the Crisis of the Colonial State.* Chapel Hill: University of North Carolina Press, 2017.

Earle, Susan, ed. *Aaron Douglas: African American Modernist.* New Haven, Conn.: Yale University Press, 2008.

Edds, Margaret. *We Face the Dawn: Oliver Hill, Spottswood Robinson, and the Legal Team That Dismantled Jim Crow.* Charlottesville: University of Virginia Press, 2018.

———. *What the Eyes Can't See: Ralph Northam, Black Resolve, and a Racial Reckoning in Virginia.* Columbia: University of South Carolina Press, 2022.

Edwards, Kathy, and Esmé Howard. "Monument Avenue: The Architecture of Consensus in the New South, 1890–1930." *Perspectives in Vernacular Architecture* 6 (1997): 92–110. doi:10.2307/3514365.

E. L. "Het Belgisch Paviljoen te New York." *Vooruit,* June 25, 1939, 8.

"Elites-Grays to Aid Bldg. Fund," *Chicago Bee,* May 4, 1941.

Exposition Internationale de New York 1939: Appel aux producteurs belges. Brussels: Commissariat Générale du Gouvernement, 1938.

Falbel, Anat. "Georgia Louise Harris Brown." *Pioneering Women of American Architecture.* https://pioneeringwomen.bwaf.org/georgia-louise-harris-brown/.

Falkenheim, Jacqueline V. *Roger Fry and the Beginnings of Formalist Art Criticism.* Ann Arbor, Mich.: UMI Research Press, 1980.

Faulkenbury, Evan. *Poll Power: The Voter Education Project and the Movement for the Ballot in the American South.* Chapel Hill: University of North Carolina Press, 2019.

Favors, Jelani M. *Shelter in a Time of Storm: How Black Colleges Fostered Generations of Leadership and Activism.* Chapel Hill: University of North Carolina Press, 2020.

Fierens-Gevaert, Hippolyte. *Nouveaux essais sur l'art contemporain.* Paris: ed. Félix Alcan, 1903.

"Flemish Tapestry on View at the New-York Historical Society." *Flanders in the USA.* https://flandersintheusa.org/FlemishTapestry.

Floré, Fredie. "Serving a Double Diplomatic Mission: Strategic Alliances between Belgian and American Furniture Companies in the Postwar Era." *Design and Culture* 9, no. 2 (2017): 167–85. doi:10.1080/17547075.2017.1325625.

Föhl, Thomas, and Antje Neumann, eds. *Henry van de Velde: Raumkunst und Kunsthandwerk, ein Werkverzeichnis in sechs Bänden.* Vol. 1, *Metallkunst.* Leipzig: E. A. Seemann, 2009.

———. eds. *Henry van de Velde, Raumkunst und Kunsthandwerk, ein Werkverzeichnis in sechs Bänden.* Vol. 2, *Textilien.* Leipzig: E. A. Seemann, 2014.

———. eds. *Henry van de Velde, Raumkunst und Kunsthandwerk, ein Werkverzeichnis in sechs Bänden.* Vol. 3, *Keramik.* Leipzig: E. A. Seemann, 2015.

"Former German Colonies Urged as Jewish Home: Hearst Sees Chance for Creation of Another Great Nation." *Times Picayune* (New Orleans), November 21, 1938.

Fortuna, James J. "Fascism, National Socialism, and the 1939 New York World's Fair." *Fascism* 8 (2019): 179–218.

Franklin, John Hope. *George Washington Williams: A Biography.* Chicago: University of Chicago Press, 1985.

———. *Mirror to America: The Autobiography of John Hope Franklin.* New York: Farrar, Straus and Giroux, 2005.

———. "Rayford Whittingham Logan (1897–1982)." *Hispanic American Historical Review* 63 (1983): 596–97.

Fry, Roger. *Vision and Design.* New York: Meridian, 1956.

Gaines, Raymond. *The Perils and Prospects of Southern Black Leadership: Gordon Blaine Hancock.* Durham, N.C.: Duke University Press, 1993.

Gasman, Marybeth. *Envisioning Black Colleges.* Baltimore: Johns Hopkins University Press, 2007.

Gavins, Raymond. *The Perils and Prospects of Southern Black Leadership: Gordon Blaine Hancock, 1884–1970.* Durham, N.C.: Duke University Press, 1993.

Geiger, Roger L. *American Higher Education since World War II: A History.* Princeton, N.J.: Princeton University Press, 2021.

G. F. "Die Paviljoens van eenige buitenlandsche deelnemers op de New York World's Fair 1939." *Bouwkundig Weekblad Architectura* 60 (1939): 359–53.

Giamarelos, Stylianos. *Resisting Postmodern Architecture: Critical Regionalism before Globalisation.* London: UCL Press, 2022.

Gillet, Florence. "La mission Cauvin ou la propagande coloniale du gouvernement Belge aux États-Unis pendant la seconde guerre mondiale." *Cahiers d'histoire du temps présent* 15–16 (2005): 357–83.

Gilmore, Glenda Elizabeth. *Defying Dixie: The Radical Roots of Civil Rights, 1919–1950.* New York: W. W. Norton, 2008.

"Given to Virginia Union." *Baltimore Sun,* December 9, 1940.

Glover, Nikolas, and Andreas Mørkved Hellenes. "A 'Swedish Offensive' at the World's Fairs: Advertising, Social Reformism and the Roots of Swedish Cultural Diplomacy, 1935–1939." *Contemporary European History* 30, no. 2 (May 2021): 284–300. doi:10.1017/S0960777320000533.

Goddeeris, Idesbald, Amandine Lauro, and Guy Vanthemsche, eds. *Le Congo colonial: Une histoire en questions.* Waterloo, Belgium: Renaissance du livre, 2020.

Goldstein, Brian D. *The Roots of Urban Renaissance: Gentrification and the Struggle over Harlem.* Cambridge, Mass.: Harvard University Press, 2017.

Goris, Jan-Albert, ed. *Belgium.* Berkeley: University of California Press, 1945.

———. *Belgium in Bondage.* New York: L. B. Fischer, 1943.

———. "De Belgische deelname aan de Wereld-Tentoonstelling van New York 1939." *Economische Tijdingen* 3, no. 8 (April 25, 1938): 126–30.

———. *Modern Sculpture in Belgium.* 2nd rev. ed. New York: Belgian Government Information Center, 1951.

———. "Souvenirs of a Great World's Fair." *Belgian Trade Review* 12, no. 7 (July 1957): 9–10.

Goslar, Michèle. *Victor Horta, 1861–1947: L'homme, l'architecte, l'art nouveau.* Brussels: Fondation Pierre Lahaut and Fonds Mercator, 2012.

Govaerts, Bert. *Dubbelman. Een Biografie van Marnix Gijsen/Jan-Albert Goris.* Antwerp: Houtekiet, 2021.

———. *Ik Alleen! Een biografie van Albert De Vleeschauwer (1897–1971).* Antwerp: Houtekiet, 2012.

Grandison, Kenrick Ian. "From Plantation to Campus: Progress, Community, and the Lay of the Land in Shaping the Early Tuskegee Campus." *Landscape Journal* 15 (1996): 6–22.

———. "Negotiated Space: The Black College Campus as a Cultural Record of Postbellum America." *American Quarterly* 51 (1999): 529–79.

______. "The Other Side of the 'Free' Way: Planning for Separate but Equal in the Face of Massive Resistance." In *Race and Real Estate,* edited by Adrienne R. Brown and Valerie Smith, 209–10. Oxford: Oxford University Press, 2016.

Green, Bryan Clark, and Lisa Meador Bricker. "Intensive Level Survey of Eleven Buildings, Virginia State University, Chesterfield County, Virginia." Unpublished report for Virginia State University, June 17, 2013.

Green, Christopher, ed. *Art Made Modern: Roger Fry's Vision of Art.* London: Courtauld Institute of Art, 1999.
Green, Kristen. *The Devil's Half Acre: The Untold Story of How One Woman Liberated the South's Most Notorious Slave Jail.* New York: Seal Press, 2022.
Gropius, Walter. *Apollo in the Democracy.* Edited by Ise Gropius. New York: McGraw Hill, 1968.
Grubiak, Margaret M. "Henry Clifford Boles (1910–1979)." In D. S. Wilson, *African American Architects,* 61–65.
Grundman, Adolph H. "Northern Baptists and the Founding of Virginia Union University: The Perils of Paternalism." *Journal of Negro History* 63, no. 1 (January 1978): 26–41. doi:10.2307/2717358.
Guisset, Jacqueline. "Art déco, modernisme et expositions internationales." In *Le Congo et l'art belge, 1880–1960,* edited by Jacqueline Guisset, 171–252. Tournai, Belgium: La Renaissance du Livre, 2003.
_______, ed. *Le Congo et l'art belge, 1880–1960.* Tournai, Belgium: La Renaissance du livre, 2003.
Hamlin, Talbot F. "Sven Markelius." *Pencil Points* 22 (1939): 357–66.
Hancock, Gordon Blaine. "Starting Something. " *Black Dispatch,* April 19, 1941, 7.
Harold, Claudrena N. *New Negro Politics in the Jim Crow South.* Athens: University of Georgia Press, 2016.
Harrison, Helen. *Dawn of a New Day: The New York World's Fair, 1939/40.* New York: New York University Press, 1980.
Hartshorn, W. N., ed. *An Era of Progress and Promise, 1863–1910: The Religious, Moral, and Educational Development of the American Negro since His Emancipation.* Boston: Priscilla, 1910.
Harvey, Melanee C. "Alma Thomas and St. Luke's Episcopal Church." In *Alma W. Thomas: Everything Is Beautiful,* edited by Seth Feman and Jonathan Frederick Waltz. Columbus, Ga.: Columbus Museum of Art, 2021.
H. B. "De Belgische deelneming aan de Tentoonstelling te Parijs." *De Standaard,* March 12, 1937.
Hecht, Gabrielle. *Being Nuclear: Africans and the Global Uranium Trade.* Cambridge, Mass.: MIT Press, 2012.
Helmreich, Jonathan E. *United States Relations with Belgium and the Congo, 1940–1960.* Newark: University of Delaware Press, 1998.
Hening, Sidney E. "A Glorious Conclusion to the World's Fair." *Missions,* February 1941, 82.
Herdeg, Klaus. *The Decorated Diagram: Harvard Education and the Failure of the Bauhaus Legacy.* Cambridge, Mass.: MIT Press, 1983.
Herskovits, Melville J. "Peoples and Culture." In *Belgium,* edited by Jan-Albert Goris, 353–65. Berkeley: University of California Press, 1945.
Hess, Janet Berry. *Art and Architecture in Postcolonial Africa.* Jefferson, N.C.: McFarland, 2006.

Hitchcock, Henry-Russell, and Arthur Drexler, eds. *Built in USA: Post-War Architecture.* New York: Museum of Modern Art, 1952.

Hochschild, Adam. *King Leopold's Ghost: A Story of Greed, Terror, and Heroism in Colonial Africa.* Boston: Houghton Mifflin, 1998.

Holder, Ann S. "The Terrain of Politics: Race, Space, and Vernacular Citizenship." In *In Search of African American Space: Redressing Racism,* edited by Jeffrey Hogrefe and Scott Ruff, with Carrie Eastman and Ashley Simone, 28–59. Zurich: Lars Müller, 2020.

Hollis, Richard. *Henry van de Velde: The Artist as Designer; From Art Nouveau to Modernism.* London: Occasional Papers, 2019.

Hood, Walter, and Grace Mitchell Tada, eds. *Black Landscapes Matter.* Charlottesville: University of Virginia Press, 2020.

Hovey, George Rice. "Virginia Union University." In Hartshorn, *Era of Progress and Promise,* 99.

Hunt, D. Bradford. *Blueprint for Disaster: The Unraveling of Chicago Public Housing.* Chicago: University of Chicago Press, 2009.

Hylton, Raymond. "University History." Virginia Union University. https://www.vuu.edu/about-union/history.

Hylton, Raymond Pierre. *Virginia Union University.* Charleston, S.C.: Arcadia, 2014.

Industries et métiers d'art en Belgique. Brussels, 1937.

"Institut Supérieur des Arts Décoratifs." Special issue, *Cahiers de Belgique* 6 (1931): 211–54.

Jacobs, Steven, Yves Schoonjans, Jan Van Vaerenbergh, and Luc Verpoest. *Tweebronnen: De recoversie van de Technische School van Henry van de Velde tot Openbare Bibliotheeek en Archief Leuven.* Leuven, Belgium: Openbare Bibliotheek Leuven, 2000.

James-Chakraborty, Kathleen. "Expanding Agency: Ethel Power, *House Beautiful,* and the Writing of the History of American Architecture." In *Rereading Women and Architecture: Female Agency and the Discourses of Architectural History,* edited by Dana Arnold. 152–68. London: Routledge, 2024.

———. "Fragile Allianz: Über die Beziehung zwischen Henry van de Velde und Walter Gropius." In *Mythos Bauhaus: Zwischen Selbsterfindung und Enthistorisierung,* edited by Anja Baumhoff and Magdalena Droste, 35–52. Berlin: Reimer, 2009.

———. "From Isolationism to Internationalism: American Acceptance of the Bauhaus." In *Bauhaus Culture: From Weimar to the Cold War,* edited by Kathleen James-Chakraborty, 153–70. Minneapolis: University of Minnesota Press, 2006.

James-Chakraborty, Kathleen, and Rachel Lee. "*Marg* Magazine: A Tryst with Architectural Modernity; Modern Architecture as Seen from an Independent India." *ABE Journal: Architecture beyond Europe,* 1 (May 1, 2012). doi:10.4000/abe.623.

Janken, Kenneth R. "African-American Intellectuals Confront the 'Silent South': The 'What the Negro Wants' Controversy." *North Carolina Historical Review* 70, no. 2 (1993): 153–79.

Jeansonne, Glen. *Herbert Hoover: A Life.* With David Luhrssen. New York: New American Library, 2016.

"John D. Rockefeller, Jr., 1874–1960." Rockefeller Archive Center. https://rockarch.org/resources/about-the-rockefellers/john-d-rockefeller-jr/.

[Johnson, Philip]. "History of Machine Art." In *Machine Art.* New York: Museum of Modern Art, 1934.

Johnson, Philip. *Mies van der Rohe.* New York: Museum of Modern Art, 1947.

———. Preface to *Built in USA: Post-War Architecture,* edited by Henry-Russell Hitchcock and Arthur Drexler, 8. New York: Museum of Modern Art, 1952.

Jones, Robbie D. "Pearl and I. T. Creswell House: International-Style at Fisk University." *Tennessee Architecture,* January 16, 2023. https://tennessee-architecture.com/pearl-and-i-t-creswell-house-international-style-at-fisk-university/.

Jones, Thomas Jesse, ed. *Negro Education: A Study of the Private and Higher Schools for Colored People in the United States.* Washington, D.C.: Bureau of Education, Department of the Interior, 1917.

Junot, Jim. "Barco-Stevens Hall—80 Years of History." *Virginia Union University Sports,* May 1, 2019. https://vuusports.com/news/2019/5/1/general-barco-stevens-hall-80-years-of-history.aspx.

J. W. B. "Die Paviljoens van eenige Buitenlandsche Deelnemers Op de New York World's Fair 1939." *Bouwkundig Weekblad Architectura* 60, no. 36 (September 9, 1939): 349–53.

Kirschke, Amy Helene. "The Fisk Murals Revealed: Memories of Africa, Hope for the Future." In *Aaron Douglas: African American Modernist,* edited by Susan Earle. New Haven, Conn.: Yale University Press, 2008.

Kollat, Harry, Jr. "Building Virginia Union." *Richmond Magazine,* March 25, 2015. https://richmondmagazine.com/news/news/virginia-union-university/.

Krauser, J. Morgan. *The Shaping of Southern Politics: Suffrage Restriction and the Establishment of the One-Party South, 1880–1910.* New Haven, Conn.: Yale University Press, 1974.

Krinsky, Carol Herselle. *Rockefeller Center.* Oxford: Oxford University Press, 1978.

Kroiz, Lauren. *Creative Composites: Modernism, Race, and the Stieglitz Circle.* Berkeley: University of California Press, 2012.

Kuenzli, Katherine M. "Architecture, Individualism, and Nation: Henry van de Velde's 1914 Werkbund Theater Building." *Art Bulletin* 94, no. 2 (2012): 251–73.

———. "'Clearing the Terrain of Art': Henry van de Velde and an Art Theory for the Twentieth Century." Introduction to Henry van de Velde, *Selected Essays, 1889–1914,* edited by Katherine M. Kuenzli, 1–34. Los Angeles: Getty Research Institute, 2022.

———. *Henry van de Velde: Designing Modernism.* New Haven, Conn.: Yale University Press, 2019.

Kuyck, Hugo van. *Modern Belgian Architecture: A Short Survey of Architectural Developments in Belgium in the Last Half Century.* New York: Belgian Government Information Center, 1955.

Lagae, Johan. "Displaying *Authenticity* and *Progress:* Architectural Representation of the Belgian Congo at International Exhibitions in the 1930s." *Third Text* 50 (Spring 2000): 21–32.

Lagae, Johan, and Paoletta Holst. "'Objects That Are Dear to Him': The Colonizer's House and the *mise en valeur* of the Belgian Congo." *E-flux Architecture.* https://www.e-flux.com/architecture/appropriations/533163/objects-that-are-dear-to-him-the-colonizer-s-house-and-the-mise-en-valeur-of-the-belgian-congo/.

Land, Ada May. "The Migration into Richmond (1775 to 1860)." Master's thesis, University of Richmond, 1949. https://scholarship.richmond.edu/cgi/viewcontent.cgi?article=1042&context=masters-theses.

Lankford, Nelson D. *The Last American Aristocrat: The Biography of David K. E. Bruce, 1898–1977.* Boston: Little, Brown, 1996.

Latouche, John, and André Cauvin. *Congo.* New York: Willow, White, 1945.

Laureys, Dirk, ed. *Léon Stynen: A Life of Architecture, 1899–1990.* Antwerp: Flanders Architecture Institute, 2018.

Lebovich, William. "Albert Irvin Cassell (1896–1969)." In D. S. Wilson, *African American Architects,* 125–32.

Leiner, Glan B. "Hilyard Robert Robinson (1899–1986)." In D. S. Wilson, *African American Architects,* 492–99.

Lemoine, Bertrand ed., *Cinquantenaire de l'Exposition internationale des arts et des techniques dans la vie moderne.* Paris: Institut Français d'Architecture, 1987.

"Le pavillon belge à l'Exposition de New-York." *La nation belge,* May 7, 1939.

Levien, Simon J. "The Crimson Klan." *Harvard Crimson,* March 25, 2021. https://www.thecrimson.com/article/2021/3/25/harvard-klan-scrut/.

Lewis, Danny. "The White House Was, in Fact, Built by Enslaved Labor." *Smithsonian Magazine,* July 26, 2016. https://www.smithsonianmag.com/smart-news/white-house-was-fact-built-slaves-180959916/.

Lewis, Earl. *In Their Own Interests: Race, Class, and Power in Twentieth-Century Norfolk, Virginia.* Berkeley: University of California Press, 1991.

"Lighted VUU Tower Enhances City Skyline." *Richmond Free Press,* August 2, 2016. https://richmondfreepress.com/news/2016/mar/08/lighted-vuu-tower-enhances-city-skyline/.

Link, William A. "Jackson Davis and the Lost World of Jim Crow Education." Albert and Shirley Small Special Collections Library, University of Virginia Library. https://small.library.virginia.edu/collections/featured/jackson-davis-collection-of-african-american-educational-photographs/related-resources/jackson-davis-and-the-lost-world-of-jim-crow-education/.

Little, Margaret Ruth. "Getting the American Dream for Themselves: Postwar Modern Subdivisions for African Americans in Raleigh, North Carolina." *Buildings & Landscapes: Journal of the Vernacular Architecture Forum* 19 (Spring 2012): 73–86.

Locke, Alain. Introduction to *Blondiau-Theater Arts Collection of Primitive African Art,* n.p. New York: New Art Circle, 1927.

———. *The New Negro.* New York: Atheneum, 1925.

López-Durán, Fabiola. "Food Capital: Fantasies of Abundance and Nelson Rockefeller's Architecture of Development in Venezuela, 1940s–1960s." In *Architecture in Development: Systems and the Emergence of the Global South,* edited by Aggregate, 303–5. London: Routledge, 2022.

Lovett, Bobby L. *America's Historically Black Colleges & Universities: A Narrative History, 1837—2009.* Atlanta: Mercer University Press, 2011.

———. *A Touch of Greatness: A History of Tennessee State University.* Atlanta: Mercer University Press, 2013.

Lucking, Maura. "Self-Suggestion in the Tuskegee Machine: Technical Drawing under Jim Crow." *Grey Room* 87 (2022): 6–43.

Luwel, M., and M. Bruneel-Hye de Crom. *Tervueren 1897.* Tervuren, Belgium: Musée Royal de l'Afrique Centrale, 1967.

Mantels, Ruben. *Geleerd in de tropen: Leuven, Congo, & de wetenschap, 1885–1960.* Leuven, Belgium: Leuven University Press, 2007.

Marlowe, Gertrude Woodruff. *Right Worthy Grand Mission: Maggie Lena Walker and the Quest for Black Empowerment.* Washington, D.C.: Howard University Press, 2003.

Martin, Reinhold. *Knowledge Worlds: Media, Materiality, and the Making of the Modern University.* New York: Columbia University Press, 2021.

"Maryland's Largest Historically Black College Named a National Treasure," Morgan State University, May 3, 2016. https://www.morgan.edu/news/morgan-state-national-treasure.

Matysek, George P., Jr. "William Gaudreau, Leading Post–Vatican II Architect, Dies at 84." *Catholic Review,* July 9, 2015. https://www.archbalt.org/william-gaudreau-leading-post-vatican-ii-architect-dies-at-84/.

McGuinn, Harry Jared. "Phylon Profile, V: Joshua Baker Simpson." *Phylon* 6 (1945): 219–24.

Meeuwis, Michael. "The Furthest Escape of All: Darkness and Refuge in the Belgian Congo." *Graham Greene Studies* 1 (2017): 56–81.

Mendelsohn, Erich. *Amerika: Bilderbuch Eines Architekten.* Berlin: Rudolph Mosse Verlag, 1926.

Metropolitan Museum of Art. *Design in America: The Cranbrook Vision, 1925–1950.* New York: Harry N. Abrams, 1983.

Ministère des Travaux Publics et de la Résorption du Chômage. *Concours d'urbanisme et d'architecture en vue de l'aménagement du Mont des Arts à Bruxelles: Rapport du jury.* Brussels, 1937.

Monument Avenue Commission Report. Prepared for the Office of the Mayor and City Council, Richmond, Va., July 2, 2018. https://static1.squarespace.com/static/597a220f579fb3cca0ab3454/t/5efe3aee34e2691d9e4c8390/1593719571758/Monument+Avenue+Commission+Report.pdf.

Morshed, Adnan. "The Aesthetics of Ascension in Norman Bel Geddes's Futurama." *Journal of the Society of Architectural Historians* 63 (2004): 74–99.

Morton, Patricia. *Hybrid Modernities: Architecture and Representation at the 1931 Colonial Exposition, Paris.* Cambridge, Mass.: MIT Press, 2000.

Muir, Laura, ed. *Object Lessons: The Bauhaus and Harvard.* New Haven, Conn.: Yale University Press, 2021.

Mumford, Eric. *The CIAM Discourse on Urbanism, 1928–1960.* Cambridge, Mass.: MIT Press, 2000.

Mumford, Lewis. "The Sky Line in Flushing." *New Yorker,* June 17, 1939, 45.

"M. Van Isacker annonce que le pavillon belge à l'Exposition de Paris sera reconstruit au Heysel." *La libre Belgique,* October 1, 1937.

Negro Education: A Study of the Private and Higher Schools for Colored People in the United States. Washington, D.C.: Department of the Interior, 1971.

Nieves, Angel David. *An Architecture of Education: African American Women Design the New South.* Rochester, N.Y.: University of Rochester Press, 2018.

Nitschke, Marie Morris. "Virginius Dabney (1901–1995)." *Encyclopedia Virginia.* https://encyclopediavirginia.org/entries/dabney-virginius-1901-1995/.

"Notable Minority-Related Grants to Higher Education." *Journal of Blacks in Higher Education* 28 (Summer 2000): 141.

O'Connor, Éimear. *Art, Ireland, and the Irish Diaspora: Chicago, Dublin, New York, 1893–1939: Culture, Connections, Controversies.* Dublin: Irish Academic Press, 2020.

Ogata, Amy. *Art Nouveau and the Social Vision of Modern Living.* Cambridge: Cambridge University Press, 2001.

Oliver, Christopher C. "Clashing Currents: Contemporary Art Exhibitions and Modernism in Richmond, 1933–1970." In *Southern/Modern: Rediscovering Southern Art from the First Half of the Twentieth Century,* edited by Jonathan Stuhlman and Martha R. Severens, 360–86. Chapel Hill: Mint Museum in association with University of North Carolina Press, 2023.

Oostdijk, Diederik. *Bells for America: The Cold War, Modernism, and the Netherlands Carillon in Arlington.* University Park: Pennsylvania State University Press, 2019.

Osayimwese, Itohan. *Colonialism and Modern Architecture in Germany.* Pittsburgh: University of Pittsburgh Press, 2017.

Packet, Tom. *Horta in Amerika: Het verblijf van Victor Horta in de Vereinigde Staten van 1915 tot 1919.* Brussels: ASP—Academic and Scientific, 2021.

Parker, Clifton B. "Picture at an Exhibition." *Hoover Digest* 3 (Summer 2014): 192–97.

"Pavillons d'Honneur, la servitude du luxe, Belgique et Hollande." *7 Arts* 3, no. 25 (April 30, 1925): 2–3.

Pelkonen, Eeva-Liisa. *Alvar Aalto: Architecture, Modernity, and Geopolitics.* New Haven, Conn.: Yale University Press, 2009.

Périer, Gaston Denys. *Stanley Goes Back to America.* Belgium, 1939.

Périer, Gaston Denys, and J. M. Jadot. *Native Arts & Craftsmanship in Belgian Congo.* Brussels: Commission for the Protection of Native Arts and Crafts, 1939.

Philippart, Georges. "Architecture." In *Belgium,* edited by Jan-Albert Goris. 274–85. Berkeley: University of California Press, 1945.

Pinder, Kymberly. *Painting the Gospel: Black Public Art and Religion in Chicago.* Urbana: University of Illinois Press, 2016.

Ploegearts, Léon. "Henry van de Velde's Only Work in the USA." *DOCOMOMO Newsletter 7* (June 1992): 56–59.

Ploegaerts, Léon, and Pierre Puttemans. *L'oeuvre architecturale de Henry van de Velde.* Brussels: Atelier Vokaer, 1987.

Pollack, Howard. *The Ballad of John Latouche: An American Lyricist's Life and Work.* New York: Oxford University Press, 2017.

Potterfield, Thomas Tyler, Jr. "Charles Thaddeus Russell." In D. S. Wilson, *African American Architects,* 510–13.

Poulain, Norbert. "De Belgische Wandtapijten op de wereldtentoonstellingen tijdens het interbellum, in het bijzonder te Parijs in 1937 en te New York in 1939." In *Liber Memorialis Erik Duverger: Bijdragen tot de Kunstgeschiedenis van de Nederlanden,* edited by Henri Pauwels, André van den Kerkhove, and Leo Wuyts, 221–54. Wetteren, Belgium: Universa, 2006.

Proctor, Tammy M. "The Louvain Library and US Ambition in Interwar Belgium." *Journal of Contemporary History* 50, no. 2 (April 2015): 147–67. doi:10.1177/0022009414552867.

Quezado Deckker, Zilah. *Brazil Built: The Architecture of the Modern Movement in Brazil.* London: Spon, 2001.

Quiñones, Eric. "'Accidental Tourist' Exhibition Provides Views of Postwar Japan." Princeton University, July 6, 2009. https://www.princeton.edu/news/2009/07/06/accidental-tourist-exhibition-provides-views-postwar-japan.

Reed, Christopher. *A Roger Fry Reader.* Chicago: University of Chicago Press, 1996.

Richardson, Joe M. *A History of Fisk University, 1865–1946.* Tuscaloosa: University of Alabama Press, 2002.

Richardson, Selden. *Built by Blacks: African American Architecture and Neighborhoods in Richmond.* Charleston, S.C.: History Press, 2008.

Rivas, Darlene. *Missionary Capitalist: Nelson Rockefeller in Venezuela.* Chapel Hill: University of North Carolina Press, 2002.

Rombouts, Luc. *Singing Bronze: A History of Carillon Music.* Leuven, Belgium: Leuven University Press, 2014.

"RPL History." Richmond Public Library. https://rvalibrary.org/about/history/.

Rydell, Robert W. *World of Fairs: The Century of Progress Expositions.* Chicago: University of Chicago Press, 1993.

Rydell, Robert W., and Laura Burd Schiavo, eds., *Designing Tomorrow: America's World's Fairs of the 1930s.* New Haven, Conn.: Yale University Press, 2010.

Sacks, Ruth. *Congo Style: From Belgian Art Nouveau to African Independence.* Ann Arbor: University of Michigan Press, 2023.

Sale, George. "One Part in the Solution of a Great Problem." In Hartshorn, *Era of Progress and Promise,* 274–85.

Savage, Kirk. *Standing Soldiers, Kneeling Slaves: Race, War, and Monument in Nineteenth-Century America.* Princeton, N.J.: Princeton University Press, 1999.

Schelfhout, Charles E. *Hugo van Kuyck, Le belge qui conquit les plages Normandes avant les armées alliées.* Deurie: Éditions de la Dyle, 2004.

Schmitz, Marcel. *L'architecture moderne en Belgique.* Brussels: Éditions de la Connaissance, 1937.

Schnaidt, Claude. *Hannes Meyer: Bauten, Projekte und Schriften.* Stuttgart: Verlag Gerd Hatje, 1965.

Schuldenfrei, Robin. *Objects in Exile: Modern Art and Design across Borders, 1930–1960.* Princeton, N.J.: Princeton University Press, 2024.

Sert, José, Fernand Léger, and Sigfried Giedion. "Nine Points on Monumentality." In *Architecture Culture, 1943–1968,* edited by Joan Ockman, 27–30. New York: Rizzoli, 1993.

Shanken, Andrew M. *The Everyday Life of Memorials.* New York: Zone Books, 2022.

———. "Planning Memory: Living Memorials in the United States during World War II." *Art Bulletin* 84, no. 1 (March 2002): 130. doi:10.2307/3177256.

Sharpe, Christina. "Black Gathering: An Assembly in Three Parts." In *Reconstructions: Architecture and Blackness in America,* edited by Sean Anderson and Mabel O. Wilson. New York: Museum of Modern Art, 2021.

Silver, Christopher. *Twentieth-Century Richmond: Planning, Politics, and Race.* Knoxville: University of Tennessee Press, 1984.

Silver, Christopher, and John Moeser. *The Separate City: Black Communities in the Urban South.* Lexington: University of Kentucky Press, 1995.

Silverman, Debora L. "Art Nouveau, Art of Darkness: African Lineages of Belgian Modernism, Part I." *West 86th: A Journal of Decorative Arts, Design History, and Material Culture* 18, no. 2 (Fall–Winter 2011): 139–81. doi:10.1086/662515.

______. "Art Nouveau, Art of Darkness: African Lineages of Belgian Modernism, Part II." *West 86th: A Journal of Decorative Arts, Design History, and Material Culture* 19, no. 2 (September 2012): 175–95.

______. "Art Nouveau, Art of Darkness: African Lineages of Belgian Modernism, Part III." *West 86th: A Journal of Decorative Arts, Design History, and Material Culture* 20, no. 1 (March 2013): 3–61.

______. "Henry van de Velde: Art Nouveau and Style Congo, 1895–1897." In *Style Congo: Heritage & Heresy,* edited by Sammy Baloji, Silvia Franceschini, Nikolaus Hirsch, and Estelle Lecaille, 7–16. Brussels: CIVA and Spector Books, 2023.

———. "'Percer les ténèbres': Traces of the Congo in Victor Horta's Art Nouveau." In *Horta and the Grammar of Art Nouveau,* edited by Iwan Strauven and Benjamin Zurstrassen, 131–40. Brussels: Bozart Books, 2023.

Siry, Joseph. *Air-Conditioning in Modern American Architecture, 1890–1970.* University Park: Pennsylvania State University Press, 2021.

Sky Lark, Taj'ullah X. "Unlocking Doors: How Gregory Swanson Challenged the University of Virginia's Resistance to Desegregation: A Case Study." *Spectrum: A Journal on Black Men* 5, no. 2 (2017): 71. doi:10.2979/spectrum.5.2.04.

Smith, Terry. *Making the Modern: Industry, Art, and Design in America.* Chicago: University of Chicago Press, 1993.

Stanek, Lukasz. *Architecture in Global Socialism: Eastern Europe, West Africa, and the Middle East in the Cold War.* Princeton, N.J.: Princeton University Press, 2020.

Stewart, Jeffrey. *The New Negro: The Life of Alain Locke.* New York: Oxford University Press, 2018.

Stitely-Moore, Julia, and Emily Chace Morash. "David S. Ingalls Rink [New Haven, Connecticut]." In *SAH Archipedia,* edited by Gabrielle Esperdy and Karen Kingsley. Charlottesville: University of Virginia Press, 2012. https://sah-archipedia.org/buildings/CT-01-009-0074.

Strauven, Iwan. *Victor Bourgeois: 1897–1962; Modernity, Tradition & Neutrality.* Rotterdam: nai010, 2019.

Stynen, Léon. "La guirlande de M. van de Velde." *Pourquoi pas?,* May 20, 1938.

Sweeney, James Johnson, ed. *African Negro Art.* New York: Museum of Modern Art, 1935.

Tauranac, John. *Empire State Building: The Making of a Landmark.* New York: Scribners, 1995.

Taylor, Jacqueline. *Amaza Lee Meredith Imagines Herself Modern: Architecture and the Black Middle Class.* Cambridge, Mass.: MIT Press, 2023.

———. "Amaza's Azurest: Modern Architecture and the 'New Negro' Woman." In *Suffragette City: Gender, Politics, and the Built Environment,* edited by Elizabeth Darling and Nathaniel Robert Walker, 33–56. Abingdon, UK: Routledge, 2020.

Thomas, June Manning. "Urban Displacement: Fruits of a History of Collusion." *Black Scholar* 11, no. 2 (1979): 68–77.

Turner, Nicole Myers. *Soul Liberty: The Evolution of Black Religious Politics in Postemancipation Virginia.* Chapel Hill: University of North Carolina Press, 2020.

Tymkiw, Michael. *Nazi Exhibition Design and Modernism.* Minneapolis: University of Minnesota Press, 2018.

Van Beurden, Sarah. "The Value of Culture: Congolese Art and the Promotion of Belgian Colonialism (1945–1959)." *History and Anthropology* 24, no. 4 (2013): 472–92.

Vandenbreeden, Jos, and France Vanlaethem. *Art déco et modernisme en Belgique: Architecture de l'entre deux-guerres.* Brussels: Éditions Racine, 1996.

Vanhercke, Karen. "Drei Latere Werken van Henry van de Velde: Het Rito in Leuven 1936–44, Het Tentoonstellingspavilijoen voor Paris 1937, Het Tentoostellingspavilijoen voor New York 1939." Master's thesis, KU Leuven, 1996.

Van Isacker, Philip. "Een bestendig Comité voor Esthetische Zorg." *Elckerlyck,* July 22, 1939, 3–4.

Van Loo, Anne. "Belgique: Henry van de Velde." In *Cinquantenaire de l'Exposition Internationale des arts et des techniques dans la vie moderne,* edited by Bertrand Lemoine, 140–43. Paris: Institut Français d'Architecture, 1987.

Van Reybrouck, David. *Congo: The Epic History of a People.* New York: Ecco, 2014.

Vanthemsche, Guy. *Belgium and the Congo, 1885–1980.* Translated by Alice Cameron and Stephen Windross. Cambridge: Cambridge University Press, 2012.

Velde, Henry van de. "Extracts from His Memoirs, 1891–1901." *Architectural Review* 112, no. 669 (September 1952): 143–55.

———. *Geschichte meines Lebens.* Edited by Hans Curjel. Munich: Piper Verlag, 1962.

———. "Les arts et la réalité contemporaine." In *L'art et la réalité, l'art et l'état,* 178–95. Paris: League of Nations, International Institut of Intellectual Cooperation, 1934.

———. *Les mémoires inachevés d'un artiste européen: Édition critique.* Edited by Léon Ploegaerts. 2 vols. Brussels: Académie royale de Belgique, 1999.

———. *Récit de ma vie, 1863–1900.* Edited by Anne van Loo. Paris: Flammarion, 1992.

———. *Récit de ma vie, 1900–1917.* Edited by Anne van Loo. Paris: Flammarion, 1995.

———. *Récit de ma vie, 1917–1957.* Edited by Anne van Loo. 2 vols. Turnhout, Belgium: Brepols, 2023.

———. *Selected Essays, 1889–1914.* Edited by Katherine M. Kuenzli. Translated by Elizabeth Tucker. Los Angeles: Getty Research Institute, 2022.

Vellut, Jean-Luc. *Congo: Ambitions et désenchantements, 1880–1960.* Paris: Karthala, 2017.

Verdavaine, G. "L'Ensemble 'Gioconda,' de Philippe Wolfers." *Le home,* n.s., 2, no. 7–8 (1925): 119.

Verpoest, Luc. "Henry van de Velde, A Welcome Home: The Technical School in Leuven." *DOCOMOMO,* July 2002, 101–12.
Virginia General Assembly, Dr. Martin Luther King Jr. Memorial Commission. "King in Richmond." http://mlkcommission.dls.virginia.gov/kinginvirginia/richmond.html.
Virginia Union University. "Virginia Union University Receives $500,000 Grant for Historic Preservation of the Belgian Building." September 19, 2019. https://www.vuu.edu/news/virginia-union-university-receives-500000-grant-for-historic-preservation-of-the-belgian-building.
Von Moos, Stanislaus. *Le Corbusier: Elements of a Synthesis.* Cambridge, Mass.: MIT Press, 1979.
Vossoughian, Nader. "Alvar Aalto, Ernst Neufert, and Architectural Standardization in Germany and Finland, 1933–1945." *Journal of the Society of Architectural Historians* 79, no. 2 (June 2020): 202–12. doi:10.1525/jsah.2020.79.2.202.
Washburn, Patrick Scott. *The African-American Newspaper: Voice of Freedom.* Evanston, Ill.: Northwestern University Press, 2006.
Waugh, Alice. "The BSU at 50: The Black Students' Union Marks a Half-Century of Making MIT More Diverse." *MIT News,* October 30, 2018. https://news.mit.edu/2018/mit-black-students-union-50th-anniversary-1030.
Weiss, Ellen. *Robert R. Taylor and Tuskegee: An African American Architect Designs for Booker T. Washington.* Montgomery, Ala.: New South Books, 2012.
West, E. James. *A House for Struggle: The Black Press and the Built Environment in Chicago.* Urbana: University of Illinois Press, 2022.
Whyte, Kenneth. *Hoover: An Extraordinary Life in Extraordinary Times.* New York: Alfred A. Knopf, 2017.
Wilder, L. Douglas. *Son of Virginia: A Life in America's Political Arena.* Guilford, Conn.: Lyons Press, 2015.
Wiley, Amber. "The Dunbar High School Dilemma: Architecture, Power, and African American Cultural Heritage." *Buildings & Landscapes* 20, no. 1 (2013): 95–128.
Williams, Susan. *Spies in the Congo: The Race for the Ore That Built the Atomic Bomb.* Washington, D.C.: PublicAffairs, 2016.
Wilson, Dreck Spurlock, ed. *African American Architects: A Biographical Dictionary, 1865–1945.* London: Routledge, 2004.
Wilson, Mabel. *Negro Building: Black Americans in the World of Fairs and Museums.* Berkeley: University of California Press, 2012.
Wilson, Richard Guy. "High Noon on the Mall: Modernism versus Traditionalism, 1910–1970." *Studies in the History of Art* 30 (1991): 142–67.
Wilson, Richard Guy, and contributors. *Buildings of Virginia: Tidewater and Piedmont.* Buildings of the United States. New York: Oxford University Press, 2002.

Wojtowicz, Robert. *Lewis Mumford and American Modernism: Eutopian Theories for Architecture and Urban Planning.* Cambridge: Cambridge University Press, 1996.

———. ed., *Sidewalk Critic: Lewis Mumford's Writings for the New Yorker.* New York: Princeton Architectural Press, 1998.

Wolfe, Brendan. "Racial Integrity Laws (1924–1930)." *Encyclopedia Virginia.* https://encyclopediavirginia.org/entries/racial-integrity-laws-1924-1930/.

Wolski, Tania, and Luc Vincent, eds. *Léon Stynen: Architecte.* Ghent, Belgium: Snoeck, 2023.

Woodson, Carter Godwin. *The Mis-Education of the American Negro.* Washington, D.C.: Associated Publishers, 1933.

"World's Fair Promotes One after Protest." *New York Amsterdam News,* January 8, 1938.

"'Y' Plans to Sponsor Fair Trips." *Lansing (Mich.) State Journal,* February 16, 1930, 30.

Zeidler, Jeanne. "The Hampton University Museum Collections." *International Review of African American Art* 11, no. 4 (1996): 46–54.

Zeidler, Jeanne, and Mary Lou Hutgren. "'Things African Prove to Be the Favorite Theme': The African Collection at Hampton University." In *Art/Artifact: African Art in Anthropology Collections,* edited by Susan Vogel, 97–111. New York: Center for African Art, 1988.

Zernike, Kate. *The Exceptions: Nancy Hopkins, MIT, and the Fight for Women in Science.* New York: Scribner, 2023.

INDEX

Page numbers in italics refer to illustrations.

Race, Place, and Justice

Race is one of the least understood forces shaping the built environment, both in our interpretations of past buildings and landscapes and in contemporary practice. As recent years have made clear, this is especially true in the North American context. In this series, we wish to curate a space that takes this intersection seriously and supports work from a younger generation of scholars for whom race and the built environment is increasingly important.

Architectures of Slavery: Ruins and Reconstructions
Nathaniel Robert Walker and Rachel Ama Asaa Engmann, editors